Italian and Italian American Studies

Stanislao G. Pugliese
Hofstra University
Series Editor

This publishing initiative seeks to bring the latest scholarship in Italian and Italian American history, literature, cinema, and cultural studies to a large audience of specialists, general readers, and students. I&IAS will feature works on modern Italy (Renaissance to the present) and Italian American culture and society by established scholars as well as new voices in the academy. This endeavor will help to shape the evolving fields of Italian and Italian American Studies by reemphasizing the connection between the two. The following editorial board of esteemed senior scholars are advisors to the series editor.

Debating Divorce in Italy

Marriage and the Making of Modern Italians, 1860–1974

Mark Seymour

DEBATING DIVORCE IN ITALY
© Mark Seymour, 2006

First published in 2006 by
PALGRAVE MACMILLAN™
175 Fifth Avenue, New York, N.Y. 10010 and
Houndmills, Basingstoke, Hampshire, England RG21 6XS
Companies and representatives throughout the world.

PALGRAVE MACMILLAN is the global academic imprint of the Palgrave Macmillan division of St. Martin's Press, LLC and of Palgrave Macmillan Ltd. Macmillan® is a registered trademark in the United States, United Kingdom and other countries. Palgrave is a registered trademark in the European Union and other countries.

ISBN-13: 978–1–4039–7271–2
ISBN-10: 1–4039–7271–0

Library of Congress Cataloging-in-Publication Data is available from the Library of Congress.

A catalogue record for this book is available from the British Library.

Design by Newgen Imaging Systems (P) Ltd., Chennai, India.

First edition: December 2006

10 9 8 7 6 5 4 3 2 1

Printed in the United States of America.

For John and Sylvia Seymour

Contents

Acknowledgments

A long time ago now, at the University of Sydney, Robert Aldrich introduced me to the pleasures of history. During the same period, several wonderful lecturers in that university's Department of Italian, including Nerida Newbigin and Paola Marmini, introduced me to the pleasures of Italy. The eventual marriage of those two pleasures led, circuitously, to this book. I would like to express my enduring gratitude to those inspiring early teachers, and also to Peter Briggs, who encouraged me to begin to study, and showed me how it was done.

Since then, many people and institutions have helped me with the work that lies behind these pages. At the University of Connecticut, it was my great privilege to work with John A. Davis, who supervised my doctoral research with exemplary knowledge, rigor, and care. I would like to record my thanks to the other members of my supervisory committee, Peter Bergman, Ronald Coons, and particularly Mary Gibson (of the City University of New York), who generously agreed to be an outside reader, and has been very supportive ever since. Special thanks also to Bill Hoglund, Martha McCormick, and Thomas Deshaies, who all smoothed my path in innumerable ways. I am grateful to the Emiliana Pasca Noether Chair, the James M. Bozzuto Foundation, and the Department of History at the University of Connecticut for their generous financial support, as well as to the Society for Italian Historical Studies, which awarded me a prize at a time when I was particularly in need of encouragement.

My debts in Italy are extensive. I would like to thank Borden Painter, Livio Pestilli, and my colleagues at Trinity College's Rome Campus for providing a uniquely congenial setting for my early research. Many librarians and archivists in Rome, Florence, Naples, and Venice helped me in ways that epitomized Italian warmth and generosity, often under trying conditions. I would like to acknowledge the particular efforts of Pina Nuzzo, Marisa Ombra, and Claudia Mattia of the Unione Donne in Italia (Rome), and Giovanna Olivieri of the Casa Internazionale delle Donne (Rome). Special thanks to Virginia Jewiss, Nino Gualdoni, and Ivana Rinaldi, for accommodation in Rome; to Angiolo Bandinelli, former Radical Party deputy, and

Adele Cambria, journalist and author, for their time and insights; to Domenico Rizzo, for answering endless questions about Italian legal procedures; and to Marco Chighine, for invaluable research assistance.

The Department of History at the University of Otago has provided a wonderful environment in which to complete this book. In addition to the support, advice, and companionship of my generous colleagues, I would like to acknowledge a University of Otago Research Grant, which supported the last stage of the research; assistance from the department's research funds; and a reduced teaching load in the first semester of 2005. The Otago interlibrary loan staff proved that distance is no impediment to research, and I am very appreciative of their work.

Various people have read all or parts of the manuscript during its preparation. These include Alex De Grand, Mary Gibson, Robert Aldrich, Nicky Page, Sue Burton, Ali Clarke and Barbara Brookes. I am very grateful to all of them, for they saved me from many errors and infelicities—I take full responsibility for those that remain. I would also like to acknowledge Palgrave Macmillan's efficient team in New York, and the painstaking efforts of the production office in Chennai.

Finally, I would like to express deep appreciation to my families and the many steadfast friends, who, over long periods in Australia, the United States, Italy, and New Zealand, have provided the sense of community, belonging, and love that not even the most nomadic individualist can do without.

Dunedin, New Zealand
August 2006

Introduction

Patria, Famiglia, Libertà!

On a cold grey morning in January 1860, General Giuseppe Garibaldi married the beautiful Giuseppina Raimondi, illegitimate daughter of a patriotic nobleman, and, at only 17 years of age, more than 35 years Garibaldi's junior. The couple had met several months earlier, during Garibaldi's first successful campaign to liberate Italian soil from Austrian rule. The wedding took place in the Raimondi family's private chapel near Como, attended by a small number of guests. One of these described the ceremony as ordinary, if somewhat lacking in joy. But the ordinary soon became extraordinary when, as the newly married couple came out of the chapel, a mysterious horseman galloped up and handed the groom a letter, which he read immediately.

Anger quickly darkened Garibaldi's face, and he ushered his young wife away from the well-wishers, giving her the letter to read. It claimed that not only was Raimondi in the throes of a passionate love affair with another soldier, but that she was already pregnant with his child. When she admitted that this was true, Garibaldi is reported to have wielded a garden chair threateningly above her head while loudly insulting her virtue (or lack of it). Raimondi had the presence of mind to reply that she thought she was marrying an illustrious general, but was dismayed to find that he was no more than a common foot soldier. She then rushed away from the scene. Garibaldi was left fuming with humiliation, and the wedding celebrations evaporated in embarrassment.[1]

This unseemly matrimonial altercation effectively ended the relationship between Garibaldi and Raimondi, who never saw each other again. But according to the ecclesiastical law under which they had been married, only death or an annulment could dissolve the knot they had just tied. The Austrian civil law prevailing in Lombardy in early 1860 gave full force to the principle of marital indissolubility, keystone of the Catholic concept of matrimony. Divorce was anathema, and annulment was hardly more conceivable in this case: it would have been beneath Garibaldi's dignity to open himself to the deliberations of an ecclesiastical court—and besides, he was already on the pope's death-list for helping to usurp the temporal power in 1848. Instead, the Garibaldi-Raimondi marriage followed a fate that was probably not uncommon in Italy before the introduction of divorce. It continued to exist before the law, but had little practical substance, as its two members went on to lead completely separate lives.

Because of the inequality of men and women before the law, the marriage arguably affected Raimondi's life more than it did Garibaldi's. It prevented her from establishing a legally recognized relationship with someone else, and also gave Garibaldi authority over Raimondi's judicial identity and financial affairs, as was the case with all married women in Italy. Since the couple had nothing to do with each other, this caused her severe inconvenience on many occasions. Raimondi's lover was killed fighting in Poland soon after her wedding to Garibaldi, and she lived a life of sad obscurity, both a wife and a widow, and yet neither.

For Garibaldi, of course, a different fate awaited. Precisely one hundred days after the humiliating wedding at Como, he set off on a mission that was to change the course of Italian history: the famous expedition of the Thousand to Sicily. As for the mysterious letter, one theory that circulated was that it had been written by some of Garibaldi's soldiers, worried that marriage to such a nubile woman would distract him from the cause of Italian unity.[2] Indeed, it is quite possible that the humiliation of the marriage was a determining factor in Garibaldi's inspired departure for Sicily in May 1860, and thus the unification of Italy itself.[3] His stature as supreme military hero of the Italian Risorgimento soon towered above the fading memories of that embarrassing morning, and many Italians never knew that for Garibaldi there was ever another woman apart from his first wife, Anita.[4] Nevertheless, for both Garibaldi and Raimondi the indissoluble marital bond remained a shackle from which they would not be liberated for nearly 20 years.

Clearly, it took less time to make a nation than to dissolve a marriage. By the autumn of 1860 most of Italy had been liberated from its old-regime rulers, and the new nation was to be governed according to liberal principles that were nourished by Giuseppe Mazzini's dream of Italian independence. The dream was summed up by Mazzini's celebrated slogan, "patria, famiglia, libertà!" (fatherland, family, liberty), which emphasized the metaphorical relationship between the family and the nation. Mazzini thought of fatherland and family as "two extreme points on the same line," insisting that *liberty* should be the governing principle across the spectrum of human communities.[5] After 1860, it remained to be seen what degree of liberty the dream of Italian unification would bring to Italians, both in their public and private lives.

Marriage and the New Italy

Occurring on the eve of Italian unification, the Garibaldi-Raimondi wedding fiasco foreshadowed many questions about the way unions between men and women would be governed in Italy, and about the relationships between marriage and the new state. As Nancy Cott has argued so elegantly, marriage, representing a formal nexus between private life and civil society, is an issue of fundamental importance in any nation, but particularly for a new one in the process of establishing its identity.[6] The Italian state attempted to refashion marriage by making it a civil procedure from 1866, but the government shied away from the institution that would have represented the most radical reform of all: a divorce law. Between 1860 and 1920 the "divorce question" came up many times in parliament, in guises ranging from isolated queries to 10 formal proposals to introduce divorce legislation. After the rise of fascism, divorce dropped from the political agenda for two decades. It returned after the advent of the Republic in 1946, but as an issue that laid bare some of the most sensitive problems in modern Italian history, it reached a final resolution only in 1974.

The most obvious of these problems is the way the divorce question influenced Church-state relations over the course of Italian history. Divorce threw into relief the contrast between Church and state over a range of issues that for the former represented the iniquities of liberalism and modernity. For practicing Catholics, marriage is a holy sacrament, symbolizing the indissoluble unity between Christ and the Church. The Church desired to protect this concept of marriage at all costs. For the Italian state of the Liberal era, ideologically rooted in the secular ideals of the Enlightenment, the Church's influence over private life had to be circumscribed. Marriage would be a contract between two willing parties, and therefore at least in theory, dissoluble when that will was somehow compromised. The question of whether marriage should be a sacrament or a contract, and thus soluble or indissoluble, lay at the base of a long series of debates that had a determining influence in the making of modern Italians.

The divorce debates also raise a second, more subtle question, because the issue foregrounds the liberal dilemma over how to reconcile notions of liberty with ideals of community and nationhood, and in turn, points to some of the fundamental ambiguities of Italian liberalism itself.[7] In Italy, as Mazzini's formula suggests and as Alberto Mario Banti has affirmed, the ideal of the family had a particular metaphorical importance that competed with ideals of individual liberty.[8] This made the divorce question in Italy peculiarly problematic, and its fate shows that the uncertainties of Italian liberalism were not resolved before the rise of fascism. Even after 1946, the question remained largely unaddressed until the 1960s.

The relationship between divorce and the problem of individual liberty poses a third question: the gendered nature of liberty in Italy, both before fascism and during the Republic. The Risorgimento gave Italian women very few new rights. Married women remained subject to the absolute authority of their husbands, and they suffered many other inequalities. The divorce question went hand in hand with the "woman question" because the idea of both men and women having equal access to divorce threatened to overturn accepted notions of the proper relationship between the sexes in Italy. Even though in some ways Italian women might have been expected to embrace the idea of divorce as an escape route from a bad marriage, in fact they largely shied away from the issue. Only from the 1960s did significant numbers of Italian women begin to show interest in such possibilities. This in turn raises questions about the ways that women in different periods, contexts, and cultures saw their own interests.

Histories of Divorce

In short, the "divorce question" provides keys to a deeper understanding of several fundamental relationships that underlay the process of making Italians. Yet, the history of Italy's "divorce question" has received relatively little attention in the historiography of modern Italy. The relationship between the Church and the state after unification has been amply examined, particularly from the point of view of how that relationship influenced the course of Italy's political history.[9] The question of divorce on the other hand, for all its potential revelations, has aroused only minimal interest, usually being regarded as an inevitable victim of the Church's increasing political power from the early twentieth century.[10] With no divorce legislation after the collapse of fascism at the end of World War II, the historical roots of the issue began to receive periodic attention from the mid-1940s, not so much from professional historians as from partisans of one view or another, who used history to support their arguments for or against divorce.

An early example was prompted by the considerations of the Italian Constituent Assembly, charged with writing a constitution after a postwar referendum abolished the monarchy and established the Republic. The Assembly came close to incorporating an article stipulating the indissolubility of marriage into the document that defined the nation's new identity. Narrowly defeated, the proposal nevertheless highlighted the close conceptual relationship between the nature of marriage and the identity of the Italian state.[11] During these debates, Giorgio Fenoaltea, a left-wing politician, wrote a study urging the Assembly to fulfill the promise of the Risorgimento and rid Italian marriage of its canon-law traces by introducing divorce.[12] Another work of the period, Giuseppe Passalaqua's *Il divorzio e la chiesa*, also attacked the Church's influence.[13] A short time later, underlining the irreconcilability of the two sides, a Catholic author argued vehemently that divorce would be the Trojan horse of "free love," and urged Italians to pay heed to the psychological benefits of the Church's teachings on monogamy.[14]

Despite the dominance of the Christian Democrats in Italian politics after the elections of 1948, the divorce question did not disappear entirely. Indeed, its old connotations as an ideological watershed resurfaced with a certain regularity. In the mid-1950s the Laterza publishing house commissioned a magistrate to write a study of the divorce issue in Italy, and although the resulting work focused on the contemporary period, it included an historical survey of divorce debates since the French Revolution.[15] At about the same time, the Socialist deputy Luigi Sansone became an active advocate of a divorce law. In 1956 he published a book consisting of testimonies sent by "matrimonial outlaws," those whose unhappy marriages had forced them to resort to various unsatisfactory arrangements outside the law. In 1957 Sansone brought the possibility of introducing divorce in Italy back to public life for the first time since 1920 with a conference in Turin, but neither of his official proposals made headway in parliament.[16]

Italy's "economic miracle" placed new pressures upon Italian families that could not be ignored, and against this background the 1960s became a decade of divorce debates par excellence. A prominent magistrate published a pro-divorce study in 1964,[17] and in 1965 Loris Fortuna, a Socialist, proposed a law that eventually changed the course of Italy's divorce debates. Fortuna's proposal gradually attracted public support, and after a concerted and long campaign, resulted in the introduction of a divorce law in 1970. The period leading up to this victory witnessed sustained interest in the history of divorce debates in Italy, exemplified by several more studies, written mainly by figures who had played a part in the divorce campaign.[18]

The political agreement that allowed Fortuna's proposal to pass through parliament successfully in 1970 provided for the divorce question to be settled by the Italian people in what was to be the first referendum since 1946. The referendum campaign, which took place in early 1974, inspired the writing of many works both for and against divorce, but only a small number of them are historical in their approach. The most useful is by Alessandro Coletti, first published in 1970, but revised in 1974 as a contribution to the pro-divorce campaign before the referendum.[19] Several other works also appeared in the 1970s and into the 1990s, including a very good treatment of the divorce question in the context of a broader study of the Italian family by Lesley Caldwell,[20] and in 2000 Diana De Vigili published an excellent political study of the divorce question in Italy from 1946 to 1974.[21]

The history of divorce in countries that introduced the institution in the nineteenth century has understandably received more scholarly attention than the Italian case. Apart from anything else, the production of records allows for research on the social history of marriage breakdown as well as the theoretical debates about the problem. The issue has been closely examined in the case of France, where the divorce question became intertwined with politics from the Revolution of 1789 onward. In English-language historiography, Roderick Philips made the field his own with a detailed social history of divorce in Rouen, published in 1980. Philips followed this with a major comparative study of divorce in Western society, *Putting Asunder*, in 1988.[22] Antony Copley has studied divorce in France within the broader context of changing attitudes to sexual morality.[23] Another study of France, more a political and less a social history, is Francis Ronsin's *Les divorciares*.[24] Clearly approving of divorce, Ronsin also displays a characteristically French awareness of the extent to which such laws signify the potential intrusion of the state into the private sphere.

England, which introduced a divorce law in 1857, has also received considerable attention. Mary Poovey's study of gender relations in nineteenth-century England treats the 1857 law in some depth, arguing that it was a landmark because it addressed the anomalous position of women in English society, and brought into question the domestic ideal.[25] The doyen of the study of divorce in English history, however, is Lawrence Stone. Stone's principal monographic study is both a social history of marriage breakdown and an analysis of the questions raised by the issue. His work epitomizes the liberal dilemma over divorce, evincing both optimism over the transition in gender relations from patriarchy to equality, and anxiety about permissiveness and the increasing brevity of human bonding.[26] A fine example of a revisionist engagement with views of the history of the family as linear and progressive is A. James Hammerton's study of conflict in marriage in nineteenth-century England, which also analyzes the divorce question.[27]

These works are the fruits of increasing interest in social history and deeper research on matters of private life. There is now a significant body of literature on such issues in many European countries, and the field was given new energy and direction by rising interest in women's history, particularly from the 1980s. In the field of modern Italy, such approaches were slightly slower to develop than in other European countries, possibly because of the strong influence of Marxist historiography and the institutional questions surrounding fascism. This has now been more than made up for, and indeed, the fascist regime's reinforcement of traditional gender roles has promoted particularly strong interest on the part of historians of women and gender. The historiography of Italian women in the nineteenth century now also covers a broad range of issues, including prostitution, religion, sexuality, and marriage.[28]

Although the divorce question raises many gender issues in modern Italian history, it has attracted little interest from specialists in women's history. At first glance this may seem surprising, but it is possible to explain. In the first place, although a limited number of women writers expressed views on divorce after Italian unification, early feminists did not do so as part of a coordinated campaign for the introduction of divorce. Even pioneering feminists of the 1860s and 1870s, such as Anna Maria Mozzoni or Paolina Schiff, who criticized the Italian civil code's subjection of married women to their husbands, had little or nothing to say about the indissolubility of marriage in Italy. From the 1890s, a generation of feminists inspired by socialism also largely bypassed divorce, because they held that the material conditions of women required primary attention and that ultimately the Socialist revolution would emancipate women by superannuating the bourgeois family.

The divorce issue also raises the question of the relationship between Italian women and the Catholic Church. The majority of Italian women were opposed to divorce: when they raised their voices collectively on the divorce question before World War I, it was in protest against it. In a provocative essay on female religiosity in modern Italy, Lucetta Scaraffia has suggested that after unification the Catholic Church consciously fostered women into the formation of an alliance of "losers," the Church and women both having lost, or gained nothing, from the progress of liberalism.[29] The undoubtedly close relationship between the majority of Italian women and the Church is an important but little-studied aspect of the broader issue of the relationship between the Church and the nation. On a different level though, given an undeveloped economy that did not offer women the chance to gain independence, it is easier to understand why the majority of Italian women saw divorce as more of a threat than a safeguard, and were suspicious of what appeared to be yet another privilege for men.[30] Issues such as these underline the need for sensitivity in assessing the ways women judged feminist issues in a context that was very different from the present.

This study follows chronological lines, though not the traditional chronology of modern Italian history. Chapter 1 shows that the legislators of united Italy regarded civil jurisdiction over the institution of marriage as a crucial aspect of making Italians, and it examines the innovations and limitations of the new civil code of 1865. One of the limitations was the deft avoidance of serious debate about divorce, even though it would have been a logical corollary of the introduction of civil marriage. Chapter 2 examines the first proposals, in 1878 and 1880, to remake Italian marriage by introducing a divorce law. These proposals were made by a remarkable proto-feminist deputy, Salvatore Morelli, who argued that a divorce law would be beneficial for women and would strengthen the institution of the family. Morelli's parliamentary colleagues met his proposals with a combination of mirth and opposition, claiming that Italians had no need for such a law. Chapter 3 investigates this claim by examining marriage breakdowns in Italy during the first decades of unification. It is true that recorded breakdowns were rare, but the difficulties and pain evidenced by those cases supported Morelli's arguments in favour of a divorce law.

Chapters 4 and 5 examine several strong proposals for a divorce law between 1881 and 1902, made by liberal and Socialist politicians. The Socialist proposal in particular came very close to success, but that success fuelled a reaction, the most visible aspect of which was a series of extraordinary popular campaigns coordinated by the lay Catholic organization, the Opera dei Congressi. Chapter 6 argues that the high profile of divorce reform by 1902 played a significant role in motivating the rise of Catholic political power in the early twentieth century. The novel political constellation resulting from the entry of Catholic deputies into parliament restricted the possibilities for innovation in, and even debate over, the private sphere. Instead, a notion of the family as a bulwark against the iniquities of modern society held increasing sway in the first decades of the twentieth century, and reached an apotheosis under fascism.

Chapter 7 examines the tensions between the postwar Italian Republic's commitment to democratize fascist families on the one hand, and the continuing hegemony of an ideal of the family as an indissoluble social cell on the other. Material conditions and Catholic familist ideology initially prevailed over more democratic ideals, and the legal regulation of the Italian family barely changed in the 1940s and 1950s. Chapter 8 shows that by the mid-1960s, the developments of Italy's "economic miracle" had placed new pressures on families, and many Italians, particularly women, began to perceive that the traditional model of the family was in crisis. This perception provided the context for a new debate on divorce in Italy, one that challenged the delicately balanced coalition governments of the 1960s. Although the debate culminated with the introduction of a divorce law in

1970, the law's approval was the result of a parliamentary bargain, which provided that the Italian people should have the opportunity to abolish the law by way of a referendum. Chapter 9 examines the famous referendum, held in May 1974. Widely interpreted as a litmus test of the nature of Italy's social fabric after the postwar boom, a solid majority of Italians affirmed the need to divorce tradition and to embrace more flexible concepts of marriage and the family. In doing so, they showed themselves to have come to the forefront of a long quest to make Italians modern.

I

Making Italians

Marriage and the Family in United Italy, 1860–1878

Once the Italian peninsula's various polities had been brought together into a united kingdom, the new nation's government was faced with the daunting task of unifying the laws of the land. The importance attributed to the family and the regulation of family relationships is indicated by the speed with which the government constituted a special commission to study the way marriage was to be regulated in the new state. On 19 June 1860 the first minister for justice, Giovanni Cassinis, presented a report to parliament declaring that since civil association arises out of the family, which is constituted by marriage, family and marriage would be the first objects of the civil law.[1] Cassinis's own speech emphasized the patriotic importance of the writing of the Italian civil code. He claimed that Italy had led the world out of the dark ages, and now had an opportunity to demonstrate that it was as capable of devising its own laws as it was of fighting its own battles. The writing of the civil code was clearly presented as a patriotic project that was intended to parlay the glories of the Risorgimento into civil society.

Cassinis's proud declarations in 1860 were also in their own way an announcement of the continuation of another battle: that between the state and the Roman Catholic Church. By making it clear that the state intended to take a deliberate and particular interest in family matters, it was throwing down the gauntlet to an institution that had hitherto considered the regulation of private life its own sacrosanct domain. The idea that marriage was the seed of all civil association was the rationale for the proposed civil code's most novel aspect: the establishment of civil marriage as the only system recognized by the state as conferring all the civil privileges of matrimony. A civil marriage was simply a contract between two willing parties of the opposite sex, blessed, as it were, by the laws of the land. This distinguished it from a marriage in a Catholic church, which is blessed by virtue of being a holy sacrament. These irreconcilably different views of the nature of marriage were a token of the tension between two fundamentally different worldviews, a tension that saw the institution of marriage become the site of a drawn-out struggle between the Church and the new Italian state. This struggle was for the most part a silent war of ideology, but occasionally it became a heated battle over particular issues. During the first 40 years of Italian unification, the possibility that divorce might be introduced into Italian law sparked controversy and bitter enmity between the two opposing worldviews of Italian liberalism and Catholicism.

The Church-State Conflict over Marriage

Conflicts between churches and states were as old as organized religion itself, but in relation to issues of family and marriage particular developments lay behind the conflicts of the late nineteenth century. The clearest and earliest was the Reformation and the Catholic response to it. The Council of Trent's edicts on marriage sought to reestablish Church authority in this area and laid down clear rules for Church marriages.[2] Those edicts represented a new page in the history of marriage in Europe, and while they helped to consolidate papal religious, social, and political power, the clarity of the doctrine on marriage later contrasted with the lack of transparency in Church practice, particularly in relation to marriage annulments. It was this contrast, perceived in so many areas, that influenced the second major development that was to have a profound effect on church-state relations in Europe. This was of course, the Enlightenment, with its insistence on the idea of the separation of church and state, freedom of religion, and other individual liberties.

The Enlightenment view of the regulation of the family was most clearly expressed in the actions of the French revolutionary governments, and eventually the Napoleonic code of 1804. In September 1791 the French Assembly declared that civil marriage, a contract entered into freely by two willing individuals, would be the only system of marriage recognized by the state. A year later the government admitted divorce for a broad range of reasons, including the most radical—mutual consent. The Assembly reasoned that since civil marriage was a contract entered into freely by two individuals, it should be possible to terminate the contract if both parties so chose.[3] From 1806, the Napoleonic code was extended virtually unchanged to most parts of the Italian peninsula, where it applied until shortly after the Restoration.[4] In Italy, unlike France, the number of divorces occurring between 1806 and 1815 was very small. Yet the short life of the code was to have great symbolic significance later in the century.[5] For conservatives, the whole idea of civil marriage and its even more disturbing corollary, divorce, became inextricably linked with the specter of revolutionary tumult. For radicals and liberals, on the other hand, both civil marriage and divorce became symbols of progress and reason in human affairs.

In Italy, as elsewhere, the Restoration meant that authority in matrimonial matters went back to the Church, but the varied ways in which canon law subsequently interacted with the civil law was symptomatic of the divisions of the Italian peninsula. After the Restoration, Piedmont, Tuscany, the Papal States and the Duchy of Modena returned to a system in which the Church had complete authority over marriage. Lombardy-Veneto, controlled by Austria, returned to Joseph II's system of 1775, in which people married in their own church, and the state conferred civil authority upon the respective religious law. This meant that Protestants and Jews could divorce, but Catholics could not. A concordat with the Holy See in 1856 renewed the Church's authority over marriages between Catholics in Lombardy-Veneto. The Kingdom of the Two Sicilies instituted a hybrid system from 1819, under which the only valid form of marriage was religious, but the ceremony had to be preceded by the couple swearing an oath before a public official. Civil recognition of the marriage was then conferred by the religious ceremony. The Duchy of Parma had a similar system.[6] In one way or another, religious authority prevailed over marriage in the Italian states, until unification in 1860.

Because of the dominance of the Catholic Church and the variety of ways in which canon law interacted with civil law on marriage all over the peninsula, the establishment of a uniform civil code presented postunification Italian legislators with real opportunities to make their mark on the new state. The mark they chose was in harmony with the formula of *patria, famiglia, libertà*: the new code united the civil law of Italy, acknowledged and reinforced the family's position as the foundation of the nation, and symbolized Italy's new liberty from foreign influence and Church domination. In this respect the most distinctive feature of the new civil code was the establishment of civil marriage as the only form officially recognized by the state.[7] This idea of marriage was in keeping with the liberal notion of the separation of church and state powers; indeed, in Liberal Italy civil marriage was to become a token of this separation.

Although in a symbolic way the introduction of civil marriage in Italy was a revolutionary break with the past, in a very important sense it changed nothing. This concerned the position of married women in society.[8] The new law continued the concept of *autorizzazione maritale*, or "husband's authorization," which meant that a married woman had no judicial identity in her own right, and depended upon her husband's authority to carry out even the simplest official act.[9] This underlines that in nineteenth-century Italy as in the rest of Europe, the Enlightenment ideals of equality that had driven much of the Risorgimento effectively applied only to men. As the early Italian feminist Paolina Schiff complained in her analysis of the Italian civil code, the new law on civil marriage "promised women liberty, but did not give it."[10]

Indeed, the legacy left to women by the unification of Italy is complex, and in many ways negative. For example, women lost the legal protection that had been offered by the ecclesiastical courts. Between 1860 and 1870 these were abolished, and poor women in particular lost a strong institutional advocate in cases such as seduction and abandonment. The civil code offered nothing to replace them.[11] Under these circumstances it is less surprising to find that very few Italian women raised their voices to protest the indissoluble nature of marriage. They may even have thought that divorce was yet another innovation that promised liberty only to men.

If in the minds of Italy's leaders the introduction of civil marriage represented a victorious break with the past, in reality it was an ambiguous rupture, with the very nature of civil marriage being among the contested issues. Clashes between the Church and the state over civil marriage had not been completely unknown during the Restoration era, but they had been rare. Twelve years before the unification of Italy, Piedmont had emerged from the 1848 revolutions as the only Italian state with any real independence from foreign domination, and it was this independence that allowed Piedmont to play the leading role in the Risorgimento. In the years following 1848 Piedmont's rulers, above all Cavour, cultivated a cautious liberalism that called, among other things, for the separation of Church and state powers. With the enactment of the Siccardi laws in 1850, named after the contemporary minister of justice, the jurisdiction of ecclesiastical courts was abolished, except, significantly, over marriage, which was considered too sensitive an issue to deal with at the time. Nevertheless, the law contained an article that obliged the government to establish a law on civil marriage at the earliest opportunity.[12]

Two years later the minister presented a law on civil marriage to the Piedmontese parliament. It was a divisive issue and the debates were drawn out. Those in favour of civil marriage used arguments that emphasized the progressive value of the state being entirely responsible for the regulation of civil society.[13] Those against it were repulsed by what they saw as the disturbing soullessness of a marriage reduced from a holy sacrament to a mere civil contract. Perhaps more to the point, they saw the possibility of divorce as a logical consequence of that change.[14] Ultimately the proposal passed through the lower house by a large majority.[15] But the bill had a more arduous passage through the Senate, where it was the main item debated between 15 and 21 December 1852. Senator Stara represented the conservative view that it was precisely the holy nature of the religious ceremony that gave marriage its solidity, which in turn provided the best guarantee of a stable society.[16] Without specifically mentioning the logical connection between civil marriage and divorce, he claimed that if marriage law were taken out of the hands of the Church, Piedmontese society would inevitably succumb to the collapse of its three major pillars: family, property, and authority.[17] A more concise expression of the same view was voiced by Senator Colli: "Matrimony is the basis of the family; together, families constitute society; take the foundation away, and the edifice crumbles."[18] Despite variations of detail, those against the introduction of civil marriage argued that the absence of a religious basis for the fundamental unit of society—the family—would inevitably lead to decadence and decline, as marriage would not be taken seriously and families would not endure.

Those arguing in favor of the introduction of civil marriage saw it precisely as an antidote to decadence and decline. Influential speakers like Cavour himself saw civil marriage as an essential symbol of Piedmont's progress. Instead of trying to combat claims that society would collapse if civil marriage were introduced, Cavour's speech argued that Piedmont's laws were harboring a fragment of the middle ages that must be purged. Civil marriage, according to Cavour, was an essential aspect of liberty and progress, and overall he saw its adoption as a first step, one that would initiate further reforms in the relationship between Church and state.[19] Typically for Cavour, the issue was also clearly an aspect of Piedmont's keeping up with other nations.

Ultimately the bill was rejected by the Senate by one vote on 20 December 1852,[20] and the next day Senator Buoncompagni, who had initiated the proposal, rather meekly closed the issue by admitting that the government was not ready to accept the principle of civil marriage, and that it would have to be re-thought.[21] It is now well accepted that the failure to introduce civil marriage in Piedmont in 1852 was a direct result of pressure brought to bear upon King Victor Emmanuel II by Pius IX himself. The issue, more than any other, had attracted determined clerical opposition from the outset. The pope added his own voice to the debate in a letter to the king as early as June 1852, and it is generally agreed that it was the king's direct pressure on the Senate that effectively blocked the law's passage.[22] Cavour's agreement to drop the civil marriage issue as a condition for forming the next government[23] meant that the issue was not to be raised again until after the unification of Italy.

The significance of the whole affair is twofold. The parliamentary debates spelled out the two main positions of Piedmontese parliamentarians on the issue of marriage. One group represented the view that religious underpinnings were an essential element, without which marriages would not last, and as a result society would fall apart. The second view was that making marriage a civil affair was the ultimate sign of the separation of Church and state powers, and a necessity in the name of liberty and progress. Above all, however, the battle over the proposed law revealed the potential for tension between the Church and the state on the Italian peninsula, and showed that, more than anything else, the Church held dear its role in the regulation of matrimony and the family. The episode in 1852 was a battle over territory that was a foretaste of things to come. In 1852 it was clearly won by the Church. The next time it was to be won by the state.

Eight years later, Italy was unified and became a nation in a way that was fairly easily made to appear as if it had been an ineluctable affair during which progress had triumphed over centuries of stasis. What was to prove much less easy was the sustaining of this myth over the coming years, as the new state struggled to conquer the loyalties of its citizens, to establish its legitimacy, and to develop a national secular culture. The first step in this process was to remove the legal traces of disunity by making the laws of the land uniform. The law that would most clearly symbolize the departure from the past was a law on civil marriage. The unification victory gave the lawmakers a powerful mandate and an inspiring purpose, and the political context was very different from the one that had prevailed in Piedmont in 1852. In June 1860, even before the new kingdom had officially been brought into being, the nation's first minister of justice announced that the government intended to claim the legal territory of marriage from the Church. Since the government administers the polity arising out of civil association, it was only natural that it should administer the seed of that association, marriage itself.[24]

Despite the zeal with which Cassinis announced the imminent change in Italian marriage law, it was several years in coming, as it was a delicate question and was studied earnestly by various parliamentary commissions. In the meantime it became necessary for parliament to pass a special law to smooth over some of the problems arising because of the variety of legal systems that prevailed until the new civil code was introduced. The most glaring difficulty arose in the south, where the marriage system of the former Kingdom of the Two Sicilies involved both Church and civil authorities. The law stipulated a procedure to be followed after the Church ceremony in order to gain the full civil effect of marriage. When newly-weds, for various reasons, had not been able to follow this procedure, the

Bourbon king had usually granted the civil effects of marriage as a matter of royal grace. After 1860 there was of course no southern king to grant these "sanatorie," and in the south, marriages that would have been perfectly legal in other parts of Italy were not valid according to the southern law that was still in force.

In May 1863 the government passed a temporary law designed to rectify this situation until the new civil code was enacted.[25] Parliamentary discussion provided an opportunity for at least one disgruntled senator, Paolo Vigliani, to ask the new minister for justice, Giuseppe Pisanelli, why the preparation of the civil code was taking so long. Pisanelli acknowledged that anything concerning the family was urgent, and undertook to expedite the matter.[26] Two months later he presented Book One of the Italian civil code to the Senate, in a speech that was laden with a sense of the historical importance of the moment. His opening words linked the notions of family, national unity, and law metaphorically: "From the moment Italians recognized the possibility of being reunited into one single family, the desire for unification of the law has spread among all educated citizens."[27] The speech proceeds with references to the major military battles of the Risorgimento, and arrives at the necessity of unifying the laws of the land. In this way, Pisanelli conflates military and legal conquest, suggesting that the work remaining to be done was merely an extension of the work of the battlefield, and no less glorious.

Less clearly expressed, but nevertheless implicit in the rhetoric, is the notion of the conquest of the Italian family. Pisanelli does not mention the opponent, the Church, explicitly, but like so many of his colleagues, he belabors the relationship between the family and the state, calling it the first link in the civil "consortium" (consorzio).[28] This harks to his opening claim that Italians were now one family. The aim of the new civil code, in short, was to make the regulation of family matters the domain of the new Italian state once and for all. Justifying the approach of the civil code, Pisanelli referred briefly to the principle of a free church in a free state, which he claimed was now an axiom of Italian public law. He delicately dismissed any possibility of a hybrid system in which the state and the Church shared the regulation of marriage, claiming that such a system would inevitably lead to unnecessary complications.

Civil Marriage and the Specter of Divorce

To devout Catholics, one of the most abhorrent aspects of civil marriage was the fact that its logical corollary was a divorce law. The potential for a clash between Church and state over this matter was defused quickly by

Pisanelli. He announced:

> It almost goes without saying that the new civil code totally excludes divorce.
> Divorce produces great harm, worse for the children than the parents; but
> the greatest harm divorce produces stems from the evils generated by the mere
> possibility. If a law . . . were to place the idea of divorce at the threshold
> and in the heart of marriage, it would poison the sanctity of the
> marriage . . . because the very idea would cause . . . a perennial and bitter
> suspicion.[29]

With these words Pisanelli laid down what was to become the official attitude of the Italian state toward divorce for more than a century. The irony,
of course, was that in its strenuous efforts to effect a clean division between
Church and state jurisdictions, the civil code created its own anomalous
hybrid: a civil contract that could not be broken. What is more, the doctrine that marriage should not be dissoluble obviously derived directly
from Church doctrine.

After Pisanelli's presentation the Senate voted that the civil code should
be examined by the Senate Commission, and in due course that commission produced its report, recommending approval of the code. It is clear
though, judging by the slightly defensive nature of the report when it came
to the principle of marital indissolubility, that the commission's members
were aware of the peculiarity of the law they were framing. The report
claimed that the new marriage law excluded divorce not for religious reasons, but in the interests of society.[30] In many ways, the Senate's report on
the civil code anticipates the central criticism of arguments presented in
the divorce debates in later decades.

From those who might have been in favor of divorce the report anticipates the criticism that the state has erred by producing a legal framework
that might admit divorce (i.e., civil marriage) while at the same time
specifically excluding it. The report defends the state's position by arguing
that human nature needs stable and constant unions between men and
women as a foundation for the procreation and education of children.
Here, it claims, religion and the state are in agreement. Against the argument that the state has no proper legal footing, unlike the Church, to make
the marriage contract indissoluble, the report counters with the idea that
marriage is effectively a contract like Rousseau's social contract. Marriage
arises out of free will, but engages the contractors in obligations to others
(to the resultant children, first and foremost, but also to the whole of society). According to the Senate report, these obligations should be sealed
with the immutable authority of the law.[31] This approach underlines the
prevailing view of marriage as the foundation of society. Once couples

volunteered to take part in the society of marriage they engaged themselves in a series of obligations that were too pressing to allow a change of mind, for whatever reason.

Yet the proposed civil code did acknowledge that marriages could fail, and while specifically excluding divorce, it proposed to continue, under state sponsorship, the long standing canon-law provision of *separazione personale* (personal separation), in certain carefully prescribed cases. These were adultery, voluntary abandonment, cruelty or injury, and mutual consent.[32] When a couple obtained a personal separation, they were permitted to live under separate roofs, and the wife had the right to financial support. But the marriage did not cease to exist: any extramarital relationship would still have been adultery, and remarriage was of course out of the question.

The civil code finally reached the Chamber of Deputies for discussion and approval in February 1865, five years after the unification of Italy. By that time its need was felt so urgently that it was expedited through the voting process with a minimum of discussion. Nevertheless, the only points that were in any way contested were the principle of civil marriage, and, of course, what that might mean for divorce. The most vocal opponent of civil marriage was Cesare Cantù, a conservative Catholic who feared that civil marriage was the thin end of a dangerous wedge that could be driven home by any subsequent government that might want to introduce divorce.[33] In a similar vein, Vito d'Ondes Reggio, who was to play a role in the battle against divorce in the 1880s, also objected to the introduction of civil marriage because he saw it as a way for divorce to enter Italian law sooner or later. In parliament he made a direct association between forms of marriage and forms of the state, arguing that in the Orient, where families are "polygamous and enslaved," the state is tyrannical. In Europe, on the other hand, where the family is "monogamous and free," the state is also free. The argument is convoluted, but it does underline the immensely strong association between family law and the polity in the minds of the new nation's lawmakers.

Discussion of the civil code went on for some days, but finally, on 22 February 1865, parliament voted to approve it by 149 votes to 77, subject only to slight modifications of detail. The code became law from 1 January 1866, thus becoming the new, single foundation stone of Italian marriage and civil society. It is often referred to as the Pisanelli Code, after the minister under whose auspices it became law. The new code's introduction of civil marriage was a victory for the principle of the separation between Church and state. But like so many achievements of the Risorgimento, it was tempered by compromise in two main ways. The first was that no law was enacted to enforce the precedence of the civil ceremony over ecclesiastical rites, and indeed many Italians continued to marry only in Church, which meant that in the eyes of the state they were merely concubines. The second was that the civil marriage law was not taken to its logical conclusion by allowing divorce.

Responses to the Civil Code

Given the historical context, the exclusion of divorce was not really surprising. Italy would have been only the second Catholic country to allow divorce (after Belgium), and given the delicacy of its historical position, however much a fait accompli the rhetoric of the Risorgimento made unification seem, compromise was the order of the day. Italy had been made in a moderate mold, and 1865 was too early to start reshaping it. Italian citizens were to be made equally moderately, and those seeking to fashion them knew that Catholic culture was one of the only things that the vast majority of Italians had in common. To risk offending those sensibilities, not to mention those of the Church itself, would have been reckless. Finally, if, as Pisanelli had said, the civil code was to be the keystone that united Italians into one family, the idea of divorce would not simply have poisoned the sanctity of marriage—it might have cast a shadow over the whole idea of Italian unity itself.

In the 1860s Italian unity was under threat from much more immediate forces than those provided by metaphors of family separation. Far to the south of the genteel quiet of parliament, battles bloodier than any of those that took place during the Risorgimento were raging, as rebels rose against the new order. The "brigandage," as it was referred to officially, absorbed the energy and attention of the new government for several years after unification and deflected attention from social questions. Furthermore, making Italians, however moderate the mold, was not going to take place overnight, and it is arguable that the majority of the public was not much interested in the new marriage laws. The inertia of decades and sometimes centuries of custom proved difficult to overcome, and this is attested to above all by the fact that even after the civil code stipulated that marriage before an official of the state was the only legally recognized form, many Italians continued to have a religious ceremony and leave it at that. This is something that Cesare Cantù had foreseen, and so his prediction that in the eyes of the law many Italians would simply be living in concubinage was correct.

Given the political climate in the first 15 years after unification, it is not surprising that there were few initiatives to change the status quo laid down by the civil code. Indeed the only further reflection parliament gave the issue of marriage was an effort to entrench that status quo by enforcing the precedence of civil marriage. The legislators who framed the civil code had hoped to evade this delicate issue simply by making the state's version of marriage the only legally recognized one. Apparently for many Italians this was not of great concern, as by 1877 the state's statistics claimed that fully 385,000 marriages since 1866 had only had a religious ceremony. Between 1873 and 1877 there were three attempts to introduce a law that would enforce the precedence of civil marriage, through some sort of sanction, either against priests who performed marriage ceremonies without informing the civil authorities, or even against the marriage contractors themselves.[34] Ultimately though, the issue was altogether too difficult, too enmeshed in the problematic relationship between the Church and the state, and the project was shelved, not to appear again for another 14 years.

If the enforcement of civil marriage was a difficult issue, at least it was only a question of actually enforcing the law as it already stood. Divorce would have been another matter entirely. The fact that it did not come up in government discussions or proposals for at least 12 years after the civil code went into effect is hardly surprising, and in some ways the fact can be read as an indication of the lack of general interest, or demand, for such a law. But it did not mean that the question had been altogether ignored. It was mainly a question that attracted the attention of legal specialists, and in some cases, fervent Catholics,[35] initially within the context of broader studies on the civil code itself. Perhaps the most representative example is Carlo Francesco Gabba's 1862 study of the civil code while it was in preparation. Gabba was an eminent jurist and professor of the philosophy of law at the University of Pisa. In his well-known comparative study of civil legislation, written precisely as a sort of aid for those then preparing the Italian code, Gabba criticized the government's plans by declaring the necessity of divorce as a logical corollary of civil marriage. Anticipating the fear of divorce,[36] he acknowledged that the idea was foreign in Italy but pointed out that since there had hardly been a single study of the question since Melchiorre Gioia's seminal work of 1803,[37] the issue would benefit from serious consideration.[38] His argument in favor of divorce was rooted in a legalistic interpretation of civil marriage as a contract entered into by two people out of free will and to mutual advantage. If, at a later stage, the marriage was no longer to the advantage of the contractors, he thought they should be able to dissolve it.

Gabba's work also provides an early critique of the institution of personal separation, which was all that the civil code proposed to provide by way of escape from a difficult marriage. Gabba regarded personal separation as a mere half measure that, by not allowing the dissolution of marriage, either cruelly enforced celibacy, or, more likely, would lead to sexual relations that were technically adulterous. In this way Gabba portrayed divorce as the morally superior solution to failed marriages. Finally, Gabba predicted that in future divorce would be available to all, and would be a major sign of the complete victory of philosophical law over theocratic law.[39] Gabba's views in 1862 were particularly advanced for their time, but although he was already an influential jurist, his views were not incorporated into the civil code. Perhaps the most interesting thing about Carlo Francesco Gabba was that when divorce appeared to become a real possibility in Italy in the 1880s, he changed his mind and became one of the leading figures in the crusade against its introduction.

A year after Gabba's work was published, a Neapolitan jurist also presented a study of the civil code as it was under preparation. Carlo Coscioni's *I prolegomeni al nuovo codice civile italiano* (Introduction to the New Italian Civil Code) must have been written rather hastily in 1863, as it was published in October, yet the book refers to Pisanelli's July 1863 speech in parliament introducing the civil code. Coscioni had been preparing an historical study of the laws of the Kingdom of the Two Sicilies a few years earlier when in 1860 Garibaldi, "Pontiff of Liberty," rendered Coscioni's effort superfluous—much to the author's evident pleasure.[40] Coscioni, like Pisanelli, saw the civil code as the symbolic completion of the work that Garibaldi had begun, and hoped that it would once again give Italy the chance to reign as "Queen of nations" on the basis of the wisdom of its laws.

While Coscioni praised the introduction of civil marriage, which he saw as a step in the right direction toward severing the ties between Church and state, he lamented the civil code's exclusion of any possibility of divorce. He pointed out that Pisanelli as well as being the minister for justice was also the minister for religions, implying that he had excluded divorce from the civil code for reasons of political delicacy.[41] In this Coscioni was almost certainly right. Like Gabba, Coscioni argued for a dispassionate view of divorce, stripped of all religious connotation, a perspective that saw divorce not as a good thing in itself, but as a remedy for particular ills. Although Coscioni saw a place for personal separation in Italian law, rather than condemning it as Gabba had done, he acknowledged that it often led to scandals, presumably adultery. Finally, Coscioni mentioned the fate of children whose parents' marriages failed. This was to be one of the most emotional issues when divorce was proposed as a law. Coscioni simply declared that it would not be divorce itself that hurt children; rather it was the domestic discord that led to the necessity for divorce that was harmful.[42]

While Gabba's and Coscioni's early pro-divorce opinions were expressed within a general commentary on the civil code, one of the earliest works specifically on divorce was by another, though less illustrious lawyer,

Giuseppe Consolo. His small pamphlet of 1864 also criticizes the proposed civil code for introducing civil marriage while at the same time specifically excluding divorce, claiming that this was an outright contradiction. Consolo's argument in favor of divorce focused on the specific issue of religious freedom, asking rhetorically how the civil code could extend a purely Catholic prohibition to those who confessed other religions, religions that were recognized by the state.[43] In fact he saw the proposed law as unfairly restricting the religious freedom supposedly conferred by the constitution. As an example, Consolo pointed out that Jewish law obliged a man whose wife committed adultery to divorce her, yet under the Italian civil law about to be enacted, that would be impossible.[44]

Consolo looked to the Napoleonic and Austrian civil codes for a solution. Under the former, marriage was a civil affair, which had permitted divorce. If couples chose to have a religious ceremony later, then they would be bound by the prescriptions of the church they chose. The Austrian code was similar, in that marriage was both civil and religious, with the civil law deferring to the prescriptions of the couple's religion on the issue of divorce. Thus under the Napoleonic code until the Restoration, and in contemporary Austria, Jews and Protestants were permitted to divorce, while Catholics were not. The logic of Consolo's argument is persuasive, but despite the much vaunted religious freedom offered to Italian citizens after unification, no such allowances for religious minorities were written into the Italian civil code in relation to marriage. For the new Italian state it was less risky to offend religious minorities by denying them the right to divorce than to introduce a principle that was offensive to the Catholic Church.

Works like those of Gabba, Coscioni, and Consolo, which examined the question of divorce from either a legalistic point of view or with regard to religious freedom, reflected the atmosphere of caution and gradualism in the new Italian state. It was not surprising that published works examining the question of divorce in a broader way were few and far between in Italy in the 1860s. This makes the small volume devoted to divorce by the Neapolitan Elviro Naclerio all the more noteworthy. Naclerio's principal tenet was that an absolute prohibition on the dissolution of pernicious marriages was uncivilized. What stands out about Naclerio's work is its sense of history, and its ready recognition of the weaknesses of the human flesh. These qualities put the pamphlet in a category apart from the rather dry treatises that his close contemporaries had written on divorce.

Naclerio felt that the century had been great for Italy, but that if a law on divorce were achieved the progress of the century would really be consolidated. He saw marriage as an institution developed by civilization to contain and direct the basic human forces: love, and the "physical tendency to reproduction." He argued that marriage could not logically be considered purely a matter of religion, because the instincts behind physical union were as old as human life (implying that religion was not). Nor, in the interests of civilization, could marriage simply be abandoned to base instincts. It was therefore obvious why marriage had always been controlled with vigilance by legislators. On the other hand, according to Naclerio, this vigilance could never completely subdue nature's laws, and it was the impossibility of forcing all marriages to live up to a supernatural ideal that made divorce, in his view, a necessary safety valve.[45]

What is impressive about Naclerio's analysis is that he saw marriage, and therefore the family, as a product of the interaction between natural human impulses and the broader processes of society—an interaction that would be subject to historical change as society developed. Indeed, one of his major arguments in favor of the introduction of divorce is an historical one. He looked back to the marriage customs of ancient Rome, mentioning the practice of *usucapione*, which permitted a couple to try each other out for a year before committing themselves to marriage.[46] Naclerio glances at Judaic law and society in ancient Egypt and Greece, all of which permitted divorce.[47] This is an attempt to underline the relatively recent nature of the Catholic Church's banning of marital dissolution. And even here, he points out that the Church interpreted its own laws with a certain elasticity when major political questions were involved.[48]

Although Naclerio argues that it is time for Italy to recognize the necessity of divorce again, his argument for it is by no means radical. His view of the family is a traditional one that would not have found trouble attracting support from conservative Catholics: that the customs of families are reflected in the state, because men bring to the administration of public affairs the same ideas and affections that they acquire within the domestic sphere. The difference between Naclerio and, for example, a conservative like d'Ondes Reggio, who used the same argument in a parliamentary speech against civil marriage in 1852, is that Naclerio viewed divorce as a moralizing institution. He thought the custom of personal separation a cruel one, having the same effects as divorce without breaking the marital bond. In his view the only possible defense for it would be the chance of a reconciliation, but he claimed that this is almost always an unrealistic hope.

Finally, Naclerio acknowledged that one of the main arguments against divorce was that it would lead to depravity, with wives seduced and abandoned. Naclerio saw divorce as a safety valve to be used with caution, and above all with the purpose of improving the moral tone of society rather than to grant greater licence. For this reason he knew that it would be imperative to surround a divorce law with safeguards that would prevent it from becoming an easy escape route from mere marital boredom.

His solution was to limit the reasons for which divorce would be permitted to those that currently applied for personal separation, excluding mutual consent adultery, abandonment, and ill-treatment.

Naclerio briefly addressed the problem of the fate of children after a divorce, the question generally considered the most difficult aspect of the entire issue. As Coscioni had done in 1864, Naclerio declared that the root of the problem for children was not divorce itself, but marital discord. He argued that at least divorce might put a permanent end to this, and even if parents entered into second marriages, happily remarried people would make better parents than those banished to the purgatory of personal separation.[49]

The conclusion to Naclerio's work broadens the focus and becomes rather patriotic. As he had suggested at the outset, he viewed divorce as an element in a battle against the pernicious effects of Catholicism's grip upon the newly woven national fabric. He saw the complete ban upon marital dissolution as a Church-inspired exaggeration, not truly representing the spirit of the Bible. He urged Italy to throw off the Catholic strait-jacket and listed the fates of those nations still enclosed in it: from Ireland, still weighed down in misery and civil war, to Portugal, dead to political life, to Poland—dismembered.[50] Italy must not succumb to a similar fate, and the introduction of divorce would be a sign that it was a nation striking out on its own. Naclerio thought that divorce would become less and less necessary as humans progressed intellectually and morally, and in the meantime marriage would become more popular if it were less threatening. All this would be to the good of the nation. According to this view, those natural human impulses that the institution of marriage is designed to contain and focus, would presumably become more and more controlled by individuals.

Here Naclerio was wrong. But in another and more important way, he was right. He had spelled out that the family and marriage were institutions that resulted from the interaction between fundamental human desires and the formative powers of custom, civil, and religious law. Catholic dogma aside, it remains unclear whether there is anything natural, in a biological sense, about a couple remaining together monogamously for their entire lives. That custom had been imposed by the Council of Trent, and by 1860 it had been accepted for so long that it was easy for rhetoric to make it seem natural. Nor did those in favor of divorce argue that it was an undesirable custom. They merely claimed that in some cases the enforcement of the ideal of indissoluble marriage was cruel. Writers who were pro-divorce were far from advocating the dismantling of the family. For them, the fundamental question was which institution should regulate marriage and the family in civil society.

The writings of Gabba, Coscioni, and Naclerio are essentially responses to what they all perceived to be the failure of the civil code to stake its claim to the regulation of marriage with sufficient conviction. It could have done this in two ways. The most radical would have been to permit divorce. As it stood, the civil code simply incorporated the characteristics of marriage that the Church had conferred upon it, with indissolubility occupying pride of place. To eliminate this would have been the clearest signal that the state had really made marriage its own, and would have followed through with the logical consequences of establishing civil marriage. The second, and less radical way, would have been to enforce with legal sanctions the precedence of civil marriage over religious marriage. But this possibility was dismissed when the civil code was introduced, in the name of a free Church in a free state. As a result, the code effectively staked its claims to the territory of marriage only in a vague way. This vagueness is a token of the compromise that characterized the relationship between the Church and the state in Liberal Italy.

The political climate of the 1860s was not auspicious for a clearer assertion of the state's claim to regulate the most intimate aspect of its citizens' lives, despite the well-reasoned arguments of legal luminaries like Gabba and others. Nor were there to be any significant changes to this climate in the 1870s, because although changes of the cabinet were frequent, until 1876 the tone of the governments continued to be dominated by the conservative elements that had been victorious in the Risorgimento. Nevertheless, divorce was a subject that continued to attract the attention of thinkers. The number of publications on the subject was not great (Pagliaini's authoritative guide lists no more than 12 works devoted to the subject published in the 1870s[51]) but it is important to indicate that although divorce was a dead letter in the legislature, it was not forgotten in society.

Women and the Civil Code

Women had a notably low profile in the debate on divorce during this early period. In a society in which public and published opinions were almost invariably those of men, women's ideas about divorce are particularly difficult to discern. This makes the scant number of works by women on the civil code, marriage, and divorce particularly important. The first woman to publish a critique of the Italian civil code's treatment of women was the radical feminist Anna Maria Mozzoni. Mozzoni was born in Milan in 1837, and was deeply imbued with the ideals of the Risorgimento. Indeed, she thought of the movement for the emancipation of women as analogous to the movement for Italian independence,[52] but she was disappointed by the little that women obtained. Although her pamphlet on the civil code applauded the principle of bringing the tutelage of family relations under the auspices of the state and away from the Catholic Church, Mozzoni was critical of the subjection of women to male authority that was the underlying principle of the code's law on marriage.[53]

Mozzoni was also sharply critical of the enormous inequality embodied in the law on adultery, which was notably indulgent to men, and also the prohibition of paternity suits, which she rightly claimed allowed men to escape responsibility for their sexual behavior.[54] It is worth noting that Mozzoni had nothing to say about the indissoluble character of marriage under the code. This may partly be explained by the nature of Mozzoni's early feminism, which was much more concerned with notions of equality than with establishing liberties for women.[55] Later, in 1902, Mozzoni was one of a small number of women who expressed herself in favor of divorce during the high point of the campaign to introduce it,[56] but shortly after unification it had not been one of her concerns.

One woman who tackled the problem of divorce directly in the 1870s was Maria Alimonda Serafini, in a pamphlet entitled *Matrimonio e divorzio*.[57] This was exceedingly rare: it is the only known work by an Italian woman dedicated to the subject of divorce published between unification and 1900. Little has been written about Serafini, but she was one of several prominent women who had played an active role in the Risorgimento. In 1859 she had taken part in a committee of national liberation in Lombardy, and in 1860 she met Mazzini and became one of his regular correspondents.[58] More dramatically, she had rushed to Aspromonte to offer succor to Garibaldi after he was wounded there in 1862.[59] Her feminism bears a clear liberal stamp, and like Mozzoni and Schiff, she was also disappointed by the little that unification had brought to Italian women.

Serafini begins her book on divorce by tackling the theme of institutional regulation of private life, claiming that Christianity asserted its control over marriage by elevating celibacy to the highest level of existence. Marriage was therefore constructed from the outset as a concession,[60] a fallen state that had to be carefully regulated. In this way Serafini underlines that marriage was invented after copulation and is society's domestication of that procedure. As she puts it, in primitive times a man laid out his property with stones, took a woman, and made her his. God's benediction came later. The idea of marriage coming later also underlines the fact that certain acts that are now morally reprehensible were actually brought into being by the invention of marriage. As Serafini herself asks rhetorically, which came first, marriage or adultery?[61]

But Serafini, like all those in favor of divorce in the late nineteenth century, was far from advocating a return to primitive times, a return to free love. She accepted marriage as an aspect of civilization. And like her male counterparts, she argued for divorce as a possibility within marriage that would help to guarantee the morality of the family.[62] Unlike those of her male colleagues, however, Serafini's comments were written from the point of view of a woman. As things stood, it was essential for a female to marry because that was the principal role society had assigned her. For a variety of reasons this could lead to bad marriages. The very pressure to marry meant that often a woman would take any man, with little concern for "homogeneity of character."[63] It was this homogeneity that Serafini suggested would be the only guarantee of a long and happy marriage. The deleterious effects of pressure to marry were often exacerbated by other factors, such as poverty (which further reduced a woman's choice), parental pressure, and female inexperience. All these could combine to undermine the future happiness of a marriage. For women, divorce would provide the possibility of escape from an otherwise permanent hell that could result from marriages entered into as a result of external pressures.

Serafini saw the question of divorce as linking broad issues concerning the position of women in society. She thought that divorce was a less pressing issue for men because even within a marriage social mores granted them more leeway to seek diversion outside the domestic confines.[64] Women, on the other hand, were effectively enslaved within those confines, and civilized societies had a duty to liberate them. Divorce would be one step toward this. But according to Serafini, divorce would not entail an exodus of women from their marriages. On the contrary, she argues that the possibility of divorce would ensure that people chose their marriage partners more carefully, with the result that families would be more stable.

Like Naclerio, Serafini shows great faith in the benefits of education and liberation, suggesting that as more people had greater access to both, divorce would become less necessary.[65] Serafini therefore places the issue of divorce within an overall scheme for national improvement, based on the notion of liberating women from the rigidities of the prevailing system of marriage. She drew attention to the availability of divorce in England, Prussia, Saxony, Belgium, and the United States, asking rhetorically why Italy should remain under the yoke of old-fashioned laws.[66] But it is important to emphasize that the main purpose of divorce, according to Serafini, was to reinforce the bonds of affection that held families together, by making those bonds more genuine. The family remained the key element in all that makes society strong and good.

Disseminating the Idea of Divorce

Serafini's technique of viewing Italy's lack of divorce in an international context was not uncommon. It was to be expected in a new nation like Italy, still in the process of establishing an identity, that its educated citizens would be sensitive to legal and social developments elsewhere. When divorce was legalized or even merely on the agenda in other countries, it sparked debate in Italy. This was the case in 1874, when divorce was introduced in Switzerland. This was the starting point for the first really major study of divorce to be written in Italy since Gioia's work of 1803. Domenico Di Bernardo's *Il divorzio considerato nella teoria e nella pratica* (Divorce in Theory and Practice), published in Palermo in 1875, dedicated more than 600 pages to the subject. The author begins by acknowledging the recent legislation in Switzerland, and lamenting the fact that more notice was not taken of the event in Italy.[67] His own work is cautiously liberal in tone, and his arguments in favor of divorce brought together many that were already familiar in the 1870s. Displaying inexhaustible legal learning, much of what Di Bernardo had to say involves the history of marriage and divorce, and even more has to do with the study of foreign legislation on divorce. In all, by sheer weight of detail the book seeks to make the lack of divorce in Italy seem, by the mid-1870s, an historical and international anomaly.

Di Bernardo's approach was legalistic rather than tub-thumping. His book advocates the introduction of divorce, but only in four cases: abandonment,[68] a criminal conviction leading to a prison sentence of seven years or more,[69] grievous injury or other acts of violence,[70] and adultery.[71] Although he mentioned it last, Di Bernardo felt that adultery was the most valid cause for divorce, suggesting, once again, that divorce was seen not so much as an escape route from an unsatisfactory marriage, but as a law that would help keep marital relationships orderly. Nevertheless, he was in complete agreement with the Napoleonic code's notion that male infidelity had to be of a more serious nature to constitute the crime of adultery, and adds dismissively that temporary affairs with one or two women would not be grounds for divorce.[72] Di Bernardo engages with Gioia, with whom he disagreed, on the question of impotence. He sympathized with the plight of older married men, but claimed that Gioia was too concerned with population increase, and he did not see impotence as a valid cause for divorce.[73]

The acid test of attitudes to divorce was the question of whether it should be allowed for mutual consent. This question had long divided the pro-divorce camp into radicals and moderates, and would continue to be a divisive issue among their ranks. Di Bernardo was a moderate, claiming that marriage was too serious a matter to be subject to personal whim, and should not necessarily be allowed to come to an end when pleasure was exhausted, even if it was mutually exhausted.[74]

Di Bernardo's moderate position on the question of mutual consent underlined his legalistic approach to the overall question of divorce. He did not in any way advocate a radical change in the position of the family within the state. His book is really no more than an argument that the civil code's position on marriage was too much a compromise with the Catholic Church. He argues that if a state allows freedom of religion, it must also accept the principle of divorce. Against those who claimed that divorce should not be offered to all citizens merely because some have a religion that does not prohibit it, Di Bernardo argues that the state should not enter into religious questions, but should simply legislate for the public good.[75] Divorce would not, after all, be imposed on people, but would simply be available to those whose consciences permitted it. While the work maintains its dispassionate and legalistic approach for the most part, toward the end it becomes patriotic. For Di Bernardo divorce was essentially a question of the application of reason to human affairs, and Italy had not gone far enough in this application: the absence of a divorce law meant that Italy had stopped half way. In order to ensure that Italy again assumed its position as "mother of every modern gentility and culture" it must introduce divorce.[76]

Books like Di Bernardo's, though a rarity, are stylistically typical of the way thinkers expressed their opinions about questions like divorce in the late nineteenth century: cautious, legalistic, dry, and aimed at a very restricted audience. By 1876 there was some evidence of a need to persuade a broader audience of the necessity for divorce legislation in Italy, and this is exemplified by two of the most important works published on divorce in that year. One is a particular curiosity, being the first known Italian novel to take divorce as its theme: Il divorzio, by Francesco Meleri. This melodramatic story is a parable about matrimonial mismatches, true love, and the way divorce would offer a solution that was then only provided by suicide. The principal characters are Elvira, daughter of a bourgeois family, and Ascanio, an orphan fostered by Elvira's parents. As children, it is clear, the two have great affinity, but as tradition would have it, Elvira is married off to an engineer, Arturo.[77]

Unfortunately for Elvira, Arturo turns out to be a gambler, and ends up in prison for life after murdering his usurious moneylender. Meleri makes much of Elvira's fate as a young wife, effectively condemned to a life-long sentence of spinsterhood because she is not able to divorce Arturo. The author intersperses the action with many scenes of earnest discussions about divorce, all of which add up to a slightly didactic attempt to dispel misinformation. The novel ends when Arturo commits suicide in prison. Before he does so he writes a note to Ascanio, saying that he knew he and Elvira had always been in love, and he was removing himself so they could marry.[78] This overdone but nevertheless poignant plot brought to life one of the scenarios referred to by the more legalistic texts, and attempted to make the scenario real for a broader audience. It was an impassioned plea for the introduction of a divorce law, presented in an unusual way, and it lives up to Meleri's promise (made in the preface) to show one way in which dissoluble marriage would be better than indissoluble marriage.

The second important work on divorce to appear in 1876 was also an attempt to popularize knowledge about divorce. Also entitled *Il divorzio*, it was a small pamphlet by the Neapolitan Giuseppe Ricciardi.[79] Ricciardi's work is not so much a theoretical consideration of the question of divorce, as an effort to persuade a broad audience of its practical necessity. The preface takes the form of a letter to the honorable Mauro Macchi, asking him to propose a law on divorce. Macchi had earlier proposed a law banning duels, and perhaps this indicated to Ricciardi that he was progressive. Ricciardi laments the fact that Italian newspapers had essentially turned their backs on the question of divorce, and also claims that there is a lack of literature on the subject. He does acknowledge Di Bernardo's massive work on divorce, but he criticizes it, first for being far too long, claiming that no one would have the patience to read it. But more seriously, Ricciardi finds Di Bernardo's model of divorce too cautious, and above all disagrees with his exclusion of mutual consent as a reason for divorce. Ricciardi's pamphlet can be seen as a reaction to this, and as an attempt to popularize an issue that in his view had remained obscure for too long.

As Meleri's novel had done, *Il divorzio* explains the benefits of divorce by developing scenarios to illustrate cases in which divorce would have a salutary effect. In the opening scene, Celia, the dutiful wife, is sewing by candlelight after midnight, patiently awaiting the return of her husband who is out drinking and accumulating debts by gambling. In another scene Roberto, the honest husband, is earnestly making a living as a goldsmith to support his family, but while he is doing so his wife is flirting with other men. Both Celia and Roberto are trapped for life with their unsuitable spouses, yet what a wonderful couple they themselves would make if their paths were to cross and they could marry. Divorce would enable such a marriage to take place.[80]

More menacingly, Ricciardi depicts a scene in which a husband's desire to be rid of his wife is so strong that he tries to murder her. As a result he is sentenced to life imprisonment, but as in Meleri's novel, the poor wife's fate is to be chained to that of her criminal husband, so she not only suffers the attempted murder, but also has to serve her own form of life sentence as a result. Nevertheless, she responds to her natural urges, and over the years has 10 lovers, to each of whom she bears a child. The implication is that if she had been able to divorce, she would have married again and had children in wedlock. So in this case the absence of divorce not only damaged her individual liberty, but also caused moral disruption to society through the birth of 10 illegitimate children.[81] As if that were not enough, Ricciardi also refers to three recent cases of uxoricide, in which either wives or husbands, out of sheer desperation, murdered their spouse rather than continue in an insufferable marriage.[82]

From these graphic and accessible illustrations of the harm that indissoluble marriage could cause, Ricciardi shifts to a consideration of marriage in jurisdictions in which divorce was permitted. He dismisses English law, which only allowed divorce in cases of adultery, and which he regarded as a reward for immorality.[83] The laws in Germany and Belgium seemed fairer to him. Even so, both required long waiting periods between official separation and divorce, and required significant sums of money.[84] Ricciardi argues that divorce should be simple and inexpensive and suggests specific adjustments to article 148 of the civil code. His concluding pages focus on women. Ricciardi regarded their position as a form of slavery, an intolerable situation in these days when all the talk is of liberty. He blamed their position upon the tyranny of priests and claimed that with women as their agents, priests exercised far too much influence within the family home.[85] Ricciardi's argument in favor of divorce reveals itself ultimately as anticlerical, and sees the chief gainers from divorce as women. Indeed, the last words of the work ask women "suffering under the cross of matrimonial indissolubility" to correspond with the author.[86] Presumably he was after true-life scenarios with which to publicize the idea of divorce further.

The fact remained that throughout the reign of the so-called Historic Right, the political climate was such that the regime of matrimonial indissolubility was an unchanging characteristic of the Italian social and political landscape. For, even though the Italian state was a fait accompli by 1861, at the time its future integrity seemed far less secure than that of the average indissoluble marriage. Apart from anything else, the Veneto and Rome, which completed the unification of the peninsula, were acquired only well after the declaration of the Kingdom of Italy. For another, the hostility of the Catholic Church to the new state, clearly expressed in the Syllabus of Errors of 1864 and Pius IX's ban on Catholics taking part in Italian national politics, known as the *non-expedit*, meant that the integrity of the nation was flawed right down to the souls of its citizens. When these flaws were first revealed in all their depth by the virtual civil war in which southern peasants rebelled against the new government in the early 1860s, it underlined the social fragility of the state and justified, in the eyes of the new government, a particularly rigid approach to an issue that went to the heart of the social fabric.

Though that attitude was firm, it was not inflexible. As even the more moderate ideals of the Risorgimento encountered the social realities of the newly created state, Italian politics became a judicious blend of outward sternness and inner compromise, thus continuing an essentially Cavourian tradition of political pragmatism. Few things illustrate this as clearly as the peculiar solution that the 1865 civil code adopted for marriage. Marriage finally became a civil affair, thus settling a question that had been opened in Piedmont in 1850, but that had been put aside by Cavour two years later as part of a political compromise. The civil code of 1865 closed that question by taking for the state a tract of legal territory that had traditionally been the fief of the Church, almost as if it were a substitute for the real territory of Rome. But by so doing, and despite its best efforts not to, the Italian government opened another question, potentially far more divisive: the issue of divorce.

Divorce as an idea hardly saw the light of day before it was put to rest by Pisanelli's comments about it when he introduced the civil code. While the code took marriage away from the institution that had made it indissoluble, it created the "juridical monster" of indissoluble civil marriage. As many commentators were later to point out, this was an oxymoronic concept, and put Italy out on a limb in terms of international comparison. But however anomalous the adopted solution may have been, it would probably have been more surprising if Italy had actually introduced divorce. Making marriage an entirely civil affair had already fulfilled the Risorgimento ideal of the separation of civil and religious jurisdictions, and given the strained relations between the Church and the state, it would have been provocative to push civil marriage to its logical conclusion. It was clearly in the state's interest to minimize provocative acts toward the Church, and in a climate of civil strife, caution and conservatism were obvious bywords. Nor, on a comparative basis, did Italy seem particularly anomalous in not offering its citizens the possibility of divorce. Indeed, even France, Italy's closest neighbor geographically and in spirit, did not have a divorce law. Among Catholic countries only Belgium permitted it in any broad way. And even England had introduced divorce only a few years before Italy's civil code was written, and only for adultery.

Ultimately, the governments that steered the new Italy over the difficult first few years of its life were determined to keep the Italian family, both national and private, protected from anything that might threaten its integrity. Introducing divorce would have widened the rift between the Church and the state, and would probably have offended many of its more pious citizens. The governments that ruled Italy for the first 15 years of unification maintained a steady concentration on ensuring the integrity of the realm. Social questions were low on the list of priorities, and divorce, while it occupied the minds of certain intellectuals, social commentators, and jurists, was certainly not an idea that would have captured the imagination of many government members between 1860 and 1876. But once this historic reign ended, and the ascent of the Left changed the air in parliament, the atmosphere was more conducive to the discussion of social questions of all types. It was only a matter of time before the question of divorce, opened by the introduction of civil marriage but ignored by politicians for reasons of political expedience, should occupy the mind of some ardent parliamentarian.

2

Unmaking Marriage?

The First Proposals for a Divorce Law, 1878–1880

The fall of the so-called Historic Right in 1876 and the ascent of the Left promised the first real mutation in Italian political life since the unification. During the intervening years the social conservatism shared by the heirs of Cavour had been justified by the insecure position of the new Italian state. Italy was made, but Italians were not, and forces both within and outside Italy would have been happy to see it return to the status quo ante. The insecurities of the 1860s were to some extent removed by the unification of Germany in 1866 and the Franco-Prussian war in 1870. The first event removed the threat of the Austrian Empire redividing the Italian peninsula among its scions, and added the Veneto to Italian territory. The second ended Napoleon III's empire in France, which had had a hostile attitude to Italy and had maintained the Pope's independence from it with military aid. France's defeat in the war of 1870 enabled Italy to claim Rome as its capital, a move that symbolized the final unification of the realm.

If the removal of external pressure on Italy in turn led to the intensification of the hostility of the "enemy within," the Catholic Church, that threat was a more subtle and less immediate one than those that had been represented by hostile foreign powers, and by the mid-1870s Italians had reason to feel more confident about their nation's future. Many Liberals and progressives now saw the powerful hold of the Catholic Church over the majority of Italy's citizens as the only major impediment to molding real Italians, and many initiatives in these years had a distinctly anticlerical tone. The fall of the Right and the rise of the Left under Agostino Depretis represents a clear changing of the guard in Liberal Italy, and it cleared the path for consideration of social questions and other matters that had hitherto received short shrift. One of these was to be divorce.[1]

Italy was not the only European country for which the year 1876 marked a turning point that would allow for freer discussion of questions like divorce. In March of that year, the elections in France had overturned MacMahon's authoritarianism and produced a progressive majority. One of the first signs of the significance of this change was the presentation of a divorce bill by Alfred Naquet in June 1876.[2] Although it was rejected, and its proponent was accused of threatening the cohesion of French families just when the republic most needed social peace, Naquet did not give up. The following year, he published a book-length study entitled *Le divorce*,[3] and in 1878 he returned to parliament with another, distinctly less radical proposal for divorce.[4] This suffered the same fate as its predecessor, but together they marked the beginning of a concerted campaign that would culminate in the introduction of divorce in France a few years later. France and Italy moved very much in tandem on the divorce issue during these years, and it is clear that the high-profile debate in France prompted a matching debate in Italy, albeit on a smaller scale.

Salvatore Morelli

It is in this context that the first proposals to modify the Italian law's categorical insistence on the indissolubility of marriage were discussed in the Chamber of Deputies. As in France, the bills were presented not by the government, but by an individual deputy, Salvatore Morelli, first in 1878, and then in 1880. Had it not been for the singular and brave persistence of this far-sighted but eccentric parliamentarian, divorce may have had to wait far longer before it was taken into consideration by the government. It was not always a straightforward matter to have a bill presented in parliament, as the members had to vote on whether they thought it was worth considering. In the case of Morelli's two proposals, both were taken up by parliament, although for various reasons neither was brought to fruition. In contrast to successive attempts by more powerful government members to introduce a divorce law into Italy, Morelli's bills did not lead to broad or significant reactions in Italian politics or society, judging by the low level of coverage the issue received in the press. Nevertheless, they were an important first step, and the seriousness with which parliament discussed divorce in 1878 and 1880 provided encouragement for the more influential politicians who followed in Morelli's footsteps.

Apart from Morelli's significance as the first person to introduce the discussion of divorce into parliament, he also deserves attention for his unusual political character. On the one hand he represented a Risorgimento radicalism that owed a great deal to Mazzini, but which in many ways appeared old-fashioned and idealistic by 1878. He was, as one of the few modern historians who has studied him claims, a classic product of the generation of 1848.[5] Yet on the other hand, the single driving force behind his whole political career was a mystical feminism, inspired by Mazzini. Morelli's proposals for divorce represented a confluence of these two currents, since it was an issue that Morelli saw as a double crusade: one for individual liberty, involving the complete rejection of all clerical impediments to the ideal state, and a second, entirely dedicated to the liberation of Italian women from the injustices of the civil code. Morelli's two proposals for divorce represent the first phase in the history of the divorce debates in Italy, and one which has a distinctive character. That character derives from the anachronistic idealism embodied by Morelli: his political views were utopian and idealistic in an age of emergent *trasformismo* (the term applied to the transformational politics of expedience that characterized the Depretis era), while his feminism anticipated the developments of far later decades.

When the honorable Salvatore Morelli presented a proposal to introduce divorce into Italian law in May 1878, he was the first deputy to attempt to persuade the government of united Italy to consider what was then regarded as a deeply radical idea. But for Morelli himself this event was not the beginning of a radical campaign; it represented the climax of a 20-year personal struggle to gain civil rights for women[6]—a campaign that was so foreign in the context of nineteenth-century Italy that Morelli seemed to be a voice in the wilderness. His 1878 attempt to introduce a divorce law had been preceded by two earlier attempts. In 1873 and 1875 he had asked parliament to consider a broad series of changes to the law in favor of women, of which divorce was simply a part. On both occasions parliament had voted not even to listen to a reading of the draft laws. The fact that parliament was even prepared to entertain Morelli's new proposal on divorce in 1878 is indicative of the new political atmosphere after 1876.

Although the tenacity with which Morelli held his views on women had earned him the reputation as an eccentric in parliament, his earlier life had furnished him with political credentials that prevented him from being altogether dismissed as a joker. Morelli was born in Puglia in 1824, in what was then part of the Kingdom of the Two Sicilies, and his career as an activist was closely tied to the history of the unification of Italy. By the time he was 24 years old Morelli had moved to Naples, where he studied law. He took part in the 1848 revolutions, and after the restoration of the Bourbons he was tried for "acts, deeds and writings" deemed harmful to the image of King Ferdinand and his queen, and with many hundreds of fellow revolutionaries he was condemned to prison. The sentence of eight years was later commuted to confinement on the island of Ponza, but in

1851 he was moved to prison again, this time on the island of Ischia, after being suspected of conspiracy. He remained there for 18 months, and was then deported to another island, Ventotene. Close to his release date, in 1857, he was accused of having made 300 tricolor flags and faced trial again, but was found not guilty.

Released, but kept under surveillance, Morelli returned to his native Puglia. When he refused to appear before the king during a royal visit to Lecce, he was again thrown into prison, and it was from within those walls that he first heard how Garibaldi's troops had overthrown the king he had refused to meet. The collapse of the Bourbon kingdom gave Morelli his liberty after more than a decade of imprisonment for his political views and activities. For Morelli, personal freedom was thus inextricably linked with the unification of Italy,[7] and his life as a politician in the new nation can be seen as a passionate crusade to ensure greater liberty for those whom the unification did not, in his view, liberate.

Morelli developed his views on the necessity of freedom for women during his imprisonment. Like Mazzini, Morelli was very close to his mother, and when she died during his confinement on Ventotene, it sparked a personal crisis that resulted in a meditation on the importance of motherhood.[8] This meditation became the basis for what was to become Morelli's best known written work, *La donna e la scienza* (Woman and Science), a book he started writing in prison and finished at Lecce in 1859. First published in 1862, the definitive third edition of 1869, which was considerably expanded, is the most important version. Morelli's thesis is that the subordinate position of women reflected male physical and intellectual force crudely parlayed into law,[9] and that society would only begin to make progress once women had been recognized as citizens with rights equal to those of men.

Morelli regarded the contemporary juridical position of women in Italian society as the culmination of a long historical process, as a result of which women had been reduced to mere items of commerce.[10] Society had corrupted women's exalted position in nature, in which she had been mystically in touch with the very processes of creation, and now she was chained to the home and the Church, "under the perpetual vigilance of the Catholic prison warden."[11] This foretaste of intense anticlericalism later developed into a major strand of Morelli's thought. But he also develops a critique of the more secular concept of female honor, which he claimed was no more than another instrument of oppression.[12] Morelli's aim was to promote the introduction of laws that would right the historical wrongs of man against woman, and set them on an equal footing. It was a campaign to which Morelli dedicated himself tirelessly for the final 20 years of his life.

This personal and rather lonely crusade for women's rights was linked to a utopian vision of a peaceful and just society that owed much to thinkers such as Saint Simon and Fourier.[13] Mazzini's "Discorso agli operai italiani" (Address to the Italian Workers) also clearly inspired Morelli's ideas about women and he quotes it early in his own work. Mazzini had claimed that the only unalloyed joys given to mankind are those of the family, through the angelic presence of woman. It was her altruistic love that ideally provided the foundation of the family, and it was this that gave the family its special quality: endurance.[14] In turn, Mazzini's ideas about the family go back to Hegel, who, rather than emphasizing the structure of the family, likened the bonds of the state to the altruistic ones that supposedly lay at the heart of the family.[15] According to Morelli, this idea of altruistic love had become perverted by centuries of male dominance, and just as the ideal of the family formed the basis of the ideal state for Hegel, so the corrupted and unequal relationship within contemporary families explained the ills of the contemporary state for Morelli. His crusade for women was therefore also a crusade for the family and in turn a crusade for the very nature of the state itself. Morelli's apparently renegade ideas ultimately expressed no more than a heartfelt loyalty to the ideals of patria, famiglia e libertà.[16] In the last years of his life, commitment to a divorce law was the vehicle through which he chose to express those ideals.

Morelli's First Divorce Proposal

The draft of Morelli's proposal for divorce was read to the Chamber of Deputies on 16 May 1878. Article 1 permitted the dissolution of a marriage without children in six possible cases: incurable impotence occurring after the marriage; infidelity on the part of either spouse, or prostitution of the wife; attempted murder of one spouse by the other; a life prison sentence for either spouse; extreme prodigality; and finally, incompatibility of character, evidenced by habitual disorder in the family. If the family had produced children, divorce could be obtained in all but the first and the last cases, that is, impotence and incompatibility of character. Although the proposal was slightly eccentric in its wording, Morelli had set an historical precedent, and most of these causes would appear in some form or other in all future proposals for a divorce law. The key issue for many, which went back to the divorce law of the French Revolution, was whether a couple could obtain a divorce by mutual consent. Although Morelli's proposal did not use this phrase, the provision for incompatibility of character would have lent itself to divorce by mutual consent.

Proffering divorce as a cure-all for society's ills seemed perverse to many of Morelli's contemporaries, but the first serious effort to alter the civil code's position on the indissolubility of marriage needs to be seen in the broader context of Morelli's thought. Despite his sworn anticlericalism, Morelli's divorce proposals were not merely attempts to provoke the ire of the Church. Above all they were an attempt to strengthen the institution of the family by remaking it along more egalitarian lines. When Morelli presented his proposal to parliament on 25 May 1878, his first rhetorical ploy was to try and forestall the criticism of those who would inevitably see in divorce an anarchic attempt to destroy the family as the basis of society. He claimed that a mere glance at the newspapers was sufficient to confirm that misdeeds and crimes plagued society. He argued that the majority of these could be attributed to the juridical inequality at the heart of the family. Aware that divorce could easily be construed as an attempt to undermine the stability of the family,[17] Morelli tried to show that the existence of divorce would actually make families stronger, as it would encourage loving partners to treat each other with respect rather than risk taking liberties of the sort that could lead to divorce.[18] Of course, if love was not part of the marriage, divorce would free partners from a life-long sentence. For Morelli, divorce had a moralizing function, and its main aim was to make better families, which would in turn improve the tone of society.

It is quite possible that there was an element of disingenuousness in the way Morelli presented his law to parliament, in that he emphasized the morality of a project whose principal motives came from an anticlerical urge or some other tendency associated with his political radicalism. But all the evidence in Morelli's published work suggests that he was genuinely profamily, while there is nothing (except perhaps his own status as a bachelor) to suggest that he had a hidden agenda. Believing that the family was a good and natural basis of society was not necessarily the same thing as having completely traditional views about the institution, and Morelli's views about the family were certainly not rigidly traditional. In the first place, his insistence upon the necessity for gender equality within marriage would have been considered deeply suspicious anywhere in Europe in the 1870s, but was all the more so in Italy, where Catholic and secular Mediterranean traditions coalesced to affirm a particularly subordinate position for women.

Despite the radicalism of Morelli's overall views, he knew that if he could emphasize his belief in the family as the fundamental institution of society, and present his project as one that aimed to reinforce the family rather than destroy it, he would have a better chance of receiving a sympathetic hearing. In *La donna e la scienza*, Morelli had claimed that the family was the "cradle of the destiny of a great society,"[19] an idea that would not have disturbed even the most conservative reader. Arguing for divorce in 1878, the overall tone of Morelli's approach was in harmony with his earlier statements about the social function of the family, but he also introduced the idea that this function could change as society developed. Rejecting the idea that the family should be an immutable and ideal institution, Morelli defended his proposal for divorce against anticipated claims that it would be the thin end of the wedge of social anarchy by promoting an historical view of the family as an institution subject to change.

Beginning with the idea of primitive promiscuity before settled society became established, Morelli underlined that the earliest families were thought to be matriarchal and then gradually mutated, through various influences, into patriarchal structures. His ideas about the historical origins of the family clearly owed a great deal to Bachofen's landmark work of 1861, *Das Mutterrecht*, which Morelli cited in his speech to parliament.[20] The idea that patriarchal society was historically conditioned provided the basis for an emerging critique of the family in the late nineteenth century.[21] Morelli was almost certainly the first Italian of any profile to apply such a critique to the patriarchal structure of Italian society.

By historicizing the family, Morelli aims to make two main points: that the family has been important since the beginnings of civilized life; and that over the centuries family structures have changed as society itself has changed.[22] Morelli thought it was the legislator's task to effect changes within the law that governed families in a way that would maximize the family's chance of fulfilling the functions allocated to it by society. But he rejected as an impossibility that such legal modifications could ever risk destroying the family. As he put it, "the extrinsic organic forms of the family can always vary, and have always varied; but the basis, the foundation . . . can never be lessened. And it is this which makes for the eternity of the family."[23]

The introductory section of Morelli's speech consists of such attempts to dissolve considerable resistance to the mere notion of divorce that he knew he would have to tackle before laying out the details of his proposal. Once he had softened the ground, Morelli moves to more specific historical antecedents, mentioning the ancient right of Jews to divorce, then that of the Egyptians and Greeks, and also the law of Republican Rome. Wisely skipping over the decadence of Imperial Rome, Morelli arrives at the French Revolution, which popularized the idea of divorce all over Europe for the first time. In certain parts of the Italian peninsula, divorce was made available for a number of years while the Napoleonic code was in force. As a counter to those who argued that divorce would inevitably lead to escalating marital dissolution, Morelli emphasizes the extraordinarily low incidence of divorce while it was available on Italian soil: 19 instances in Milan, 6 in Naples, and 2 in Palermo.

As a final part of his general address Morelli presents a harsh critique of the law on personal separation, the only relief from a difficult marriage permitted by the civil law. Morelli again underlined the eminently moralizing aim of his divorce law by pointing out the potentially immoral consequences of personal separation. When couples separated, he argued, it was almost inevitable that both partners would form new relationships. The indissoluble bond of the first marriage would mean that the later partnerships could never be sanctified by law, and if children were born they would have to bear the stigma of illegitimacy. Morelli claimed that this was a far more anarchic situation than a divorce, which would leave each party free to remarry. Using statistics rather loosely, Morelli estimated that the law admitting legal separation created at least three thousand ruined families every year in Italy. First, he counted the "decomposition" of approximately a thousand marriages per year; then he assumed that each individual became involved in a second partnership, creating a family unit unrecognized by the state, thus adding 2000 more "ruined" families to the total. Morelli condemned the law as cruel and destructive.[24]

After a break in his speech due to faintness, Morelli wanted to schematize and sum up. He promised the audience, which was now showing signs of impatience, that divorce was necessary for four reasons: logic, morality, economy, and politics.[25] The reason of logic, as might have been expected, harked back to the introduction of civil marriage. Morelli reminded the Chamber that this had been one of the great liberating acts of the new government of Italy, because above all it meant that the questions of religion and marriage had been disengaged, and non-Catholics were at no disadvantage compared to Catholics. Morelli claims, as many legal experts had done before him, that the Italian government, having established civil marriage, had denied its logical consequence by excluding divorce.

The "moral" reason was related to Morelli's vision of marriage as a contractual arrangement. He argued that, especially among the poor, many people were lured and tricked into marriage. This, he felt, often befell women, who, through pressure from relatives or even venal matchmakers, could easily find themselves married to someone who was not the person they thought they were marrying. Given the importance of economic considerations over sentiment, the scenario Morelli describes was probably quite common. And it was certainly true that daughters, who had no juridical identity before they were 21, suffered much more as a result of these machinations. Morelli argued that it was immoral for innocent people to be chained for life to a partner under such circumstances, and just as the Church permitted annulments for "error," so the state should allow divorce to cover such cases. The state should no more coerce the continuation of a marriage entered into in ignorance than it should one in which the partners no longer loved each other and wished to part. Morelli suggested that divorce would become an agent of improved morality, and would even increase the number of marriages, since people would not fear it as a trap.

The economic reason for introducing divorce was also related to the ignominy deriving from unhappy marriages, and the costs, both financial and social, that could ensue. In a general sense there were the usual "costs" associated with marriage failure, ranging from the deleterious effects on the rearing of children, to crimes of passion that could result from marital tension. Morelli mentions the high number of trials that passed before the courts as a result of these ills. Carried away slightly by his own rhetoric, Morelli goes on to claim that at least a third of all suicides are the result of unhappy marriages, from which death is the only escape. He also mentions the strife caused by duels, and the cost of prisons, which he estimates would be a third less populous if the institution of the family were better regulated. In this way, Morelli presents indissoluble marriage as economically costly to society.

The fourth and final reason Morelli gives for the necessity of introducing divorce is political: it would be an antidote to the menacing threat of socialism. Morelli claims that socialism is to be heard rumbling all over the place, and his implication was that governments have never had a more pressing need to use the civil laws to reform social conditions in order to avoid political unrest. The implicit notion is that allowing people to divorce would reduce the social pressure that might otherwise force them to resort to socialism. In an era when less than 2 percent of the population had the right to vote in Italy, and socialist parties were a thing of the future, it seems that Morelli is using the term socialism as a sort of metaphor for civil strife, rather than a political movement. This was clearly a deliberate tactic on Morelli's part to try and break the conceptual association between divorce and the political upheaval of the French Revolution. In this sense it would also underline the responsible nature of Morelli's motives for wanting to introduce divorce.

This shows an essential duality in Morelli's political vision, in that he was both radical and conservative. For Morelli the family was a bulwark of social stability, but at the same time it could be a test-bed for experiments relating to individual liberty and social freedom. Moreover, the bringing of notions of liberty to the domestic sphere was an essential way to maintain social cohesion. As the final flourishes of Morelli's speech claim, Italians had "proclaimed liberty in the town square, but maintain despotism within the family . . . . We have abolished the papal temporal power in the legislative arena, but we permit the adoration of its symbols in the home." Morelli concludes by expressing the fervent hope that his colleagues in parliament will accept the proposal, bringing to the family itself the benefits of liberal reform, mitigating the havoc of the present, and "exorcizing the disasters of the future."[26]

Morelli ended his speech with the same techniques of persuasion that he had used at the outset. He advocated an essentially radical reform of family law, attempting to make it palatable to a ruling class that was timid about such things by claiming that divorce was a strong medicine that would heal, rather than a drug that would corrupt. This was to be a constant motif of future proposals for divorce. In 1878 Morelli's proposal and the philosophy behind it were in some ways quaintly old-fashioned and idealistic, but also far ahead of their time. The reaction of Morelli's parliamentary colleagues during his speech reflected both admiration and a sense of ridicule. In contrast to presentations on the budget, or railway lines, and other weighty matters, the opportunity to discuss divorce offered some light relief.

Partly in reaction to the irreverent style that had already earned Morelli a reputation as an eccentric, his speech was frequently interrupted by laughter, especially in response to his barbs against the Catholic Church. At one point Morelli claimed that the newly elected Pope, Leo XIII, planned great reforms, including permitting the clergy to marry. For some reason this appears to have particularly tickled the parliamentarians' sense of humor. And when Morelli finally ended his impassioned speech, he was greeted with cheers and shouts of "bravo!," although that may have had more to do with the entertainment value of his speech than with its content.

The response of the Minister of Justice Raffaele Conforti, who took the stand to respond to Morelli, restored sobriety to the Chamber. Conforti politely praised Morelli's perennial concern for the rights of women, but warned that his proposal to introduce divorce presented "many and grave difficulties." He chose not to engage with the theoretical aspects of divorce, but went straight to the practicalities. Looking back to the drawing-up of the civil code, he said he knew the question of divorce had been in the air, but no one had "dared" to propose it.[27] This choice of words is revealing. When the civil code was introduced, Pisanelli had blithely dismissed the idea of divorce as a custom foreign to the Italian people, and for that reason it had barely even been considered. But the fact that Conforti now let it slip that no one had dared to propose it is further evidence for the argument that this had been for fear of aggravating relations with the Church. The logic of civil marriage led inexorably to the admission of divorce, but that logic had been sacrificed on the altar of political expedience.

Conforti did not consider the passage of a few years since the introduction of the civil code sufficient time to justify the introduction of a change as radical as that proposed by Morelli. But rather than explain that presentiment with reference to political risk and tension, Conforti introduced for the first time an issue that would plague those in favor of divorce, known as *divorzisti*, for several decades: the almost complete absence of any public clamor for a divorce law. Conforti contested Morelli's argument that it was the legislator's task to develop laws for the good of society regardless of whether that society demanded them or not. He thought such a substantial revision of the law should first be called for by public opinion.

As an example, he referred to a recent proposal to abolish the death penalty, which was in turn a response to a call by many academics and jurists. The example shows that by "public opinion" Conforti did not mean that of the masses, but rather, the weight of learned opinion. Divorce, although it had been the subject of several scholarly works in Italy by 1878, did not have that weight of opinion behind it, and it was a far more divisive issue. And just as Morelli had used the small number of divorces in Italy during the Napoleonic era as an assurance that society would not unravel if divorce were introduced again, so Conforti used those statistics to argue that there was insufficient demand for divorce in Italy to justify the introduction of so radical a change to the civil code.

Surprisingly, given his chilly response to Morelli's proposal, Conforti did not express formal opposition to the possibility of parliament taking the proposal into consideration. Morelli had already won a victory in being permitted to propose the law to parliament, but the vote on whether it would take the proposal into consideration was crucial if it were to go any further. The deputies voted to take the law to the next stage.[28] It is important to realize that the stance of the minister of justice on such an issue would have been highly influential in parliament, and Conforti's tacit approval of a discussion of divorce already represented a significant step forward from the 1860s.

Although Morelli's speech was a novelty in that it was the first time that the question of divorce had been proposed in the Italian parliament, the press's reaction was limited. Outside Rome, the speech was generally reported as part of the regular chronicling of parliamentary events.[29] In the capital itself, however, where the newspapers tended to be more clearly divided along "Roman question" lines (that is, on the question of church-state relations), the responses of two newspapers gave the first hint of two irreconcilable positions on divorce.

The official organ of the Vatican, the *Osservatore romano*, had already given a foretaste of its position when it announced the imminent presentation of a proposal on divorce by "Salvatore Morelli(!)."[30] The exclamation mark almost implies a suppressed snort, and indeed, when the usually sombre newspaper reported Morelli's speech some days later, it described the event sarcastically as a comedy at the "Theatre of Montecitorio" (Montecitorio houses the Italian parliament), held to benefit those who were tired of one husband and wanted to move on to another. In a cruel parody of Morelli's southern accent, the editorial described the deputy's dedication to female "emangibadzione" (as opposed to "emancipazione"), and claimed that this "paladin of the weaker sex wants to make skirts into trousers." The conclusion continued the sarcasm to the end, claiming that not every parliament could boast a resident comic.[31] This was, however, both the first and the last occasion on which the *Osservatore* would be able to take the divorce question so lightly.

Representing the other end of the journalistic spectrum, the progovernment and deeply anticlerical *La Capitale*[32] expressed delight over Morelli's proposal. The day before he was due to present it, an article drew attention to the occasion, and described Morelli as an "indefatigable crusader for the solution of problems concerning women and the family."[33] Some days after Morelli's presentation, the newspaper ran a prominent editorial on the front page entitled "Il divorzio." Describing divorce as one of the great social questions of the day, the editorialist was clearly pleased, and perhaps rather surprised, that parliament had voted in favor of taking the proposal into consideration. The article criticized the minister for justice, Conforti, for the cool reception he had given the proposal, and argued that his claim that there was no visible public demand for divorce was misguided: the proof of the need for a divorce law was obvious from the number of crimes of passion and other indications of marital disorder.[34] This difference of opinion over how to interpret "public demand" would be one of the divorce cause's principal obstacles for many decades to come.

It was difficult to spark lasting debate on the divorce question in Italy, especially in 1878. Perhaps this is best illustrated by the fact that even *La Capitale*, after one final mention of divorce on 1 June 1878, ceased to follow the story as the proposal moved to the next stage in parliament. The newspaper's silence may well indicate that journalists with good parliamentary connections knew that the smooth passage of Morelli's proposal through the first stage in the Chamber would not continue behind the scenes.

The Parliamentary Hinterland

According to standard procedure, the vote to take the proposed law into consideration meant that discussion of the issue was delegated to nine parliamentary committees, known as *uffici*. Each committee consisted of nine deputies, who discussed and voted on the issue at hand. After forming a majority view, each committee elected a representative of that view who would form part of a commission, which would then discuss the issue in detail. The commission would report its views on the proposed law to parliament, according to whether the majority was favorable or not. Sometimes, if opinions were irreconcilably divided, there would be both a majority and a minority report.

These procedures, admirably democratic in conception, also amounted to a dangerous parliamentary hinterland in which it was quite common for proposed laws, especially if they were contentious, to become impossibly mired. If in the meanwhile a legislative session closed or a cabinet fell, the parliament's mandate to consider a question would no longer be valid and the procedure had to begin again. Several proposals for divorce fell foul of the dangerous combination of labyrinthine parliamentary procedure and frequently shuffling governing coalitions that marked Italy's parliamentary government.

One of the few dated records among the deliberations over Morelli's divorce law was the initial meeting of the first committee, which took place on 6 June 1878. Morelli himself presided over the committee, and it reached a conclusion without delay. It voted that the committee "in principle accepts divorce as a necessary consequence of civil marriage and only needs to ascertain by careful study whether it is opportune to introduce it." This was the opinion that Morelli took to the commission in his role as representative of the first committee.[35]

Discussions within the remaining eight committees revealed the full range of contemporary opinion about divorce in Italy. For example, the second committee's first speaker simply demanded the outright rejection of the proposal on the basis that it would be a disturbance to the family. Another contradicted him, saying that divorce was the logical corollary of civil marriage, and that it should be accepted, though with more restrictions than Morelli proposed. Others variously welcomed the project, said it was inopportune, or worried about the fate of the children of divorced parents. Finally one member of the committee tabled a motion that the proposal be rejected, and it was carried by a majority.[36]

The third and fourth committees rejected the proposal peremptorily. It seemed for a moment that the fifth committee welcomed the idea, since they recognized the need for divorce in the case of life imprisonment of one spouse, but one conservative member interjected that even a single reason for divorce would deal a blow to the institution of the family. In the end they rejected the proposal, on the basis that the principle of the indissoluble family was so sacrosanct that its integrity warranted the sacrifice of a few individuals who would remain bound to spouses condemned to prison for life.[37] The sixth, seventh, and eighth committees cautiously approved the idea of divorce, and voted that the commission should study the articles making up Morelli's proposal. Even among those committees agreeing with divorce in principle, none of them fully approved the breadth of Morelli's proposal, and several deputies expressed particular concern about the fate of children.

One argument against divorce conspicuous by its absence in these discussions concerned religion. Only one deputy said he was against the idea for religious and moral reasons, even if the concept of divorce was admissible in an abstract way. In general, the most common argument against Morelli's proposal was that it was "inopportune."[38] Even many of those in favor of divorce suggested that Morelli's broad proposal be modified so that it was more in conformity with "the spirit of the times."[39] This was not a suggestion that divorce was inappropriate for Italian society. It was an argument that the timing was wrong, a claim that Italy was not yet ready for divorce. This suggests that there was still an overriding sense of the fragility of Italian society, and that it was too early to start making significant changes to the civil law. Although the idea was not voiced explicitly more than once, it is very probable that the deputies felt that the state's relationship with the Church should not be made more difficult than it already was.

If the normal procedures had reached their conclusion, a commission of nine deputies, each representing the majority view of their *ufficio*, would have produced a report, called a *relazione*, according to the majority view. That report would have formed the basis of a broad parliamentary discussion of the proposal, and eventually, a vote. Morelli's proposal did not reach that stage. Indeed, it never found its way back into the Chamber, because the parliamentary session closed prematurely. In any event, it seems unlikely that the commission would have written a favorable *relazione*. Although the records of the proposal's passage through the *uffici* are inconclusive, at the last recorded meeting four had voted to reject the proposal outright, four had hesitatingly recommended further discussion, and one had yet to make a decision.[40]

Causes Célèbres: Annulments or Divorces?

The failure of Morelli's first divorce proposal in mid-1879 sent him back to the drafting table, and nothing was heard of divorce at a legislative level until he reappeared with a new proposal in early 1880. In the intervening period Italians who read the newspapers witnessed an extraordinary court case in Rome that illustrated to the public some of the potential consequences of indissoluble marriage. The case involved none other than the quintessential hero of the Risorgimento, Giuseppe Garibaldi, who, 19 years after that fateful day in 1860, was still formally married to the Marchesina Raimondi, even if he had not seen her since the wedding. In 1879, Garibaldi finally began legal proceedings with the aim of asking the state to annul the marriage.

Both Garibaldi and Raimondi had long wished to be free of the shackles represented by their matrimony, but under the prevailing law there was simply nothing that could be done, except perhaps a supplication to the Pope for an annulment. Garibaldi was too proud to subject himself to the vagaries of what he would have seen as papal whim. One motive that pressed Garibaldi in 1879 was the decline of his health and his sense of the approach of death. He was keen to marry his de facto wife, Francesca Armosina, with whom he had lived for many years, and to legitimize the children she had borne him. The fact that Morelli's divorce bill was being considered by the parliamentary commissions may well have suggested to Garibaldi and his lawyer, Pasquale Stanislao Mancini, both of whom were deputies themselves, that the circumstances for a dissolution of the old marriage were more propitious than they had ever been.

In a country where divorce was not permitted, Garibaldi's request for what could easily have been interpreted as a divorce raised a number of serious and awkward complications. These were exacerbated by Garibaldi's position as a supreme hero. Both Garibaldi and no doubt many members of the government were anxious to obtain his release from an absurd situation, but nobody was eager for the rather shabby details of an episode best forgotten to tarnish the hero's image. Nor, when some deputies had very recently claimed that even one case of divorce would be a blow to the institution of the family, did the state want to be seen making exceptions for its privileged citizens.

These problems also go some way toward explaining why Garibaldi had for so long tried to forget that episode in Lombardy in 1860. But as long as he and Raimondi were man and wife in the eyes of the law, it was impossible for Garibaldi to legitimize his children, and in the Spring of 1879 Garibaldi and his lawyers decided that the time had come to act. Garibaldi and Raimondi had been married in Lombardy in 1860, under the prevailing Austrian civil code. This code delegated jurisdiction over matrimony to the appropriate religious authorities. Those married with the rites of a religion that allowed divorce were permitted by Austrian law to divorce, but Garibaldi and Raimondi had married in a Catholic ceremony, and their marriage was indissoluble as a result. With Italian unification and after the enactment of the Pisanelli code, this marriage, like all others, gained civil recognition, and the Italian state had become the sole arbiter over marital questions of this kind. The only possibility for Garibaldi's lawyers was to find some technicality that would have meant it was an invalid marriage according to the ecclesiastical law that prevailed when the marriage had taken place. Ideally this would also be something that would obviate the need to exhume too much of the past.

When the case came before the Rome civil tribunal in July 1879, lawyers representing Garibaldi claimed that the wedding had not taken the proper form, in that Raimondi, as the illegitimate daughter of the Marchese Raimondi, needed the consent of her legally appointed custodian, her *tutore.* Consent had only been obtained from her father.[41] They added that the marriage had not been "cemented" by any form of cohabitation, hinting heavily but not quite claiming that the marriage had not been consummated. Without resorting to it at this stage, the lawyers reserved the right to proceed according to a much more potentially scandalous reason for dissolving the marriage: article 58 of the Austrian civil code had specified that a marriage would be considered null if it was found after the ceremony that a woman had been impregnated by someone other than her husband at the time of marriage.

The court rejected the claim on all counts, arguing that it considered the consent of Raimondi's father to have been sufficient under the circumstances and that the marriage had been valid. The court also rejected the possibility of declaring the marriage null under the terms of article 58 of the Austrian code, unless there was good evidence of Raimondi's pregnancy. They specifically excluded as evidence the idea of a statement from Raimondi. Knowing that both Raimondi and Garibaldi wanted the marriage dissolved, the court ruled that even if Raimondi were to testify that she had been pregnant to another man in January 1860 (something she always refused to admit anyway), this could easily be regarded as collusion between Garibaldi and Raimondi. The only path left open, in the court's view, was the presentation of some concrete evidence that would allow a release under article 58.[42]

Garibaldi and his representatives knew how difficult this would be because they had already searched for such evidence, and there was none. In May and June 1879, before the case went to court, Mancini's agent Fazzari made two trips to Lombardy with the intention of finding witnesses who would be able to testify about Raimondi's "condition" in January 1860. They interviewed various people who remembered the wedding, including the Marchese Rovelli, a relative of the Raimondi family, who acted as a liaison between Garibaldi's lawyers and potential witnesses. Something of a scandalmonger, Rovelli happily supplied details of the most lurid kind about the loose morals of Raimondi and her family, including his opinion that she had lost her virginity at the age of 11,[43] and that even her own father enjoyed her sexual favors.[44] But the eager legal team could not find any satisfactory evidence of the alleged pregnancy.

The clearest evidence, of course, would have been the birth of a child. Although a search of the parish registers revealed nothing, Rovelli was able to secure several witnesses who claimed to know about the birth of a child to the Marchesina in the late summer of 1860. The problem was that there were as many different opinions as there were witnesses. One was Raimondi's former chambermaid, Stella Arrighi, who claimed at first that a child had been stillborn in August or September 1860, then later denied all knowledge of such a child. Another witness was an erstwhile neighbor of Raimondi, who said there had been a child, passed off as the nephew of Raimondi's chambermaid. A third witness, the doorkeeper at one of Raimondi's residences, had a similar story.[45] But no one knew what had become of this mystery child, and it must have been reasonably clear that the discrepancies between the various stories would have made any legal court suspicious.

Frustrated by the lack of progress, Fazzari decided to investigate the idea of a negotiated settlement of some sort. He visited the house of Raimondi's lawyer, Gatti, to ask whether Raimondi would be willing to sign an admission that she had been pregnant with another man's child in 1860. Gatti had given to believe that his client was as anxious as Garibaldi himself to settle the matter. Fazzari presented a statement for Raimondi to sign, the essence of which was this: "Even though I could defend myself against these accusations [the pregnancy] I will not; because I too desire an annulment and in so doing will bring tranquility to the man to whom Italians owe so much." Fazzari, while emphasizing the importance of discretion for Garibaldi, showed no such sensitivity toward Raimondi herself. In an effort to persuade her lawyer that she should sign a full admission, he clumsily threatened to air the Raimondi family's linen in court, even alluding to the alleged incestuous relationship between father and daughter.[46]

Evidently these strong-arm tactics backfired, because when Fazzari returned to Como on 8 June 1879 to retrieve Raimondi's statement, he found that she had decided to defend her honor, and would not cooperate by signing any statement at all. Clearly, it would have been much better for both Garibaldi and Raimondi if the marriage could have been declared null on the basis of some less sensitive technicality, and this, combined with the absence of any real evidence about Raimondi's alleged pregnancy, explains the eventual choice to apply for the annulment on the basis that Raimondi had not had proper consent before the marriage.

The court's decision that the marriage should not be dissolved can be interpreted in a number of ways. It was amply evident that in reality there had been no relationship between Garibaldi and Raimondi after the wedding ceremony, and it was equally evident that the continued existence of the marriage bond did harm to both parties. Yet the court's black-letter approach to the law revealed that the principle of indissoluble marriage had more strength than any reasoned consideration of the circumstances. It is also possible that the judiciary, in an attempt to show its independence, took a particularly cautious approach to the case, lest it should be accused that the law was applied less rigorously for citizens of Garibaldi's stature. This hypothesis was actually formulated at the time by the President of the Court of Appeal in a letter to Garibaldi's lawyer, Mancini.[47] And it was to the Court of Appeal that the case now progressed.

The appeal document was lodged on 21 July 1879, and it spared no effort to obtain Garibaldi the equivalent of a divorce. The first part makes an attempt to establish which laws were actually applicable in Lombardy in 1860. All the previous legal work had assumed that the Austrian civil law still applied, but the appeal claimed that after the cession of Lombardy to Piedmont following the armistice of Villafranca, Piedmont's civil law applied.[48] The appeal then proceeded with a three-pronged approach to its claim that the marriage between Garibaldi and Raimondi should be annulled. The first again concerned the lack of proper consent on Raimondi's part.[49] The second was a new claim that conceded that even if the Austrian law were still considered to apply, the marriage should be annulled on the basis that it had not been consummated.[50] The third basis of the appeal simply claimed that it was unjust for the Tribunal to have excluded the possibility of a statement from Raimondi as good evidence that she had been pregnant to someone other than Garibaldi in 1860.[51] This point of course referred to the provisions of article 58 of the Austrian civil code. Since the preamble to the appeal had already argued that that code did not apply in January 1860, the inclusion of an appeal on this basis again showed how unclear were the laws of the time, and revealed the appeal's determination to cover all possible interpretations.

The first part of the appeal elaborates the earlier claim that Raimondi had married without the proper consent of her guardian. In 1858 Como's local magistrate had cancelled the wardship of Raimondi's earlier guardian, a certain Martinez, and nominated her father as the official guardian. This was done on the basis that in 1842 Marchese Raimondi had acknowledged his paternity of Giuseppina. But Mancini pointed out that this spontaneous recognition on the part of the father was not sufficient to qualify him as an official guardian, as *patria podestà*, or paternal authority, was specifically denied to fathers of illegitimate children.[52] He also claimed that in any case the Marchese was an unsuitable guardian, as his combination of prodigality and pompous ambition were well known.[53] Furthermore, the magistrate of Como had had no jurisdiction to remove Martinez's wardship, which had been established by the higher authority of Como's provincial tribunal.[54] Finally, referring both to the authority and flexibility of canon law, the report claimed that the Church's Congregation of the Council in Rome had annulled marriages on similar grounds, even when the marriage had been consummated and had produced children. In this case "all the world" knew that the marriage between

Garibaldi and Raimondi had never had any real substance, and it should therefore be annulled.[55]

The second major argument presented in the appeal also referred to the procedures of ecclesiastical law. It was no less than a request for an annulment of Garibaldi and Raimondi's marriage on the basis that it was not consummated. This is the most interesting aspect of the appeal, not only because in the end it was for this reason that the appeal was successful, but also because it shows the way the civil law had taken over the territory of canon law, and could still apply principles of canon law retrospectively. The statement prepared by Garibaldi's lawyers is minutely argued, but essentially it claims that there were grounds for seeking a papal annulment under the law that had prevailed at the time of the marriage. If a properly performed religious marriage was for some reason not consummated, the marriage could be declared null. This procedure was known as a *dispensa* and, like all annulments, as opposed to divorces, a sentence of this sort declared that a marriage had never existed. The peculiarity of this particular case was that Garibaldi's lawyers were asking the Italian civil court to act as if it were an ecclesiastical court.[56]

The written statement hastened to point out that such powers had actually been granted to the Italian civil courts in the rules that regulated the transition from ecclesiastical to civil law. Article 6 of these regulations specifically gave responsibility for any cases already under way in the ecclesiastical courts to the civil tribunal. Moreover, as the statement emphasized, new laws never retroactively removed previously existing rights unless they stated the fact specifically.[57] The Court of Appeal thus found itself about to grant an annulment under the terms of the ecclesiastical law that had prevailed in Lombardy in 1860. The only real task was to establish the fact that consummation had never taken place.

That was a somewhat delicate matter, but the report pointed out that under the procedures of canon law, a sworn statement from seven family members amounted to adequate proof.[58] The report also made reference to Garibaldi's fame and stature, which meant that anything to do with him was "avidly investigated and researched,"[59] and it was common knowledge that Garibaldi had departed from the scene of the wedding after finding that his new wife had been less than pure, and had never seen her since. The statement concludes with the assertion that the sentence of the tribunal should be revoked and the marriage annulled, either because Raimondi did not receive proper consent for the marriage or because the marriage had never been consummated.

The Court of Appeal, consisting of five judges, heard the case on 10 December 1879.[60] First they established that, although in January 1860 Lombardy had already been united with Piedmont, Austrian civil law still applied, as it did until the enactment of the Italian civil code from 1 January 1866.[61] Under the imperial patent of 1856, marriage had fallen under the jurisdiction of canon law. This was decisive for the first element of the appeal, because under canon law the lack of a guardian's consent could not give rise to an annulment.[62] Moving to the second claim, the court declared that nonconsummation was indeed a ground for annulment.[63] After making a brief nod of assent to the claimants' arguments about their witnesses' statements, and public knowledge that consummation could not have taken place, and taking into account all the other factors that had made the marriage a sham[64] (even though they had no relevance to the law), the Court of Appeal declared Garibaldi and Raimondi to be free from the marriage bond that had tied them since 1860.[65]

Later that month, the liberal press discreetly reported on Garibaldi's marriage to his de facto wife, Francesca Armosina, and the legitimization of their children.[66] The conclusion of the case was of course a relief and a joy to all concerned. Raimondi gained the least; and she returned to a life of obscurity, although at least she now had the right to control her own property. Garibaldi, the nation's great hero, had freed himself from an absurd albatross, and was able to enjoy his last few years, secure that his children were now his legitimate heirs. But would this landmark decision have any real significance for Italian marriage law?

It so happened that the publication of the news about Garibaldi's annulment and remarriage helped to make the early months of 1880 particularly significant in the history of the Italian debates. Coincidentally another famous marriage was also annulled in January 1880, this time by the Vatican itself. The case concerned the Prince of Monaco and his English wife, the Duchess of Hamilton, who had been married since 1869, and whose two children were testimony to the fact that consummation had perfected the religious ceremony. The press had been observing the deliberations of the ecclesiastical court concerned, the Sacred Congregation of the Council, since the case began at about the same time as Garibaldi's. When the court finally announced the annulment in January, *La Capitale* did not miss the opportunity to make the obvious comparison with the contemporaneous Garibaldi-Raimondi case. In a scathing attack on the decision, which had been made on the basis that the Duchess claimed to have had "mental reservations" at the time of the marriage, the front page editorial, entitled "Il Vaticano ed il divorzio," (The Vatican and Divorce) lambasted ecclesiastical procedures, which it claimed treated royalty one way and commoners another.[67]

Further events in early 1880 heightened tension between religious and secular jurisdictions over marriage. In France the divorce debates had reached a new peak, and this had ramifications in Italy as well. After the failure of his proposal of 1878, Alfred Naquet had undertaken a major campaign of public meetings and speeches all over France.[68] This campaign reached a high point with the publication of *La question du divorce* by Alexandre Dumas (*fils*), which was serialized in *Le Figaro* in late 1879, and caused an immediate sensation.[69] Soon after this the book, which promoted divorce and was highly critical of the Church, was translated and published in Italy.[70] This new level of dissemination about divorce deeply concerned the Church hierarchy, resulting in a papal encyclical, *Arcarnum divinae*, published in February 1880.

The Pope notionally reclaimed marriage as the natural jurisdiction of the Church, and sternly warned against the introduction of divorce because of its inevitably pernicious effects. Particularly noteworthy was the suggestion that any wise state would avail itself of the support offered by the Church in the supervision of human morals.[71] This clear cry against the notion of the separation of Church and state underlined that the Pope still felt that the Church had a strong role to play in the regulation of private life. The timing of the encyclical could suggest that it was an attempt to thwart Salvatore Morelli's second proposal to introduce divorce in Italy, which began with the presentation of the new draft to parliament on 21 February 1880. However, as Francis Ronsin has pointed out, *Arcanum* was more likely to have been prompted by the high profile of Naquet's pro-divorce campaign in France, where the whole question had advanced much further than it had in Italy.[72]

Morelli's Second Proposal for a Divorce Law in Italy

The combination of two celebrated annulments, Dumas's book, and a papal encyclical on marriage and divorce, all in the space of the first two months of 1880, created a heightened sensitivity to the question in Italy. It was in this context that Morelli presented his second proposal for divorce shortly after the opening of the parliamentary session, on 21 February 1880. His introductory remarks unsurprisingly made rhetorical use of some of these events. He claimed that the Catholic Church itself allowed divorce, which it gave under the name of diriment impediments, and cited the recent example of the Prince and Princess of Monaco. He also referred to *Arcanum*, questioning the Pope's claim that marriage was rightly the exclusive jurisdiction of the Church, again underlining the way the divorce issue was a touchstone for this question.[73]

Morelli's exposition of the law to the Chamber of Deputies on 8 March 1880 was an impassioned combination of serious motivations and outlandish claims that made the deputies roar with laughter. He mentioned the backwardness of the Latin race, and contrasted the absence of a divorce law in Italy, France, and Spain with the progress of Belgium, Holland, Sweden, England, Russia, Poland, and Greece.[74] Divorce was a matter of catching up with the faster pace of the world. Morelli promised that this pace would soon be represented by air travel, which would allow a couple to go to America to get married, and then return to Italy for their honeymoon. The deputies thought this was an hilarious idea. The notion, apart from illustrating Morelli's farsightedness, also suggests that he foresaw the day when Italians would escape the rigid marriage laws of their nation simply by getting married elsewhere. That day was not far off, although it would not involve air travel for a few more decades.

The speech also focused on church-state relations, making much of the recent decision that had annulled the marriage of the Prince and Princess of Monaco and allowed them to marry again. To the great amusement of his colleagues, Morelli suggested that the granting of annulments had a fiscal importance to the Church similar to a grist tax. But Morelli's comic flights of fancy should not distract too much attention from the new version of his proposal, which, although unsuccessful, had lasting significance. Unlike his previous proposal, he based the new one upon the existing legislation for personal separation, providing for an existing separation to be converted into a divorce after a certain period of time: three years if there were no children, or six years if there were. This simple formula became the template for all subsequent proposals for divorce in Italy until 1901, and was politically astute in that it merely took a very familiar law to a conclusion that many advocates of civil marriage considered completely logical.

The political astuteness behind Morelli's new proposal may very well have been owed to Tommaso Villa, who had taken over as minister for justice. In contrast to his predecessor, Conforti, who had given Morelli's first proposal a guarded reception, Villa welcomed Morelli's proposal warmly in his comments following the deputy's exposition. Villa's comments put great emphasis on the need to modernize Italian marriage law by completing the process of making marriage an entirely civil matter. As he put it, "where the eye of the civil legislator does not penetrate, religious morals retain the power to do so." This was a subtle but clear indication of Villa's conception of divorce as a symbolic separation of church and state spheres. Villa also tried to temper the frivolity that Morelli's personal style had given to the divorce proposal. He stressed that the government considered divorce only as a final remedy in extreme cases, and that it would review Morelli's proposal carefully to ensure that there was no room whatsoever for abuse of the law. After Villa's words, the deputies duly voted to take the law into consideration.[75]

Although there is no doubt that the initiative behind the proposal was Morelli's, the extent of Villa's sponsorship was revealed a few days later, when newspapers reported that the minister had sent a circular to the heads of the nation's courts explaining the importance of the divorce law. It also informed them that within a week they would be required to compile a statistical study of all applications for personal separation in their jurisdictions since the inception of the civil code in 1866.[76] This significant sign of commitment on Villa's behalf suggests that he was very much behind Morelli's proposal, and although there is no direct evidence that he had a hand in revising its wording before it was presented, it is very likely that the decision to base the proposal on the existing law for personal separation was the result of Villa's influence.

Villa's support for the divorce proposal also made a difference to the level of attention paid by the press. For example, the *Corriere della sera* only reported Morelli's 8 March speech in a rather cursory way, using most of the eight lines spared for the item to point out the hilarity Morelli's speech had provoked in the Chamber by likening the pope to Nero.[77] The following day, however, when news of Villa's circular to the courts came out, the newspaper devoted significantly more space to the divorce question, reprinting the text of Villa's message. The Catholic *Voce della verità* was particularly alarmed by Villa's intervention, publishing a long article that claimed the ministerial involvement indicated how serious the government was about divorce. In fact this article could be regarded as an early clarion cry to Catholic action against divorce, a call that would mature to great significance within a few years. The *Voce* argued that the divorce proposal provoked the Church and insulted the pope's recent encyclical on marriage and was an attempt to dismantle the family. It suggested that *Arcanum* should be heeded as a call to action addressed to all those who wanted to save the Christian family from dissolution.[78]

On the other hand, the ever-lofty *Osservatore romano* was not yet ready to descend into the fray, merely dismissing Morelli's speech as a "disgusting parliamentary episode."[79] This dismissal was in fact more in line with the true degree of threat posed to indissoluble marriage by Morelli's proposal, because in the event it made very little progress. After the vote to take the law into consideration, the parliamentary *uffici* duly met, and even though a commission was formed where five out of nine members were in agreement with the principle of divorce, their deliberations were inconclusive because the parliamentary session was again prematurely dissolved in April. Elections for the Chamber were held in July, but Morelli was too ill to campaign properly[80] (his failing health had impeded the delivery of his last speech to the Chamber, that on divorce), and he was not reelected. His proposal could not proceed without him. Morelli retired to Pozzuoli, a seaside village near Naples, where he died on 22 October 1880.[81]

Morelli's death marks the end of the first phase of what was to be a long series of debates over divorce in Liberal Italy. Divorce for Morelli had represented a battle on two fronts: one for the improvement of the condition of women in Italian society; another for the full fruition of the secular ideals of the Risorgimento. Morelli's feminism made him unique, but his anticlerical ideals had a clear provenance in the ideals of 1848, and when, 30 years after taking part in these revolutions, he had the opportunity to present a law on divorce to the Italian parliament, it was both an eccentric and a logical outcome of those ideals. It is well accepted that for various reasons Italy had been steered in a conservative direction after 1860, but the victory of the Left in 1876 had briefly given some hope that the more radical ideals of the Risorgimento's democratic origins would have an opportunity to flower. Morelli's proposals for a divorce law were without doubt the most radical examples of such ideas. Their fate was emblematic of the direction Depretis's governments were to take: they disappointed progressive thinkers then as much as they disappoint many historians who look back on them.

If Morelli's death represents the passing of an era, few people would have noticed it at the time. A century after he conceived them, his ideas about divorce, women, and even air travel, made perfect sense. At the time, however, Morelli's ardent ideals had to be adapted to the increasingly complex realities of Italian politics. Morelli had provoked discussion about divorce, he had mobilized pens and words, he had stimulated reflections[82]—but it would be up to others to try and steer those debates to fruition.

Tommaso Villa was the natural heir to Morelli's divorce legacy, and he was to oversee it for the next two decades. Despite sharing many ideals with Morelli, his personal style was very different, and although he believed passionately in divorce as a symbolic ideal, he felt that the best way to convince the Italian ruling classes that Italy needed a divorce law was to prove it empirically. In other words, Villa wanted to address the reservations that his predecessor, Conforti, had expressed on behalf of many conservatives in relation to Morelli's first proposal: surely the Italian population could do without such a law. Despite its eventual resolution, the case of Giuseppe Garibaldi and Giuseppina Raimondi had suggested that a divorce law could have a certain utility in extreme instances. But no one was keen to make too much of that particular example. The pressing task for the *divorzisti* who followed Morelli was to show that there could occasionally be a need for a divorce law in the lives of ordinary Italians.

3

Divorce Italian Style?

Marriage Breakdown, 1860–1880

Even with colorful advocates like Salvatore Morelli, in the nineteenth century divorce in Italy remained a theoretical question that was debated only in limited circles. Opponents of divorce pointed out that there was no public clamor for divorce, and therefore no need to introduce it. Those who took this position generally relied on two arguments. The first was that the number of marriage failures was so negligible that it did not justify an attack on what the anti-*divorzisti* saw as the very essence of marriage, its indissolubility. The second was that the law already made sufficient provision to relieve couples who did encounter severe difficulties. Two obvious questions arise from such arguments: was Italy a land of marriages made in heaven, and if not, what did Italians do if married life should become an unremitting hell?

The problem for any qualitative investigation of married life in the past is that the vast majority of couples rarely left a trace on the historical record. Even in Italian literature, specific treatment of the theme of marriage failure was extremely rare until the early twentieth century.[1] Yet the silence of the records cannot simply be taken to mean that married life was bliss for the majority of couples. In an age when divorce is almost as popular as marriage itself in many Western countries, it has become easy to idealize the apparently solid marriages of earlier times. Realistically, it seems unlikely that marriages in the past were unsullied by the frictions that cohabitation can generate from time to time. What seems more likely to have changed is the way in which married partners responded to those problems, and to some extent those responses were conditioned by the possibilities offered by the law.

An important point to keep in mind is that in nineteenth-century Italy married women had fewer rights and less license than their husbands. The clearest example is provided by the different legal definitions of adultery: any sexual contact outside marriage on the part of a woman could be considered adultery, whereas a man had to keep a concubine in the marital home, or allow his affairs to become "notorious" in order to be considered an adulterer. The inequality exemplified by this law, which derived directly from the Napoleonic code, is an aspect of a larger question,[2] but it must be kept in mind that, both legally and according to custom, men and women were as unequal in a good marriage as they were in a bad one. For a woman, this inequality would obviously have mattered more in the latter case.

For certain anticlerical intellectuals in Italy, the original "divorce Italian-style" was the annulment of religious marriages by the courts of the Church. Salvatore Morelli spoke for many when he claimed, during a speech in parliament arguing for the introduction of divorce, that the pope, too, allows divorce. In his words, "The Papacy . . . has eighteen motives for divorce, which take the name diriment impediments. But the name does not change the nature of the thing . . . and from the effects it is clear that diriment impediments are synonyms for divorce."[3] "Diriment impediments" were conditions that prevented marriage, such as consanguinity, and if discovered after marriage, could give rise to an annulment. Morelli claimed that the Church's interest in marriage was above all an economic one, because the seven sacraments were an important source of income. This, he said, was especially true of marriage, because it was a "broad-based source."[4]

Such arguments provoked hilarity in the Chamber, and were typical of Morelli's iconoclastic style, but his claim that annulments were divorces by another name was inaccurate. Although it was true that the Church's control of marriage and power to grant annulments had given it considerable social power in the past,[5] Morelli exaggerated the idea that the Church reaped great profit from these procedures. Although annulments became less and less historically important toward the end of the nineteenth century, it is important to put Morelli's claims into perspective.

The impediments to which Morelli referred were long-established religious rules that determined who could marry and under what circumstances, and any marriage that did not conform to the strict requirements of canon law could be rendered null. Many of the religious rules on marriage were adopted by the civil laws of Western nations, the more familiar ones relating to consanguinity, age, and the extraction of consent by force. There were several others, such as impotence, or where the consent of one party was in some way "defective." An annulment was an acknowledgment that such an impediment had existed before the marriage had taken place, and a declaration that the marriage was null and void; in short, that it had never existed. In the view of the Church, such a procedure was very different from a divorce, which, on the basis of some ground arising after the ceremony had taken place, could dissolve a properly constituted marriage.

One reason to consider Morelli's claim that annulments were an important source of income for the Church as untenable is that they were very rare. Between 1860 and 1908, for example, the curial courts of the Vatican heard a total of about 390 applications for annulment, just over eight per year.[6] Not all cases came to the Vatican, of course; certain cases could be heard locally, after which the Vatican acted as a Court of Appeal. Others, particularly cases involving sensitive and difficult matters, such as defective consent, impotence, or alleged nonconsummation, had to be heard in Rome. The figure of 390 cases referred to the entire Catholic world, not just Italy, so it is clear that the overall numbers were too small to be a significant source of funds for the Church, or, for that matter, to be considered a substitute for divorce.[7]

Anticlericals like Morelli tended to seize upon the fact that the canon law was a law unto itself and occasionally seemed to work in favor of the exigencies of the rich and the prominent. It is more than likely that the judgments of the ecclesiastical courts were subject to influence according to the wealth and position of the supplicants, but the ecclesiastical courts were not solely the preserve of the rich, if the Church publications that made the cases public can be taken as an indication. A significant proportion of the matrimonial causes treated by the Vatican involved people of humble station, and sometimes there was no charge at all to the petitioners.[8]

Although annulments may have retained a symbolic value, their small number, combined with later developments in the civil law, made them progressively less important in the late nineteenth century. As far as Italy was concerned, the factor that most diminished the significance of annulments is that after the civil code took effect from 1 January 1866, civil marriage became the only form recognized by the state, and of course only the state could annul a civil marriage. Technically, ecclesiastical annulments became irrelevant at this point, even though in effect the law moved faster than custom.

It is well known that the civil code's failure to enforce the precedence of civil marriage resulted in a grey area of couples who, whether from custom, ignorance, or deliberate deceit, married in Church and left it at that.[9] In the late nineteenth century several attempts were made to introduce a law enforcing the precedence of civil over religious rites, beginning with two government projects in 1873. The preamble to the second law claimed that during the first five years after the civil code came into effect, a total of 120,421 religious marriages had not been subsequently made official by a civil ceremony.[10] The failure of this and all subsequent projects underlines the unwillingness of the governments of Liberal Italy to exacerbate the rift between the Church and the state. Enforcing the precedence of civil marriage would certainly have rubbed salt into the wounds suffered by the Church when religious marriage ceased to have civil validity.

Under Italian law from January 1866, couples who married in church but did not have a civil ceremony were concubines, and their children were illegitimate. The papal response to the introduction of civil marriage specifically urged local priests to ensure that the couples they married in church subsequently legitimized their union in the eyes of the state,[11] but the Ministry of Justice's figures show that this did not always happen. According to a French-language review of pontifical jurisprudence, from the inception of the civil code it had become "common practice" for Italian couples to marry in church and then wait before making their marriage legally binding with the civil procedure. If their marriage remained only *ratum* (that is, canonically valid), but not *consummato*, "whether through impotence or the disposition of the spouses," they could ask for a papal dispensation that would annul the marriage.[12] However, the suggestion that the two marriage systems were played off against each other as a sort of insurance policy against impotence or even sexual repulsion is certainly not borne out by the number of dispensations for marriages that were *rati et non consummati*: 134 such cases were considered in Rome between 1866 and 1899, and again, these covered the world, not just Italy.

In short, although the procedures of the ecclesiastical courts in relation to marriage were shrouded in mystery, annulments and dispensations were really a straw target for the *divorzisti*, as they had less and less practical relevance as far as the law was concerned. There is no doubt, though, that the civil law paid homage to religious traditions, because of the extent to which the new marriage laws echoed ecclesiastical laws, and indeed, did not displace them by force. The best examples of this are of course the exclusion of divorce itself, and the adoption by the civil law of the Church's compromised substitute, personal separation. Although the occasional annulment might have startlingly resembled a divorce by another name, as Morelli claimed, annulments did not amount to the equivalent of divorce, "Italian-style," at least in the nineteenth century.[13] The civil code remained true to Church doctrines, and the closest thing it offered to divorce was the centuries-old custom of personal separation.

Separazione Personale in Italy

The few existent records of troubled Italian marriages are mostly the result of people resorting to the civil law on personal separation, and these do suggest that Italians had fewer serious marital problems than some of their

European neighbors. Those who were against the introduction of divorce in Italy were fond of using statistics to show that Italians did not need such a drastic remedy. The figures they particularly liked to cite concerned the revolutionary period of the late eighteenth and early nineteenth centuries. After divorce was introduced in France during the First Republic in 1792, there were thousands of divorces within a few years. By contrast, when the Napoleonic code introduced the possibility of divorce on Italian soil for the first time, there was only a handful of divorce cases, mostly in Milan, in the six years before the divorce law was abolished by the Restoration rulers. On the other hand, these figures were also pressed into service by the *divorzisti*, beginning with Morelli himself, who argued that these low numbers proved that Italians had nothing to fear from divorce legislation: while it would be a useful remedy for a small number of desperate cases, it would clearly not be the undoing of society.

Despite their opposite aims, both arguments made use of the notion that Italian marriages were for the most part happily solid. This may have been so, but Italians may also have embraced a culture of resignation and tolerance in marriage, and a tendency to keep such matters private. Even so, the civil code acknowledged, by the inclusion of personal separation, that even in Italy married couples needed to be provided with some sort of escape route from marriages that went wrong. The principle of personal separation had been introduced into canon law in the twelfth century. Effectively, it was a dispensation from the "conjugal debt" of a married couple to live with each other and to have sexual intercourse, and could only be granted after a judicial process. According to canon law there were three main grounds on which a separation could be granted: adultery, cruelty, and apostasy.[14] Such a judgment did not, of course, dissolve the marriage bond. Consequently, couples who formally separated and who did not want to be sinners faced a life of celibacy, at least until one partner died.

The Italian civil code of 1865, following the example of the Napoleonic code, essentially incorporated this ancient tradition into the marriage law of Italy, although with a few modifications. The most significant change was that a separation could be obtained on the grounds of mutual consent, and unsurprisingly, apostasy no longer gave rise to a separation. Other grounds on which separation could be requested were similar to those that had been provided by canon law: adultery, abandonment, cruelty, threats and serious injury, as well as the husband's failure to establish a fixed abode.[15] If the couple had children and the plea for separation was not by mutual consent, the court could decide the fate of the children. Usually the children were given to the care of the spouse who was not guilty of the offence giving rise to the separation. The law also provided for an order of support, which usually meant that the husband paid maintenance to the wife.[16]

Between 1866 and 1879, 11,431 Italian couples were involved in petitions for personal separation. This represented an average of 817 cases per year, and of these an average of 612 separations were actually approved. In about 10 percent of cases the spouses were successfully reconciled during the proceedings. The remaining cases were either abandoned or dismissed by the court for lack of evidence.[17] Personal separation had always been conceived by the Church as a temporary measure, and the same spirit applied to the civil law. The effects of a judgment of separation under the civil code became void automatically if the couple began to live with each other again, so there was no need for a formal process.[18] For this reason it is impossible to develop any idea of the fate of these separated couples. One authoritative jurist of the period felt that few couples, once officially separated, would reunite,[19] and this view was accordingly echoed by all *divorzisti*.

Although those on both sides of the divorce argument liked to make much of the customary stability of Italian marriages, emphasizing either the irrelevance of divorce or the minimal application it would have, the statistics on separation suggest that Italian marriages were not immune to the vagaries of human nature. A comparison with some other European countries suggests that Italy was neither the best nor the worst country when it came to marriage failure. During the decade from 1871 to 1880, in Italy there was an average of one separation for every 44,550 people each year. In Belgium over the same period, where divorce was permitted, there was one divorce for every 43,815 people each year. The real contrast was with France, where divorce was not permitted (it was reintroduced in 1884), but there was one personal separation a year for every 18,055 people. In other words, for Italy's 612 separations per year, in Belgium there were 120 divorces, and in France there were 2150 separations.[20] Although the number of personal separations in Italy was reassuringly low overall, the problem was far from nonexistent: there were more than 15 requests every week, and more than 11 of those were granted.

Variations on a Theme

The average figures say little about variations over the Italian peninsula, which were significant. The statistics were compiled by the 20 different Courts of Appeal, rather than by region, so the territorial units do not correspond exactly with contemporary divisions. Nevertheless, it is possible to make broad generalizations about patterns of personal separation during the first decade and a half of the operation of the civil code.[21] The most obvious is that personal separation was a solution embraced far more often by couples in the north than in the south. For example, in the areas under the jurisdiction of the courts of Milan, Turin, and Florence, which covered a population of 5.25 million, there were 5,873 applications for separation between 1866 and 1879. By contrast, in the area covered by the courts of Naples and Palermo, which covered 5.29 million people, there were a mere 828 applications over the same period.[22] There were exceptions to this general rule that make it difficult to draw any simple conclusions. The territory covered by the court of Venice included more than 2.6 million people, but the number of separation cases between 1866 and 1879 was a mere 512, a rate that was only slightly higher than that of Naples and Palermo.

Although it is not possible to explain such variations with any certainty, some speculations can be made. One possibility that can be dispensed with rather easily is the idea that separation was an urban phenomenon. The way the statistics were kept makes it unfeasible to examine the question in a detailed way, as each court did not make distinctions between urban and rural areas. But the case of Naples points away from the supposition that separation was concentrated in urban areas. Naples was still the largest city in Italy during the 1870s, yet the Court of Appeal based there reported one of the lowest rates of separation in the whole country. Another possibility, even less susceptible to empirical analysis, has to do with the relationship between citizens and the state. The indifference and indeed recalcitrance of many southern Italians toward their "Piedmontese" overlords in the period after the unification was legendary. Going to court to ask for a personal separation implied an acceptance of and engagement with the state that may have been foreign to southern culture.

Putting aside the considerable variety in the incidence of marital breakdown dealt with by the state, it is worth charting some of the more general characteristics of Italian couples who sought separations. The first point that needs to be made is that while the civil procedure did cost money, personal separation was by no means only the preserve of the well-off. The statistics collected by the courts divided the financial position of the applicants into two main classes. The first, *possidente* or "possessor," described those with property. The second class was *nullatenente*, having no property at all. There was also an "unknown" category. Of the 11,431 couples who applied for a personal separation between 1866 and 1880, 4,142 women owned property, 6,035 owned nothing, and in 1,254 cases their status was not known. Of the men, 4,637 owned property, 5,438 did not, and the position of 1,356 was not known.[23]

The statistics on the possession of property also display strong regional variety, pointing toward further possible generalizations about the great differences in number of applications between north and south. In Florence, for example, where there were 1,660 applications between 1866 and 1879, a minority of applicants came from the propertied classes: 344 propertied males, as opposed to 873 male applicants without property. This ratio, not unexpectedly, was similar for the women. The distinction was not as great in Milan, but propertied applicants were still fewer: 962 as opposed to 1,341 without property. In Naples, where there was a total of only 466 applicants, the trend is starkly reversed: 373 of the male applicants had property, against a mere 93 who did not. Again, the ratio of women was very similar. In Palermo, the difference between propertied applicants and nonpropertied was not as stark, but there was still a significant preponderance of those with property.[24]

Beyond the rather crude classification of applicants for personal separation into haves and have-nots, the state's statistics provided a breakdown of their economic activity. These figures again confirm in a more detailed way the impression that the need for marital separation was not dominated by one group. In Milan, the area that dealt with the highest absolute number of applications (2,656), the largest occupational group was represented by workers and day-laborers (556 men and 581 women). The same applied in the area administered from Florence, where 523 men and 387 women came from this category. This was a particularly high proportion of the total of 1,660 applications.

It is important to know something about the demography and class background of personal separations in Italy, but the most important question concerns the sorts of problems people had in marriage and why they separated. The records provided by the statistics on separation do not, of course, tell the whole story. Since the law provided certain clear grounds for separation, petitioners were obliged to proceed on those grounds, even if in reality other motivations propelled them to separate. Indeed, the problem with using court records to study aspects of private life in the past is that the laws themselves inevitably influenced the accounts of marriage problems. Bearing this in mind, it is nevertheless valuable to know how those who wanted to separate presented their cases to the courts.

Of the 11,431 cases recorded in the early statistics, just under half the total (5,106) of the unhappy couples applied for separation on the grounds of mutual consent. This was the simplest way to proceed, because it meant that there was no need to air private problems before a court, or to prove any misdemeanor or offense to the satisfaction of the tribunal. The president of the court simply went through the required process of trying to reconcile the couple, but more often than not this was little more than a formality, and the separation was approved by the court.[25] Usually in such cases the couple agreed upon the way they would separate their property and the sum of any maintenance to be paid. It should be borne in mind, though, that this process, which could appear quite simple and even amicable in the records of a court, could mask emotional situations that were fraught and complex.

If cases of separation by mutual consent may have occasionally masked some more pressing cause, the remaining 6,325 cases were brought by one aggrieved spouse against the other, who would have allegedly been guilty of one or more of the offenses that were grounds for separation. Women initiated 4,945 cases, whereas only 1,269 were brought by men. This is not surprising, given the lesser constraints on men, and women had fewer avenues through which to seek relief from the pressures of a difficult domestic life. The trials of a bad marriage would therefore have been more difficult for women to tolerate, which explains why they turned to the state for a solution more often than men.

The sorts of problems that might drive married women to court to seek a separation are elaborated by the breakdown of the specific motives for which separations were sought. Domestic violence accounted for 4,462 of the total number of cases. This figure combined 2,787 for "excesses and cruelty" and 1,675 for "threats and grievous injury," although the exact ways in which these categories differ is unclear. Although the statistics do not expressly state that cases made under these categories were sought by women, it seems much more likely that in the majority of cases, threats, cruelty, and physical injury were suffered by women at the hands of their husbands. In a marriage in which a woman was subject to violence, she could either resign herself to her fate, or seek a personal separation. Another important category that motivated separations was voluntary abandonment. Here again women were more likely to have made such requests, because it was more difficult for a woman to abandon the security of the domestic sphere than it was for a man.

Again, it is worth noting how some of these statistics varied across the peninsula. The national average for separations by mutual consent was 44.6 percent. Of the cases initiated by an aggrieved party, 11 percent were moved by men, and 43 percent were moved by women. The data from the Appeals Courts of Turin, Milan, Florence, Naples, and Palermo show that with one exception there was not a great variation in these figures, with between 42 percent and 50 percent of cases being for mutual consent, 6 percent and 14 percent being moved by the husband, and between 39 percent and 44 percent of cases being moved by a wife. The exception was Palermo, where a mere 11 percent of cases were brought by mutual consent, 14 percent of separations were sought by the husband, and 75 percent of separations were sought by wives. Explaining this variation would require a careful anthropological study; but it is also the exception that proves the rule that there was a reassuring similarity between the other major areas of the peninsula in terms of how couples seeking personal separation brought their cases to court.

Such national similarities do not apply to the major motives of separation. The most peculiar case was Milan, where 73 percent of cases were sought for "other" reasons, and more scandalous causes, such as adultery (at 2 percent) and violence (at 17 percent) were correspondingly diminished. It is very likely, though, that the records again coyly hide more specific reasons under this vague category. It is worth remembering that if a couple separated by mutual consent there was no need for them to state a particular reason for their decision. Another anomalous case is again provided by Palermo, the city where 75 percent of the 366 cases were initiated by women. It is therefore surprising to find that in this area of Sicily only 29 percent of cases were motivated by violence, whether threatened or actual. This figure is significantly lower than those of Naples or Florence, for example, where around 50 percent of cases had violence as a motivation. In Palermo the main reason for seeking an official separation was for voluntary abandonment, which accounted for 37 percent of cases. Abandonment also motivated 25 percent of separation cases in Naples, and the two southern cities also took adultery seriously. It accounted for 16 percent of cases in Naples and 13 percent in Palermo. By contrast, in Turin and Florence adultery was the motive behind only 6 percent of cases.

What Will Happen to the Children?

One of the most frequently recurring arguments against the introduction of a divorce law in late-nineteenth-century Italy was that the lives of the children of divorced couples would be ruined. A common riposte to this argument was that children suffered most harm as a result of living with parents who were at each others' throats, and the law needed to ameliorate situations of this sort. Those in favor of divorce argued that personal separation made things worse for children, because it prevented their parents from forming legally recognized new unions.[26] It is not possible to generalize whether it is better for children to live with a single parent or one who has remarried, but the *divorzisti* argued that many separated parents would inevitably develop new relationships, regardless of whether these were formalized by the law or not. And they argued that if children had to see their parents in new relationships, it would be better if they were officially recognized rather than illicit.

By the time of the first parliamentary proposals for the introduction of a divorce law in Italy, the courts had had a certain degree of experience with making provisions for the offspring of parents who had legally separated. Of the total number of applications up to the end of 1879, 50 percent of the couples concerned had children, although in about 10 percent of these cases the children were already of majority age or had come from prior marriages (or both), so that there was no need for the court to decide their fate. Overall, the courts registered decisions in relation to children in a total of 4,653 cases, or very close to 40 percent of the total number of separations.

The courts' decisions could be interim or definitive, but putting that distinction aside, in the majority of cases (59 percent) the children were given to the care of the mother against the 36 percent that were given to the father. A very small proportion of children (4 percent) were given to the care of "others," most likely a close relative. The remaining 1 percent were placed in institutions. Overall this meant that 95 percent of the children of separated couples were placed with one of their natural parents, most often to the mother. If divorce had been introduced, much the same would have occurred. The difference is that the parents would have been free to marry again. The idea of children having to live with a new "parent" struck horror into the hearts of many, but the *divorzisti* claimed that it was the lesser of two evils, because divorce offered a cleaner break from a past best left behind.

However small the absolute number of personal separations in Italy in the late nineteenth century, there was undoubtedly a continual demand from people who wished to be released from the most basic of their marital obligations, and overall figures show that this demand increased steadily throughout the rest of the century.[27] Although the national statistics show a significant variety of numbers and motives for separation in different parts of the country, this constant demand also suggests certain uniformities in human nature. People from all walks of life, and all "conditions of fortune," from agricultural day laborers to leisured aristocrats, occasionally found married life so intolerable that they chose to expose the most intimate aspects of their lives to the state in search of a solution.

This is a reminder of something that cannot be captured by statistics: in the vast majority of cases, failed marriages were the cause of emotional pain. A sense of the human dramas that lay behind the applications for personal separation is revealed by the records of the Tribunals that heard the cases. These records also add further detail to the variety suggested by the national statistics, as well as revealing interesting exceptions. Above all the more personal records are a reminder of the ways in which marriages could go wrong, even in the city whose Church espoused the doctrine of indissoluble marriage.

Separations in Rome

Italy's civil code of 1865 only applied to Roman citizens after their city had become the capital of the Kingdom of Italy in 1870. Shortly after this last bastion of ecclesiastical law was taken over by the Italian state, jurisdiction over the marital affairs of Rome's citizens passed to the Kingdom of Italy. Perhaps surprisingly, Romans did not hesitate to take their marital woes to the new civil courts. Between 1871 and 1879, there was an average of 66 applications for personal separation each year. Although this is a small absolute number, measured as a ratio of the population covered by Rome's Court of Appeal, the figure was 250 percent higher than the national average.[28] Moreover, applications by Romans were to increase by 50 percent in ensuing years: between 1882 and 1892 there was a total of 1,187 requests, or over 100 per year.

The procedure for obtaining a personal separation was reasonably simple, especially if the couple proceeded by mutual consent. The first step was to appear in court, where a clerk would take down the details of the case and fix a date for a hearing before the president of the Tribunal (the lowest Italian court), usually about a week later. When the couple appeared in the court, the president would listen to the details, and if the separation was not desired by mutual consent, he would hear the partners independently.

The next step was always an attempt to reconcile the couple. The fact that the law required at least an attempt at reconciliation was a vestige of the canon law procedure, in which one of the most important figures in a hearing for annulment was the *difensore vinculae*, or the defender of the marital bond, whose function was to show why the marriage should not be annulled. In the procedures for annulment the defender of the bond turned every legal stone in order to deter the giving of an annulment, with regard only to the law, and none whatsoever to the happiness of the couple. In separation cases before the civil courts, the cursory way in which the attempt at reconciliation was usually recorded suggests that it was now little more than a polite formula, although such attempts were successful in about 10 percent of the cases on a nationwide basis between 1866 and 1879.

The proceedings were recorded in a *verbale* (a statement), and finally a "record of voluntary separation," which recorded the terms of the separation, noting any financial arrangements or an order for the children to be given to the sole custody of one of the parents. This document made the separation official. The court also levied charges for the procedure. A charge was made for the official paper recording the hearing, and for "access" to the law and the court's time. A straightforward case might cost 16 lire, a complex or drawn-out one considerably more. This was not enormously expensive, as it was common for a male in an unskilled occupation to earn about a hundred lire per month.[29]

Behind the Scenes

An examination of individual cases heard in Rome confirms the overall tendencies indicated by the national figures on personal separation. It also reveals a sense of the human dramas that lay behind those numbers, adding nuance, detail, and serving as a reminder of the limits of statistics. For example, two cases heard at the Tribunale di Roma in early 1882 suggest that officially approved separations were the visible part of a much more widespread phenomenon that generally went unrecorded in the official statistics.

In the first case Antonio and Palmira Belli applied for a separation in January 1882. The court records show that they had been married in 1870 but had separated after five years of marriage because they found life together intolerable.[30] By granting a personal separation to the couple, the court simply gave official recognition to an established situation. A similar case occurred a few days later, when Carlo Zendrini and his wife Lida also sought to convert a "separazione di fatto" into a legally recognized separation. They got married in 1869 and had gone separate ways after two years, finding their characters to be "absolutely incompatible."[31]

Neither the Belli nor the Zendrini gave reasons that explained why they had suddenly been inspired to formalize separations that had been in effect for six and eleven years respectively. Neither couple had children, nor was any arrangement for financial support made in either case. In fact it is far from clear what exactly was to be gained by the process, which was not expensive, but hardly free, except perhaps the satisfaction of tying up the loose ends left by their unofficial separations. Above all though, it is most likely that these two cases were exceptions that proved a rule: for every official personal separation there must have been many cases of de facto separation that were never formalized and never recorded.

Not all separation cases were as simple as the court giving its official blessing to a separation that had either already taken place or been agreed upon by mutual consent. Cases involving adultery were among those that were most emotionally charged and more likely to be contested. For example, in May 1882 the Rome court heard the case of Adele and Pietro Castigliano. Adele had abandoned the marital home in 1876 after only 11 months of marriage because she discovered that her husband was having an affair with his young niece. The niece lived in the marital home as a ward of Pietro Castigliano, and she had borne him a son in August 1881. Italian law did not make it easy for a woman to prosecute her husband for adultery, but the separation of the Castiglianos was one of the rare cases in which the husband was technically guilty of adultery, and the incestuous aspect added further scandal.

Ironically, Signor Castigliano tried to obtain a separation from his wife on the basis that she had wilfully abandoned the marital home. In reply, she mounted her own case, carefully mentioning her right to commence proceedings against her husband for his concubinage. This veiled threat was a way of pressuring Castigliano into accepting terms of separation that were entirely in his wife's favor (as of course they should have been).[32] The court ordered that the signora could keep all the income from her dowry, and that her husband should pay her 1,200 lire per year (equal to an average salary), as well as the court costs.[33] But for the satisfaction of seeing her husband in jail for adultery, the woman's triumph was as complete as it could have been under the law, and she moved to Turin. The benefits of obtaining a personal separation are much more evident in this case than the previous matters, but it should be remembered that despite the apparent finality of the Castigliano's separation, they remained legally married until one of them died.

Separation cases for nearly all the legally admitted reasons appeared quite regularly in Rome. In general the court cases dramatize the broad picture established by the general statistics on personal separation. But they also underline the great variety of marital experience, with cases that range from the unconventional to the lurid. These warrant attention, not for the sake of prurience, but because they add complexity and detail to a picture that might otherwise be constructed with the cliches of the anti-*divorzisti* who claimed that marriages in Italy were so solid.

Cases cover the breadth of the class spectrum and illustrate different priorities. For example, when the Marchese Andrea Venturi and his wife the Principessa Valeria Santacroce wished to separate in March 1884 after 12 years of marriage, financial considerations and social decorum were paramount. Clearly both parties had consulted lawyers, who presented extremely detailed statements of the terms under which the couple were prepared to settle. The Marchese kept his rights over the princess's dowry, but she kept control over her nondowry property (under Italian law a married woman had to obtain her husband's permission before making any dealings with her own property). The three eldest children (aged 11, 8, and 7) went to the father, while the mother kept the two younger ones (aged 6 and 5). While she received maintenance at the extraordinary level of 2000 lire per month (much more than most Italians earned in a year), the agreement punctiliously stipulated that if she desired to use agricultural products from their estate she would have to buy them at the market price.[34]

The painful truth and the bitter disagreements that lay behind many couples' decisions to seek personal separation were more often than not revealed in the course of the legal proceedings. For example, in May 1882 the Rome court heard the case of Melanie Rayner and Pietro Carnevali, involving the marriage of a genteel 39-year-old widow in comfortable circumstances to a penniless butcher of 25. The wedding took place in September 1880, by which time a child had already been born to the couple, and another arrived only six months later. In her statement Rayner emphasized the extent to which the marriage had represented an improvement in material circumstances for the young butcher, who was welcomed into the comfortable house she had inherited from her first husband. It was therefore all the more puzzling to her that within a few months of the wedding her new husband started to visit upon her "every sort of cruelty," requiring recourse to the police on more than one occasion.

Pietro Carnevali, for his part, stressed that only the purest sentiments of affection had been his motive for the marriage. He felt this was proved by a consideration of the fact that the widow Rayner was not rich, that she already had a large family, and that she was 13 years his senior. According to Pietro, immediately following the marriage, his new wife had revealed a restless and unstable character, and even though he had not given her the slightest reason for suspicion, she was perpetually jealous. He claimed that she was a bad housewife, failing even to attend to the most basic task of feeding her family. Eventually she had even prevented him from showing affection toward his two children, had had his personal effects removed from her house, and refused him entry. His desire to seek a resolution to these wrongs had propelled him to seek a personal separation. The case was resolved by the judge's decision that the two young children should remain with their mother. Carnevali was required to pay 30 lire per month toward their maintenance, and he was allowed to see them once a week.[35]

Apart from the fact that by law this unfortunate marriage would remain in existence until one of the spouses died, the official treatment of the separation has something remarkably contemporary about it, as indeed do the circumstances of the marriage itself. There is a tendency to believe that in the nineteenth century there was a clear distinction between respectability and immorality, and that respectable people generally married within their own age and class. The case of a marriage between a respectable widow and an evidently lusty young butcher is an example of the fact that not all families in the past fitted rigid models of respectability.

It is of course in the nature of court records on marital separation to reveal the things that could go wrong with marriages. In doing so they also provide evidence that marital relations in late-nineteenth-century Italy were as subject to the vagaries of human whim and caprice as they are now, and that peculiarities, variations, and even perversities are not a monopoly of modernity. For example, in July 1887 Giuseppe Frattini petitioned for an immediate separation from his wife on the basis that she had on several occasions encouraged him to have sexual relations with her 14-year-old daughter Maddalena (apparently he was not her father). Frattini claimed that his wife's motive was to cover up the "damage" already done by someone else. He demanded custody of their 10-year-old daughter Teresa to protect her from the risk of suffering the same treatment as Maddalena. The court granted the separation, but for reasons that remain unclear, custody of the daughter Teresa was granted to the mother, and Frattini was ordered to pay maintenance of 45 lire per month.[36] This suggests that to the court the main issue was the separation, not the moral welfare of the young girls.

A case in 1892 also involved incest. Giovanni Cicchetti, a cook aged 34, claimed that from the moment he had married Giulia Franceschini five years earlier, he had not had a moment's peace. Violent family scenes had constantly been provoked by her immorality, and the last straw was the discovery of her in flagrant adultery and what was worse, with her own brother. Cicchetti claimed that because of his peaceful nature he did not want to prosecute her adultery, but wanted a personal separation. They separated by mutual consent on 28 March 1892, with no financial settlement.[37]

What became of people like Giulia Franceschini and Giovanni Cicchetti after they separated is impossible to say. Franceschini was a "housewife," and turned out of that position, with no support, she would either have to find some sort of job, return to her family, or perhaps resort to prostitution. Remarriage was not a possibility unless her first husband died. Cicchetti himself was denied the pleasure of a happy marriage because of his first wife's incestuous adultery. Clearly, personal separation was an area of permanent limbo, but the unjust aspect was that there was no distinction between the guilty and the innocent, and there was only one way for the limbo to end: the death of one spouse.

Usually, the cases of personal separation in Rome confirm the generalizations that can be made about the national statistics. For example, it seemed reasonable to assume that if the motive for separation was violence, that violence was directed by a man toward a woman. If there was some sort of financial settlement, the husband would usually make payments to the wife. Most of the Rome cases support these assumptions. In a sense the frequency of acts of violence on the part of a husband is suggested by several cases in which the woman had resigned herself to violence for many years,[38] and only lost her patience, for example, once the children had grown up. But for every woman who did lose her patience, even after many years, there must have been many more whose patience never ran out.

On the other hand, the direction of the violence was not always a hard and fast rule. One Achille Ferini pleaded for separation from his wife in

1892 because of mistreatment he had received at her hands. According to his account, she had made room for a male "relative" of hers in the family home with whom she played a game known colloquially as "footsie" at the dining table. Not only that, "cruelty and beatings" had become the order of the day for Achille, who reported that he was deaf and a stutterer (these conditions were, however, antecedent to the beatings). When he had asked the "relative" to leave his house, he was set upon by his wife, the visitor, and even his daughter. They delivered him to an asylum, claiming that he was demented, and he was rescued only two days later by his sister, who had received an anonymous letter detailing her brother's whereabouts.[39]

A male suffering violence at the hands of his wife (albeit with a male accomplice) is the exception that proves a rule about domestic violence. Similarly, in a world that offered women few opportunities for self-sufficiency, it was much more common for maintenance to be paid by a husband to his wife after separation. The most common exception to this was when no maintenance was paid at all. But neither were those conventions completely rigid. For example, in the first case to come before the Tribunal in Rome in 1892, the couple had decided to separate after a mere six weeks of marriage. The separation was amicable and by mutual consent, for reasons of incompatibility of character. What made the case particularly unusual was that according to a private agreement the wife was to pay her husband the sum of 1,500 lire in monthly installments of 100 lire.[40] This sum represented a partial payment of the cost of the wedding. It made the couple's six-week foray into matrimony an expensive affair, since that sum was more than a typical annual salary for a clerk or manual laborer. And as always, the bond still prevented a more felicitous marriage for either partner as long as both remained alive.

Although personal separation at least allowed the possibility of an escape from marriages that had become insufferable, it is easy to see why those in favor of divorce argued that it was a half-measure. Above all, it made no allowance for the possibility that after the first marriage human passions could ever again rise beyond the lukewarm. Or perhaps more to the point, by ignoring the fact that they clearly could, it meant that the state's laws virtually encouraged the existence of a nether world, a sort of black economy of relationships that were never acknowledged by the laws of the land. In this sense, while the institution of marriage had been so urgently embraced by the new Italian state as a symbol of the new relationship between the law and the people, the denial of a divorce law meant that the state hypocritically turned its back on the problems of couples after having offered them only half a solution.

Divorce by Murder

Reflecting an inheritance that went back to the Council of Trent, according to Italian law, death was the only way by which a marriage could be dissolved. This meant that if passions became particularly inflamed, murdering a spouse was the only way to effect a "divorce" that would allow remarriage. This notion of divorce "Italian style" was made famous by Pietro Germi's film, *Divorzio all' italiana*, in the 1960s.[41] The film was made just as the final campaign to legalize divorce began, but the crime itself was of course much older, and had been acknowledged as a problem during the early years of the Italian kingdom. Indeed, when Salvatore Morelli proposed the adoption of a divorce law in parliament for the second time, he made reference to several notorious murder trials, all of which he implied were attributable to the indissolubility of marriage in Italy.[42]

In the same vein, when in 1881 Tommaso Villa, the then minister of justice, took up Morelli's crusade by presenting a divorce law designed by the government, one of the documents he presented with his law was a table of statistics showing the number of homicides (both attempted and successful) by one spouse against another that had come before the courts between 1866 and 1880. The total was 699 for all of Italy. A note claims that the table does not include spouse murders that were "manifestly independent of the indissolubility of the marriage bond."[43] The table therefore represents a statistical argument for the introduction of divorce on the basis that marital indissolubility could have murderous results.

Just as personal separations showed considerable regional variety, this form of "divorce" in Italy also shows striking variations in different parts of the peninsula. In the area administered by the Court of Appeal in Milan, which had a population of approximately 1.7 million, a mere 14 cases were heard between 1866 and 1880. The area covered by Florence (1.3 million people) had 21 cases, and Rome (approximately 837,000 people) had 19. The much more alarming figures apply to Naples, which had a large population (approximately 3.6 million) but the extraordinary number of 211 cases, and Palermo (with a population of approximately 1.66 million) with 100 cases.[44]

It is worth remembering that Naples and Palermo were the areas that had had relatively low levels of application for personal separation over the same period. For example, Naples, with over twice the population of Milan's area, had had 466 cases against 2,656 in Milan. Yet when it came to spouse murder, Naples and Palermo stood out from any other area in Italy. This suggests that while the residents of those areas were reluctant to take their marital problems to court, they were rather more willing than Italians elsewhere to take matters into their own hands and "solve" marital problems privately.

The Fadda Case

The Italian newspapers frequently reported cases of spouse murder. One of the most notorious murder cases was tried in Rome in the late 1870s, just as the divorce question was awakening in parliament. It was mentioned by Salvatore Morelli,[45] and was known as the Fadda case, the name of the murder victim. The accused were Pietro Cardinali and Raffaella Saraceni, two illicit lovers who had allegedly plotted and carried out the murder of Saraceni's husband, Captain Fadda. Saraceni and Fadda had been married in 1871. She was a well-to-do Calabrian woman; he was a career officer originally from Sardinia, promoted to captain after the marriage, then posted to Caltanisetta, in Sicily. Shortly after this posting the marriage had begun to fall apart, and eventually the couple separated. This was a de facto separation rather than an official one. Nevertheless, Fadda returned Saraceni's dowry to her, and she returned to reside with her mother in Calabria.[46]

This failed marriage could have remained typical of so many others of its day, suspended in the permanent limbo of unofficial separation, unrecorded and known only to friends and family. The shift from an empty marriage to a murder whose purpose was "divorce"[47] was sparked by the arrival of a circus in Raffaella Saraceni's town, Cassano Jonio, in the summer of 1878. Raffaella fell in love with one of the acrobatic horse riders, Pietro Cardinali, and they began a passionate affair. Saraceni's husband was murdered on 6 October 1878, and the illicit couple were accused of the crime, Cardinali as the murderer, Saraceni as the "principal agent."[48]

The murder trial began just under a year later in Rome, where the murder had taken place. The proceedings attracted enormous public attention, and were reported avidly and in lurid detail by the major newspapers of the nation, while in the capital itself, huge crowds flooded into the courtroom from the first day. The whole affair was watched much like a modern-day television soap-opera, and the correspondent of Milan's respected *Corriere della sera* assiduously pointed out the preponderance of women in the audience.[49] The high numbers of women attending the trial says as much about who had the time during the day to attend a court case as it does about their interest in the case itself, but what is certain is that the case had all the elements necessary to grip the attention of a large public: a loveless marriage, illicit passion, and a gruesome murder. Putting aside the murder, the case pitted the idea of a dutiful, sexless, but respectable marriage against notions of love, romance, and, implicitly, sexual gratification. This gave the case a moral intensity that helps to explain the fervent following it received.

As the court proceedings outlined the events, these elements were woven into a dramatic narrative. Although Saraceni was not directly accused of murder, a great deal of the attention of the public and the news-papers focused on her plight. Trapped in an unsatisfactory marriage, she had been torn by her love for Cardinali, and together the two had plotted the only measure that could make way for their marriage. The question of sexual love and satisfaction was never very far from the surface. Early in the trial a document came to light certifying that Saraceni's husband, Captain Fadda, had received a groin injury during the battle of San Martino in 1859, one of the early battles of the Risorgimento. Apart from establishing Fadda's credentials as a patriotic son of Italy, the document raised the question of Fadda's sexual potency. It was rumoured that Saraceni had long lamented Fadda's genital incapacity, and the figure of Pietro Cardinali, described by the newspapers as good-looking, sensual, and vigorous, all suggested that in him Saraceni had found a potent antidote to her marital shortcomings.[50] Saraceni's choice was between a respectable but compromised bourgeois marriage, and the chance to ride off with a virile but common horseman. It was this dilemma that clearly had the Rome audience transfixed.[51]

The sensational trial revealed how Cardinali and Saraceni had fallen in love. He was 35; she was 25 (which meant that she had been 17 when she married Fadda in 1871). Over a hundred witnesses were called, and the story of the lovers' plot to do away with Fadda so that they could marry came together very quickly. Initially two circus women in whose company Cardinali traveled had offered 100 ducats to the circus clown, Carluccio, to murder Fadda, but he had refused. Eventually Cardinali himself had trav-eled to Rome, where Fadda had been stationed at the time. Fadda was stabbed with a stiletto that was later found lying on the steps of the build-ing in which he lived. He rushed into the street in his underpants to raise the alarm, and Cardinali was seen running off.[52] Fadda died soon afterward; he had been stabbed twenty-three times.[53] When Cardinali was caught, he claimed that the blood on his hands came from a nosebleed incurred after he had fallen off his horse.[54] Saraceni was arrested three days later, accused of complicity.[55]

Cardinali's direct involvement in the crime was proved, at least as far as the audience's sighs and murmurs were concerned, fairly quickly. The question of Saraceni's guilt was a more subtle matter, absorbing much more of the court's time and the audience's attention: each day the open-ing of the session began with an avalanche as the public scrambled for seats, and the correspondent's superlatives for a full house were soon exhausted. Although Saraceni calmly denied everything, witnesses made it clear that many people had known about her affair with the horseman.[56]

The question of Saraceni's involvement in Fadda's murder was opened by the use of the word "divorce" by another defendant accused of complicity,

Antonietta Carrozza. Carrozza was part of the circus troupe and passed for Cardinali's sister, although rumour had it that she was also part of the horseman's harem. During her first interrogation Carrozza referred to the crime, apparently ingenuously, as a "divorce." She claimed that she had heard Saraceni discussing with Cardinali her desire for a divorce from Fadda. The *Corriere della sera*'s correspondent was stunned to hear the word "divorce" issue from "that ignorant mouth" and speculated that this was a sure sign of premeditated murder: "What could divorce be, if not death, the other not being permitted by the law," the correspondent asked rhetorically.[57]

If this murder was a divorce "Italian-style" par excellence, then the principal ground, according to the understanding of several witnesses, was impotence. Although the newspapers did not again refer to the document mentioning Fadda's groin injury, the reports seemed to take it for granted that Fadda's presumed impotence was the source of Saraceni's marital misery.[58] During Saraceni's first cross-examination, her interrogator homed in on the question of Fadda's lack of virility. Saraceni claimed that she was unaware of his injury, but did not deny the rumours that he was not up to his matrimonial obligations.[59] Later, Saraceni's hairdresser claimed she had heard her client lament her husband's incapacity.[60] The next day another woman made the same claim, adding that Saraceni had openly stated that in order to free herself from her husband it would be necessary to kill him.[61]

After the testimony of many ancillary witnesses, the proceedings reached the point of the lawyers' summing up. Cardinali's guilt was so taken for granted that the prosecution barely wasted breath on him. Instead, they focused their attention on Saraceni, and what they clearly regarded as her dereliction of her duty to womanhood. Revealing open prejudice, Professor Ponsiglioni claimed that Saraceni had been brought up in too "southern" a way, possibly even an "American" way, and as a result was dedicated to the gratification of sensual pleasure. She had been the wife of an honest soldier of the cause of Italian liberty, but rather than being loyal to a man "whose body carried the indelible record of the Austrian bullets," she had allowed herself to fall for a vulgar show-jumper. He urged particularly severe treatment for Saraceni, claiming that it would be an insult to honest women if she were to leave the court "free and triumphant."[62]

The onslaught on Saraceni's betrayal of her class and her sex continued the next day with another prosecutor, Rutigliano. He made the audience weep with his description of the honest Fadda's last moments, "knowing that his wife had caused his death because of an ignoble passion for a contemptible circus performer." He claimed that Saraceni could have lived an honorable life with a proud soldier, but she became delirious with "shameful love for a worthless man."[63] In sum, Rutigliano urged the audience that public morality, so atrociously offended by Saraceni, should be avenged.

The prosecutors created a picture of a woman who felt passions she ought not to have felt, who lusted after a virile horseman rather than her impotent husband. Saraceni had stooped beneath her class, was a traitor to the ideal of the family, and had threatened the bourgeois order with sexual chaos. The irony is that according to canon law, Saraceni would have been able to get an annulment of her marriage to Fadda on the grounds that he was impotent, and the marriage would therefore not have been able to fulfill its purpose according to God's will, that of procreation. But the Italian civil law was more rigid in this regard, and there was no legal way for the contractual bond between Saraceni and Fadda to be dissolved.

Rutigliano's speech in particular drew deep murmurs of approval from the audience,[64] and it would be easy to assume that to a bourgeois audience Saraceni's transgressions were beyond doubt. However, the arguments of the defense show that it would be wrong to assume that there was no sense of a woman having the right to sexual gratification, nor that women should always be expected to sublimate sexual passion to matrimonial duty. For example, Saraceni's first defense lawyer argued that Saraceni was a sensual woman, ardent and in need of "strong emotions and continual physical pleasure."[65] He would not have used such arguments if they had run counter to prevailing mores. Furthermore, he asked the public to imagine what would happen if the courts had decided to try all men and women who had illicit relationships: "we would need a court room as large as Rome itself."[66]

The proceedings continued to suggest the existence of socially acceptable but unofficial sexual license. Saraceni's first defense lawyer claimed that there was no motive for murder, because Fadda had given his wife enough freedom to do as she wished. He claimed that effectively they had had "a sort of divorce."[67] This implies that at least some of the license extended to men who had separated from their wives may also have been taken by women. Indeed, the second lawyer launched his defense by turning to the audience and asking which woman would care to throw the first stone. The audience, far from being sanctimonious, laughed, showing that illicit affairs were probably a common and open secret.[68]

Finally, the last lawyer to speak on Saraceni's behalf claimed that the obstinate obsession with proving her guilt had distorted the trial, at which point he was interrupted by a burst of applause. He painted a picture of Saraceni as an unfortunate woman, worthy of compassion. Suggestively, he claimed that the "the torch of love" had not entered Saraceni's "house," and instead there reigned "inertia, cold, and impotence." The fact that the crowd went wild with delirious cheers shows that, far from being stern moralists, much of the audience felt strong sympathy with Saraceni's marital predicament.[69]

Despite the public shows of support, no such sympathy was manifested when it came to the verdicts and sentences, handed down on 31 October 1879. Cardinali was convicted of murder, after a short deliberation. Saraceni was convicted of being a primary agent to the murder, because the jury agreed that she encouraged Cardinali in actions she knew would conclude with murder. The principal lawyer of the prosecution requested the death sentence for Cardinali and life imprisonment for Saraceni, and these sentences were granted.[70] Peculiarly, given the almost obsessive attention paid by the newspapers to the moods of the audience, there were no comments about the public reaction to these sentences. The only mention was reserved for the fate of Antonietta Carozza, Cardinali's "sister," who had also been accused of complicity. She was not convicted, as she was considered by the jury to have been subject to influence that she could not resist. Her release gave rise to huge applause from the crowd.[71] These verdicts officially closed one of the most notorious and closely followed cases of divorce "Italian-style" during the early years of the Italian state. A few months later the state showed clemency toward Pietro Cardinali, whose death sentence was commuted to life imprisonment.[72]

Spouse murder was of course the most extreme way of escaping from a painful marriage in a nation where divorce was not possible. If the figures of the Ministry of Justice are accurate, between 1866 and 1880 there was a murder or attempted murder related to the indissolubility of marriage virtually once a week in Italy. This was a rate sufficient to keep the matter in the newspapers, and indeed the Fadda case had not even concluded when the *Corriere della sera* almost triumphantly announced that a new case, involving the poisoning of a rich, elderly husband by his young second wife (and her lover), would go to trial the following month.[73] In themselves, notorious murders that were obviously connected with the desire to be rid of one spouse and to marry another, did not amount to a cogent argument in favor of the introduction of divorce. But for Italians interested in making marriage dissoluble, such murders were a gruesome manifestation of the inadequacy of the Italian law to provide a remedy for the small number of people whose marriages, whether because of repulsion from their partner, or for other reasons, went irremediably wrong.

Conclusion

The number of Italians who resorted to murder obviously represented a tiny, desperate fraction of the overall number of people who found marriage unsatisfactory. Even those who were willing to engage the state in their marital affairs by requesting a personal separation still underrepresented the number of Italian marriages that remained marriages in name only. It is impossible to know how many couples dealt with insuperable marital difficulties simply by living separate lives, the way Fadda and Saraceni had done before the murder, and the way Garibaldi and Raimondi had done before their annulment. An assessment of what was to be gained by turning an informal separation into one that was officially recognized shows that in most cases the process offered limited tangible benefits.

In late-nineteenth-century Italy, expectations of marriage, and standards of resignation in cases of abuse, particularly for women, were clearly different from those of society more than a century later. Nevertheless, even a limited analysis of a small number of petitions for personal separation shows that marriages in the past were subject to frictions and difficulties just as they are today. Those who thought that the introduction of divorce would sully the very concept of marriage argued that personal separation was an adequate solution to problematic marriages. For various reasons, this view had carried the day in the mid-1860s when the civil code was written. But by 1880 more people were becoming convinced that personal separation was a half-measure that was cruel and hypocritical.

People like Morelli saw it as a medieval relic, compromising the progress supposedly represented by the introduction of civil marriage. His voice had seemed impossibly ahead of the times in 1878 and 1880, but those years marked a turning point in the history of the debates over divorce in Italy. The demise of Morelli, and with him his divorce bill, might very well have been the last that was heard of divorce in Italy for some years. But 15 years of life for the Italian civil code, and with it the accumulation of 15 years of national statistics on marriage, separation, and marriage-related crimes, were enough to prompt the rise of a phoenix from Morelli's ashes.

This was Tommaso Villa, the minister for justice who had supported Morelli's second divorce proposal. Villa, who had signed the decree that commuted Pietro Cardinali's death sentence into life imprisonment, took up the crusade to introduce divorce after Morelli's death. He was to dominate the pro-divorce lobby for at least 12 years. And the Church, which had been able to dismiss Morelli's ideas as those of a parliamentary misfit, could not do so in the case of Villa, who was powerful and well-respected. From the moment Villa took up the leadership of the divorce campaign, the debate took on a different, and much more serious, tone. In fact, the progressive elements of the state would now be locked into an intermittent battle with the Church over the divorce issue, until one of them established a clear victory over the question of whether divorce would become legal in Italy, or whether couples would continue to resolve serious marital disputes with one or another variation on the "Italian-style" theme.

Real Italy versus Legal Italy

Catholic Mobilization, Conservative Traditions, and Divorce, 1881–1900

One of the recurrent themes in the history of Liberal Italy has been the apparent discontinuity between the *paese legale* and the *paese reale* or, in other words, the separation between Italy's law-making class and the masses. Although it is clear that Italians were no more immune to occasional marital strife than the couples of any other nation, the issue of divorce was hardly a subject of public clamor, or even concern, in Italy at any time before 1880. During the following two decades, however, this was to change, as the question became the object of much broader national attention. If there was a single driving force behind this change, it was the vision and dedication of Tommaso Villa, the Italian minister for justice from 1879 to 1881, and an indefatigable crusader for the introduction of divorce right up to the early twentieth century.[1]

Although Villa was the key figure behind the escalation of public debate over divorce, the forces of resistance and opposition to the idea were ultimately responsible for making divorce into a contested public issue, rather than merely a polite debate restricted to parliament. In the broadest sense, that opposition was inspired by the Catholic Church, but it was the zeal of a particular movement within the bosom of Catholicism that gave the divorce issue its distinctive profile. That movement was known as the Opera dei Congressi Cattolici, the earliest national movement of Italian social Catholicism. The Opera dei Congressi, representing the Church, and Tommaso Villa, representing the state, were at loggerheads over divorce from the early 1880s. The resulting clash of ideologies was an exemplary meeting of religious and secular ideals, and naturally attracted the attention of intellectuals, but because of the tireless efforts of the Opera dei Congressi, for the first time the issue was also brought to the attention of millions of ordinary Italians. The divorce question inspired such passion among the faithful and resulted in so much organization that it must be concluded that the divorce question was a crucial catalyst in the conversion of social Catholicism into a mass-based political Catholicism in Italy by the early twentieth century.

For good reason, the rise of socialism has traditionally been regarded as the principal reason for the politicization of Italian Catholics, with Leo XIII's encyclical *Rerum Novarum* (1891) representing the first papal clarion cry.[2] Nevertheless, the issue of divorce preceded the rise of the Socialist movement by more than a decade. Divorce can therefore be seen as one of the most important inspirations for Catholic political organization. For this reason, Villa's attempts to introduce divorce into Italian law in the 1880s and 1890s represent not only the coming of age of the divorce debate in Italy, but also the beginnings of a new, more determined mobilization of the Church's lay organizations. That development would come to fruition with the entrance of Catholics into parliament by the early twentieth century. This chapter examines the early stages of those developments.

Tommaso Villa was born in Piedmont in 1832 and was the embodiment of low-key Piedmontese anticlerical liberalism. Villa's commitment to introducing a divorce law in Italy had already been demonstrated by his support for Morelli's second proposal in 1880. As the minister for justice, he had warmly welcomed Morelli's plan, urging the deputies to vote for the proposal to be taken into consideration. Although Villa shrewdly expressed some reservation about the way Morelli's proposal was framed, his recommendation was nevertheless a contrast to the one his predecessor, Conforti, had given to the proposal of 1878.

In fact, Villa's support for Morelli had gone much further than mere words of recommendation. In the speech following Morelli's presentation of the law, Villa mentioned that he had already commissioned a statistical study of marriage and marriage breakdown in Italy since the inception of the civil code in 1866. He intended the study to be a "faithful mirror of our customs," and to give a sense of the true state of marriage under the new civil law.[3] Villa's initiative demonstrated the depth of his commitment to the divorce cause, and the resulting study became the centerpiece of his own design for a divorce law, which was ready to be presented to parliament in early 1881.

Catholic Mobilization

It was one thing for an amusing deputy like Morelli to propose a divorce law as a private initiative, but quite another for the government itself to present a *disegno* (draft) of its own for a divorce law.[4] The difference was most immediately evident in the response of the Italian Catholic world. Villa presented the law to parliament on 1 February 1881, but the plan was public knowledge well before that date. A week before the law was presented, the deep concern it provoked at the Vatican was suggested in two articles decrying divorce published in the Church's organ, the *Osservatore romano*.[5] One of these claimed to be puzzled by the "strange" reaction of the liberal press to the Opera dei Congressi's planned opposition to the law.[6] The liberal press also picked up the news, and Rome's lively and iconoclastic *Messaggero* published a leading article entitled "Divorziamo." This was the title of a new play by French dramatist Victorien Sardou, and under the guise of a review of the play the newspaper took the opportunity to condemn the Opera dei Congressi's fear of divorce as "congressomania."[7] Such altercations between the Catholic and anticlerical press, sometimes quite humorous, were actually symptomatic of a deep and irremediable cleft that ran through the Italian nation.

From Villa's proposal of 1881 onward, the divorce question became a lightning rod that ignited the forces on either side of the issue, revealing an unbridgeable gulf between them. Since unification Pius IX had inveighed ceaselessly against the modern evils of liberalism, secularism, and socialism. In the Church's view divorce was a concrete manifestation and natural culmination of these abstract concepts, and it came to represent the worst extremes of all that was wrong with the secular world. Beginning in 1881, Villa's proposal and others that followed provided the Church with an emotive issue around which to rally the faithful.

Catholic forces lost no time in applying themselves to this project, with the actual organization being left to the lay social movement. It is nevertheless evident that the original idea and impetus for what was essentially an intervention in the nation's political processes emanated from the pope himself. Nearly three weeks before Villa was due to present his law in parliament, the national president of the Opera dei Congressi, Count Scipione Salviati, conferred privately with Leo XIII over the divorce problem. On 13 January 1881 Salviati wrote to the vice president of the movement, Giovanni Aquaderni, saying that earlier in the day he had had an audience with the Holy Father. He reported that the pope had asked that the Opera dei Congressi to "take the initiative" in preparing a petition to be presented to parliament against the projected law on divorce.[8] Even though the pope preferred to appear aloof from politics, this is clear evidence that when an issue threatened a Catholic principle, as divorce did, he was more than ready to intervene.

Within two days the administrative wheels of the Opera dei Congressi were in motion, providing insight into the political potential of the Church's unique capillary organization, extending throughout the nation.

In Bologna, where the Opera had its headquarters, the vice president drew up letters that would accompany blank petition forms to all the Opera's regional committees, to every bishop in Italy, and eventually to all local parishes.[9] Meanwhile, Salviati worked on the text of the petition itself in Rome. He sent this to be printed on 17 January,[10] and on the same day he sent a circular to the presidents of the regional committees explaining the petitions of protest and urging them to collect as many signatures as possible.[11] The whole correspondence covering the few days between Salviati's audience with the pope and the sending out of circular letters is suffused with an enormous sense of purpose and urgency, and is a testament to the dedication of the men running the Opera dei Congressi.

The wording of the petition itself, which was to be directed to both deputies and senators (meaning that each signatory would have to sign two petitions), was a revealing exercise in fire-and-brimstone that was a foretaste of the passionate opposition of the Catholics to divorce. It began: "A deplorable projected law is threatening to strike the sacred bond of conjugal union." The second paragraph explained that, in the name of religion and the public good, divorce should never be allowed even the slightest foothold. If it were, there would be no stopping the terrible consequences. The petition concluded with a dark description of what some of these would be:

> You could not wish to bring such a calamity upon Italy: you must not permit, by introducing mutability into matrimony, that conjugal love and faith should be weakened; that the education and upbringing of children should be compromised; that the seeds of discord should be sown upon the hearth; that the very basis of society should be rocked. We implore you: do not allow such a fatal blow to be struck against the Family, if you do not want to destroy the *Patria*.[12]

Although the petition does not downplay the role of religious principles in the battle against divorce, the association between the institutions of family and *patria* received much more emphasis. Given the intended audience, a supposedly secular parliament, this makes perfect sense. But it also raises questions about the very nature of the Opera dei Congressi, and about where the organization lay on the political and ideological spectrum of post–Risorgimento Italy. These questions need to be answered in order to understand the significance of the movement's opposition to divorce in the context of late-nineteenth-century Italian politics.

The classic liberal view of church-state relations in unified Italy is exemplified by the work of Giovanni Spadolini, whose analytical framework is that of a continual power struggle. Spadolini regarded Pius IX's *Syllabus of*

Errors of 1864 as the font of all Catholic activism up to 1900,[13] and in this sense the issue of marriage (and by implication divorce) was simply one of the major sites of the struggle.[14] Although in broad terms it makes sense to see church-state relations in Liberal Italy in this way, it would be wrong to see the two entities as simply pitted wholeheartedly against each other as a matter of principle. This view tends to overlook nuances such as the variety of opinions in each camp and even the extent to which the two sides overlapped. Even if the Catholics, variegated as they were, intended to recover a position of lost influence, Catholic action from the 1880s involved a recognition that change could not be ignored, and revealed a determination to have a hand in shaping the new status quo.

This is not to deny that the Opera dei Congressi originally grew out of the traditional Catholic hostility to liberalism and the ideals of the Risorgimento. Its origins can be traced to the Catholic groups centered in Bologna that formed even before 1860 with the chief purpose of combatting liberalism.[15] An intermediate stage was the group of Catholics centered around the journal *Il Conservatore*, founded in 1863 by G. B. Casoni. Casoni had been inspired by the Catholic societies he had seen in Belgium, and his group was an early Italian example of a Catholic organization with national pretensions.[16] But the most direct seeds of the Italian Catholic social movement lay in the efforts of the Venetian lawyer, G.B. Paganuzzi, to unite those Catholics who were intransigently opposed to the Italian state in the early 1870s.[17] The resulting organization held its first congress in 1874, and by 1876 the movement had its own statute and had received the blessing of the pope. In 1881, the statutes and regulations of the Opera dei Congressi e Comitati Cattolici, to use the full name, were published. The main aim of the organization was to "unite and order" Italian Catholics for the purpose of defending their rights.[18]

Even though there was undoubtedly a link between the contemporaneous rise of socialism and the Opera dei Congressi on the plains of the Po river,[19] a group that aimed to unite and defend Catholics needed more defined poles around which to rally its forces. It was not mere happenstance that the Opera dei Congressi came into the public view in 1881, just as a divorce law began to look like a serious prospect for the first time. By that year, however, the political context of church-state relations was not the same as it had been in the 1860s. The intervening period had witnessed important changes, such as the rise of the Left to power in 1876, and the election of Pope Leo XIII, who was less hostile in his attitude to the Italian state than his predecessor had been.

Changes such as these, as well as the fact that by 1881 the Italian state looked more secure than it had 20 years earlier, meant that mere opposition to liberalism (or socialism) was not enough to hold a Catholic movement together. Indeed, by 1881 divisions between transigent and intransigent Catholics (that is, those who were prepared to work within the framework of the Italian state, and those who refused to accept it) were becoming evident. These differences of opinion were also present within the organization of the Opera dei Congressi,[20] and this was probably another reason why it tended to focus so single-mindedly upon issues such as divorce, over which few Catholics could have the slightest doubts.

Because of the relative security of the Italian state after 1870, as well as Crispi's laws for its internal defense, the Opera dei Congressi could not afford to be subversive, and the way it chose to operate is significant. Spadolini's overall picture of intransigent opposition too easily obfuscates the skillful way in which Catholic organizations by the late nineteenth century were making use of essentially liberal principles, such as associationism, the press, and lobbying tools such as meetings and petitions, to promote their interests. A Jesuit named Taparelli had pointed out as far back as 1848 that it was the nature of liberal governments to allow particular interests to be promoted by interested groups. By the 1880s Catholic groups had taken that lesson to heart, and were beginning to compensate for their official ban from Italian politics by Pius IX through extra-parliamentary tactics.[21]

Moreover, having accepted the existence of the Italian state, a large number of Catholics were beginning to find it expedient to promote themselves as defenders of the new *patria*, rather than simply wanting to dismantle it. This subtle but important change of Catholic mood is reflected in the journal *Rassegna nazionale* (National Review), founded in Florence in 1879. The first aim of the progressive Catholics centered behind the new journal was remarkable: "the conservation of unified Italy under the house of Savoy." Issues of freedom of conscience and the determination to combat any interference with the rights of families, above all in relation to the education of children, followed the opening patriotic flourish.[22]

Despite an essentially conciliatory stance toward the Italian state, among the first targets of the *Rassegna* were civil marriage and Villa's divorce law.[23] These foreign imports could be attacked in the name of protecting the nation from external corruption. The Opera dei Congressi, far less conciliatory (though not internally uniform) also attacked divorce on the grounds of protecting the *patria*. Accepting the existence of Italy as a fait accompli, Catholics were now seeking to occupy the moral high ground in its defense. For them, the Church had represented the spiritual unity of Italy for centuries,[24] and they saw liberal ideals destroying the spiritual patrimony of the land.[25] No law yet devised by legal Italy had represented a clearer threat to this patrimony than Villa's divorce law, as the wording of their petition against it suggested.

Tommaso Villa's First Proposal

What of the wording and intent of the divorce law itself? Was it really such a radical attack on the roots of the nation? The preparation that went into the proposal shows that there was an unparalleled determination behind the law. While the printed matter associated with Morelli's proposal the previous year had consisted of a scant two pages (a brief introduction and the law itself, consisting of five short articles), Villa supported his law, which consisted of 22 articles, with a comprehensive address of 22 pages, seeking to persuade the Chamber of Deputies of the law's necessity. Furthermore, the design was followed by 70 pages of documentation, mostly about foreign divorce laws. They included the divorce laws of the French Revolution and the Napoleonic code, as well as copies of the 1876 and 1878 laws proposed by the contemporary apostle of divorce in France, Alfred Naquet. Others included those of Prussia from 1875, the Swiss federal law of 1874, the Russian law of 1873, the Scandinavian countries, Belgium, nine American states, Great Britain, and even Turkey and Haiti.[26] Clearly, Villa aimed to make Italian lawmakers feel at once behind the times, and reassured by the idea that they would be following in the footsteps of other nations.

The imposing quality of the law for those who feared it was already significant because of its proponent's ministerial position, and this impression was reinforced by the amount of preparation that had gone into it (it was unusual for such meticulous documentation to accompany a design for a law). The spirit of the law itself, however, was far from being radical. It was in fact inherently gradualist and conservative, paying due heed to tradition. It proposed that divorce could be granted under two principal conditions. The first was if one spouse was condemned to death or to a life sentence in prison (a condition that corresponded to the concept of "civil death" in the Napoleonic code, which had also given rise to divorce[27]). Second, divorce could be applied for by a couple who had been officially separated for either three or five years, depending upon whether they had children.

Because a personal separation could be obtained by mutual consent, effectively under the proposed law a divorce could be obtained for the same reason, albeit after a lengthy delay. Mutual consent, which was a divisive issue even among those in favor of divorce, was buried deep beneath a variety of restrictions that were designed to ensure that a divorce could only take place when all hope of reconciliation was lost. The waiting period between personal separation and divorce already made this intention clear, but more significant was the consultative role envisaged for the couple's closest relatives. This involvement was to be regulated by four articles of the proposed law, which specified the requirement to constitute a "consiglio di famiglia," or family council, for each process.

According to Villa's design, a family council of four members would be constituted to consider each application for divorce.[28] The members of the council were ideally to be the parents of both spouses, but if that was not possible, brothers and uncles, in respective order of preference, could be substituted.[29] If the couple had children, they too had to be called as witnesses.[30] The law stipulated that the family council had to listen to the case and then make "remonstrances aimed at reconciling them." If this failed, the council could express an opinion about the necessity of divorce, about provisions for the education and maintenance of the children, and the "interests" (presumably matters of property) of the pair.[31]

Although the final decision would be made by the tribunal itself, the law's tacit acknowledgment of the influence of other family members upon a married couple is revealing. The divorce proposal was heavily based upon the existing law for personal separation, but that law did not require the intervention of a family council. This meant that technically couples were able to separate independently of the opinions of the immediate family members. The provision in Villa's design indicates the great caution with which he was approaching the question of divorce. In some senses though, the design probably reflected elements of the prevailing culture that the law on personal separation had ignored, thus proposing to give formal recognition to a process that was likely to have occurred regardless of the law. Villa's scheme for divorce acknowledged the extent to which marriage was a truly social institution, subject not only to the free will of the participants, but also to the intervention of close family, and ultimately, in concert with them, the state.

The cautious elements of the design were those Villa chose to stress in his detailed introduction to the law. This warrants a close examination because it is a particularly eloquent expression of a classic liberal-juridical view of the necessity for divorce. Beginning with a revealing historical analysis of the first 20 years of Italian unity, Villa acknowledged that in 1865 the introduction of civil marriage had been an enormous step, and that introducing divorce at the time would have been considered too much of an offense to Catholic religious sentiment. He went on to say that "today the Church's power has providentially been returned to within its proper confines" and now that Italy was free and strong, the legislator had to focus attention on the lacunae that were left in 1865 due to the "special conditions of immaturity at the time."[32] A more tactful analysis of the compromises made by the 1865 Pisanelli code could hardly have been made, and it suggests that Villa saw his divorce law giving renewed impetus to the progressive elements of the Risorgimento.

The way Villa encapsulated the divorce question for his fellow deputies was to ask whether the civil law should incorporate the "mystical doctrine of the union between Christ and the Church represented by the sacrament of marriage." Did reasons of public order require the "legal fiction" of the maintenance of the marriage bond, even when in reality that bond no longer existed? He argued that the civil law did not create marriage but merely recognized the matrimonial state after subjecting it to certain conditions in the name of the public interest. The ultimate question, as Villa put it, was to decide whether the civil law could legitimately refuse to recognize the effective dissolution of a marriage bond after a couple had separated.[33] In a liberal vein, Villa emphasized the contractual nature of marriage, in which the essence of the contract lay in the free consent of the two individuals concerned.[34] He argued that the improvements of the modern world owed a great deal to the tendency for relationships, whether between nations or individuals, to be contractual in nature rather than based upon force.[35] The contractual view of the basis of marriage was anathema to Catholics, for whom the "mystical doctrine" of the sacrament that Villa had rather lightly dismissed was its true essence. These worldviews were fundamentally irreconcilable, and for all Villa's elegant argumentation, he must have known it.

It was perhaps this knowledge that lay behind the most peculiar aspect of Villa's presentation. This concerned his claim that "marriage must be indissoluble." An odd statement in an argument in favor of divorce, at first it seems to be a rhetorical ploy designed to arrest attention. In fact Villa put a great deal of effort into emphasizing the ideal of indissoluble marriage, almost certainly with complete sincerity, and in accordance with the moral values of the time and the place. The way he reconciled the idea of indissolubility with the occasional practical necessity to allow divorce is curious. He describes "absolute indissolubility" as "nothing less than the submission of the civil power to religious dogma," and argued that it should be replaced by "relative indissolubility."[36] This seems no less a legal fiction than the idea that the symbolic value of a marriage bond was unaffected by the separation of a couple.

Nevertheless, the idea of "relative indissolubility" perfectly represents the tenor of Villa's entire design, which consisted of divorce as an extreme measure to be resorted to only in rare circumstances. He fought, as Morelli had done, against the idea that divorce was intrinsically corrosive of the ideals of marriage, and tried to argue that it could help to preserve them. According to Villa, marriage and the family were an "element of conservation, the school and training ground of civil virtues." But to maintain those ideals it had to be possible to purify marriage itself of evils that could bring "perversion and moral degradation."[37] Villa referred to these as a plague upon the social organism that needed to be healed. The present system was no more than the "systematic negation of the illness," rather than a remedy. In short, Villa presented divorce as a painful but necessary cure that would cauterize the sores of society if it were applied in carefully measured doses.

Women and children, according to Villa, were most susceptible to the harm created by the absence of any remedy for the social malady of failed marriages. In the case of children, Villa used the already-familiar argument that offspring were harmed by the failure of marriage itself, rather than by what happened afterward. Many of those against divorce claimed that second marriages would be disastrous for children, but Villa rather neatly dismissed this argument in a mere footnote, suggesting that if second marriages were so dangerous for children, then widows and widowers with children should not be allowed to remarry either.[38]

More detailed is Villa's revealing analysis of the position of married women in Italian society, and the effects of the present law on separation. He considered no life more difficult than that of a young woman, married for a few years, and then separated, forced either to return to her family, or to be "among the perils of isolation."[39] Even if she remained virtuous, her life would be continually subject to the harsh scrutiny of society and her virtue would win her no credit anyway. She would probably abandon herself to "other affections" and thus a formerly honest woman, despite the best intentions, would become an adulterer. The fate of a separated woman was therefore tantamount to being condemned to perpetual misery and sadness, or a life of guilt, especially if she had children.

Villa described the social attitude toward separated men as completely different. If a man chose to live with a woman after separating from his wife, he could do so almost with impunity, as society was disposed to be indulgent and to forgive him, even to consider him a victim of his wife's failings.[40] This straightforward assessment of the different ways men and women experienced personal separation holds no surprises, but coming from the pen of a minister it is a particularly sobering collective epilogue to the individual cases analyzed in the preceding chapter. It permits inferences about the lives of separated men and women that would be difficult to corroborate in any systematic way from historical records.

After a general consideration of the need for divorce, Villa's introduction to his law proceeded through the provisions of each article, attempting to forestall criticism and emphasizing with an ineluctable logic the concept of divorce as a painful but necessary remedy. Complementing the logic of the jurist was a sense of the high moral purpose of the philosopher, and it was this purpose that Villa's concluding remarks left ringing. Returning once again to the ideal of perpetual conjugal union, Villa's final words actually said nothing about divorce. He simply said that the ideal of perpetual union cannot be imposed by force, but should be the natural product of "freedom and morality."[41] Villa's statement of 1881 amounted to a landmark position on divorce, a consolidation of ideas destined to launch polemics that would set the tone of the Italian divorce debate for more than two decades.

By the time the parliamentary committees met to discuss Villa's project in April 1881, the activity of the Catholic social movement that had been set in train even before Villa had presented his design, had resulted in the collection of 637,712 signatures to the petitions against divorce.[42] In addition to the petitions, the government received letters of protest from clergy all over the peninsula, including an 11-page example from the Bishop of Naples, representing some 111 bishops, abbots, and prelates from the south of Italy.[43] Among other things the letter claimed that since woman had been made from Adam's rib, not some independent material, she must clearly be indissolubly bonded to man. Furthermore, because God had created only one man and one woman, he clearly meant that a man could have no more than one wife, and vice versa.[44]

Arguments such as these were hardly likely to influence the opinion of members of a government ostensibly committed to the principle of a free church in a free state. The letter probably hit a more sensitive nerve with its claim that it was the duty of a government to express the will of the people, and because the vast majority of Italians were Catholic, divorce was necessarily against their wishes.[45] The question of whether the government had any interest in introducing a law that could very well run against the religious conscience of the majority of its people had been a stumbling block for divorce in the past, and was destined to remain one for more than 90 years.

On the other hand, there is something peculiar about the fact that a parliament elected by less than 2 percent of the population should have been so concerned about the feelings of the remaining 98 percent on the issue of divorce, but this argument clearly did strike the conscience of some parliamentarians. In relation to Villa's proposal the issue was noted during the deliberations of the *uffici* when one deputy raised the "problem" that divorce was not something for which the public had manifested any desire. He was answered by another who pointed out that divorce would never be the object of broad public interest, as, for example, electoral reform might be, because it would concern only a minority of marriages.[46]

Variations on this theme were to be heard during all future debates on divorce, but references to the lack of public support were a specious argument. First, the principles of liberal government upon which Italy was based had little regard for broad democratic representation. If it had, many progressive measures, civil marriage among them, would never have been introduced into Italian law. In fact, one of the great fears of the Italian government was the idea of mob rule, and throughout the Risorgimento leaders were conscious of imposing progress upon an indifferent or even hostile populace. References to the lack of public clamor for a divorce law reflected fears about exacerbating the rift between state and society, and such fears could well have been fuelled by a sense that the state's purchase on society was no match for that still held by the Church.

These concerns are an aspect of the residual disappointment over the Risorgimento's failure to "make Italians" and a latent fear on the part of politicians about the future relationship between society and the government. Even though such doubts may have been in the air in 1881 they did not discourage a majority of the *uffici* from voting in favor of Villa's divorce law.[47] They subsequently elected one member from each *ufficio* to form a nine-man committee that would study the law in detail and produce a report on which parliament's deliberations would be based. The election of a committee favorable to the law was an important step in the passage of the law from draft to statute book, but it was by no means a guarantee of that passage.

For reasons that are not clear, it took a great deal of time for the committee to discuss the law and write its report, and it was presented to parliament only on 23 January 1882, nearly a year after Villa introduced the law.[48] It was presented by Cesare Parenzo, a well-known anticlerical, who warmly recommended the law to the Chamber. But the long delay between the constitution of the commission and the presentation of its work probably cost the initiative its life, because the parliamentary session was closed early due to a technicality in May 1881, and with the closure Villa's initiative fell.

The early closure of the parliamentary session temporarily stalled the divorce project and prevented it from reaching the crucial discussion stage in parliament. This meant that the full range of opinions on divorce at the parliamentary level was not expressed. However, the early 1880s saw a marked increase in the publication of works on divorce in Italy, revealing some of the most important dissenting opinions. The most direct reason for this increase was certainly the government's expressed intention to introduce divorce, and probably went back to Villa's serious interest in Morelli's project. There were other factors too, from the pope's encyclical of January 1880 on marriage, to the interest inspired by the contemporaneous debates on the subject in France.

Antonio Salandra and Secular Conservatism

The most significant work on divorce to be published in Italy during this period was by no less a figure than Antonio Salandra, who was to become one of Italy's most important politicians in the early twentieth century. In his book, *Il divorzio in Italia*, published in 1882 as a direct response to Villa's proposal, Salandra made much of the idea that the "divorce ferment" was blowing across the Alps from France.[49] The significance of Salandra's work, which was widely read and went through new editions right up to 1920, was that it lent a prestigious liberal voice to the cause against divorce, revealing the disunity among liberals on the issue. Salandra's view was also portentous of the direction Italian politics would take from the early twentieth century. This is because from the outset he declared that he had little interest in the question of whether marriage should be dissoluble or not from a social perspective, but instead aimed to study the question as a matter of politics, arguing that from this point of view the introduction of divorce in Italy would be "gravely inopportune."[50]

Salandra's emphasis on the connection between the Italian *divorzisti* and France was itself an opportune way of discrediting the movement. At the time he wrote, the divorce wave in France was building steadily, and Salandra foresaw the victory of Naquet and the French *divorzisti* two years in advance.[51] Relations between France and Italy had deteriorated badly since 1881, when the French occupation of Tunis had deeply offended many Italians.[52] Painting divorce as "French" in 1882 was therefore a shorthand way of depicting it as another menace to Italian national security, and this was no doubt what Salandra intended. He made further efforts to taint divorce as a threat by associating it with the most radical phase of the French Revolution, invoking images of sexual chaos and social decay.[53]

These were standard tactics commonly found in all works hostile to divorce, but Salandra's argument went beyond them. He came to the nub of the problem with a critique of the liberal view of marriage as a contract resulting from the will of two individuals. The liberals, he claimed, knew that marriage was also a social institution, and that the family as an institution had to be protected from the arbitrary will of its individual members. They had failed, however, to reconcile the ideal of liberal individualism with the social function of the family in a coherent liberal theory of marriage.[54] Salandra claimed that the family protected the destiny of humanity, and this should not be overridden for the sake of the happiness of a few individuals. In his view, only the conscientious preservation of this ideal would make the state a worthy successor to the Church in the tutelage of marriage.[55]

As a liberal, Salandra accepted the principle of the state taking responsibility for marriage, but as a conservative he argued for continuity in the way that responsibility was used. He admitted that the introduction of divorce would have been a powerful symbol of the triumph of secular power over the Church, but argued that because divorce was neither needed nor wanted in Italy, its introduction would be no more than an act of pre-meditated hostility toward the "national religion."[56] In short, divorce would amount to the introduction of an unwanted law that was "foreign" to Italian culture and was being pressed by a minority of "divorzisti franco-italiani," as he repeatedly referred to them.[57]

Referring to the broader framework of Italian politics since the Risorgimento, Salandra admitted that the fall of the "Destra" in 1876 had had much to do with their having exhausted the political credit they had inherited from the Risorgimento. On the other hand, he claimed that the "Sinistra" was only driven by a determination to oppose the Right, not by an overall vision of Italy. He ended his book on this note, hoping that the radicals of Italian politics would not abandon their desire to assault the family and offend the "inveterate traditions of national sentiment," pre-cisely because it would drive Italians away from the politics of the Left and turn Italy rightward.[58] The final pages of Salandra's work on divorce can be read as a subtle rallying cry to renew the forces of the political right, whose aim would be to unite the nation around traditions such as its "national religion." In 1882 the time was not ripe for such views. The rift with the Church was too deep, and the anticlerical ideals of the Risorgimento were still too strongly felt for such a formula to be successful.

Twenty years later the climate would be much more suitable, and divorce was to be intertwined with a deep shift in Italian politics, with Salandra again playing a pivotal role. That shift was able to take place partly because Salandra's claim about the Left's lack of vision in the early 1880s proved to have been well grounded. However, his use of divorce as an example of the Left habitually opposing the Right was mistaken. In fact, Villa's and later Zanardelli's sympathy for the divorce law in some ways represented the last gasps of the ideals of Risorgimento liberalism, and although the complexity of Italian politics would eventually suffocate them, the fresh air of those ideals would still be breathed for a few more years.

Giuseppe Zanardelli's Proposal

Shortly after the government reshuffle that put an end to Villa's divorce project of 1881, a new government was formed under Depretis, with Villa's friend Zanardelli as minister for justice. Villa's draft was given a new lease of life by Zanardelli, though all the momentum of the previous project had been lost. On 10 April 1883, Zanardelli announced to the parliament his intention to present six laws, among which would be one on divorce.[59] The draft of the law, which was identical to Villa's original draft of 1881, was printed and circulated on 30 April 1883.[60] Zanardelli clearly felt no need to support the draft with a lengthy statement as his predecessor had done. Instead, the draft was accompanied by a relatively brief introduction, referring to the support obtained for the earlier draft, shown by the report of the *uffici* charged with the task of evaluating it. Indeed, with an almost haughty reference to the fact that divorce had already been adopted by nearly all the "civil nations," Zanardelli suggested that he virtually took for granted the acceptance of the law by parliament.[61]

The *uffici* delegated to examine the law took their task seriously and proceeded slowly. They had their first meeting on 19 June 1883, but did not discuss the law in any depth until February of the following year. All but one *ufficio* approved of the proposal in varying degrees, which meant of course that an affirmative report would be written.[62] The man elected to complete this task was Domenico Giuriati. Like Parenzo, the *relatore* of Villa's 1881 draft, Giuriati happened to be Jewish, and he had published his own monograph on love, marriage, and divorce three years earlier.[63] Giuriati presented a summary of his colleagues' opinions to parliament on 23 June 1884. His very carefully prepared 25,000-word document was a worthy sequel to the one written by Parenzo. Unsurprisingly, many of the arguments were very similar, especially the emphasis on divorce as a salutary, profamily measure, designed to hem the fraying edges left unfinished by the inadequate law on personal separation.

In contrast to Parenzo's report on the same law, however, Giuriati's reveals the influence of two important developments in the 1880s, one intellectual, the other concerning Italy's place in relation to other nations. The first was the increasing prestige of the social sciences, in particular sociology. Barely five years earlier, Morelli's arguments in favor of divorce had principally rested on political ideals of freedom. Even in 1882, Parenzo had only fleetingly referred to some of the statistics made available as a result of Villa's massive effort to collect data on Italian marriage, initiated in 1881. Giuriati's report, on the other hand, frequently referred to statistics and other figures, as well as to the writings of prestigious sociologists such as the senator and famous author on family matters, Paolo Mantegazza.[64] Giuriati cites figures to show that Italy (with France) had the highest rate of illegitimate births in Europe, and that the figure was on the increase.[65] He laments the lack of statistics for the majority of marital separations, which went unrecorded, and speculated that the official figures probably only represented about a tenth of the real number.[66]

On the historically difficult question of the fate of children after divorce, Giuriati did not follow his predecessors, who rather limply argued that children were better off with one or other divorced parent than two adults who lived together in perpetual hatred. Instead he allowed the prestigious voice of Mantegazza to do much the same job, by quoting a large excerpt from *Fisiologia dell'amore* (*Physiology of Love*).[67] Giuriati then added that for every 100 recorded separations involving children, in 95 cases the children went to the care of one or other of the parents, while only five went to the care of third parties. This he adduces as evidence that parental love does not end with the exhaustion of marital love, and that under a regime allowing divorce, any new brothers and sisters could be legitimate.[68] In short, Giuriati's report was the fullest statement yet made in Italy of one of the aims of the modern state: the proper scientific "management" of the institution of the family.

The second significant novelty in Giuriati's report was the impact of the recent developments in France. The debates over Naquet's third proposal to introduce divorce in France had also dragged on since late 1881 but, by mid-1884, even the obstacle of the conservative French Senate seemed to have been overcome. At the time Giuriati was writing his report there was a strong sense that the French divorce law was a fait accompli.[69] The French debates clearly had the potential to influence Italian thinking profoundly, but from the point of view of those in favor of divorce, the timing in this case could not have been worse. Relations between the two states were at a nadir, and this had provided an opportunity for anti-*divorzisti* such as Salandra to depict divorce as a sort of French Trojan horse, allowing the invasion of pernicious revolutionary ideas.

It is therefore not surprising that Giuriati's frequent references to the debates in the French legislature display no sense of triumph at all. Nevertheless, the recent debates in France provided Giuriati with a rich font of statistical data and persuasive detail for his arguments. He made ample use of them in his report, without over-emphasizing their provenance. Instead, he chose to emphasize that Italy had allowed itself to be left behind during the past twenty years, now that, apart from Italy, Spain, and Portugal (the last two seen as bastions of reaction), all European nations and the United States permitted divorce.[70]

In this Giuriati was following in the footsteps of his pro-divorce predecessors. Evidently he thought appealing to a sense of the need for Italy to catch up with more developed countries was an effective tactic, but Giuriati went further than his colleagues by foreshadowing an issue that was to become a significant complication in Italy in later years. This concerned the potential clash of laws if Italian citizens should marry foreigners and obtain divorces elsewhere, which Italian courts would be obliged to recognize; or if an Italian couple should change citizenship with the express purpose of obtaining a divorce outside Italy. Effectively, Giuriati was telling the Italian political class that Italy needed to fall into step with the rest of the Western world for reasons of both modernity and practicality.

It is on this basis that Giuriati's report sweeps aside the problem of lack of public support for the law and dismisses the assiduous campaign on the part of the Opera dei Congressi. He said that any engagement with their arguments would be a "superfluity,"[71] since the collection of the petitions was coordinated under a single authority. Since that authority wanted not simply to block divorce, but also to effect a return to Church authority over marriage, its claims were not worthy of the slightest consideration. Giuriati's conclusion suggested that instead of being intimidated by imposing but irrelevant petitions, Italian legislators should listen to the many Italian intellectuals who were already converts to the idea of divorce. He also pointed out that the first work to appear on divorce in the nineteenth century had been by an Italian, Melchiorre Gioia,[72] and that ever since 1803, Italians of all political colors had been inspired by Gioia's ideas. Giuriati's rather contrived "heritage" for Italian ideas on divorce had its greatest flowering in the significant pro-divorce outpourings of contemporary professors, and he mentioned well-known names from all over the peninsula. Under the authority of these illustrious names, Giuriati warmly and urgently recommended the law on divorce to the Chamber.

For all the interest of Giuriati's carefully prepared report, it suffered the same banal fate of its predecessors: the closure of the parliamentary session prevented the draft from reaching the crucial discussion in the Chamber. The draft thus disappeared with hardly a whimper, and the flurry of newspaper interest that had begun with Villa's initiative three years earlier had also strangely died out by 1884. This is evident from the newspapers of the day, which allowed Giuriati's report to pass almost without comment. Rome's *L'Opinione* reported the event in two lines,[73] and Florence's conservative *La Nazione* gave it one.[74] Many other newspapers did not mention the event at all, including Rome's virulently anticlerical *La Riforma*.

Just as the failure of Zanardelli's draft divorce legislation marked the end of an historical period initiated by Morelli and continued by Villa, so this failure marked the beginning of a long hiatus in the divorce debates in Italy. Giuriati had invoked the authority of jurists and professors in his effort to win acceptance for a divorce law. After 1884 the debate passed almost entirely into their hands, so it did not altogether die out. In fact at least eight books or pamphlets on divorce appeared in 1885, and throughout the remainder of the decade anywhere between two and five works appeared each year. In the political sphere, however, the environment was not propitious for such a reform, and nothing more was heard of it for several years. The second half of the 1880s was absorbed with increasingly difficult economic problems, particularly in the agricultural sector, as cheaper grains imported from the Americas began to make inroads in Europe. The tariff war with France after 1887 was also a major issue, and although the prime minister from 1887, Francesco Crispi, was notably anticlerical, his authoritarian political regime was not auspicious for the introduction of a divorce law.[75] Without the incentive of divorce as a legislative issue, those who wrote about it were like sheep without a shepherd.

The Masonic Connection

The issue found leadership again in 1890 under the auspices of the Masons. The Catholic Church was to make much of the idea that the plan to introduce divorce was a Masonic-Jewish (and later, Socialist) plot, and indeed, there may have been some truth in this. Villa and Zanardelli, for example, were well-known members of the Rome lodge. Parenzo and Giuriati were both Jews, and Alfred Naquet was also of Jewish origin. There is little to suggest that there was any particular organized support by the Masons for the draft laws of Villa and Zanardelli between 1881 and 1884, but it is clear that there was an organized Masonic impulse behind the campaign that began in 1890. The key figure behind this change was Adriano Lemmi, elected as Grand Master of the Italian lodges in 1885. Lemmi's election was a turning point in the history of Masonry in Italy, marking the beginning of a new period of energetic activity. One of the main aims of the Masons was the establishment of true liberty of conscience, which for them meant that the state had to be completely secular. Lemmi gave this aim a new imperative from 1885, and the goal of establishing a divorce law became a symbolic plank in the Masonic program.[76]

In September 1890 the Mason and lawyer Camillo De Benedetti founded the "Comitato centrale per la propugnazione del divorzio" (Central Committee for the Promotion of Divorce). The following month Lemmi wrote a circular to the lodges in which he urged members to support the committee. The committee began to publish a journal, entitled *Il Divorzio*, in November 1890.[77] From May 1891, the committee changed its name to the "Comitato promotore della legge sul divorzio" (Divorce Law Promotion Committee), and the journal, which began as a new series in the same month, adopted the subtitle *Rivista critica della famiglia italiana* (Critical Review of the Italian Family).[78] The journal listed a prestigious group of collaborators, including Villa, Zanardelli, and many other deputies, but also many well-known figures such as Alfred Naquet, Paolo Mantegazza, and Cesare Lombroso—all names that give a sense of the growing importance of the divorce question. The first editorial explained that the primary aim of the journal was to lobby for the introduction of a divorce law, but it also maintained that Italian family law needed to be reviewed more broadly.[79] It claimed that the particular areas needing attention were the ban on paternity suits, the inferior position of women within the family, and the question of enforcing the precedence of civil marriage.[80] In short, the journal promoted the modernization and laicization of the Italian family in accordance with emerging social theories.

The founding of *Il Divorzio* represented part of a new and concerted effort to bring the divorce question back into the public domain. A sense of the energy put into this is given by reports on the number of public meetings held to discuss divorce, beginning with a major meeting in Rome on 6 April 1891, whose main speakers were Tommaso Villa and Alfred Naquet. This was held in the Grand Salon of Italian Journalists,[81] and it ceremonially marked the beginning of what would be a major new campaign on the part of the *divorzisti*. The campaign began with a flurry of publicity, and with the second issue of *Il Divorzio* the publishers sent their subscribers advertising posters for the journal, asking them to pin them up in prominent places such as reading rooms and cafés.[82] The public meetings and assemblies were by no means confined to a handful of major cities. The second issue of the journal reported that conferences had been held or were planned in smaller cities up and down the peninsula, in Siena, Avellino, Sondrio, Foligno, and Naples. Subcommittees on divorce were reportedly set up in Siena and Foligno and probably many other cities as well.[83]

One of the immediate goals of the Comitato promotore della legge sul divorzio was to ensure that the question had a high profile at the Third National Juridical Congress that was to be held in Florence in September 1891.[84] There is little doubt that this meeting was a major legal event that placed the divorce question squarely before a large number of educated Italians. Initially the committee entrusted with choosing the questions to be debated did not want to include divorce, regarding it as too politically divisive. Eventually, however, for fear of seeming to be out of touch, the committee allowed the divorce question to be put on to the agenda.[85] Milan's *Corriere della sera* wondered how the committee could have shied away from a question that had recently received so much public attention. The same newspaper reported a high state of tension and excitement preceding the opening of the conference, because of the inclusion of the divorce question,[86] which eclipsed all other topics in its report on the opening of proceedings.[87]

The congress was held in Florence between 7 and 12 September. One of that city's main newspapers, *La Nazione*, expressed a certain civic pride in the fact that Florence was hosting the conference, and estimated that 500 people would take part.[88] The debate on divorce took place between 9 and 11 September, and it focused on a motion written by Tommaso Villa, who had once again become the figurehead of the divorce camp. Villa opened the first session on divorce by announcing the following motion, which bore all the hallmarks of his political subtlety: "The congress should express its vote that while the general concept of the indissolubility of marriage remains untouched, the law recognises the practical necessity of divorce only in cases where the matrimonial state has become morally and absolutely impossible."[89] Put to the first round of voting, the motion was supported by 86 votes to 54. Villa was elected to write the majority report in favor, and the conservative professor of civil law Giampietro Chironi was to write the minority report.[90]

The crucial day for the divorce question was the concluding debate of 12 September. One of the most important speakers against divorce was Carlo Francesco Gabba, who had written in favor of divorce in his book on the civil code of 1862,[91] but had since changed his mind.[92] His address criticized Villa's motion for its lack of specific cases allowing divorce, which he claimed would result in the indefinite multiplication of reasons for divorce. Gabba also claimed that divorce was antidemocratic, because only the rich would be able to afford a second marriage. The *Nazione* journalist enthused that Gabba's "brilliant" speech won "unanimous applause."[93] The closing words went to Villa and Chironi, and the question was finally put to the vote: 106 were for divorce and 77 voted against it.[94]

This was a landmark victory for the divorce cause, and it sparked much excitement in the liberal press. The *Corriere della sera*, which had published an editorial in favor of divorce describing the frenetic, impassioned atmosphere with which the question had imbued the congress, enthusiastically reported the results of the vote. It dedicated half of its front page to the issue on 12–13 September, describing the session as immensely crowded and exciting. The article gave all the credit for the victory to the wisdom of Villa, whose motion had stressed the value of indissoluble marriage and whose address had shown that divorce was not a contradiction of the principle. In the journalist's view, this judicious approach had won over even the most conservative lawyers to the divorce cause.[95]

Rome's irreverent *Messaggero* saw the result of the Congress's debate on divorce in a similar light. Reporting on the results of the vote with great joy, it concluded that the need for divorce in Italy had "a new and authoritative sanction"[96] and lambasted *L'Opinione*'s claim that the issue was not yet "mature." This was nearly always a euphemism for the desire not to exacerbate the unresolved tensions between the Vatican and the Italian state. The view expressed in *Il Messaggero* was that the Vatican was doing everything in its power to undermine the Italian nation and its monarchy, and that the diplomatic approach of the conservatives was an excuse to avoid the issue.[97] This implied that the anti-*divorzisti* were simply making room for the conspiracies of the main enemy of the Italian state.

The association between anti-divorce conservatives and the Church was an easy one, and one that could put conservative liberals in an awkward position. Salandra's 1882 book on divorce had been a deft statement of the political arguments against divorce in Italy. After the conference in Florence the conservative newspapers also defended their position, usually by attacking the liberals. A good example is *La Perseveranza*'s editorial response to the victory of the divorce motion, which was that the jurists at the conference in Florence were laboring under the misapprehension that being liberal simply meant being against every principle of the Church. For its part, *La Perseveranza* did not add anything particularly cogent to the conservative liberal argument in favor of marital indissolubility, but it is a good example of the oft-heard defense that to be against divorce was not the same as being in favor of the restoration of the pope's temporal power.

The organ of the Vatican itself, the *Osservatore romano*, drew some of these ideas together in its response to the juridical conference, with its unmistakable tone of implacable condescension. The newspaper had only given the briefest notice of the event,[98] and it only deigned to comment several days after the excitement of the other newspapers had died down. The editorial, like that of *La Perseveranza*, characterized the "iniquitous" vote in favor of divorce as driven largely by anticlericalism. But it mocked the lawyers at the conference by suggesting that their support of divorce was also motivated by professional self-interest. Finally, the paper expressed confidence that divorce would not be introduced in Italy because the Italian public did not want it.[99]

Villa's Final Attempts

After the success of the congress in Florence, the moment seemed propitious for another divorce proposal. On 17 March 1892, Tommaso Villa, no longer a minister but simply a deputy to parliament, proposed a divorce law for the third time, worded exactly as it had been in 1881. Because this was a proposal from a deputy, rather than a ministerial project, as it had been between 1881 and 1884, parliamentary procedure required that the Chamber vote on whether to take the law into consideration or not. This meant that Villa had to explain the proposal and persuade the Chamber to take it up. Villa made his address on 4 April 1892, and there was an element of pathos in the words of a former minister trying to persuade the assembled deputies to take up a project that was clearly so close to his heart.

Most of the arguments were completely familiar to all deputies, but Villa went through them eloquently nevertheless. He touched upon the idea that Italy was surrounded by countries that allowed divorce, making reference to the potential for awkward situations when Italians married to foreigners obtained divorces elsewhere. He summarized the fate of earlier proposals and drafts, beginning with Morelli's pioneering gesture in 1878, and emphasized that in the meantime divorce had conquered much territory.[100] Notably, Villa resisted the temptation to boast about his victory with divorce in Florence, only referring to it in passing. This was testimony to both his rhetorical restraint and to the fact that the divorce question had matured significantly since 1878.[101]

The issue may have matured significantly in intellectual terms, winning over a number of influential thinkers, but since 1878 the divorce cause had still not made inroads into the consciousness of Italian society. When the minister for justice, Bruno Chimirri, whom parliamentary protocol called upon to comment on Villa's proposal, spoke to the Chamber, it was upon this problem that he chose to dwell. His cold response erected the old stumbling block of Italian public opinion, claiming that the favorable opinion of the "jurist class" (clearly a reference to the Florence conference) was insufficient evidence that the country was ready for a law on divorce.[102]

Going right to the heart of conservative fears about social unrest, Chimirri claimed that in a new nation like Italy, the government had to proceed cautiously before intervening in the one area that remained solid in the midst of such upheavals. Chimirri's rather obscure metaphors referred to the political, economic, and moral renovation of the Italian nation as a result of the Risorgimento. He portrayed the indissoluble Italian family as the only vestige of the old regime, one that he felt should be left untouched for now, at least until the new edifice had "solidified." For Chimirri, the indissoluble Italian couple was to be a stable bridge between the old society and the new. He concluded his speech saying that he did not oppose the law being taken into consideration, but only "for the usual reason of courtesy."[103] The Chamber then voted (by standing) and the law was taken into consideration.[104]

A writer in *Il Divorzio*, the journal started a year earlier, clearly knew that Chimirri's words sounded the death knell for Villa's proposal. The leading article of the issue published after Villa's parliamentary address bitterly criticized the official stance, embodied by the minister, who took refuge behind the "conscience of the country." The writer wondered whether taxes had been imposed with this in mind, or whether civil marriage had been requested by the nation's conscience. What did the government expect people to do about divorce, as the *Messaggero* asked rhetorically? Riot? Erect barricades?[105] The committee behind *Il Divorzio* claimed that it had received 4,000 letters from people suffering unhappy marriages,[106] and pledged that it would do its utmost to keep the project alive, with meetings, conferences, and encouragements to the press to support the idea.[107] The frustration of the pro-divorce lobby was beginning to overflow previously polite boundaries, and there was an air of defeat to be found in that issue of *Il Divorzio*, which had been so boundlessly optimistic after the Florence conference only a few months earlier.

The most poignant symbol of the coming defeat lay in the misleadingly bulky file containing what should have been the discussions of the parliamentary *uffici*. The unforeseen fall of the government on 15 May 1892 forestalled what would perhaps have been a more ignominious defeat of Villa's proposal on divorce. As a result, the *uffici* never even met, and the file opened to record their discussions and votes has a completely blank cover page.[108] Instead, the entire file consists of hundreds of letters of protest from every corner of Italy, coordinated no doubt by the Opera dei Congressi, which had launched its anti-divorce campaign within days of the first reading of Villa's proposal in parliament in March 1892.[109] The tenacity and determination of the Catholic organizations was impressive, a seemingly endless torrent of words about the impending catastrophe of divorce. Phrases like "the destruction of the family and the rendering of the society weak and effeminate,"[110] and "this immoral law, subverter of the family and society, legalization of polygamy,"[111] set the tone for these protests "in the name of religion, fatherland and family."[112]

It is as difficult to do justice to the imposing quality of this vast outpouring of feeling as it is to assess the extent to which it really represented the "conscience of the country," or "real" Italy. Prior parliamentary groups had had no qualms about dismissing these protests as the contrived voice of just one element of the nation's conscience, and the overwhelming impression of the strength of anti-divorce feeling would certainly have been reduced if some of the alleged 4,000 letters of support for the Committee for Divorce had arrived at Montecitorio to balance the Catholic protests. None of those unhappy couples, however, seems to have thought of writing to parliament. It also has to be kept in mind that while appearing to express the innermost convictions of every *signore* and *signora* who signed them, the anti-divorce petitions resulted from a well-organized project, coordinated from above, and hardly representing a spontaneous groundswell. In this sense, a hierarchical and authoritarian organization like the Catholic Church could appear to represent heartfelt democratic feeling, but the question of how true an expression of feeling this was remains problematic.

In the case of Villa's 1892 proposal, such questions are made less pressing by the fact that once again, it was the capricious turning of Italy's parliamentary wheels, rather than a defeating vote, that brought an end to its progress through the legislature. Nevertheless, the significance of those anti-divorce petitions, with their millions of signatures, would come to the fore again early in the twentieth century, and would be fiercely debated. But for the spring of 1892 it is enough to note that the momentum of the Opera dei Congressi machinery far outran the headway made by the proposal itself.

The divorce question in the nineteenth century did not quite end with the failure of Villa's proposal. Despite the air of defeat that had fallen over the divorce camp after the parliamentary response of the minister for justice, Chimirri, Villa did not yet give up. With apparently indefatigable zeal he resuscitated his proposal for the next session, notwithstanding the onerous need to breast the parliamentary procedures from the very beginning again. Perhaps one incentive was that in the new cabinet Chimirri was replaced as minister for justice by Teodorico Bonacci, who intended to design a law that enforced the precedence of civil marriage over ecclesiastical marriage.

Since the application of the civil code of 1865, which had made civil marriage the only legally recognized version, but had done nothing apart from that to enforce its precedence over Church marriage, there had been two attempts to address this peculiar loophole in the Italian law, neither of them successful. There was a certain pleasing logic in the idea that the parliamentary session of late 1892 was to discuss laws on both the precedence of civil marriage, and divorce. Rome's anticlerical *Tribuna* was particularly excited by the confluence of the two proposals, regarding both as symbolic steps toward clarifying the relationship between the Church and the state. On the divorce question in particular, the paper enthused rather over-optimistically that the "port was close" and could now be reached "with only a few gentle strokes of the oars."[113]

The Vatican was no more thrilled about the prospect of the precedence of civil marriage being legally enforced than it was about the introduction of a divorce law. The *Osservatore romano* expressed the Church's conviction that the two laws together represented a Masonic plot. The Masons had recently held a conference in Naples that the *Osservatore* interpreted as an open declaration of war against the Church, with the two main weapons being the promotion of civil marriage and divorce. The newspaper saw the presentation of Bonacci's law on the former and Villa's on the latter as emanating directly from the conference.[114]

Needless to say, the machinery of the Opera dei Congressi had already been brought back to life, and once again, the response of the Opera dei Congressi outran the driving force behind the divorce project. Indeed, although this, Villa's last proposal on divorce, went marginally further in procedural terms than the one he had presented several months earlier, in many ways it was no more than a coda to the former proposal, and even to the history of the divorce debates in Italy in the nineteenth century.

The text of the proposed law, which was unchanged since 1881, was read to the Chamber on 8 December 1892, and Villa's address to support the law took place on 25 January 1893. It must have taken a special effort for Villa to make the speech, which began with an acknowledgment that this was the fourth time he had asked his honorable colleagues to consider the divorce question.[115] It must have been made even harder by Villa's certain knowledge of parliament's preoccupation with Italy's deteriorating economic condition, which was reaching crisis level that very year. Villa blithely dismissed those material preoccupations and expressed confidence that his colleagues still had an inclination to study grave moral and juridical problems.

The Rise of Conservative Tradition

Villa's long address was as eloquent and learned as ever, but it did no more than rehearse familiar arguments in favor of divorce and against personal separation. Nor could it have been expected to do more. The significant aspects of that parliamentary session occurred in response to what Villa had to say. Antonio Salandra had requested the right of reply, and he rose to speak as Villa concluded. His extraordinary opening words were ominous: he felt that it was indispensable that at least one voice be raised in protest against the proposal, "so that when the Chamber, out of courtesy, votes to take the law into consideration, that vote should not be taken for unanimous assent to a reform that the country does not want, and that the great majority of Italians absolutely reject."[116]

These words sparked an outburst of protest from the Left of the Chamber, which took some moments to settle. Salandra then proceeded with a speech decrying the evils of divorce that was almost as long as Villa's initial address. The essence of Salandra's sentiment exemplifies the rise of late-nineteenth-century doubts over liberalism and a renewed fear of the divisive forces acting upon society. As he had done in his book in 1882, Salandra claimed that divorce was a result of the individualistic tendencies of the prior century, tendencies that had "reached their highest expression in the French law [on divorce] of 1792."[117]

That shorthand for revolutionary chaos was an easy way of making divorce guilty by association, but the key words, the words that really reveal Salandra's appeal to conservatism, are not those of a nervous reference to rampant Jacobinism, but an appeal to "family values." Salandra posed the following question: "at a time when we are trying to reinforce social ties, when we are trying to inspire the spread of altruism in all walks of life and in the state, why would we seek to destroy the only truly socialistic institution of our laws, the indissoluble family?"[118] This corporative vision, of a state constructed of altruistic, forcibly indissoluble families, pointed to a loss of faith in the ideals of liberalism that had driven the Risorgimento. Divorce was becoming an ideological dividing line between those who still upheld liberal ideals, those who had lost faith in them, and those who had never believed in them in the first place.

If Salandra's speech gave ideological reasons for rejecting divorce, the words of the minister for justice, who customarily made comments on any such proposal, were more mealymouthed. Bonacci's statement that he saw Villa's proposal as completely in conformity with the highest principles of natural law drew shouts of "bravo!" from the Chamber.[119] But his initial stance was soon tempered by weak hedging about the Church, about the idea that Italy was still laying foundations, and finally about the claim that such an important question should really be looked at in a period of calm and serenity. Given the fact that urgent financial and economic issues pressed upon the parliament, Bonacci suggested that the divorce question should be held back for a more "opportune" moment.[120]

Villa was of course offended by Bonacci's words. He claimed that consenting to the Chamber's taking the law into consideration while in the same breath saying it was inopportune was as good as asking the deputies to vote against it.[121] Regardless of all this, the Chamber did vote for it, as everyone knew it would. While this had seemed like a great victory for Salvatore Morelli in 1878, by 1892 it was a rather familiar routine, with a sadly predictable outcome. Even though the proposal reached the stage of discussion by the *uffici*, of which initially at least a majority were in favor of the law, the commission never got as far as producing its report before the dissolution of the government.

After that, the financial problems that were incipient in 1892 mushroomed into a crisis that was one of the most difficult confronted by the Italian state in its short history. The clearest sign of crisis was the collapse of one of the six issuing banks, the Banca Romana, in late 1893. The problems were not resolved before the disastrous imperial war in Ethiopia in 1896. With anarchist terrorism and increasing social unrest also troubling the political landscape of Italy right up to 1900, it is not difficult to see why a social question like divorce, for all its symbolic value, was easily swamped by more immediate issues for the remainder of the nineteenth century.

The failure of Villa's last proposal to introduce a divorce law in Italy in 1893 represented an ignoble end to a campaign that had begun so promisingly and so idealistically in 1881. That year, with the full force of his ministerial office behind him, Villa had turned the divorce question in Italy from an amusing parliamentary event into a major national issue. As an indirect result of his initiative, numerous books and pamphlets had been published, many public meetings had been held, and large numbers of journalists had published articles about divorce. Yet the disappearance of the question from the parliamentary agenda after 1893 confirms that for all the activity, no tangible progress had been made. In fact, if anything, more progress had been made on the part of the anti-divorce side: the activities of the Opera dei Congressi began as a step into the unknown in 1881, in response to Villa's law, but by 1893 it had become clear that the Church was able to call on an imposing extra-parliamentary machine to wield political influence.

Conclusion

Was there any particular reason for the failure of the Italian *divorzisti* in the nineteenth century? Without a proposal or draft ever having reached the important stage of full parliamentary discussion, it is difficult to assess the true majority opinion of the Italian political class. The fact that Villa never had any trouble getting parliament to vote in favor of taking the law into consideration probably says more about parliamentary courtesy than anything else, as the incident with Salandra suggested. In the deliberations of the *uffici*, which were chosen by lot and represented a cross-section of parliamentary opinion, each proposal had a majority on its side. The outcome of the Third Juridical Congress debate also shows that there was broad sympathy for the idea of divorce, at least in an abstract sense, within the legal profession (and a majority of Italian deputies were lawyers). Despite all this, each proposal for a divorce law, whether put up by individual deputies or as government projects, failed.

It seems an unsatisfying explanation, but one element of the failure of the divorce cause in the last two decades of the nineteenth century certainly related to the way parliament functioned. The many checks and balances of parliamentary procedure may have been workable under a regime of long-lasting and stable governments, but they combined unproductively with the unstable and often short-lived parliamentary sessions that were a reality in Italy. In consequence, controversial or delicate questions like divorce tended to run foul of a system that moved slowly in the parliamentary hinterland of the *uffici* and commissions, but could move fast and unpredictably at the level of changes of government. The era of "transformism" (*trasformismo*), in which governments changed rapidly, but nothing really moved, was not propitious for divorce, or for any issue of philosophical importance for that matter. As Villa complained during his final address on divorce, "it is in vain that anyone would wait to hear the echo of some grand question in this Chamber."[122]

Ultimately, a certain pall had fallen on the politics of Liberal Italy. The 1880s and 1890s were some distance away from the height of the Risorgimento, memories of which were fading. At the same time, Italian politics started to become weighed down with crises and complications that overshadowed issues that had once seemed symbolically paramount, such as divorce. This was certainly the case between 1893 and 1900, even though the question still surfaced from time to time in pamphlets and newspapers. Then, in 1900, a small incident in the annals of Italian legal history sparked the issue all over again.

In the meantime, the emergence of a major new political force, that of socialism, upset the transformist balance of the Italian parliament. When divorce came up again, it would be a full-scale political battle whose resolution would set the country on a new path that represented a departure from the "individualistic tendencies" of 1792, and an ineluctable turn toward the corporate ideals outlined by Salandra in his remarkable objections to divorce in January 1893.

5

Divorce between Liberalism and Socialism, 1900–1902

The issue of divorce effectively lay dormant for several years after the failure of Tommaso Villa's proposal of 1893. Although the flame was kept alive by the occasional publication, and particularly the short-lived journal of 1895–1896, *Divorziamo*, the issue was easily obscured by the pressing crises of the fin de siècle. In Italy these crises were particularly painful. Against a background of enduring economic problems, the nation lurched from the banking scandals of the early 1890s to a humiliating defeat at the hands of the Ethiopians at Adowa in 1896. Italy ended the nineteenth century with worker riots from Sicily to Milan, and began the new one with the assassination of the king in July 1900. These events exacerbated fears about the rise of socialism, and governments under various leaders struggled to maintain economic, political, and social stability. It is hardly surprising that contentious reforms such as divorce legislation temporarily slipped off the agenda.

The assassination of Umberto I at the hands of an anarchist was the symbolic apogee of a general sense of crisis during which the ability of Italy's institutions to contain the jostling forces of modernity was put severely in doubt. The assassination, which might have been expected to touch off further unrest, in fact had the opposite effect, with the national shock drawing attention away from the social tensions of the period just long enough to reestablish stability. As the twentieth century opened, the governing institutions of Italy emerged intact, and Italy joined the rest of Europe in a period of economic growth and industrialization that would later be regarded as a *belle époque*. However, while in some ways this epoch saw Italy draw closer to the rest of Europe in terms of economic and social development, it was also a period during which Italy began to take a distinctive political path.

Historians have long recognized that this period brought significant changes to the political system of Liberal Italy, particularly in relation to liberal disenchantment with the Socialists, and the entrance of Catholic deputies to parliament after the so-called Gentiloni pact of 1913. Less attention has been paid to the beginnings of those changes very early in the twentieth century, and still less has been given to the way divorce acted as one of their major seeds. For a brief period between late 1900 and early 1902, the torch of divorce reform was taken from the liberals by two Socialists, who seemed to come very close to establishing a divorce law. This was the high tide of the divorce question in Liberal Italy, but it was also a turning point, because the apparent imminence of that success began to shift the currents of Italian politics in a way that helped to set a new course for Italy in the twentieth century.

The broader context of the reemergence of the divorce question in Italy had much to do with the intellectual and political climate in contemporary France. For progressive Italians, France had long been the main beacon of liberal and democratic principles,[1] and toward the end of the nineteenth century a new wave of anticlericalism there undoubtedly helped to stimulate such sentiments in Italy. The key event in France, of course, was the Dreyfus Affair, which ended a period of *ralliement* between the Vatican and the Third Republic.[2] Waldeck-Rousseau's government, formed in June 1899, restored order after the chaos of the Affair, and focused anticlerical feeling in a determined effort to root out any organization that posed an implicit threat to the republic. This effort was expressed officially in July 1901 with the passing of the Associations law, which aimed particularly at clerical congregations,[3] and would be the first clear step in a series of moves that eventually led to the separation of Church and state in France in 1905.

These initiatives in France inspired comparisons in Italy, where the state was inevitably seen as weak in the face of the Church.[4] While France had obtained divorce in 1884 as part of a great wave of secularization whose best-known aspects related to education,[5] no such changes had been achieved in Italy. Anticlerical sentiment in Italy certainly existed, as indicated symbolically by the erection of a statue commemorating the heretic Giordano Bruno in Rome in 1889, or Prime Minister Crispi's declaration of 20 September (the date the Italians troops seized Rome from the pope) as a national holiday, in 1894. But at the government level this was a capricious anticlericalism that had ebbed and flowed with Crispi's fear of the collusion between Catholics and Socialists.[6] More significant measures, such as the introduction of divorce, had been avoided because of Italy's particular problems during the 1890s, when such a law would have been too open a declaration of war. Furthermore, in Crispi's case divorce was a sensitive issue, because he would not have wanted to run the risk of exhuming the disgrace of his bigamy, over which he had had to resign from parliament in 1878.[7] By the end of the 1890s, however, partly inspired and certainly helped along by events in France, there were fresh moves for a clearer separation of Church and state in Italy.

Much indigenous Italian anticlericalism came from Masonic quarters, and even before the significant event of the formation of Waldeck-Rousseau's government in France, there were signs that the Masons were encouraging a new wave of secularizing projects in Italy. In early 1899, Ernesto Nathan, the influential Grand Master of Italian masonry, and for a time mayor of Rome, had urged his Masonic brethren to fight for the twin causes of divorce and the enforced precedence of civil marriage.[8] This was the first sign of the divorce issue coming to life in Italy after the early 1890s, and it was just one aspect of an incipient anticlerical ferment that would soon be buoyed up by the new anticlerical climate in France. In many ways the divorce question in Italy between 1900 and 1902 had a similar histori-cal significance to the Dreyfus Affair in France, in that it laid bare many old political tensions, and it prompted the beginning of a new era of political arrangements. In an Italy that had very often looked to France for the lead in progressive politics, this was the context of the resurgence of Liberal Italy's most important divorce debates.

The Problem of "Foreign" Divorces

The spark that brought divorce back onto the agenda in Italy early in the twentieth century was of a different nature from those in the past, which had without exception depended on the personal commitment of a partic-ular deputy or minister. In 1900 the question was brought to the attention of the public in a circuitous way: the revelation of yet another style of Italian divorce, one that was in fact not Italian at all. Since 1884 a handful of well-to-do Italians had obtained divorces outside Italy. Taking advan-tage of a loophole in the law, they moved elsewhere and took foreign citi-zenship (usually in Switzerland, Germany, or France), obtained a divorce, then returned to Italy and applied for renewal of their original citizenship. Because of the way the international law worked, the Italian courts were obliged to give executive force to foreign sentences of divorce, which meant that the way was then clear for these Italians to marry again in their home-land. Clearly, moving abroad for the purposes of obtaining a divorce involved expenses that only a small number of Italians could meet, and indeed, between 1884 and 1900 only about 28 such divorces are thought to have taken place.[9]

The possibility of eluding Italy's cast-iron marriage laws in this way had been noted as far back as 1876, when an eminent professor of civil law and enemy of divorce, Francesco Filomusi Guelfi, had published an article in *Giurisprudenza italiana* alerting the legal world to the potential problem.[10] The essay focused on a case in which a married French woman had taken German citizenship in 1875 with the express purpose of obtaining a divorce. She subsequently married a German prince. Filomusi Guelfi felt that the case merited attention because, although it had not yet happened, it was theoretically possible for Italian and German laws to become similarly entangled.[11] Indeed, one celebrated victim of Italy's marriage law who is said to have threatened to make use of that potential was Giuseppe Garibaldi himself. Two years after the publication of Filomusi Guelfi's article, Garibaldi was to commence the campaign to dissolve his longstanding but effectively nonexistent marriage to Giuseppina Raimondi. In September 1879, at least two major newspapers reported that Garibaldi was threatening to renounce his Italian citizenship and become French so that he could obtain a divorce.[12] The idea of the personification of Italian patriotism giving up his Italian citizenship in order to get a divorce must have appalled many Italians, but in effect the whole story seems to have been the result of an over-eager journalist's flight of fancy: for one thing, at the time France had no divorce law, so the whole exercise would have been pointless.

The episode nevertheless serves to underline that the possibility of going abroad to obtain a divorce had been brought to the attention of the public well before anyone actually took advantage of it. The first known case of Italian recognition of a foreign divorce took place in 1884 and involved the German consul to Ancona, Count Ermanno Bremen von Oldenberg, who had married an Italian woman in 1879. The woman had left her German husband and moved to the United States, where she had obtained American citizenship, divorced her husband in absentia, and promptly married again.[13] According to Italian law von Oldenberg was still married, and his wife was a bigamist. He applied to the Tribunal of Ancona for a divorce on the basis of adultery. The court accepted the charge of adultery but refused to hand down a divorce to the plaintiff. This harsh application of the law attracted the intervention of the minister of justice, and on 22 March 1884, the Italian court granted executive force to the American divorce so that von Oldenberg could also be considered divorced.[14]

Initially this was a unique case. Nevertheless it provided cause for concern in legal circles, and Filomusi Guelfi criticized the decision, arguing that it was a signal that divorce was being admitted to Italy through the back door.[15] It should be remembered that between 1881 and 1884 parliament debated the introduction of a divorce law several times, so it was a sensitive issue. On the other hand, more liberal minds saw the absurdity of refusing to acknowledge a divorce that had already effectively taken place abroad, and argued in fact that it was much more immoral to insist that a spouse was married to someone who had divorced and married again.[16]

By the end of the nineteenth century foreign divorces for Italians were becoming more common, as there had been 28 of them in the previous 16 years. Although this was not a great many, juridical interest in such cases was disproportionate to their number. This interest reveals the extent to which divorce was an ideologically fraught issue, but it also shows a growing sense of unease among Italian jurists about the way Italian marriage law was increasingly out of step with that of its European neighbors. This unease in legal and then government circles reached a peak in 1900, and ironically it was the expression of this unease, and the rather clumsy efforts of the judicial system to close the loophole, that initiated the next attempt to introduce divorce officially into Italian law.

Official unease over the problem of Italians obtaining divorces abroad and then returning to take up their citizenship was felt at quite high levels. In August 1900 the Ministry of the Interior (responsible for matters of citizenship) officially requested an opinion on the legality of regranting Italian citizenship when it had been renounced for the express purpose of obtaining a divorce abroad. The ministry sought the opinion from the Consiglio di Stato, the highest court in the land with responsibility for administrative matters. The Consiglio di Stato convened a special commission on 17 September to consider the problem. It concluded that technically, permission to regrant citizenship to former Italians should not be given when they had renounced it with the "manifest scope" of obtaining a divorce.[17] It is important to remember that this view was handed down only as a "parere," or opinion, and was not legally binding. As if to underline the point, only the following month the Court of Appeal in Venice gave executive force to a "foreign divorce" obtained by an Italian, who presumably settled back into Italian life and probably remarried soon afterward.[18] The opinion of the Consiglio di Stato seems to have gone unnoticed by the press, despite its significance,[19] but as a signal it was very much noticed in judicial circles and in parliament itself.

The first concrete response to this signal came in the form of a judicial review by the Court of Cassation of Turin on 21 November 1900, when the district attorney launched a vituperative attack on what he regarded as the increasing tendency of the Italian magistracy to see divorce as a "desideratum of an advanced society."[20] He regarded the increasing number of foreign divorces as a sign that the Italian courts were beginning to sanction divorce tacitly. The attorney reviewed four recent cases in which courts under Turin's jurisdiction had given recognition to foreign divorces involving Italians who had temporarily renounced their Italian citizenship and then reobtained it. Although the lengthy report (over 100 pages) strives to maintain an appropriate tone of legal objectiveness, there is an unmistakable sense of mission under the surface. The attorney clearly found the increasing number of Italian couples resorting to this method of divorce a disturbing development, and he claimed that the question of whether a marriage contracted in Italy was dissoluble or not needed to be resolved once and for all. The full court, which consisted of seven judges, accepted the district attorney's case and annulled the four sentences handed down by the Courts of Appeal. This annulment was entirely academic in the sense that it had no retroactive effect. It was simply a peculiar but significant example of finger-wagging by a higher legal authority to a lower one.

Although the Turin case was effectively no more than an exercise in legal theory, it was destined to reopen the Italian debates on divorce that had faded away since the failure of the parliamentary proposal of 1893. The case underlined several aspects of the entire issue. First, even in a country where marriage was indissoluble, well-off and determined Italians could find ways of escaping their marriage bonds, although at great cost in time and money. Second, by 1900, the Italian position on divorce had become increasingly isolated as other nations adopted the law. And finally, the starkly contrapuntal positions that the divorce issue had hitherto evoked in various ways in Italian society had finally been expressed at the level of the Italian judiciary itself, in which an essentially ideological question had become the subject of an unseemly judicial power struggle.

The Socialist Divorce Proposal

The Turin decision was much debated in judicial circles,[21] and these polemics made the whole question all the more pressing at the level of government. The first sign of the coming pressure was a formal question put to the Ministry of Justice by two Socialist deputies, Agostino Berenini and Alberto Borciani, during question time in parliament on 25 November 1900. Their question was whether the recent decision on foreign divorces might prompt the government to present a law on divorce.[22] The reply, delivered during the parliamentary session on 14 December 1900, was a barely elaborated negative given by the under-secretary of the Ministry of Justice, followed by a reprimand that such a delicate question should be discussed at a more opportune moment.[23] Berenini lamented the "monosyllabic nature" of this response, pointing out that the disparity between Italian legislation on marriage and the legislation of its neighbors required urgent attention. He then announced a plan for a divorce law proposal, gallantly claiming that he would have the great fortune to present the law while a *divorzista* like Zanardelli presided over the Chamber.

By drawing attention to the great liberal heritage of the divorce question Berenini may well have been trying to attenuate the idea that as a Socialist his proposal for divorce would be an essentially subversive project. For the Church and conservatives the allegedly intimate relationship between divorce and socialism had always been enough to condemn the idea. But the truth is that the Italian Socialists as a party had an ambivalent position on divorce, one that alternated between attraction to its anticlerical, libertarian character, and dismissal of the question as a bourgeois issue whose need would be obviated by socialist revolution.

The latter view is best expressed by Anna Kuliscioff, a leading figure of Italian socialism and an important feminist. Kuliscioff was the partner of Filippo Turati (her socialist principles ensured that she refused to marry him[24]), founder of the Italian Socialist Party (PSI). In 1891 Turati and Kuliscioff had started a periodical, *Critica sociale*, which soon became the most important forum of Italian socialism. It was here that Kuliscioff published an article in the early 1890s that provides valuable insight not only on the official Socialist view of marriage and the family, but also on women in relation to divorce.

Responding to a male reader who had expressed surprise that *Critica sociale* did not devote more space to the question of women, Kuliscioff wrote that everything that could be said about women had already been written over the past 50 years. The reader had suggested that women's problems could be solved by abolishing indissoluble marriage, and he had suggested renewable five-year marriage contracts as an alternative. Kuliscioff scathingly dismissed the idea that "sentimentalisms" such as liberty, equality, and fraternity would ever change society, including relationships between the sexes. She reminded readers that the true agent of female emancipation in both public and private realms would be industrialization and the advent of economic independence for women.[25]

When women had achieved this, marriage would become a mere accessory, and they could choose to enter into "free unions"[26] with a simple advice to the local authorities. But the time was not yet ripe. In Kuliscioff's view the present marriage regime had the advantage of protecting the weak (women and children).[27] This surprising statement from one of Italy's most prominent feminists underlines the complexities of Socialist feminism, which, while passionately committed to the notion of equality between men and women, regarded mere adjustments to bourgeois marriage as an unproductive distraction. Indeed, proposing such adjustments risked bringing unnecessary bad publicity to the Socialist cause. Kuliscioff claimed that many people already thought that *Critica sociale* had invented the class struggle, and invited her readers to imagine the results if it were now to advocate the destruction of the family.

Yet a significant number of Socialists, representing a group that were to become known as reformists (as opposed to revolutionaries), were interested in promoting social change within the existing system, rather than waiting for economic development to do the work. It is from this wing of the PSI that the next initiative for a divorce proposal came. Little was done about the issue until the following March, when another deputy, Giovanni Curioni, presented a parliamentary question on the issues raised by the Turin judgment on Italians divorcing abroad. In essence Curioni denounced the court's decision, but his main purpose, as Berenini's had been, was to suggest that it was high time the government introduced a divorce law, which would solve the problem at its source.[28] Some days later further questions from two other deputies, Sorani and Pavia, also sought to pressure the government into taking the initiative on divorce, and the minister for justice, Francesco Cocco Ortu, said he would consider the matter.[29]

In the event, though, it was not the government that took the next step. The Socialist deputy, Berenini, who had declared his intention to propose a divorce law the previous November, had already initiated the procedure necessary to present the proposal. The draft, presented in the names of Berenini and Borciani, as well as 36 other "adherents" representing a spectrum of leftist deputies, was dated 9 March 1901, and was read to parliament three days later.[30] This almost bureaucratic step passed with barely a ripple in the media. Of all the major newspapers, only the *Osservatore romano* mentioned the proposal, in its regular column chronicling the business of the Chamber, but no editorial comments followed over the next ten days.[31] *Il Messaggero* mentioned the questions presented by Sorani and Pavia,[32] but remained peculiarly silent about Berenini and Borciani's proposal. The strangest silence was that of *Avanti!*, the organ of the PSI, which did not mention the Socialist proposal either. This may be explained by the fact that parliament's wheels moved slowly, and there was no opportunity for the proposal to be elaborated before the long summer break. The issue that had sparked so suddenly into life with the contentious issue of foreign divorces was left untouched over the summer months of 1901.

The first signs of the question stirring again came in the form of several newspaper articles mentioning divorce in anticipation of the next parliamentary session. The *Osservatore romano* dolefully announced that it was expecting a new season of "religious persecution" to emanate from government and Masonic circles, citing the divorce project as an example.[33] Milan's *Il Secolo* revealed itself once again as a stalwart supporter of divorce, announcing in mid-October that Berenini and Borciani were planning a series of public lectures to promote the cause and garner support for their proposal in Alessandria, Turin, Modena, and Rome.[34] A few days later the same newspaper approvingly reported a pro-divorce meeting held by the two Socialists in Milan, referring to the possibility that the government itself (that is, the minister of justice) was also preparing a project. The writer concluded happily that this was a sure sign that the popular parties were laudably fulfilling their proper role by providing the impetus for civil reforms.[35]

The potential for not just one but two divorce projects had been in the air for some time, although Berenini had taken his cue to prepare one after a government spokesman had denied that there were any official plans. There remained the "promise" extracted from Cocco Ortu in response to the questions raised by Sorani and Pavia, and indeed it does appear that *Il Secolo*'s analysis was correct: regular questions from the floor, and the Berenini-Borciani project, prepared with the support of a wide range of deputies, clearly kept pressure on the government, which had already been embarrassed by the disagreements over "foreign divorces." Prior to the opening of the parliamentary session in late November 1901, several newspapers speculated over whether the Socialist project or a government proposal would prevail. For example, the *Corriere della sera* announced that the government proposal, whose key figures were the prime minister, Zanardelli, and the minister for justice, Cocco Ortu, had been abandoned because Giolitti, the minister of the interior, was against it.[36] The paper corrected this the next day, admitting that there was no evidence that Giolitti was against the project, but it still claimed that the idea had been put in abeyance.[37]

Later in the month the *Corriere della sera* reported continuing debates within the government about whether or not to present a divorce law, but the correspondent remained cynical and stated that he was certain there would be no government project. Instead, he claimed, the government would feign a welcome for the Berenini-Borciani proposal but then allow it to founder during the considerations of the *uffici*.[38] *Il Secolo* also referred to the contradictory reports emanating from Rome about whether the government would proceed with its own law, describing "hasty deliberations" and "hostile currents" in parliament. In fact, though, *Il Secolo*'s correspondent cut through the confusion and offered a prescient summary of what would happen: the Socialist proposal would be presented shortly after the reopening of parliament, and the government would present its own draft in the following parliamentary session.[39]

Parliament reopened on 26 November 1901, and on 6 December Berenini presented the proposal to parliament. According to normal parliamentary procedure, the deputy responsible for the proposal was able to explain the law to parliament, at the end of which the deputies voted on whether it should be taken into consideration and studied further. Berenini's speech was neither as long nor as eloquent as those Tommaso Villa had made in 1881 and 1891, but it merits some analysis, not only because the proposal was to come closer to success than any of it predecessors, but for two further reasons. It was the first time that a Socialist deputy had made such a proposal, and the way Berenini tried to fit divorce into Socialist ideology is of inherent interest. The second, and related reason, is that the proposal differed in significant ways from its predecessors.

Berenini was the first to admit the apparent awkwardness of a Socialist deputy proposing such a law, by anticipating the question of why a Socialist would propose a law that was really only likely to have been of benefit to the bourgeoisie (because those with property interests had more need for state recognition of the status of their private lives). Such a question could only be valid, Berenini argued, if he were presenting the law as a Socialist Party law, but he claimed he was not doing this. He paid lip service to the idea of the class struggle and alluded to the day when, through Socialist efforts, social life "will have given the family a more stable basis and better conditions of moral life,"[40] but essentially he was presenting the law for moral reasons, not as a member of a particular party.

Once Berenini had made polite reference to socialism, there was little that distinguished his argument for divorce from those of his liberal precursors. He spoke, as they had done, of the family as the "elemental cell of the social organism," although he added, appropriately, that the family was subject to "successive transformations." Essentially this phrase was Socialist window-dressing for an argument that stressed the nuclear family as the moral foundation of the "vast human family" and equated defending the family with defending society.[41] Conceptually, then, the Socialist proposal was not fundamentally different from the proposals it followed. As for the ways in which divorce would defend and invigorate the family, Berenini lightly skipped over that obligation, claiming that it would be otiose and vain to repeat all the reasons already put forward by philosophers, jurists, and sociologists. Berenini relied on the idea that by now all deputies were so familiar with these arguments that there was no need for him to spell them out once again.

More important for Berenini was the question of "national dignity."[42] He asked rhetorically how Italy could continue to refuse even to confront the question when divorce laws were securely in place in surrounding nations. This argument clearly alluded to the problem of foreign divorces that had been a catalyst for the revival of the issue in Italy, and indeed the speech was suffused with subtle goading about Italy being out of step with "more civil populations."[43] Berenini challenged those who were against divorce to prove either that the inferiority of Italians meant divorce would bring ruin to them, or, conversely, that their superiority meant their marriages were so secure that divorce would be superfluous.

This approach was fresh and challenging when compared with the cautious and defensive arguments in favor of divorce heard in the Chamber since 1881. In fact, Berenini's speech skillfully blended familiar arguments and new circumstances, as well as taking his divorce proposal further than his liberal predecessors had done. Some of his justifications for divorce were entirely familiar, such as the claim that all divorce did was permit formal recognition of a situation that existed de facto. Similarly, Berenini condemned personal separation as a half-measure that simply drew a veil across the "repellent spectacle" of conjugal battles, but in fact violated biological laws and generally aggravated an already difficult situation.[44] And even if the phrase "biological laws" had a distinctly fin-de-siècle ring to it, the sentiments behind the overall argument barely differed from those of Tommaso Villa and Giuseppe Zanardelli and others who had spoken in favor of divorce in the past.

On the other hand, the Berenini project did present new ideas, especially in relation to the crucial area of the causes that could give rise to divorce. As well as the provisions of the law's precursors, Berenini and his colleagues also proposed to include the onset of mental illness lasting for more than three years, as well as impotence, even if it occurred after marriage, as motives for divorce. More vaguely, article 3 of the proposal included as possible causes for divorce "all those repellent diseases, incurable and transmissible, and in general all those serious things that threaten the stability of the conjugal union so profoundly as to render cohabitation dangerous or incompatible."[45] The elasticity of this provision was a clear departure from the extremely cautious and restrictive approach that had been taken by Villa and Zanardelli during the last few attempts to introduce divorce.

The innovation most important to Berenini concerned the possibility of legitimizing children born out of wedlock.[46] The civil code treated illegitimate children harshly, placing several impediments in the way of their recognition and legitimization. The code also banned paternity suits, a feature that, like the unresolved problem of enforcing the precedence of civil marriage, had also been the subject of several failed proposals for legislation. Under Berenini's divorce law, the articles barring the legitimization of "adulterini" (illegitimate children) would no longer have any effect once a divorce was granted, so children born of adulterous relationships would have been legitimate once a divorce and a new marriage had taken place.[47]

This aspect of the proposal sums up the spirit of the law and underlines the contrast between progressive and conservative politics in relation to the family. The civil code of 1865 embodied an authoritarian approach to human relationships, prohibiting the dissolution of marriage, banning forever the recognition of children born out of wedlock and prohibiting paternity suits, all with the intention of maintaining moral standards. It sought to improve human behavior by stern tutelage, informed by the idea that the stigma of failed marriages or illegitimate children would discourage those eventualities. It imposed ideals that were too high to be achieved by everyone, and, without the allowance for derogations that had been built into centuries of canon law practice, its provisions for those who erred were severely limited. In effect, the civil code condemned many individuals to a limbo unrecognized by the law, and meant that their private lives were outside the jurisdiction of the state itself.

Berenini's divorce law epitomized another philosophy, one that made more provision for human weaknesses. Rather than pretending that they did not exist, it accommodated them within the law. Berenini and Borciani represented a long line of thinkers who believed that society would be improved if the state made room to acknowledge and ameliorate failed marriages and illegitimate children. Their opponents believed this permissive approach would open the way to decadence and social degradation. The debate over divorce in Italy had always been one between those two views, but in the early twentieth century, as traditional controls broke down, there was more at stake, and this time it would be a fight to a more certain conclusion.

The first hint of the resistance that would be mounted came immediately after Berenini had taken his seat following his speech urging the Chamber to vote for the law to be taken into consideration. Deputy Emilio Bianchi rose to speak against divorce, offering token objection in the way that Salandra had done against Villa's proposal in 1893 (and to which Bianchi made reference). His opening argument claimed weakly that the civil code needed to be reformed in so many other ways that it would be counterproductive to go straight to the most controversial issue.[48] Bianchi claimed that divorce would be a catalyst of degeneration,[49] and would be an offense to the majority of Italians because of their religion. Against these claims Bianchi had to fend off vociferous opponents from the Left, and the contentiousness of the issue was expressed through constant murmurs, comments, noises, and interruptions. After Bianchi's closing comment that divorce endangered the nation, emotions were running high, but they were neatly summed up in the parliamentary account: "Applause from the right, noises on the left, shouts of disapproval from the press gallery."[50]

The proceedings were brought to a close by the minister of justice, Cocco Ortu, who, as the relevant minister, was obliged to give his opinion on the validity of the proposal. He immediately laid his pro-divorce cards on the table, proudly referring to the days when he had assisted Zanardelli in the preparation of the proposal of 1883, and saying that he had no hesitation in giving his assent to the present proposal.[51] While agreeing with the principle of divorce, Cocco Ortu not surprisingly expressed strong reservations about the wording of Berenini's proposal, which in his view lacked the prudence and caution of its predecessors. Nevertheless, he gave his full backing to a vote in favor of its being taken into consideration, in the hope that the state would finally "perfect civil marriage, thus rendering the moral fibre of the family more strong and vigorous than ever."[52] The law was taken into consideration by a standing vote.

This vote to take the Socialists' proposal to the next step marks the beginning of a remarkable period, during which the divorce issue came to be a debate that animated the Italian press, the government, intellectuals and writers, the Church, and quite probably, a significant number of ordinary Italians. The matter had been simmering since August 1900, when the Ministry of the Interior had discreetly asked the Consiglio di Stato for its advice on what it obviously perceived as the growing problem of foreign divorces. The press had shown intermittent interest, particularly around the time of the Turin court decision of November 1900 and the inquiries made about the government's intentions on divorce in March 1901. Speculation had grown around the autumn of that year, and there was some confusion about whether the government would live up to the promise it had given in March. Once the divorce proposal was again part of the machinations of government there was a veritable explosion of interest and activity, creating a great sense that divorce's moment in Italy had finally arrived.

Naturally this state of affairs provoked horror on one side and a great sense of expectation on the other. The excitement was clearest in the Socialist newspaper, *Avanti!*. Although it had not paid particular attention to divorce in the past (even when it was clear that a Socialist deputy was working on the project), from the date of Berenini's speech in parliament *Avanti!* became the proposal's leading supporter. On the day of the speech the front page featured a leading article by Professor Arnaldo Lucci, a Socialist lawyer, urging Italy to throw all its democratic energies behind the project. He mentioned the possible government project, claiming that it would be too restrictive. Drawing on his own personal experience as an advocate, Lucci claimed that he had obtained decrees of personal separation for at least 70 couples, and many had formed new relationships that had no chance of being recognized officially unless a divorce law was introduced.[53] In the same issue, the paper dedicated much space to Berenini's proposal, taking special care to point out the large number of women in the audience of the Chamber of Deputies that afternoon, implying that the issue was one that concerned them particularly. On page three the proposed law was printed in its entirety, an unusual appearance that underlined the extent to which the newspaper supported the project and recognised its symbolic importance.[54] That December hardly a day went by without *Avanti!* publishing some article on the divorce issue.

One of the crucial events relating to the passage of the law was the constitution of the committee that would study the law and make its recommendations to parliament, on the basis of which parliament would then debate the question and vote on the law. A sense of the particular excitement and expectation surrounding the proposal comes across even from the title page of the file set up to record the deliberations of the *uffici*. In contrast to the normally sober style of the parliamentary record keepers, some enthusiastic clerk typed the title page of the volume like this:

"DISPOSIZIONI SUL DIVORZIO"
!-!

According to normal procedure the nine ad hoc *uffici* discussed the matter briefly, voted on whether they were in favor or against the law, and each elected a member, representing the majority view of the *uffici*, to the nine-man committee that would study the law in detail and make recommendations to parliament. By the end of the initial proceedings, which took place on 10 December 1901, the resulting commission consisted of an extraordinary eight members in favor of divorce, and only one against it.[55]

The Catholic Response

This vote represents the high point of the divorce campaigns in Liberal Italy, one that would not be reached again until 1970, when divorce was finally introduced. Unsurprisingly, this signal of official favor also acted as a clarion cry to the forces of opposition, and if the pro-divorce campaign revealed both differences from and similarities to its predecessors, the same can also be said of the campaign against divorce. This effectively began with the intervention of the ageing Leo XIII himself. On 16 December, Leo pronounced an allocution on the subject of divorce to the Consistory, in direct response to the proposal. The essence of the allocution was terribly familiar, ringing with phrases like "an open injury to God," "a grave and pernicious error," and so on. The novelty of the allocution lay in the final words, which made a direct though subtle appeal to the Italian national parliament, expressing the fervent wish that its members would decide against divorce.[56]

This appeal may have been a small step for the pope himself, but in terms of Italian church-state relations it was a very important turning point that underlines once again the importance of the divorce issue in the history of that relationship. Never before had a pope said anything that might have implied that he sought some sort of alliance with a government whose authority the Vatican had never recognized. This unprecedented opening seems largely to have gone unnoticed in the liberal press at the time, with the exception of Turin's *La Stampa*, which ran an article entitled "L'Allocuzione del Papa contro il divorzio. L'appello al parlamento," commenting on the significance of this new development. Although that significance was missed by many, it was a signal that ultimately marks the beginning of a new era in Church involvement in Italian politics, in which an overriding preoccupation with the "safeguarding of immutable principles and values" gave way to the Church's preoccupation with the "problem of political behaviour."[57] While a full transition was still some way off in 1901, the event marked an important chink in the armor of the Vatican's feigned indifference to the activity of Montecitorio.

The papal allocution also gave an added note of legitimacy to the activity of the Opera dei Congressi, which, as in previous years, assumed the mantle of leadership in the anti-divorce campaign. The day after the pope's address in Rome, the Consiglio Direttivo of the Opera dei Congressi printed the text of an anti-divorce petition addressed to parliament. Among many other things, the three-page petition claimed that divorce would bring nothing but disaster to "our fatherland." The closing paragraph drew the deputies' attention to the pope's words of the previous day, reinforcing the point that he had addressed them specifically, and urging them to save the "shared fatherland of the august pope from such a calamitous proposal."[58] There was more than a whiff of neo-Guelfism to be discerned here, and even if the arguments against divorce were all very familiar, the pope's direct appeal gave the petition a new air of authority.

This energy was immediately apparent in the dedication and speed with which the anti-divorce campaign came together. Just as *Avanti!* hardly let a day go by without mention of some pro-divorce meeting, so the *Osservatore romano* reported the activities of anti-divorce committees springing up once again all over the peninsula. The Opera dei Congressi's petition forms were sent out to the parishes within a few days of being printed on 17 December, and there is no doubt that the clerics set to work with unprecedented zeal. The Consiglio Direttivo received dozens and dozens of letters and telegrams from parish priests, detailing their efforts to send as many signatures against divorce as possible. Many made requests such as "beyond the original 500 forms please send 1000."[59] Some described concern over the illiteracy of their parishioners, apologizing for the number of people who merely placed a cross on the form because they could not sign their name.[60] Other priests proudly claimed that their flocks were "united in their expression of horror and execration of the ill-omened law."[61] Another letter, however, indicates that the populace of small parishes was not always unanimous in its views on divorce: a priest wrote to apologize for the delay in returning the petitions, reporting that there had been a struggle because of opposition to the petitions, due to the large number of Socialists living in his parish.[62]

While the parish priests were hard at work in the field combatting obstacles such as illiteracy and Socialist opposition (the former was likely to have been much more widespread than the latter), the upper echelons of the Opera coordinated the campaign from Venice and Rome. A noteworthy novelty that distinguished the campaign from previous efforts was the publication of a special anti-divorce broadsheet, entitled *Il Divorzio*, the same title as the short-lived pro-divorce Roman journal of 1892–1893. This was of course part of the anti-divorce armory, and consisted of one large newspaper sheet folded in two, thus making four pages. It was a one-off publication produced in Rome around mid-December (although it was dated January 1902). In the capital it was distributed by means of "strilloni," or news criers, on the first Sunday after the pope's allocution, probably to take advantage of the Sunday churchgoers. Three thousand copies were sent to the Venice headquarters of the Opera for distribution to regional committees.[63] The large letters of the broadsheet's title were flanked to the left by a quotation from Matthew XIX: 6, about what God hath joined, and on the right by articles 56 and 148 of the Italian civil code, which referred to the indissolubility of marriage. This unusual combination of biblical and civil law provides another example of a newly emergent sense of alliance between the dominant religion and the Italian state, even if the overtures were made only by the Church.

How much this new attitude had to do with divorce per se, and how much it was related to the fact that the current proposal had been put forward by the Socialists is difficult to distinguish, since in the Church's view both socialism and divorce were coextensive harbingers of social ruin. In any case, the second article presented in *Il Divorzio*, entitled "Divorce and the Catholics" may just as well have taken the title "Divorce and the socialists," because it made as much of the fact that the law was proposed by the Socialists as it did of the notion that divorce was anti-Catholic and an offense to nature, religion, morals, women, children, love, family, fatherland, and civilization. The article explained that even though the law's protagonists claimed that the causes of divorce would be restricted, the introduction of the principle would inevitably lead to free love, or the "free infamy" of sex for the sake of pleasure. This was what the Socialists wanted, for they were materialistic and radically antireligious.[64] This interpretation was a far cry from the sober intentions expounded by Berenini in favor of divorce, but it was also absolutely representative of the way divorce was depicted by the anti-*divorzisti* at the popular level.

The remaining three pages of the newspaper were taken up with a variety of articles all aimed at giving divorce the most negative publicity possible. One focused on the "depopulation" of France, seizing upon contemporary French concerns about the low birth rate and implying that France's demographic problems could all be traced back to the 1884 divorce law.[65] The back page reported on the progress of the anti-divorce campaigns and listed all the planned meetings. It put special emphasis on the number of women who were against divorce, with a section devoted to female protest. The particular relationship between Italian women and the Church and its organization was one of the great strengths of Catholicism in Italy. Indeed, when women's voices were raised collectively on the divorce issue, it was most often to decry the institution. Women were often organized under religious auspices, and *Il Divorzio*'s special report gives several examples. One, the "Pious Union of Catholic Women," composed their own anti-divorce petition to be sent to the government, opening with the declaration that "As women, jealous custodians of the inviolability of the domestic hearth, we protest energetically against this insane proposal."[66]

The special number of *Il Divorzio* put out by the Opera dei Congressi and the circulation of anti-divorce petitions combined with a particularly noteworthy effort on the part of the pro-divorce activists to create the most widespread battle of publicity over divorce that Italy had ever seen. All the major newspapers mentioned the spectacle regularly, while the organs of the main protagonists of each view, the Socialists and the Catholics, reported on the divorce question assiduously between mid-December 1901 and February 1902. *Avanti!* ran a regular column that reported the intensifying agitation on both sides, though naturally focusing more attention on the committees and meetings in favor of divorce. A typical example was the report of a pro-divorce rally at Spinazzola on 3 January 1902, held at the Circolo socialista. The meeting was followed by a "calm demonstration in the streets . . . to shouts of 'long live divorce, down with the priests, long live the Socialist deputies promoting divorce.' "[67]

On other occasions *Avanti!* mentioned vast audiences gathering in favor of divorce, such as a meeting of 2,000 people in Parma,[68] and even 5,000 at Andria.[69] Ultimately though, the lack of enduring evidence of the pro-divorce ferment contrasted so starkly with the imposing petitions of the Opera dei Congressi that a shadow of doubt is cast over *Avanti!*'s reporting of the pro-divorce campaign in December and January. On the other hand, there were doubts over the legality of the Catholic petitions themselves, reported eagerly by *Avanti!*. For example, one story reported that a priest near Rovigo was so unhappy with the number of parishioners who had signed the petition that he had locked the doors of his church after mass one Sunday, and would not permit people to leave until they had signed.[70] *Avanti!* also claimed that beyond the use of such techniques, the priests also included the names of all sorts of people who did not qualify to sign petitions, such as minors, breast-feeding babies, and even the dead.[71]

Some of the petitions themselves have survived, and it is clear that the three and a half million signatures that the directors of the Opera dei Congressi so proudly boasted of later in 1902 were not the result of an equal number of different hands. In some cases the "signatures" are simply lists of names, written in the same ink, in identical handwriting, most likely that of the priest who visited the homes of individual families (very often the arrangement of surnames suggests that families were visited one at a time).[72] As the correspondence between parish priests and the Consiglio Direttivo of the Opera dei Congressi had revealed, there was much concern over whether illiterates could be represented on the petitions, and even though only the literate were supposed to sign, the listing of illiterates, rather than the mere fraudulent listing of invented names, is a more likely explanation for the occasional irregularities found among the petitions' much vaunted signatures.

Even if the occasional corpse or breast-feeding baby expressed an opinion on divorce through the petitions, a century later it would be counterproductive to be preoccupied with that level of misrepresentation, even though the pro-divorce side had every right to be indignant at the time. What the petitions and their three and a half million signatures bear witness to now is the extraordinary adaptation of the Church's capillary organizational structure to the ways of a modern democracy. Even if Italy had not quite entered the age of mass politics (universal manhood suffrage came in 1913), the successful activity of the Opera dei Congressi over the divorce issue showed that the Catholics were as well if not better prepared for the advent of mass politics than any other interest group.

One of the best signs of the effectiveness of the campaign was revealed at the next step in the parliamentary procedure, when the physical evidence of public opinion was presented in parliament. Throughout December and January, while the public debate on divorce was at its height, the parliamentary commission elected by the *uffici* carefully considered the proposal and made adjustments to the wording of the law. The report of the majority view of the commission, in favour of divorce (eight out of nine members) was written by Berenini, but the minority member, Enrico Scalini, also insisted on writing his own report. These were presented to parliament on 24 January 1902. Apart from the notable speed with which the law had passed from the first stage to the second, the most striking aspect of the reports was the addition of a list of "petitions, appeals, memorials, telegrams, etc." that had arrived at parliament in relation to the proposed law.

Two full pages listed a vast mass of telegrams and petitions of protest from every corner of Italy. Many items claim to represent large numbers of people, such as the "Telegram from Parma of 558 Italian cooperatives," or the "Telegram in the name of 13,200 citizens of the diocese of Fano" (improbable as it was that each of these citizens had expressed an individual opinion). By contrast to the 72 anti-divorce protests, the mere seven messages sent in support of divorce amount to an almost pathetic afterthought appended to the main list. The fact that four of them were from individuals, such as "Appeal from C. M. Zini of Milan" sadly underlined the plaintive and feeble nature of the pro-divorce turnout.[73] What had happened to the meetings of 2,000 and even 5,000 people in favor of divorce, so proudly reported in *Avanti!* just a few weeks earlier?[74]

This state of affairs could not have failed to make some impression upon the parliamentarians concerned, however true it was that there were certain matters in which popular opinion could have little bearing upon legislative change (as had clearly been the case with the introduction of civil marriage itself). Scalini's report drew most of its rhetorical strength from the fact that the "immense majority" of the Italian nation was against divorce. The report emphasized the Socialist provenance of the proposal, underlining the idea that for some time Socialists had been battling against the principle of marital indissolubility as part of their ideological battle against private property. The report also suggested that if a referendum were held on the divorce issue it would be so thoroughly defeated that it would be abandoned for "at least ten years."[75]

Scalini's report did not deign to engage with the individual articles of the proposal, claiming it was a proposal to be rejected a priori. Another argument was that introducing divorce in Italy would be much more favorable to men than women. The reason for this, Scalini argued, was that Italian women were still "several centuries" behind those of other nations in terms of social and economic independence, and as a result divorce would be disastrous for them in a way that it was not for English, German, Russian, and North American women. Obviously Scalini was not susceptible to the argument that just because more advanced countries had divorce, Italy should emulate them. On the contrary, by referring to "our virgin provinces," he argued that Italy was particularly free of the sort of social corruption commonly found elsewhere. As numerous scholars had pointed out for decades, Italy's families were not immune to irregularities; it was just that Italian law had a way of ignoring those problems. But Scalini's was not a reasoned argument. A speaker who had the weight of all that anti-divorce material behind him did not need to refer to more detailed statistics of Italian family life to make his point.[76]

The majority report, prepared by Berenini himself, exuded the confidence that came of knowing eight out of nine parliamentary *uffici* had voted in favor of divorce. The introduction sought to build on this unprecedented official success by sketching a rapid history of the fate of the divorce question in parliament since Morelli's initiative of 1878, presenting the current proposal as the result of careful study on the one hand, and the groundswell of learned support on the other.[77] The tone of the report betrays no sense of unease about the much more tangible groundswell of Catholic protest against the proposal that undoubtedly provided part of the backdrop to the commission's considerations. In the spirit of the theoretical separation between Church and state, all Berenini's report said in relation to the religious question was that the divorce law would never be imposed upon anyone, and that Catholics do not have a right to disallow those who do not share their faith from obtaining the benefits of divorce.[78] In short, the document is a sober and scholarly report of the results of the commission's work that calmly ignores the storm raging over the issue in the press and in the parishes.

Despite broad agreement on the principle of divorce within the commission, in the end its proceedings were not completely free from storminess themselves. Although the parliamentary records left no trace of the deliberations, they were clearly marked by disagreement. One of the commissioners, Palberti, objected strongly to the possibility that separation by mutual consent could eventually result in divorce.[79] He also disagreed with the inclusion of mental infirmity and impotence among the causes of divorce.[80] These objections eventually led Palberti to resign from the committee, but as Turin's *La Stampa* remarked, these disagreements would be insignificant in the long run. Much darker clouds had already cast their shadow over Berenini's proposal: not only was the closure of the parliamentary session imminent, but according to *La Stampa*'s correspondent, the presentation of a ministerial project on divorce, something that had been speculated about for more than a year, was now a certainty.[81] A few days later the parliamentary session ended, and the most promising divorce proposal Italy had ever witnessed was stopped in its tracks. A few weeks later, the Socialist project was sidelined, to be overtaken by the more prestigious government project.

Conclusion

After the failure of Villa's proposal in 1893, the divorce issue had been submerged by other more pressing events for seven years, but had sprung back to life almost unexpectedly, as part of a complex campaign of anticlericalism that had much to do with Italian admiration for the politics of the French governments of Combes and Waldeck-Rousseau. Although divorce had long been associated with the Jacobin phase of the French Revolution, it was something of a surprise in Italy that the divorce proposal emerging from this ferment was made by a Socialist deputy.

Although the prime minister, Zanardelli, the president of the chamber, Villa, and the minister for justice, Cocco Ortu, were all convinced *divorzisti*, the Berenini-Borciani proposal came from a quarter that was very much their junior in this field. The liberal dilatoriness in 1900–1901 showed that there was a certain timidity, a certain lack of initiative on their part, and the Socialist project only threw this into relief. Not to be outdone, and very likely encouraged by the warm reception given to the Berenini-Borciani proposal by the parliament, the long-rumored government project was finally readied for what all *divorzisti* hoped would be the triumphant crowning of a long but fitful campaign that had begun more than two decades earlier.

There would be a final attempt, and in some ways it would be quite spectacular. But even before it began, two things that were crucial for the future of Italian politics had been revealed by the latest episode of the divorce campaign. The first was the lack of coordination between the progressive forces in government and their extra-parliamentary supporters. This is revealed by the inherent sense of competition between two different approaches to the divorce question: the Socialist project, and the government project that was about to overtake it. It is also revealed more starkly by the lack of tangible support for the divorce cause sent to parliament. By contrast, the successful adaptation of the centuries-old organization of the Catholic Church to an ideological crusade against divorce is all the more impressive. This was not the first time it had happened, and each time the Opera showed itself more efficient and better organized.

The fact that the campaign was effectively launched by no less a figure than the pope, and that in so doing he addressed himself to the Italian parliament for the first time in the history of the new nation, has to stand as an indication of a new level of Church involvement in Italian politics. Indeed, the successful campaigns masterminded by the Opera dei Congressi paved the way for further campaigns in the Giolittian period, notably on the teaching of the catechism in schools. Ultimately, though, what was most important about the pope's appeal to parliament and the success of the popular campaign was that it revealed the emergence of a new attitude on the part of the Church to parliamentary politics. The Church was poised to enter a new age of mass politics with an advantage that was to distinguish Italian history throughout the twentieth century. The threat of the introduction of divorce revealed just how much religious faith could count in modern politics. All that remained was to harness that faith in order to defeat the menace as permanently as possible.

From the Failure of Reform to the Lateran Pacts, 1902–1929

A t the end of January 1902, the divorce question was like a wave that had been unnaturally stilled by the closure of the parliamentary session. The succeeding 18 months would reveal that moment to have been the issue's historical peak during the Liberal epoch. Between January 1902 and June 1903, changes within the Italian parliament effectively absorbed the turbulence caused by the debates over divorce. All this is not to imply, however, that during those 18 months the divorce debates were only a fin-de-siècle disturbance, caused by Italy's adjustment to the realities of the twentieth century. On the contrary, as the Catholic Church's unprecedented direct appeals to the political class had already foreshadowed, the divorce question was itself a watershed that helped to define the landscape of Italian politics in the Giolittian era. This in turn laid out a trajectory for the better part of the twentieth century. The divorce threat galvanized influential Catholics into action and gave them confidence to enter politics. Contemporaneous instability in the broader political arena made the Liberals willing to accommodate them. Once that had happened, divorce was mentioned rarely in parliament, and it never aroused the passions of 1902. All divorce proposals were kept in abeyance until the rise of Fascism, after which the possibility of establishing a divorce law was soon extinguished.

Although hindsight reveals the closure of parliament to have been an important turning point in the narrative of divorce's rise and decline, outside the confines of Montecitorio the public debate maintained a high profile throughout the year. An extraordinary expression of public opinion reached a peak in 1902 and continued well after the issue was put to rest. By February of that year the issue had already prompted the intervention of many of Italy's most esteemed intellectuals, including Benedetto Croce and Gaetano Mosca. The divorce question also became a woman's issue, as several important Italian women voiced their opinions through works of literature, newspaper articles, and pamphlets. Even so, vocally pro-divorce women in early-twentieth-century Italy were notable more for their rarity. Even though the period between 1890 and 1910 was particularly important in the mobilization of Italian women,[1] divorce was not one of the issues that motivated them. Nevertheless, women's voices comprise an important element in a spectrum of intellectual responses to divorce's high tide in 1902. What follows is an interweaving of these responses with the broader narrative that brought the divorce debates to an end upon the altar of political expedience as Italy entered the twentieth century.

From the first inklings of the reappearance of divorce as a political issue in March 1901, when Berenini and Borciani had launched their initiative with a minimum of fanfare, the most novel aspect of the whole affair was that the proposal had been made by members of the PSI. For the forces that had historically opposed divorce, this new political sponsorship was merely a revelation of the true nature of the institution: a plot harking back to the Jacobin phase of the French Revolution. Now that divorce was clearly draped in Marxist robes, conservatives felt doubly certain that it was a harbinger of the destruction of the family and private property, and a vehicle of that ultimate symbol of social chaos, "free love."

While Berenini's proposal had revealed itself as a sheep in wolf's clothing, in that it was no more than a respectable descendant of its liberal forbears, from the outset there had been an implicit tension between that proposal and the possibility that the government might itself decide to repossess the ideological territory of divorce for its own initiative. After all, for Zanardelli as prime minister and for Villa as president of the Chamber, it may have been slightly disturbing to see the issue commandeered by members of the upstart Socialist Party. When the government did finally unveil its own divorce proposal, it was the first step in a sea change in the relationship between divorce and Italian politics.

The ministerial plans for divorce, over which there had been speculation since early 1901, were not disclosed until late January 1902, when the government's intention to go ahead with such a law were confirmed by several newspapers. As the *Corriere della sera* pointed out, the existence of a ministerial project inevitably resulted in diminished interest in the Socialist proposal.[2] Turin's *La Stampa*, which sustained more interest in the issue than most other newspapers (except the partisan *Avanti!* and the *Osservatore romano*), also referred to the ministerial project, claiming that the executive had decided that such an important initiative should come from the government itself.

It is likely of course, that the eight to one vote in favor of the proposal in the parliamentary offices also gave the government courage. Parliament was in recess for the first three weeks of February, so official machinations over the issue were not recorded from within parliament. However, it is evident that the contentious question of how to present the divorce issue was one that greatly preoccupied the relevant ministers, and ultimately led to the resignation of a minister, Gerolamo Giusso, from the cabinet.[3] Apparently he objected to Zanardelli's plan to have the king announce that a divorce law was part of his government's program at the opening of parliament. Giusso's resignation was the perfect political scandal to add piquancy to an already tense situation, and the press had little time for anything else.

The tension of those few days underlines that the transition from the Socialist proposal to the ministerial one was no smooth matter. Under the Socialists the issue had always seemed to have something of the air of a public festival, whereas Giusso's resignation was evidence of bitter contestation and reflected an altogether different mood. Nevertheless, after more than a year of hesitation, Zanardelli now pushed the cause with iron determination. Nothing showed this better than his success in ensuring that, despite objections, the plan to introduce a divorce law was announced by the king during his brief "Discorso della Corona" (Crown speech) at the opening of parliament.

The King Announces a Divorce Law

The newspapers had built up considerable expectations over this speech, particularly in relation to the way the announcement of the government's project would be phrased. For example, *La Stampa* had declared that the divorce project would be titled a law "on the ordering of the family."[4] Similarly, the day before the king's speech and in the midst of the ministerial crisis, the *Corriere della sera* reported that the Council of Ministers had desperately tried to prevent Giusso from resigning by adopting a formula for the king's speech that did not include the word "divorce." On 20 February, the king finally uttered his much anticipated words. Among other worthy projects, he promised, somewhat anticlimactically, that his government planned to "temper the ideal of marital indissolubility . . . in line with neighbouring countries."[5]

Reactions to both the phraseology and the very fact of the announcement predictably divided along lines similar to the divisions of opinion over divorce itself. *Il Secolo*, a stalwart supporter of divorce, was one of the few newspapers that unequivocally praised the king's speech, which, in its view, announced a "good practical programme that adhered to liberal principles." In particular the paper regarded it as a program "infused with modernity" and claimed that the foreign press had also praised it as being "in line with the times." As for divorce, the editorial expressed relief that the government had remained steadfast on the issue despite Giusso's resignation, and it found that the wording "revealed the juridical mind of Zanardelli, and could not have been better."[6]

The *Osservatore romano* took umbrage, reporting emotively that the pope was particularly disturbed that the king's "divorce speech" came not just during the pope's jubilee year, but on the very day of the twenty-fifth anniversary of his election to office.[7] The *Corriere della sera* found the king's euphemistic words "infelicitous" and felt that the government was artificially maintaining the pretense that divorce was an entirely juridical question, when it so clearly entered the field of national sentiment. For this and other reasons, particularly a sense that Italy was going through a decisive and difficult period, the *Corriere* felt, in contrast to *Il Secolo*, that the government's stance on divorce was insensitively out of step with the times.[8] The *Fanfulla* was more pointed, saying that the government was only concerned with its liberal image, and completely oblivious to matters of opportunity.[9] Most of the newspapers that expressed reservations about or hostility toward divorce also underlined that the deputies of the Chamber gave the king's speech a cool reception, although their interpretation of the degree of coolness ranged considerably, from merely cold to "glacial" (*Osservatore romano* and *Corriere della sera*). Even *Avanti!*, which up until this moment had been a fervent supporter of divorce, was reserved in its response to the king's speech, describing the obfuscatory phrasing as more befitting of the Vatican.[10]

For several days after the opening of parliament the press devoted large amounts of space to the divorce issue in general and the government's position and the king's speech in particular. In terms of journalistic attention the king's timorous words of 1902 signified another high point for the divorce issue in the century between 1860 and 1960. Having as prestigious a voice as that of Victor Emmanuel III announce the government's intention to introduce a divorce law was a publicity triumph for Zanardelli, the apogee of a trajectory that had been launched in 1878 by Morelli. But it was a pyrrhic victory, for it also marks the turning of the tide against divorce and the beginning of an ineluctable ebb that was foreshadowed by the press's lukewarm response to the king's words.

Mixed Reactions

At the core of this ebbing support was the sense that it was inappropriate for one of the nation's few symbols of unity to speak on so sensitive an issue.

Another problem was that the king's speech appears to have accentuated divisions of opinion among the *divorzisti*, and even more seriously, to have galvanized the nonclerical but conservative liberals into more concerted action against divorce. As *Il Secolo* commented, the government's enemies began to increase in number in response to the speech.[11] The *divorzisti* had never been a compact lobby group, but there had been a certain esprit de corps among pro-divorce Socialists and progressive liberals, who had hitherto been able to count on the resigned silence of those whose true feelings were ambivalent. The approaching end of that fragile status quo had already been signalled by Palberti's resignation from the commission studying the Berenini-Borciani proposal in January. The resignation of one of the government ministers over the issue of the king's speech was a more ominous sign that the pro-divorce coalition was quickly losing whatever cohesion it had previously possessed.

Another indication that the divorce lobby would soon face new obstacles came in the wake of the king's speech with news from Naples about a significant development in the anti-divorce camp: the conservative liberal deputy, Emanuele Gianturco, had launched an initiative to form a new anti-divorce committee. His motive, echoing Salandra's memorable parliamentary intervention in 1893, was that he did not want it said that all the opposition to divorce was clerically inspired.[12] *Avanti!* quickly picked up on this news, scornfully questioning how a committee could describe itself as liberal and laic when its two key figures, Gianturco and Salandra, were clearly "reactionaries tied to the Neapolitan curia."[13] Despite the condescending tone of the article, there was an unmistakable sense that the wind was slipping out of the sails of the divorce cause, at least as far as *Avanti!* was concerned. It concluded with the not particularly reassuring news that "meanwhile, the pro-divorce committees' work continues." Compared with the confidence of former articles, there was an air of flagging determination in this limp Parthian shot.[14]

While the ideological stance of *Avanti!*'s correspondent would have explained this peremptory dismissal of the significance of the new committee, the development was actually of crucial importance for the future of the divorce question in Italy. This is because it heralded an emerging conservative turn in Italian politics that would eventually help to ensure the defeat of the divorce issue. Gianturco was interviewed by the popular Milan newspaper, *Il Pungolo*, and the account was subsequently published in several other newspapers, including *Il Messaggero* in Rome. In a statement that typified the conservative attitude to divorce, he claimed that divorce sacrificed the collective interests of society to the individual will. By implication, this meant that Gianturco valued the idea of personal sacrifice in the interest of the collective good more than the other way around.

Even if the whole purpose of his new committee was to establish a liberal nonclerical voice against divorce, this sort of social philosophy still had more in common with Catholicism than it did with liberalism, which is why *Avanti!* was so scathing.

That broad underlying philosophy would always have seen divorce in a negative light, but Gianturco added further comments that made his views more interesting than the predictable anti-divorce stance they seemed to represent. The first was that he sensed a particularly acute threat to Italy's social cohesion at that time, for he claimed that Italy's unity was "menaced everywhere," and divorce was therefore the last thing Italy needed to introduce at that moment. It was as if Gianturco regarded Italy as so much knitting, and one dropped stitch would lead to the unraveling of the entire garment. But it was a garment made of two parts, for here Gianturco introduced another argument against divorce that had not hitherto been much used. Gianturco argued that, however unpleasant the phrase might be, as far as divorce was concerned there were "two Italies." While from Rome northward divorce might find some favor, Italy to the south was totally against divorce.[15] This was an interesting new twist on the divorce question, touching the emotive issue of the incomplete cultural and social unification of the nation. In effect Gianturco claimed that the introduction of divorce would be a further impediment to the completion of this process.

Regardless of the actual effects of a law on the north and the south, the emergence of a conservative, southern, but nonclerical stance against divorce is also evidenced by a speech given by a Calabrian deputy, Pasquale Murmura. At the invitation of the mayor of Catanzaro, Murmura gave a lecture on divorce in that city on 11 May 1902. His views are important because they reinforce those of Gianturco, and show that the divorce debates were becoming considerably more complex than they had been even a decade earlier. Murmura's major point was that it was politically inexpedient to introduce divorce at that particular historical juncture. Gianturco had said the same thing, and so had many others. Murmura's first reason for this claimed inopportunity was that the whole question exacerbated the historic rift between the Church and the state, and that the introduction of divorce would give the Church the opportunity to increase its popularity by converting the majority of Italians into comrades in arms.[16]

Murmura's second argument against divorce involved regional, particularly north–south, divisions. Like Gianturco, Murmura warned that the introduction of divorce might aggravate the regional cleavages that had never disappeared after unification, and in fact seemed to be getting wider. He claimed that in the south of Italy divorce might be regarded as an attack on the family, which he described as "our refuge."[17] Nevertheless, Murmura did concede that he would condone the possibility of divorce provided a marriage had produced no children,[18] although later he claimed that the only real advantage of this would be to take power away from the Church.

Overall, Murmura's stance is ambiguous. It projects a family-oriented conservatism that is not completely insensitive to the arguments of liberal jurists, but emphasizes the need for political caution in order not to disturb the delicate marriage between Italy's north and south. In sum, Murmura argues for a gradualist approach that is barely distinguishable from complete immobility. It would hardly have merited attention at all, but for the fact that, put more eloquently and forcefully a year later, this philosophy of leaving the status quo undisturbed for the sake of political opportunity was broadly responsible for putting the divorce issue to rest for more than six decades.

Apart from the clique of powerful southern politicians centered around Gianturco and Salandra, there was little if anything to distinguish between northern and southern views on divorce. Southern intellectuals had contributed much to the pro-divorce debate since the 1860s,[19] and of course Salvatore Morelli, who had first brought the question up before parliament in 1878, was a southerner. In the debates that had been sparked by Berenini and Borciani's 1901 proposal, which were given new impetus by the announcement of a ministerial project, southerners also made an important contribution to the pro-divorce arguments.

The most notable of these was Benedetto Croce, the celebrated Neapolitan philosopher and historian who added his views to those of the *divorzisti* on several occasions. A decade earlier Croce had published a study of divorces in Naples during the Napoleonic era that was a subtle argument in favor of the reintroduction of divorce.[20] In January 1902 Croce also authored several newspaper articles that were more explicitly pro-divorce than his 1891 scholarly essay.[21] The truth is that among intellectuals the divorce debate did not reflect geographical divisions in any obvious way. Rather, the divisions were religious, ideological, and, as Hartmut Ullrich has suggested, "scientific" and "moral."[22] Among the myriad newspaper articles and pamphlets by authors ranging from well-known jurists to obscure amateurs, Croce's voice stands out, but two other intellectuals who made their mark on Italian history in the twentieth century also made significant contributions.

In February 1902 Enrico Corradini, soon to become the prophet of a new form of Italian nationalism, published an article entitled "L'agitazione ecclesiastica contro il divorzio" in *Rassegna nazionale*, organ of the moderate Catholics. Corradini was particularly interested in the implications of a divorce law for the relationship between the family and the state, arguing that divorce might be the first step toward the establishment of a closer relationship between the institution of the family and the state.[23] In his view the ideal family structure fostered by the Church was too closed to the outside world, too self-contained.[24] Corradini argued that giving the state a greater role in the case of marriage breakdown would create a greater sense of engagement between state and citizen.[25]

Corradini's assertions about the potential of divorce to bring the family and the state closer together touches an important theme in Italian history: the alleged sense of distance between the state and its citizens, resulting in mutual mistrust. Although Corradini does not focus on the Church, the title of the article draws attention to the clergy and implicitly reinforces the idea that the powerful presence of the Catholic Church in Italy was one of the reasons for that gulf. The Italian state had a competitor for the allegiance of its citizens, and the ecclesiastical agitation against divorce to which Corradini referred was effectively an agitation against the state gaining a greater hold on its citizens through its complete control of marriage and divorce. Even though there would only have been a relatively small number of divorces, its introduction into law would have been so radical a change that it would have been a far more powerful symbol of the state's new tutelage of the family than the introduction of civil marriage had been in 1865.

The question of state-family relations also had a bearing on the north–south question raised by Gianturco, since the level of acceptance of the state by southerners had traditionally been low. The very low level of applications for personal separation in the south of Italy probably revealed more about a southern tendency to avoid recourse to the state than it did about the number of successful marriages there. Indeed, the exceptionally high number of spouse murders in the southern cities of Naples and Palermo could be taken as an indication of preference for "resolving" personal matters within the private sphere rather than taking the matter to court. Under these circumstances, the introduction of divorce might have been regarded as an offense to southern mores, as Gianturco argued; but, to side with Corradini, it may eventually have had a salubrious effect on southern marriages. Ultimately, the way Corradini poses the question of what divorce might mean for the relationship between state and citizen makes his views particularly worth noting. Moreover, they foreshadow his later insistence upon a nationalism that would privilege the state, anticipating fascist concepts of the proper relationship between state and citizen.

A similar view was expressed by another prominent intellectual who entered the divorce debate at its peak in early 1902. Gaetano Mosca had become known in the 1890s for his theories about the way states are dominated by elites. Mosca published an article on divorce, "Pro e contro il divorzio," in the *Corriere della sera* in February 1902, just as the legislative session was about to open. His position was ambivalent, as he had no objection to divorce in principle when a married couple had no children, but was against it if they did. Mosca claimed that his view went to the heart of new currents of thinking about individual liberties, arguing that as a social body develops it has an ineluctable tendency to impose more restrictions and to restrain the passions of its members.[26] Indeed, he suggested that "progress" was no more than a continual sacrifice by individuals of the present generation in favor of those of the future.[27] He pointed out that the passionate tendencies leading to adultery fade with time, and that the family generally remains intact.[28] If divorce were introduced it might allow families to disintegrate when they would otherwise have outlasted the effects of short-lived passions.

Mosca's article is noteworthy for several reasons. In a final flourish he claimed that the principle of rigid monogamy was one of the glories, and at the same time one of the hypocrisies, of civilization, representing the struggle between the highest ideals and the basest human instincts.[29] He also argued that divorce should be allowed in rare cases despite the ideal of monogamy. To this extent he was cautiously pro-divorce for reasons that aligned him with the arguments that had been adopted by liberals like Tommaso Villa and Giuseppe Zanardelli. In other ways, though, Mosca's reasoning represents a departure from the classic liberal view in a conservative direction. His argument that progress is made by individual sacrifice in favor of society and its future generations is infused with a peculiar combination: Catholic rejection of liberal individualism, together with a new valorization of the body politic. In this there is a link between Mosca's and Corradini's views on divorce: both saw the most significant "family" as the state, because in their view only the state could be the motor of progress.

Mosca and Corradini are just two names that stand out among many who contributed to the divorce debates in 1902. The countless other contributions ranged across the spectrum for and against divorce. Professor Giovanni Marchesini's scholarly pamphlet on the divorce debates as the ultimate struggle between dogma and progress was a perfect example of the classic liberal view.[30] Professor L.M. Bossi's *La legge sul divorzio considerata dal lato ginecologico* (The Divorce Law from a Gynecological Perspective) illustrates the development of new ideas about social hygiene and sexual health, claiming that enforced celibacy led to precocious atrophy of the sexual organs.[31] Emilio Federici, president of the Court of Appeal of Venice, viewed divorce and socialism as practically coextensive, decrying even very restricted access to divorce as the thin end of a wedge that would eventually lead to the chaos of "free love."[32] In a similar vein, but from an explicitly Catholic point of view, Salvatore Brandi inveighed against Zanardelli's "Jacobin" insistence upon imposing the view of a "shabby minority" on the majority.[33] Brandi, like many Catholics, regarded divorce as the Trojan horse of a collusion between Socialists and Masons, arguing that anyone who wanted to destroy society would attack it at its base—the family.

In much of the writing about divorce at the height of the debate in 1902, little was notably new. Mosca's and Corradini's words presaged a view of the state that would become more prevalent later in the twentieth century. Ideas about the gynecological aspects of divorce were unusual, but were more important for their novelty value than for any influence they might have had. While Brandi's ideology was firmly rooted in the Council of Trent, his article did make a subtle reference to a characteristic that distinguished the early-twentieth-century divorce debate in Italy from its nineteenth-century predecessors: the visible involvement of Italian women. Brandi drew attention to this new development in a footnote, celebrating the great success of the campaigns against divorce, and acknowledging the part played by women, who, as "women, wives and mothers," had risen together to protest divorce as an attack on the institution of the family.[34]

Women's Voices on Divorce

Brandi's reference to women underlines a peculiarity of the divorce issue in Italy: the low profile of women's opinions on divorce, and their tendency, when expressed, to defend the existing marital arrangements. Although marital problems and personal separations were very much women's concerns in the private sphere, between 1865 and the turn of the century, very few women expressed opinions about these questions in public forums. One modern commentator on the relatively slow development of women's movement in Italy, Fiorenza Taricone, ascribes a major reason to the fact that under the civil code married women could not make any legal transactions without their husbands' permission. This in turn led to practical difficulties in renting meeting space or establishing an association in a formal sense.[35] It could also be argued that the position of married women under the Italian civil code both reflected and helped maintain a sense of subordination among women that was a psychological factor in the slow development of a collective female consciousness.

As a result, female associationism was "hardly known" in Italy in the early 1890s,[36] and it was not until the height of the Giolittian period that the Italian women's movement achieved national and international visibility, with the Congresso delle donne italiane, held in Rome in 1908.[37] By that date though, the divorce debate was a dead letter, and the issue was not raised at the congress.[38] Before that, and only after the turn of the century, a small but significant handful of women made public contributions both for and against divorce, but those in favor did so as individuals, not as representatives of any collective opinion. One example was Anna Maria Mozzoni, who had pronounced herself in favor of divorce in the pages of *Avanti!* in 1902.[39] As Franca Pieroni Bortolotti put it, Mozzoni was one of the very few women to take a pro-divorce position, because "custom" prevented most others from doing so.[40]

Another significant example of a lone Italian woman making a contribution to the divorce debate is Teresa Labriola, who published a work on divorce in November 1901. Labriola herself was unusual, in that she pursued an academic career at the University of Rome long before it was common for women to attend a university even as students. Labriola's father Arturo was a well-known Marxist and one of the leaders of the PSI, but Teresa, who had recently won a position as professor of the philosophy of law, did not follow her father's line. Nor does Labriola's analysis in *Del divorzio: Discussione etica*,[41] present a specifically feminist argument. Rather, as the title suggests, she presents an ethical analysis, with particular reference to Italy's contemporary condition.

Labriola stresses the family's essential function in the reproduction of the human race. For this reason alone, those who follow an "exaggerated cult of unlimited personal liberty" must realize that the existence of the family cannot be left entirely to individual whim. Labriola explains that marriage restrains the base instincts, thus safeguarding the family as a unit of reproduction. It is this responsibility to society that makes the family an ethical institution.[42] But she also argues that when a marriage no longer exercises this social function on its individual members, ethically the marriage ceases to exist. At that point the ethical bonds between a family and broader society are damaged, and Labriola disagrees with those who think that damage can be limited by forcing a marriage to exist juridically when the psychological basis of the marriage has dissolved.[43] For this reason, Labriola sees divorce as ethically valid, because rendering marriage dissoluble acts as a deterrent against potentially harmful acts. This argument had been used by *divorzisti* since Morelli, but the path by which Labriola arrives there is more elaborate and more sophisticated.

In relation to contemporary Italy, Labriola agrees with those who argue that divorce cannot simply be a matter of principle but must answer to differing moral and material conditions of time and place. She felt that conditions in Italy would only allow divorce on an extremely restricted basis, because the family was still essential in fulfilling functions that might later be provided by the state. Implicitly, for Labriola, as for Corradini, the introduction of divorce would be a step toward the development of a closer relationship between the state and the family, but that relationship was something that could change only as material conditions allowed. In her view these conditions were a greater impediment to the introduction of divorce in Italy than the Catholic conscience,[44] and in fact she expressed the hope that with time the state would take over from religion in the tutelage of the family.[45]

Ultimately Labriola spells out that divorce in Italy should be allowed only in cases when ethical harm has been done to a marriage, principally in cases of adultery or violence.[46] The result would be a social-Darwinist purification of marriages, through the elimination of "morally inferior" examples, which would in turn elevate society as a whole.[47] Overall, Labriola's work amounts to a cautious statement in favor of divorce, not for the benefit of individuals, or women, but for the organism of society itself.

Although significant for many reasons, Labriola's views on divorce do not express an avowedly feminist position. The most significant forum through which Italian women expressed their ideas about marriage and divorce was through fiction. An important example is *Una donna*, by Sibilla Aleramo, begun in 1901.[48] Acknowledged as the first example of Italian feminist literature, this autobiographical novel narrates the rites of passage of a girl to womanhood, and the tragedy of her married life. As a child the main character suffers at the hands of her stern father, and witnesses her mother's unhappy marriage and eventual suicide. In her teens the girl is raped by one of her father's employees, whom she is then forced to marry. The marriage is a disaster, and the couple separates, and as a result the main character loses access to her children. The novel is a harsh critique of Italian marriage laws and the way in which they oppress women, and although it does not mention divorce, implicit in the narrative is a criticism of its absence. *Una donna* met with immediate success and Aleramo became a prominent personality, but she did not become a public advocate of divorce.

Among the first works of Italian fiction to treat the question of divorce explicitly was *Dopo il divorzio*, by the Sardinian author Grazia Deledda, who later won a Nobel prize for literature. Published in 1902, it is a poignant work that presents divorce as a complex moral problem, and was unquestionably inspired by the contemporary debates. Set in Sardinia, the novel begins two years in the future, in 1904, and is a fictional example of the effects of a law that must have seemed imminent when Deledda wrote the novel.

The main character is Giovanna, whose husband Costantino has been (wrongly) charged with murder and is about to be sentenced to 30 years in jail.[49] The story of their marriage unfolds around the dinner table of the Porru household, where Giovanna is a guest. Members of this family are the other main characters. The young Paolo, a law student on the mainland, represents modern liberal views, and predicts that within a couple of years Giovanna will be remarried. Members of Paolo's family, particularly his mother, are shocked by this, because in their view not even God can dissolve a marriage.[50] The remainder of the first half of the novel depicts the emotional agony of the divorce, which Giovanna accepts because remarriage is the only solution to the problem of her material survival.

The second half of the novel opens in 1908. Giovanna is again a guest of the Porru family, and has been shopping, buying fabrics for her dowry. She is about to marry her wealthy neighbor, Dejas Brontu, whom she had considered marrying in the first place, before choosing to marry the penniless Costantino for love. This second marriage is to be limited to a civil ceremony (the Church would obviously not have recognized the divorce), and is to take place in utmost secrecy: the whole town is still scandalized by the divorce, and this wedding is "worse than the marriage of a widow."[51]

Giovanna's second marriage has divided the Porru family along the same lines Italian society itself was divided by the divorce question. Paolo, now a young lawyer, argues that couples should be free to unite and separate as they please (a clear reference to the much feared "free love" of the Socialists). His mother, on the other hand, still values the sacrament of religious marriage. For her part, Giovanna claims that she has to marry to survive. Up to this point Deledda presents the question of divorce rather evenly, with Paolo the progressive idealist, his mother the devout Catholic, and Giovanna the dependent woman, all representing different aspects of the question. For a moment it is possible to look forward to a conclusion that supports divorce as the lesser evil, an acceptable remedy *in extremis*, as the Liberals argued.

Deledda does not provide such a conclusion. Giovanna's second marriage is ill-starred, and even the mayor, whose job it was as representative of the Italian state to perform the ceremony, felt uncomfortable about it.[52] Married life for Giovanna becomes an inferno, as her position is little different from that of the family servant. The novel's conclusion is protracted and does not really offer a resolution. Eventually Costantino is released, old and pale. He returns home to Sardinia, but for at least two months cannot bear the idea of seeing Giovanna again, and decides to abandon the place forever. Finally though, he hears that she is alone in the house, and, full of terror, he goes to see her. At first she jumps up in horror, as the past she has "divorced" returns, but after the initial shock the couple embrace tightly and the novel ends.[53]

This ambiguous conclusion means that the novel is neither for or against divorce. Perhaps above all it laments the position of women in Italian society, for whom life independent of a husband was particularly difficult. Regardless of the author's intentions, the novel is significant because it represents an unusual female contribution to the divorce debates of 1902. It allows the full complexity of the question to be played out, revealing why the pro-divorce lobby had as difficult a battle as it did. Italians like Paolo Porru were in the minority; many more of them would have resembled the Sardinians who did not understand why marriage after divorce was not bigamy.

In contrast to Deledda's poetic, spare, and unpolemical work, the second novel about divorce published by a woman in 1902 took a very clear position. This was Anna Franchi's *Avanti il divorzio*, a largely autobiographical novel of which several thousand copies were sold.[54] Franchi's novel was as polemical and outspoken as Deledda's was subtle and literary, and it takes its place alongside Sibilla Aleramo's *Una donna* as a clear rallying cry to remedy the position of women under Italian marriage law. Franchi represents divorce as a symbolic step toward righting the many inequalities between women and men. The plot of *Avanti il divorzio* is a literary summa of the pro-divorce arguments made in parliament since the question first arose, complete with a chronological structure that faithfully follows the major parliamentary proposals for divorce from 1878 to 1902. It presents a detailed scenario of all the worst things that could happen to a married woman, including an arranged marriage to a violent man who gambles, has affairs, and contracts syphilis, as well as true love, an illegitimate baby, and the desperation of forever living in sin.[55]

The novel complements Franchi's more direct plea for women to unite in favor of divorce, *Il divorzio e la donna*, also published in 1902.[56] Franchi wrote that she was puzzled about why so many words were wasted over a law that was obviously needed. The most revealing aspect of the pamphlet is that it laments the number of Italian women who had risen against the introduction of divorce.[57] In Franchi's view this uprising was inspired by Catholic morality, but she suggested that Christian resignation offers little succour in a bad marriage.[58] Nor could she understand female Catholic activists who claimed that women must defend their "marital rights," because the only marital rights Italian women had were those of slaves.[59] Franchi's conclusion referred to that great defender of the true rights of women, Salvatore Morelli, and urged women to support the 1902 divorce proposal.

In the early twentieth century women with views like Franchi who spoke their mind were in the minority, and even though her novel sold well, her arguments did not have the ready audience that Catholics such as

Luisa Anzoletti had. To Franchi, Anzoletti's success was unfathomable. In fact the two women embody the Janus-faced nature of early Italian feminism, summed up by historian Laura Lilli's description of the early women's press as torn between ideals of liberation, and the myth of the "angel of the hearth."[60] Although the divorce question was not the preferred battleground of either camp, women's reactions to it do exemplify the fundamental division outlined by Lilli. Anna Franchi's writing epitomizes a radical feminism that regarded Italy's marriage laws as a cruel and antiquated trap for women. On the other hand, Catholics like Anzoletti saw indissoluble marriage as the principal guarantor of female security and honor.

Luisa Anzoletti was an indefatigable crusader against divorce. A poet and writer from Trento who had moved to Milan, she was one of the first Italian women to elaborate a Christian feminist theory.[61] In January 1902, just a few days before the king was to announce his government's intention to introduce a divorce law, she held a conference on the question in Milan. Soon afterward, her speech was published as an 81-page pamphlet entitled *Divorzio e la donna italiana*, dedicated to Leo XIII.[62] The occasion of the Milan speech was the first time that a woman had spoken out against divorce in public. Anzoletti later presented her ideas in Bergamo, Florence, Pisa, Pistoia, and other Italian cities.[63] Anzoletti therefore exemplified the Catholic women's activism that flowered after Italian unification and reached into strata of society that were never touched by the secular women's press.[64]

According to Anzoletti's argument divorce would be a desecration of the tradition of Latin dignity that stretches back two millennia. Yet she also argues that divorce should not be introduced in Italy because of the impetuous passion of the Latin race. Italians lack the "equilibrium, calm and regularity of the northerners that makes it easier for them to be moderate in their customs."[65] Hers is an argument that oscillates between seeing divorce as an insult to Latin dignity and indissoluble marriage as a bulwark against Latin impetuosity. Regardless, Anzoletti's view is that Italian women have a special role in maintaining Latin family traditions against the dangers of Latin impulsiveness, not only in the name of the family, but for the nation itself. Her advice to women in miserable marriages is to pray and pardon, that is, to sacrifice their own individual happiness in the name of an ideal.

Anzoletti's final flourish is an appeal to the patriotism of Italian women, urging them to be ready to sacrifice all, as they did during the Risorgimento, "for the liberty of their religious consciences, the defense of their children, the honor of women, the inviolability of the family, the fatherland and the Christian faith."[66] She may just as well have said that divorce would be an attack on Mazzini's famous formula of *patria, famiglia e libertà*. In this way, Anzoletti's speech perfectly represents the adaptability of the Catholic position. Its stand on matters such as indissoluble marriage was carefully represented as the defense of an ancient status quo that was an emblem of the Latin race, and more subtly, a metonym for the integrity of the *patria*. Thus the Church, united Italy's most serious traditional enemy, in defending its own traditions, was also becoming the *patria*'s strongest pillar.

Anzoletti's speech also represents the far end of a spectrum of women's opinions about divorce in early-twentieth-century Italy. At the opposite end is Anna Franchi, whose writings about divorce represent the most radical, and probably the least supported, extreme of the same spectrum. Grazia Deledda's novel represents the medium between the radical and conservative ends, with a story that contrasts the practical value of divorce with a poetic yearning for the ideal of indissoluble marriage. While each work was written from a woman's point of view, this spectrum of opinion corresponds with the more familiar range of opinions that had been expressed by men on divorce since Morelli's first proposal in 1878. Franchi's emphasis on individual liberties for women reinforces Morelli's entire argument, which observed that the liberal revolution of the Risorgimento did not have the same results for women as it had for men. Anzoletti's appeal to women to pray and pardon and think of Italy when marriage went wrong was a more explicit statement than ever of the conservative view that indissoluble marriage was a symbolic and fundamental sacrifice of individual sentiment in favor of society as a whole.

Divorce had been an open question in Italy since the unification had brought the peninsula together under a new political framework. When, after long debates, the question finally began to close in the early twentieth century, it was because it was easier to defend tenets like those expressed by Anzoletti than it was to argue that a few failed marriages warranted such a radical change as the introduction of divorce. The real question, though, is why Italian sentiment seemed more receptive to the former argument than to the latter. The closure of the divorce question provides an answer, and reveals as much about the limits of the Risorgimento's ideal of a separation between Church and state as any other single issue.

Zanardelli's Proposal in Parliament

When the young king Victor Emmanuel III had announced his government's intention to introduce a divorce law, the potential publicity triumph quickly faded. The more significant effect was to reinforce the already noteworthy division of opinion over the issue. Zanardelli and his minister for justice, Cocco Ortu, pressed on implacably, despite the lukewarm response to the king's words, and above all despite internal difficulties within the cabinet. Nevertheless, they did not rush: the draft of the law was not revealed until 27 November 1902, almost 10 months after the king's speech. When the law was finally presented, there was a noteworthy contrast between the government's hubris early that year and the rather timorous project that went by the ambiguous title of "Dispositions on the ordering of the family."[67] Ostensibly the reason for this title was that the draft contained two laws in one proposal. The first was a divorce law; the second was a proposal to allow paternity suits in cases of illegitimate birth.

The rationale for this decision to combine the two proposals is not clear, but it was almost certainly part of a strategic approach. One possibility is that Zanardelli and Cocco Ortu thought that the less controversial nature of paternity suits may have acted to minimize the controversy over divorce, or at least to deflect attention from it. Allowing paternity suits was one thing over which Liberals and the Church could agree; the former on the basis that it emphasized individual responsibility, the latter because it might act as a brake upon the passions. Indeed, proposals to change the law to allow such suits had been made in the past mainly by two of the conservatives who figured prominently in the battle against divorce (Gianturco and Filomusi Guelfi). Yet, the very first proposal of this type had been made by none other than Italy's prophet of divorce, Salvatore Morelli.[68] This was a clear indication that even figures who might disagree fundamentally on divorce could share the same opinion about paternity suits.

As it turned out, the euphemistic title of the draft did nothing to hide the fact that it contained the most controversial law in Italy. Newspapers tended to refer to it simply as "the divorce law,"[69] and divorce's opponents, unsurprisingly, were not hoodwinked at all. A few days after Cocco Ortu had circulated the draft of the joint law in parliament, the *Osservatore romano* published an editorial entitled "Two opposing ministerial projects in one single act," arguing that the two ideas were intrinsically contradictory. It described paternity suits as a "just reaction against liberal theories," while divorce represented the "rancid dregs" of such theories. In short, if the government's tactics were to try to cloak divorce in different garb, the editorialist of the *Osservatore romano* saw straight through them. As the closing line of the editorial put it dismissively, "They have put divorce arm in arm with a gentleman to make it, too, seem like a gentleman."[70]

The claim that permitting paternity suits was a reaction against liberal theories and a contradiction of divorce was not strictly true, and underlined the extent to which the Catholic organ associated liberalism with "free love." Both divorce and paternity suits were admitted in Britain,

Austria, Germany, Sweden, the German cantons of Switzerland, Finland, and many of the North American states. In Italy, one of the main articles in defense of both proposals was published in *Avanti!*, which saw the current prohibition of paternity suits as bourgeois hypocrisy. Pointing out that the civil code did allow these suits in rape cases in which pregnancy was contemporaneous, the article suggested that they should also be allowed in cases of adultery. The writer claimed that because adultery, a punishable crime, most often occurred between lower class women and bourgeois men, precisely those who could afford to maintain their illegitimate offspring knew they were safe from the obligation to do so.[71]

Even if the government had placed the divorce law arm in arm with a gentleman, in fact the new version of the law was itself gentlemanly, in that it was notably gradualist and conservative. The design proposed that divorce would be permitted in four instances: adultery, voluntary abandonment, physical violence, and a prison sentence of more than 20 years.[72] Completely absent was any element of mutual consent, which had been a feature of all prior divorce proposals in Italy through the admission of divorce after a certain period of personal separation. The exclusion of personal separation as grounds for divorce meant Zanardelli's and Cocco Ortu's 1902 design was the most restrictive divorce bill ever to have appeared before the Italian parliament. It stood in stark contrast with the Socialist proposal of the previous year, which had received the approval of an extraordinary majority of the parliamentary *uffici* that examined it.

In the event, Zanardelli's and Cocco Ortu's design was not conservative enough, and its fate was sealed in a comparatively short time. The week after the law was presented in parliament, the nine parliamentary *uffici* met to discuss the law and elect a commissioner to represent each *ufficio*'s majority view. Even though the composition of parliament was unchanged, the deputies making up the *uffici* had rotated since their vote in favor of the Socialist proposal, and they were now considerably less favorably disposed. By 2 December 1902, they had elected a commission that was against divorce by a majority of one; and two days after that the commission elected divorce's long-term enemy, Salandra, as *relatore*, or reporter, and Pietro Carmine, also anti-divorce, as its president. The election of a hostile commission, and two well-known opponents of divorce to its most important positions, was a final blow. This was a remarkable about-face in a very short space of time.

One of the main aspects of this change was simply the element of chance involved in which particular deputies were rostered to do duty as part of the parliamentary *uffici*. Nevertheless, it is worth examining some of the reasons that would explain why those deputies shied away from an issue that their colleagues of a year ago had so enthusiastically embraced.

In broad terms the discussions of the *uffici* do not reveal the strong influence of any major new arguments for or against divorce. Most deputies rehearsed arguments that would not have sounded out of place 30 years earlier. For example, Alfredo Bertesi argued that divorce was "highly moral," in response to Rizzo, who argued that even strictly limited divorce would be a direct attack on the sanctity of marriage.[73] However, several deputies did make comments against divorce that help to explain the swing against. There is a strong indication of a heightened sense of political sensitivity, suggested by the frequent mention of divorce's potential not only to divide married couples, but also the country. Pietro Carmine felt strongly that the deputies' deliberations should take account of the "contrary current prevailing in Italy." Francesco Aguglia said that the law was throwing the country into a bitter struggle, which alone was reason to reject it.[74] Raffaele De Cesare also focused on the potential political divisiveness of the law, claiming that the issue exacerbated cleavages even within political parties.[75]

Two deputies made comments about the disservice divorce would do to Italian women, suggesting that they needed the security of indissoluble marriage.[76] No one argued that divorce would be an advantage for women. Several made comments about the plight of countries that had introduced divorce. This was the period in which the "depopulation" of France had become a matter of concern in the Third Republic,[77] and Italian enemies of divorce liked to suggest that France's declining birthrate was directly linked to its galloping divorce rate. They also referred to France to show that even very restrictive divorce laws tended to be relaxed over time.[78] A further distinguishing feature of the debates was a regret that divorce and paternity suits had been placed under one law. Several deputies expressed unease about this, particularly those who were in favor of paternity suits but not divorce.[79] Given that in the end the entire proposal was rejected, the government's strategy effectively tainted another progressive law, and failed to introduce either.

If the deputies were preoccupied by one aspect of the politics of divorce above all others, it was the question of public opinion. The campaign initiated by the Opera dei Congressi in response to the Socialist proposal of 1901 had simply continued when that project was subsumed by the government's own draft for divorce. The campaign had been running for close to a year by the time the discussions in the *uffici* took place, and it had clearly succeeded in making a significant impact on the collective conscience of the deputies concerned. De Cesare, like Carmine, urged his colleagues to take account of the petitions, which he said were a clear indication of the country's views. Antonio Di San Giuliano felt that "public opinion" was important, and although he did say that discussion of such a large issue should not be stifled, he clearly thought the manifest opinion of several million petitioners should be taken into account.

Several deputies made counterarguments, the tenor of which was already familiar. For example, Ettore Socci, responding to a colleague's preoccupation with the tide of opinion against divorce, pointed out that anti-divorce sentiment was not a spontaneous expression, but one that had been coordinated from the pulpit and the confessional.[80] Similarly, Borciani rebutted De Cesare's claim that the petitions reflected the nation's view, saying that everyone knew how the petitions had been collected.[81] By pointing out that there had been much less agitation at the time of his and Berenini's proposal a year earlier, Borciani points to why the Catholic agitation weighed much more heavily on this set of *uffici* than it had done earlier. Even so, at least one deputy made an argument that harked back to those made by Morelli and Villa some 20 years earlier: Luigi Bianchi claimed that in certain cases legislators must direct, not follow, public opinion. True as that may have been, politics in Italy had changed significantly since the 1870s, and even if universal manhood suffrage was still a long way off, well-organized interest groups could certainly exert pressure on the minds of parliamentary deputies. Few issues made this clearer than the divorce question.

The idea that the pressure exerted on parliament by the unprecedented efforts of the Opera dei Congressi against divorce acted in a straightforward way may need qualifying. The divorce question tended to be a matter of conscience and personal conviction, with little permeability between *divorzisti* and anti-*divorzisti*. Although the pressure of public opinion came up more frequently in the deputies' discussions in late 1902 than it had in the past, this did not mean that previously pro-divorce deputies had suddenly changed their minds because they realized their constituents were against it. Frequent references to the agitations against divorce were most likely used rhetorically by deputies already against divorce.

The powerful agitation of the Opera dei Congressi in late 1902 was the most influential of a range of factors that contributed to a change of heart within the *uffici*, resulting in five voting against divorce, whereas only four voted for it. Another important difference was the lack of unity within the government, already demonstrated by reactions to the king's speech, and a growing sense that the divorce law was becoming something of a personal obsession for Zanardelli.[82] Combining the divorce law with a second law had exacerbated these divisions and obviously created a further sense of unease. And last but certainly not least, the personnel of the *uffici* had changed and now included some particularly powerful enemies of divorce. All these factors explain what might otherwise seem to be a mysterious reversal, from an eight-to-one vote in favor in 1901, to a five-to-four vote against divorce in 1902.

The majority against divorce already spelled doom for the law; the election of Carmine as president and Salandra as *relatore* would have made it difficult for those in favor of divorce to argue their case. The committee lost no time in pushing for the desired result, and the fate that awaited the law was obvious even at the first meeting, which three of the four favorable members did not attend.[83] It came as no surprise that at the next meeting, on 16 December 1902, the committee voted on article 1 of the divorce law, voting five to three to reject it.[84] Time revealed that this was a definitive vote that would bring to an end a period when *divorzisti* had been able to hope, with some justification, that Italy would soon have a divorce law. The significance of the vote was reflected in the reactions of the press: first, there was interest and a degree of perplexity over the fate of an issue that had seemed so close to victory just a year earlier.[85] Catholic newspapers evinced a sense that an enormous danger had been narrowly avoided. The *Osservatore romano* printed recent statistics about the huge number of divorces in France, and sighed that Italy had been saved from the same fate.[86] Soon, though, the newspapers lost interest as the issue fell into oblivion.

The most telling rejection of the divorce issue appeared in *Avanti!* two days after the commission's vote.[87] To mark the occasion, the editorialist[88] felt it was necessary to note that divorce was not part of the Socialist program. Finally, after two years of ambivalence, the position of the PSI had retreated from the enthusiasm inspired by the Berenini-Borciani proposal, and had returned to the austere, orthodox position that had been so clearly laid out by Anna Kulisioff in *Critica sociale* a decade earlier. Even though the idea of freer marriage relationships was obviously part of the Socialist vision, it was something that would follow naturally with the overthrow of the present system. To chase after "bourgeois reformettes" was not the business of true Socialists. Acutely, the editorial observed that the whole battle over divorce had provided conservatives with an excellent excuse to obtain their much-hoped-for alliance with the "priestly phalanx."

Salandra's Death-Knell for Divorce

The divorce issue was now a dead letter, and it remained only for Salandra to show why, and to foreshadow a new alliance in Italian politics. Salandra's *relazione* urging a vote against divorce is a brilliant, complex piece of argumentation, but its essence is an unalloyed conservatism. The clearest indication of this, and the greatest contrast to even his anti-divorce predecessors, is Salandra's open acceptance of the moral role of the Catholic Church in Italian national life. He carefully pays lip-service to notions of the proper separation of church and state by shaming the fathers of the divorce law for having provoked the nation to rally around the clerical flag. Yet the gist of his argument is not that militant Catholics have imposed their view on the majority of Italians, but that those forces took advantage of a broad sentiment that was ancient and cultural, not necessarily religious.[89] Nevertheless, Salandra welcomes the religious influence in the maintenance of marital indissolubility. He justifiably takes to task the fiction of "tempered indissolubility," begun by Villa, continued by Zanardelli, and uttered most recently and memorably by the king himself.[90] Instead, as a true conservative, Salandra urges not only the recognition of the influence of religious beliefs on Italian marriage, but their full acceptance, even as the state asserts its right to control the family.[91]

If it were clear that Salandra's voice was that of an alarmist and dated fogey, the *relazione* would have less significance than it really does. But his words sum up the emergence and increasing acceptance of a new climate of opinion in which such reforms were likely to wither. Soon after the report was distributed, Zanardelli's government fell, and the divorce bill that had been announced with such fanfare 18 months earlier went with it. This had been the fate of all its predecessors, but this, as time would tell, was a more definitive end for an era of attempted divorce reform. For this reason Salandra's *relazione* is a figurative conclusion to a long-running battle that began in 1878. Salandra's *relazione* explained why divorce could not be introduced in Italy: the cultural and moral values of the vast majority of the Italian people were still those of their religion, and Italian conservatives, even if they were more liberal, were not prepared to take steps to sever that fundamental nexus. The introduction of a divorce law would have symbolized a radical separation of Church and state that was fast becoming inexpedient.

Salandra's essay was far from being a voice in the wilderness. He was simply expressing a view that he knew had the tacit support of large numbers of Italians. Nor were his views a hangover from the past. Indeed, they were peculiarly avantgarde in that they foretold of a new truth: the Italian state and the Catholic Church would soon join hands, quietly, almost secretly, in an attempt to slow the progress of ideas for which divorce was the most alarming symbol.

Toward the Lateran Pacts

The dissolution of Zanardelli's cabinet in the autumn of 1903 took with it the best chances for divorce reform in Italy's Liberal era. After that, the political constellation of the nation changed subtly but fundamentally, with the result that the divorce question did not achieve the high profile it had had in 1902–1903 until more than 60 years later. The essence of that change was the entry of Catholics into the Italian political arena. The key figures behind the first steps of what Giovanni Spadolini referred to as the "silent reconciliation" between the Church and the state were two new leaders.[92] In August 1903 Pope Pius X succeeded Leo XIII, and in October 1903 Giovanni Giolitti became prime minister. Together, they represented the beginning of a new era in both Italian church-state relations and in Italian politics. Leo XIII had adhered to the spirit of Pius IX's *non-expedit*, prohibiting the involvement of practicing Catholics in Italian national politics, but his most famous encyclical, *Rerum Novarum* (1891), had been a rallying cry to the Catholic social movement to reinforce the Church's position against the spread of socialism. The Church's most important lay organization, the Opera dei Congressi, had existed since 1874, but received a significant ideological impetus from the encyclical. Its leaders, above all through their anti-divorce campaigns, learnt how to apply political pressure in Italy without entering into the political fray directly. No issue aroused more passion and energy among members of the Opera than divorce, and no example illustrated the latent political power of the Catholic machinery more clearly than the anti-divorce campaign of 1902–1903.

During the same years, the tendency for this latent power to fuel an open struggle among the factions of the Opera dei Congressi also came to a head as the national profile of the organization reached its peak. The internecine squabbles between the more liberal "Christian democrats," led by Romolo Murri, and the old intransigents, led by Paganuzzi, was a matter of deep concern for the newly elected Pius X. This was precisely because the Opera dei Congressi was showing the potential to be used by leaders like Murri as a means to create an autonomous Catholic political movement.[93] The irreconcilable nature of the disagreements between Catholics like Paganuzzi, who declared themselves "more papal than the Pope,"[94] and new leaders like Murri, who wanted the Church to abandon its intransigent separation from the state, threatened to undermine the unity represented by the pope himself.[95] For this reason, Pius X decided to dissolve the Opera dei Congressi in July 1904, almost exactly 30 years after its first congress. The movement that had so successfully opposed the introduction of divorce was thus removed at a stroke.

This did not mean that the introduction of divorce would now be easier. The vacuum left by the dissolution of the Opera dei Congressi had to be filled, and historians such as Emilio Gentile have suggested that from the outset, Pius X had already been prepared to turn a new leaf and overlook the *non-expedit*.[96] One of the most important impulses behind Pius X's need to secure a relationship with the Italian state had to do with contemporary developments in France. In the wake of the Dreyfus Affair, tactical errors committed by the French clergy had given great strength to secular forces. This resulted in several stinging defeats for the Church, culminating in the law of the separation of Church and state in 1905. Faced with such developments, Pius X felt the need to establish a more secure relationship with the Italian state, but he had to do it very delicately.[97] The result was an unprecedented search for an understanding with the less radical of Italy's "modern" political forces, the Liberals. And just as divorce had been a symbol of all that was iniquitous about the "old" modern Italy for the "old" Church of the Opera dei Congressi, so Giolitti's attitude to divorce would be the signal of a new potential for compatibility between Church and state in the twentieth century.

Giolitti's personal attitude to divorce was ambiguous, but his approach to the issue was that of a political pragmatist. This is best summed up by his brief mention of the 1902 draft divorce law, which he described dismissively as deriving from Zanardelli's "old convictions."[98] The comment made it clear that for Giolitti divorce was part of an era of ideals that were no longer expedient. While Giolitti never expressed disapproval of divorce in principle, he quietly let it drop from his government's program. For example, in December 1903, Berenini, the Socialist who had revived the idea of divorce in 1900, questioned Giolitti in parliament over whether divorce would be part of his government's plans. Giolitti's answer displayed his mastery of obfuscation. He replied that it was not only up to him, but when someone asked for it to be inscribed in the order of the day, at that point he would decide. As Spadolini concluded, Giolitti was certainly not going to foster a divorce law personally (as Zanardelli had done); instead he would allow the issue to be decided by "the wolves of the Chamber."[99]

Giolitti's position was an early but definitive blow for divorce reform. A second, closely related to the first, was provided by Pius X's initial careful steps toward tempering the ban on Catholic involvement in Italian national politics. This came in the wake of the general strike of September 1904, which, as well as giving Giolitti the opportunity to call elections at a time that would exploit the fear caused by the strike,[100] also inspired several influential Catholics to suggest to the pope that it would be an appropriate moment to reconsider the *non-expedit*. The fact that the general strike prompted Pius X to change the Church's official policy in relation to national politics has tended to reinforce the overall interpretation that the Church's hostility to socialism was the main motive for the pope's actions.[101] Although this interpretation is unarguable in a broad sense, at a more detailed level it has obscured the critical role of the divorce question in the Church's reversal of attitude toward Italian national politics in the early twentieth century.

In the first place, it is clear that on several occasions concern over the divorce question gave rise to unprecedented interventions by the Church in the political sphere of the nation. This was evident as far back as 1881, when Leo XIII had made a personal request to the leader of the Opera dei Congressi to mobilize its forces against Villa's proposal for divorce. It was much more explicit in 1901 when Leo XIII made the first direct papal appeal to the Chamber of Deputies, asking them not to permit divorce to enter Italian law. Further evidence of the special role of divorce in encouraging the lifting of the *non-expedit* can be seen in the figures who influenced the pope in his decision. Chief among these was the very conservative Bishop of Cremona, Monsignor Geremia Bonomelli.[102] Bonomelli had also been a lifelong enemy of divorce, and had published a virulently anti-divorce pamphlet in 1881.[103] In 1904 he was one of the main figures urging the pope to consider allowing Catholics to participate in Italian national politics, as a counterweight to the "subversive and irreligious" elements in parliament.[104] Although he did not mention divorce specifically, it is abundantly clear that for the Church hierarchy divorce legislation represented the most extreme example of irreligious subversion.

The first relaxation of the *non-expedit* occurred relatively simply and quickly. On the government side of the arrangement was Giolitti's minister of foreign affairs, Tommaso Tittoni. He arranged for one of the most influential Catholic organizers, Paolo Bonomi of Bergamo, to urge the pope to allow Catholics to stand for election and to vote. The pope gave tacit permission for a limited suspension of the *non-expedit* by telling Bonomi to "do what your conscience dictates."[105] As a result, at the elections of November 1904, for the first time in the history of modern Italy, two Catholic deputies were elected. As might have been expected in the wake of a general strike, Giolitti also found himself leading a much more conservative Chamber than that elected in 1900.[106]

The first breach of the *non-expedit* was as significant for the future of divorce reform as the breach of Porta Pia had been for the pope's temporal power in 1870. After 1904 the "wolves of the Chamber" increased in number, and Giolitti knew he could rely on them to keep anticlerical proposals such as divorce at bay. What the new political constellation meant for reforms like divorce was not the complete elimination of the issue, but its effective disappearance from the corridors of power. Giolitti had famously said that the church and the state should be like two parallel lines that never met. Even if under Giolitti's reign they did not meet, after 1904 those two lines were much closer together, and more importantly, they were on a converging path.

After 1904 no proposal for a divorce law was made for a decade. The question came up from time to time, but it did so in a way that ironically underlined the increasing particularity of Italy's position. In 1902, the Hague Convention, to which Italy was a signatory, had clarified the law requiring member states to recognize divorces granted by other members. This highlighted Italy's old problem of "foreign divorces," by which Italians with substantial means could take the citizenship of another country, obtain a divorce which the international law forced the Italian civil authorities to recognize, and then regain their Italian citizenship. In November 1905, a law was passed in Italy that made it harder for individuals to use this loophole.[107] But those who could afford to stay out of the country long enough to make it appear that they had not adopted foreign citizenship for the sole purpose of evading Italy's marriage laws still managed to obtain divorces. The practice was much decried by conservative jurists.

In the Chamber of Deputies the question of divorce was mentioned rarely, and usually with a resigned tone, with the deputies lamenting the Church's increasing grip on Italian politics. For example, the Socialist Enrico Ferri, responding to the king's speech opening parliament in 1904, drew attention to the absence of plans for social reform, and in particular claimed that the dropping of the previous legislature's divorce proposals was a sure sign of the warming relationship between the Church and the state.[108] In 1909, again in response to a royal speech, the reformist Socialist Claudio Treves claimed that the disappearance of the divorce question showed that politicians were fearful of Catholic power in parliament.[109] In 1913, the Socialist deputy Ubaldo Commandini asked the government whether it had any plans to introduce a divorce law. Giolitti, still prime minister, replied uncharacteristically clearly that he did not feel the majority of the country was yet ready for such a reform.[110]

Why this sudden clarity? The answer is that the election of 1913, the first since the introduction of almost-universal manhood suffrage, had been preceded by a secret pact between the president of the Catholic Electoral Union, Count Gentiloni, and a large number of individual deputies. The arrangement, which came to be known as the Gentiloni pact, promised Catholic electoral support for liberal candidates in return for certain policy undertakings. Among these, obviously, was the prohibition of divorce.[111] When Giolitti had claimed that Italians were not ready for divorce reform, what he really meant was that divorce was no longer politically feasible.

The Gentiloni pact was the culmination of a process that had begun in 1904, and represented the irreversible entrance of Catholic electoral power into the Italian parliament. The arrangement had still been confidential when Giolitti had rejected Commandini's suggestion that divorce be included in the government's program, but when it became public some time later, Giolitti was forced to resign. The fact that Antonio

Salandra succeeded Giolitti as prime minister is sufficient to explain why Commandini's subsequent proposal for a divorce law, presented to the Chamber on 2 February 1914, was not taken up by parliament.

If the tacit political arrangement of 1904 represented, as Emilio Gentile has claimed, an initial search for an understanding between the Church and the state,[112] the Gentiloni pact of 1913 represented a prenuptial agreement. In both cases, it was understood that divorce was to be excluded. In the revolutionary tumult of the years after World War I, the divorce question did manage to make a brief appearance in the form of another proposal by a Socialist, Guido Marangoni. The whole debate was set alight again, but the proposal was blocked by the early closure of the parliamentary session.

Two years later, Mussolini came to power. Despite an attitude in favor of divorce expressed in the manifesto of 1919, the fascists also had to reckon with the Church, and their initially radical ideas were soon overtaken by a social ideology that reinforced the primacy of the family in Italian life. Mussolini's government provided an early indication of its approach by eliminating a divorce loophole that been opened by Italy's acquisition of the provinces of the eastern Adriatic after World War I. Under the law that applied when these areas had been part of the Austrian Empire, non-Catholic couples could obtain a divorce. After these areas became part of Italy in 1919, but before Italian civil law was officially extended to them, there was a brief period during which a divorce could be obtained in one small part of Italy. However, Mussolini's minister of justice, Aldo Oviglio, hastened to remove this possibility by extending the Italian civil code to these provinces. In his summing up of the matter in parliament, he justified the imposition of indissoluble marriage law on a region where divorce had been possible for more than 100 years by asserting that all Italians regarded divorce with "repugnance."[113] The elimination of the possibility of divorce in the Adriatic provinces was to be the last time divorce figured in the deliberations of the Italian government before 1946.[114]

From its earliest stages, the fascist approach to the family was little more than a reinforcement of the Catholic family ideology that had permeated Italian society so strongly in the nineteenth century, and that the liberals had failed to modify. Indeed, when the prenuptial agreement of 1913 became a formal union between Church and state in 1929, with the Lateran Accords, one of the Church's greatest victories was that the civil marriage law of 1865 was overturned and control of marriage was once again returned to its canonic bosom.

In this way, by 1929 marriage law in Italy had arrived where it began, and the defeat of civil marriage, which had once been one of the symbols of the Risorgimento's promise to make Italians in a more secular mold, in fact underlined the failure of that project.

Remaking Italians? From Fascism to the Republic, 1929–1964

During the two decades of Mussolini's rule, fascist policies attempted to remodel the Italian family into a microcosm of his vision of the ideal state: hierarchical, fecund, and indissoluble. The fanfare surrounding the myriad fascist family initiatives signaled a clear break from the studied disinterest of the Liberal regime regarding the family, but the fascist approach was less a break with the past than an exaltation of certain values that had long permeated the fabric of Italian society.

Before fascism, these values, above all of marriage and the family as restraints against individualistic sexual urges, had found their most enduring champion in Antonio Salandra, who always claimed his inspiration was ethical rather than religious. Under fascist rule, however, these same notions, more loudly trumpeted, resonated in harmony with Catholic ideals of the family. For all the limits of the fascist-Vatican *connubio*,[1] as well as the limits of fascist efforts to turn Italian families into fasces,[2] it made sense that the regime was happy to share its labors toward this vision with the Catholic Church through the Lateran Pacts. As far as divorce was concerned, of course, the Lateran Pacts were a tomb for a debate that had long since been a dead letter.

The ignominious demise of Mussolini's regime in July 1943 and the subsequent 20 months of German and Allied occupation left the Italian state morally and materially at its lowest ebb of the twentieth century. Perhaps ironically, this ebb provided a clean slate onto which reemergent democratic forces inscribed their visions for the renaissance of democratic society.

One of the most important features of this new democracy was the elevation of women to the same civil stature as men. In early 1945, women obtained the vote for the first time in Italian history, and they first used it in the historic elections of 2 June 1946. On that day, the Italian people decided that Italy should become a republic, and they also determined the composition of the Constituent Assembly. Women won 44 seats, or 6.3 percent of the total.[3] Among the tasks to be tackled by the Constitutional Assembly was the redefinition of the relationship between the institution of the family and the new state.

In a nation lacerated and divided, the cultural heritage and ideal of the indissoluble family once again took on the quality of a powerful metaphor of national integrity across the political spectrum. Even if all political forces might agree that the Italian family required a new model, one in which, as with the new state itself, men and women should find themselves on an equal footing, ultimately the culture of indissoluble unity became the most important aspect of the family as a social metaphor. The ideals of Italian family unity and indissolubility remained symbolically crucial in the formative years after the collapse of the fascist regime in 1943, and they would not be seriously questioned again until the mid-1950s.

The Family in the Republican Constitution

After 20 years of families living in service to the state, including five years of war and two of foreign occupation, Italians were more than ready to repossess their private lives by the end of World War II. *Noi donne*, the fortnightly magazine of the Unione Donne Italiane (UDI), the women's section of the Italian Communist Party (PCI), expressed the relief of being able to return to the bosom of family life, on the cover of its first postwar issue. This shows two women juxtaposed, one in military uniform holding a large rifle, the other seated, breast-feeding a baby nestled in the crook of her arm. The caption says "Having dropped our guns, we will reconstruct our families."[4] This image of a return to "normality" suggests that even among the most militant and progressive Italian women, the normality they had fought for, and wanted now to embrace, was the right to build their families in peace.

At a political level, commitment to the family as an essential building block of postfascist Italy provided a common foundation across the political spectrum from Left to Right, helping to bridge fundamental ideological differences. The Christian Democrats (DC) had no need to stake their claim as upholders of family unity, but the Left and the PCI in particular found it politically expedient to underline their commitment to the family as the fundamental unit of society. In the Italian context one of the most effective ways to do this was to exclude any interest in radical measures such as a divorce law.[5]

Palmiro Togliatti, leader of the PCI, laid out his party's lack of such an interest clearly in a speech to the first conference of women Communists, held in June 1945. He emphasized the need for the family to be relieved of the feudal vestiges still found in many regions of Italy. But above all the family was to be a "centre of elemental human solidarity," and for this reason, Togliatti declared, the PCI was against anything that might impinge on the ideal of family unity.[6] Togliatti's speech prefigured his party's commitment to renew and modernize the family, particularly in relation to gender parity. But he also made explicit reference to a nation shocked and torn to pieces and the consequent need to defend family unity.

The constitutional relationship between the family and the new state was to be worked out by the first subcommittee of the Constituent Assembly in late 1946. The entire assembly would then vote on the wording put forward by the subcommittee. Much of the committee's time was spent not in heated ideological argument—there was clearly broad agreement on the "preeminent and fundamental nature" of the institution of the family in Italian society—but in trying to work out a written formula to express the relationship between the family and the state that could then form part of the nation's constitution. In general terms, the Communists proposed a formula that recognized the family as the basis of the material and moral prosperity of the nation.[7] The Christian Democrats were concerned to inscribe the family with an ethical element, as a "società naturale," a natural society antecedent to the state.

Ideological differences appeared over two main questions, the first of which concerned the gender relationship at the heart of the family. In line with a new commitment to legal equality between men and women, expressed in the granting of women's suffrage in September 1944,[8] the subcommittee's first article stated that marriage "is based on the principle of moral and legal equality of the spouses." Some Christian Democrats felt uneasy about this formula, not wanting to do away with the notion of the head of the family, which, "by the very nature of the family itself, must be the father."[9] During the discussion, Giorgio La Pira requested that the preeminent position of the father in relation to the children be made clearer, suggesting the formula "first among equals."[10] Ultimately the subcommittee agreed on the principle of conjugal equality,[11] even if the civil law still accorded married women inferior status.

The second point of disagreement, over whether the indissolubility of Italian marriage should be enshrined in the national constitution, proved more difficult to resolve. By 7 November 1946, Camillo Corsanego (DC), with the help of Aldo Moro (DC), had framed the following article: "The law regulates the legal condition of the spouses, with the aim of guaranteeing the unity of the family."[12] The Left interpreted this as an attempt by the

Christian Democrats to provide a constitutional block against the future introduction of a divorce law. Though some months earlier Togliatti had declared the PCI's commitment to avoiding anything with a whiff of divorce about it, Nilde Jotti objected to this formula and put the question up for discussion by the whole subcommittee.[13]

Togliatti was anxious that the question of family indissolubility should not become cause for disagreement. Once again he took pains to underline his own conviction that a divorce law would be unnatural and even dangerous for Italian society under the present circumstances.[14] La Pira insisted that divorce should be barred by the constitution, arguing that this is what the Italian people wanted and expected. Perhaps alerted by Togliatti's reference to the "present circumstances," La Pira declared that he could never accept a formula that might permit a future legislator to introduce divorce into Italian law.[15]

The issue gave rise to a deadlock within the committee. The Left, led by Togliatti, was firmly convinced that it was unnecessary and inappropriate to mention marital indissolubility in the constitution. The Christian Democrats insisted on a full discussion of the original formula, and by the end of the day on 13 November 1946 the subcommittee voted to retain its wording, with nine votes in favor, two against, and three abstentions.[16] This decision echoed Pisanelli's emphatic exclusion of divorce law from the civil code of Liberal Italy in 1865. Now, in 1946, it looked as if divorce law would be even more formally barred from Italian law than ever.

There remained, however, the hurdle represented by the collective opinion of the Constituent Assembly, which appraised the proposals of the first subcommittee in April 1947. By this time the wording of the first article was "The Republic recognizes the family as a natural society based on indissoluble marriage." This formula reveals a double victory for the Christian Democrats, to whom the ethical construct of the family as a natural society had been important early in the discussions, and the indissolubility of marriage paid homage to Catholic values. But the inclusion of the word "indissoluble" disturbed the Left of the Assembly and sparked a debate on the relationship between marriage, the family, and Italian society, which lasted a full week.

Despite the fact that "indissolubility" genuflected to the spiritual values of the Christian Democrats and the Church itself, the overall willingness of the Left to compromise in the interests of national unity became evident in the general debate. For example, Francesco Saverio Nitti and others felt strongly that bringing the whole question of family law into the constitution was unnecessarily divisive, and should have been left to a discussion of the civil code.[17] Christian Democrats such as Ennio Avanzini pressed the metaphorical relationship between the united family and the nation further. Picking up on Nitti's plea, Avanzini argued that if the salvation of the nation lay in unity and indissolubility, then "the same law must be applied to the family."[18]

The debate on the family sparked by the question of its indissolubility went right to the heart of the relationship between the family and the state, as it had done during the preparatory work of the subcommittee. However, it did not divide the Assembly down clear party lines, and in fact gender divisions were equally significant. For example, Togliatti and other Communists, as well as Socialists such as Pietro Nenni, consistently maintained that details of family unity were not appropriate issues for a national constitution. By contrast women such as Nadia Gallico Spano, of the PCI, was pleased to see the institution of the Italian family protected by the constitution. She and others saw this as a safeguard against the sort of interference in the family that had been perpetrated by the fascist regime—interference that had weighed particularly heavily on women. Spano argued that the silence of Italy's previous constitution, the 1848 Statuto, on the family, had allowed the fascist regime to humiliate women and the institution of marriage through the demographic campaign and other attempts to influence private behavior. Spano claimed, like many others, that only a new, democratic model of the family could contribute to the renewal of Italian life.[19]

Maria Maddalena Rossi, also a member of the PCI, claimed that it was vital for the constitution to mention the family. She argued that fascist rule had reinforced particularly antidemocratic characteristics within the family, and it was the task of the new constitution to foster and safeguard the new democratic family, exemplified by the parity of husband and wife. Rossi disagreed with the constitutionalization of marital indissolubility, however, claiming it would prevent future legislators from addressing the problem of illegitimate families. Rossi's allusion to the potential utility of dissolving marriages in the future went beyond the official position of the PCI, but her contribution to the debate underlined the need for the constitution to protect gender parity within marriage, which she saw as a democratic safeguard for the nation as a whole.[20]

While the Communists argued about whether the family should or should not fall under the purview of the constitution, a little-known Socialist deputy finally took a fateful stand against the constitution describing marriage as "indissoluble." On 23 April 1947, Umberto Grilli proposed an amendment to remove the adjective.[21] The proposal seemed to come out of the blue and caused a small uproar in the Assembly, but Togliatti took the opportunity to reaffirm that marital indissolubility was not a matter for the constitution, and announced that his party would support Grilli's proposal. Grilli's amendment to the constitution passed by a tiny margin: 191 deputies voted to retain the word "indissoluble," while 194 voted to remove it.[22]

This vote meant that at least a divorce law was not constitutionally banned in Italy, but it could not hide the fact that the constitution ultimately reflected the hegemony of a Catholic conception of the family, and indeed the unprecedented influence of Catholicism in the new Italian Republic.[23] Nothing illustrated this better than the continuation of the Lateran Pacts through their incorporation into the constitution in article 7, voted by a large majority of deputies to the Constituent Assembly, including the Communists.[24] Overall, the institution of the family emerged from the discussions of the Constituent Assembly reinforced as a fundamental institution of the Italian Republic. As Anna Rossi-Doria has emphasized, a pervasive familist culture set the tone of Italy's postwar years, much reducing the value of many of the rights promised to women in the constitution.[25] Arturo Carlo Jemolo, an eminent legal historian and himself a Catholic, felt that the family had become a "capsule of steel" within Italian society, to the detriment of other institutions.[26] It was this capsule of steel that the postwar divorce debates would have to prize open.

Matrimonial "Outlaws" and *Piccolo Divorzio*

After the resounding victory of the Christian Democrats in the 1948 election, the Cold War set the tone for European politics in the austere 1950s. It might have been thought that in a country like Italy, divorce would have fallen off the political agenda. Jemolo wrote that divorce was never mentioned in public in the 1950s,[27] but that ceased to be the case from 1954, when Luigi Sansone, a lawyer and Socialist deputy, took it upon himself to agitate for the introduction of an Italian divorce law. Sansone was a native of the southern region of Puglia, but he had lived in Naples since his university days. He had been a Socialist since the age of 18 and a member of the first democratic junta in Naples after the collapse of fascism. He was elected to the Italian parliament as a deputy in the 1948 election, and again in 1953. He became a senator from 1958.

Sansone's interest in a divorce law came from his personal knowledge of the harmful effects of indissoluble marriage, rather than a politically motivated desire to introduce secular laws. This is clear from much that Sansone wrote and said about the issue, beginning with an important article that appeared in *L'Europeo*, a liberal-democratic weekly newspaper, in October 1954.[28] The article, written by Sansone himself, shortly before he presented his proposal for divorce to parliament, coined two phrases that were destined to reappear countless times in the ensuing 20 years.

The first, *fuorilegge del matrimonio* (matrimonial outlaws), referred to those unfortunates whose marital status had become irregular, usually due to the formation of a new relationship after a first marriage had broken down.[29] Sansone calculated that at least 40,000 Italian marriages failed each year, with most men and women proceeding to new relationships. Whether the individuals concerned sought official recognition of their separation or not, the new relationships were technically adulterous, and the children they produced were illegitimate and could never be made legitimate. It is little wonder that in the 1950s, the divorce question was a particularly frequent subject of letters addressed to Italy's "agony" columns.[30] Sansone claimed that at least four million Italians were "outlaws," whether they were adults living in relationships the state did not recognize, or the offspring of such relationships. It was a simple concept, and as a dramatic expression of the disparity between Italian family law and the realities of society, it captured the imagination of many commentators.

The second concept introduced by the article was Sansone's proposed remedy for these outlaws: *piccolo divorzio*, or "little divorce." Sansone later claimed that the epithet was applied by the editors of *L'Europeo* because of the very restrictive nature of his proposal.[31] The phrase stuck, probably because it was both ironic and accurate. The irony lay in the effective impossibility of having degrees of divorce. The accuracy lay in the fact that Sansone's proposal was so extraordinarily conservative that it was barely a divorce law at all.

It provided for divorce under the following instances: when a spouse had received a prison sentence of 15 or more years; in cases of attempted spouse murder; after abandonment or consensual separation lasting 15 or more years; in cases in which one spouse had an incurable mental illness and had been in an institution for five or more years; and if a foreign spouse obtained a divorce ruling from a court outside Italy. By way of contrast, the last proposal for divorce to get a serious hearing in Italy, the one made by Giuseppe Zanardelli in 1902, had provided for divorce after one year of separation if there were no children, or three years with children. This difference underlines the caution with which Sansone felt he needed to proceed, and adds credence to Rossi-Doria's claim about the familist culture of 1950s Italy.

Nevertheless, Sansone assembled familiar arguments in an attempt to persuade his parliamentary colleagues. He began by presenting a survey of the history of discussions about divorce in parliament, from Morelli's proposal of 1878, to Grilli's constitutional amendment of 1947.[32] He presented statistics on personal separation, which had almost doubled in the previous two decades, from 4,523 in 1933 to 8,152 in 1952[33] (these figures were of course far lower than his famous estimate of 40,000 marriage breakdowns per year). Finally, Sansone argued that Italian marriage laws were out of step with the rest of the world. He stressed that in Europe, divorce was available in all nations except "Franco's Spain," Portugal, and the "feudal Republic of Andorra." He stressed that the Catholic populations of France, Belgium, Hungary, Poland, and Switzerland all had access to divorce, and nowhere had the availability of divorce damaged the "sense of family"; on the contrary, violent crimes within families occurred infrequently.[34]

The proposal fell on deaf ears in parliament, and it never reached the crucial stage of parliamentary discussion.[35] The same fate befell a subsequent proposal, which Sansone presented jointly with Giuliana Nenni to the Senate, in June 1958. Although both Sansone's attempts to introduce a divorce law failed in parliament, his initiatives, including his book on matrimonial outlaws, marked the cautious beginnings of what was destined to become a battle for divorce.

The opening and broadening of the debate is illustrated in several ways. First, the publication and subsequent notoriety of Sansone's own book, urging the introduction of a divorce law, suggest that a significant number of Italians recognized a need for a divorce law. Prompted by the news of Sansone's plans for the law, many Italians who found themselves in situations of matrimonial illegality wrote to the deputy to tell him their story, urging him to press parliament on their behalf. Sansone chose 36 of these letters to form the core of his book. He tried to let the situations of ordinary Italians make the argument that some sort of divorce law was necessary.

The letters revealed a variety of typical cases of people whose lives had been ruined by the lack of a divorce law. In keeping with the spirit of extreme caution in Sansone's proposal, all his cases represented situations of long standing. For example, one man, married in 1915, returned from fighting in World War I to find that his wife had taken up with another man. He began to live with another woman, hoping that Guido Marangoni's divorce proposal of 1920 would be made law. His wife emigrated to Brazil and had not been heard of for 34 years. He now had seven illegitimate children by the woman he had lived with for 35 years.[36]

The disturbance of war provided a common theme. One woman had married an American solider at the age of 15. He had disappeared three days later, leaving her unable to marry again for the rest of her life. This also raised the problem of cases in which partners who lived outside Italy had obtained a divorce elsewhere, while the partner left in Italy remained married according to Italian law. For example, a man whose wife had lived in San Francisco for 30 years, and had obtained a divorce there, was still married to her, according to Italian law.[37]

Another strand of the pro-divorce argument addressed through these letters was the inadequacy of Church annulment. One woman had married in 1936, but separated by mutual consent four months later without the marriage having been consummated. Her letter claimed she had tried to get an annulment but could not afford the 100,000 lire to pay for the first two hearings. Even though in theory she could have availed herself of the legal aid for cases heard in Rome, the fact that the process could take four years made it an intimidating prospect.[38] Such examples were evidently only the tip of a large iceberg, and part of Sansone's argument was that there must have been thousands of cases in which a divorce law would have regularized situations that were grotesquely unfair to one or both marriage partners. Sansone's proposed legislation, his *piccolo divorzio*, had been designed to address such extreme cases.

Sansone's parliamentary proposals may have fallen upon deaf ears, but there were signs that the question was coming to life at a broader level in the mid-1950s. For example, in 1956, the publishing house Laterza invited the magistrate Domenico Peretti Griva to write a short book on divorce and the family. Peretti Griva's introduction makes it clear that the context of the invitation was a sense of the decline of the integrity of Italian families as they faced the social and economic exigencies of postwar Italy. For the most part the book is a rehearsal of the history of divorce from the French Revolution, and a survey of legislation elsewhere, but in the final chapter the author makes his own proposal for an Italian divorce law, with adultery the principle factor.[39]

A more significant signal that the echo of Sansone's proposal was larger than it may have seemed is the fact that the story was taken up, albeit with a slight delay, by one of the most important women's magazines of the era, the PCI-sponsored *Noi donne*. In the 1950s, *Noi donne* still represented the curious combination of ideals of women's liberation and traditional notions of womanhood that Maria Casalini has noted for the founding period in the 1940s.[40] For example, in January 1954, articles on the Miss Italy competition, lavishly illustrated with starlets, held a prominent position in one number,[41] while a sober enquiry into maternity and motherhood among Emilian sharecroppers showed the more dedicated side of *Noi donne*'s editorial character.[42] In July 1955, some eight months after Sansone's proposal went to parliament, *Noi donne* presented its first article in favor of a divorce law.[43]

In early 1957, *Noi donne* went much further, with a series of six articles dedicated to the question of divorce. Revealing Sansone's influence, the first article is simply entitled "I fuorilegge del matrimonio" and it summarizes his book's arguments. The first lines introduce Italian women to the essence of the debate, announcing that although Italy's civil and religious laws proclaim marriage as indissoluble, there is a great gulf between the proclamation and the reality. It explains that the gulf is populated by millions of unfortunates who stand outside the law because their marriages have effectively ceased to exist, but in ways that cannot be recognized by the law.

The article also provides a few egregious examples of the anomalies of Italian marriage law. One was exemplified by a woman who claimed she had been forced to marry a Polish soldier in 1945 to save her father from the accusation of being a fascist spy. The couple had had a civil wedding rather than a Church ceremony. The soldier then went to the United States, and was never heard from again. Under canon law the woman would, in theory at least, have been able to obtain an annulment, since she had been forced into the marriage. The Italian civil law had no provision for an annulment on that basis and the young woman could never disentangle herself from the absent Pole and marry again.

An Italian man who had married a French woman in France in 1927 found himself in an even more absurd situation: in 1948 his wife obtained a divorce under French law and married someone else. Yet under Italian law her first husband remained married to her, and was also the legal father of the children from his wife's subsequent marriage. *Noi donne's* introductory article underlines the cautiousness of Sansone's proposed step, which aimed not so much to introduce "the principle of a true and proper divorce," but to legalize certain extreme cases in which reality and the law simply did not match. In this way the outlaws would be brought into the fold and Italy itself would be brought into line with nearly all nations of the world.[44] This article was followed by five others, each covering the divorce question from a different angle. The second featured a roundtable discussion with six participants covering the political spectrum. Further articles consisted of letters from readers, all detailing awkward matrimonial situations that a divorce law would have solved. The concluding article, entitled, "The salvation of marriage is also in 'little divorce' " was a plea to parliament that Sansone's proposal be discussed and approved, in the cause of healing the institution of marriage.[45]

As always, the supporters of a divorce law, whether parliamentarians or editors of a popular, Communist-supported women's magazine, or its readers, talked of divorce not as a revolution in the private sphere, but a small adjustment that would allow the law to take account of social reality when a marriage broke down. Since the 1870s this argument had failed to overcome the resistance of an influential anti-divorce bloc composed of an inextricable alliance between social conservatism and Catholic principles, which saw the idea of divorce, however restricted, as a dangerous breach of a fundamental principle.

By the late 1950s, however, arguments for divorce had begun to circulate in Italian society at a more popular level than ever before. Sansone's proposals, though they failed in their immediate intent, came at a time when Italian society had embarked on a process of restructuring that would result in changes of outlook and mentality. The broader discussion launched by Sansone's notion of divorce and exemplified by *Noi donne*'s series of articles showed that the divorce taboo had started to give way. The institution of the Italian family, though not by any means ready for revolutionary dissolution, was at least up for serious and sustained rethinking, not just by the cultural and political elite, but by the Italian people themselves.

The "Economic Miracle"

Increasing sensitivity to shifting ideas about marriage and the family structures around it was part of Italians' awareness of the enormous transformations wrought by their nation's rapid economic development. *Noi donne*'s pioneering articles on divorce in 1957 provide early examples, and the magazine, for obvious reasons, remained at the forefront of popular publications advocating recognition of social change, particularly as it affected gender relationships. Another early example from *Noi donne* came with a more general inquiry on the state of modern marriage in Italy, published in the summer of 1959. Entitled "Is marriage the tomb of love?" the article consisted of interviews with married couples living in public housing in Bologna. The respondents had been married from as few as 2 years, to as many as 50. The editorial introduction made it clear that an awareness of the "new demands" of daily life motivated the enquiry. It gave away the conclusion before the interviews even started, claiming that a "new mentality" was taking root in Italy, one which struggled against entrenched prejudices and the daily difficulties deriving from a situation that was in many ways still backward.

In essence, the "new demands" had to do with urban life and its expensive complexities, the cost of supporting children through many years of schooling, the need (and right) for women to work outside the home, and the shift in gender relationships that this entailed. The article aimed to portray at the grassroots level the way Italy's economic miracle both required and fomented a change of mentality in relation to marriage and the family.[46] Although this article did not mention divorce specifically, the accumulation of such inquiries documenting change at the everyday level helped to make sure that the sociological language of transformation became familiar to many Italians.

By the late 1950s, this sense of change at the level of family structures was not just a figment of the imagination of Communist journalists insisting that structural shifts must lead to superstructural modification. An equivalent sense of impending mutation in marriage and family life is also evident in Catholic women's associations at about the same time, though the thrust was to contain rather than promote such mutation. For example, in 1958 *Cronache*, the monthly bulletin published by the largest Catholic women's association, the Centro Italiano Femminile (known as CIF), warned that the family could disappear if it were not carefully fostered. As proof it announced that the Russian family "had ceased to exist" because the education system kept children away from their parents day and night. According to the writer, under the Soviet system the state had effectively taken the place of the family, which in any case had been watered down by divorce law. The only function still carried out by the family was the production of new citizens for the state.[47]

The task for Catholic women in Italy was to make sure that economic modernization and the ideas it brought with it did not effect a similar transformation of the Italian family. On the one hand, CIF's writers expressed confidence that Italian women believed above all in family values ("not because of their traditionalism, but because of a tradition of spiritual maturity").[48] On the other, by 1960, they were beginning to acknowledge that economic development had placed crisis-level pressures on families.[49] In their view the crisis had been brought about by the large-scale entry of women into the paid workforce. While accepting and even embracing the benefits paid work brought to women, Catholic feminists resisted the left-wing view that such work was the sole condition for the emancipation of women, arguing that a woman's role in the family had no substitute.[50]

What Communist women interpreted as promising, though demanding economic and social developments, would continue to be a "crisis of the family" for conservatives and Catholics. The crisis was incipient in the late 1950s, but at this stage for Catholics, both women and men, a divorce law remained a grotesque spectre that epitomized the soullessness of Communist society. For Communist women, the difficulty in speaking about divorce was an example of the sort of taboo that prevented discussion of the way economic forces affected modern Italian women and their families.

Fèfè, Rosalia, and Angela

While the debate between Catholic and Communist women regarding the family was significant, it had a fairly restricted audience, and focused on the urban regions of the north. One of the most popular landmarks of the emerging debate about divorce in Italy was produced by a man who stood outside the Catholic-Communist political division that marked so much Italian cultural production of the 1950s and 1960s. It also shifted the focus of the debate away from the industrial north to a mythical southern Italy. This was Pietro Germi's *Divorzio all'italiana*, a major feature film released in 1961,[51] which did much to place Italy's divorce question before a world-wide audience.

Set in Sicily, at the center of the plot is Baron Ferdinando Cefalù (Fèfè), played with almost palpable ennui by Marcello Mastroianni. The principle cause of his boredom is Rosalia, his cloyingly attentive wife, played by Daniela Rocca. The object of Fèfè's escape fantasies is Angela, a nubile cousin from a more successful branch of the same family. Fèfè yearns to be rid of his wife and to wed Angela. With divorce out of the question, he looks to other means, and hits upon the idea of a murder, committed under the mitigating circumstances of finding his wife *in flagrante delicto*. This will allow him to count upon the clemency of the court under section 587 of the criminal code, which imposed a minimal sentence of three years' imprisonment for the murder of a spouse or daughter committed in a state of rage caused by offense to personal and family honor.[52]

Fèfè embarks upon an elaborate scheme to contrive a situation that will justify his uxoricide. Rosalia has eyes only for Fèfè, so it is not easy, but eventually he succeeds in reigniting his wife's affections for an old flame, the artist Carmelo, by commissioning her portrait. Carmelo's solicitous kindness to Rosalia and her response to it are nothing if not platonic, but Fèfè makes sure he publicizes the growing affection between the "illicit" couple. The climax of the film features an ironic twist of gender roles, because Fèfè's hand is forced by Carmelo's outraged wife, who shoots her husband in a genuine (but unwarranted) fit of jealous passion. Fèfè rather half-heartedly follows suit and shoots Rosalia—though in line with the film's lightheartedness the shootings occur unseen, on an idyllic promontory where Carmelo had decided to paint Rosalia's portrait.

Fèfè is sentenced to just under three years in jail for the murder of his wife, during which time Angela waits patiently for him, and eventually, they are married. The final scene amusingly undermines the prospect of many years of married bliss for Fèfè by turning the whole motive force of the film on its head: on their honeymoon, as Fèfè settles down to embrace his sunbathing wife on the deck of a yacht, the camera moves slowly down her half-naked body, coming to rest on her toes, as they engage with the toes of the handsome young sailor at the wheel of the boat. This ironic final frame ensures that the film's ultimate message is that subterfuge begets subterfuge.

Divorzio all'italiana had great success both in Italy and internationally, and it placed some of the anomalies of Italian law before a very large audience for the first time. The question of divorce itself, slumbering since 1947, had been reawakened by Sansone's 1954 parliamentary proposal, his 1956 book, and the second proposal with Giuliana Nenni in 1958. These events had clearly animated a significant number of people for whom the issue was politically resonant, as well as the many thousands of individuals who had personally fallen foul of Italy's stringent marriage laws. The question had even trickled down to the thousands of readers of *Noi donne*, but until *Divorzio all'italiana*, it had not reached a truly mass audience.

Yet, it is important to point out that the film's appeal lay in its subtlety. It denounced certain aspects of Italian law (the provision for "crimes of honor" even more than the lack of a divorce law), but it was not didactic. In fact, by choosing Sicily as a setting, Germi made a film that was as much about regional customs as it was about national laws. Apart from the relentlessly stultifying atmosphere of Sicilian "immobilism," the point is made clear by a clever intertextual device: at one point the people of Agromonte pack the local cinema to watch *La dolce vita*, made the previous year by Federico Fellini. Doubly playful since that film's leading role was also played by Mastroianni (he is not seen in the clips shown in *Divorzio all'italiana*), the effect is to emphasize the distance between Rome's sweet life with its sexual license, and the simple folk of a Sicilian village.[53] Yet Germi, who was from Turin, loved Sicily and Sicilians, and *Divorzio all'italiana* is far from being a facile portrait of the customs of Italy's southernmost people.

It makes more sense to see Baron Cefalù as an extreme incarnation of Italian men in general. This is suggested by comments made by one of Germi's friends, who claimed that the director saw Italian men as incapable of liberating themselves from customs that no longer matched reality, because of their emotional complexes and religious and atavistic cultural roots.[54] Nor, of course, was the film only about Fèfè and other men. Germi had a passionate interest in the subordinate position of women in Italian society. This is exemplified by Rosalia, whose feathery shadow of a moustache marks her as stereotypically southern, and who is even more a victim of seemingly unshakeable customs than her husband. Yet the younger Angela is endowed with powers of agency that herald the demise of traditional gender hierarchies in Italy.

The film's universal appeal is attested by its critical acclaim and success with audiences not just in Italy, but around the world. Among Anglophones, the title itself became inextricably associated with the absence of a divorce provision in Italian law. Historians of the cultural turn have no difficulty with the idea that cultural products make revolutions, particularly when it is possible to point to a growing number of such products that might amount to a cultural humus. In Italy in the early 1960s the humus in favor of introducing a divorce law was still shadowed by the cultural weight of tradition, but Germi's film was all the more visible a milestone in an otherwise unpromising landscape.

Noi donne, which regularly reviewed films in a paragraph, devoted four pages to *Divorzio all'italiana*, illustrated with stills from the movie. It is salutary to remember that the film, which in retrospect appears charming and innocent, was a pioneer in Italy in 1961. Twice in four pages *Noi donne*'s reviewer referred to Germi's "courage" in dealing with the divorce question. This is a reminder that divorce remained an emotive taboo.[55] In Italy, perhaps more than anywhere else in Western Europe, the 1960s represented a decade in which the clash between the new realities created by extraordinary and sudden economic advancement and the customs portrayed in *Divorzio all'italiana* reached a high point.

The Early 1960s: A Weakening Taboo

There seems little doubt that throughout the 1960s the Italian taboo against divorce weakened. Prophetically, the chief judge of Trieste referred to this taboo in his speech at the opening of the judicial year in 1960. Justice Grieb exclaimed that the Italian fear of the word "divorce" puzzled him, particularly since it was clear that bonds that had become insupportable dissolved of their own accord, regardless of the limitations imposed by the law. It was unusual for a public official to mention divorce at a public ceremony, and Grieb's words rippled through the press. But Grieb had perhaps sensed that the divorce question, raised timorously in the 1950s, would become clamorous in the 1960s.[56]

The new openness with which divorce would be discussed in this decade was also foreshadowed at the 1960 congress of women lawyers, who met that year in Turin. Another signal that the divorce question was once more breaking into the Italian public sphere was the publication in 1960 of a special number of the journal *I problemi di Ulisse*. Each issue of *Ulisse* provided a close analysis of a contemporary problem, and the number on divorce presented four articles by legal experts, either practicing or academic lawyers.[57] The choice of authors underlines that in an Italian context the divorce question was still the domain of legal specialists, rather than that of sociologists and other social scientists. In other words, in the public and official sphere at least, in 1960 divorce was a question for legal Italy, as it had been since 1860. What happened in the 1960s, and relatively quickly, is that family questions, including divorce, began to be part of a wider public discussion. The divorce question genuinely became part of the discourse of real Italy.

In January 1960, the women's section of the leadership of the PCI prepared a position paper on the family that coyly affirmed commitment to the principle of divorce. The document, which remained unpublished, reveals a painstaking effort to maintain the coherence of what had been a fundamentally ambiguous position of the PCI in 1946–1947, when the constitution had been written. The 1960 document proclaimed that the PCI had been opposed to the constitutionalization of indissoluble marriage but maintained the validity of not pressing for a divorce law during that delicate postwar phase. The explanation for that position, from the perspective of 1960, was that the economy had excluded the majority of Italian women from positions of financial independence. In other words, economic conditions had not been sufficiently mature for the introduction of a divorce law in Italy.

Thirteen years later, the paper argued that millions of people had fallen outside the scope of the law, and in such cases a divorce law would provide the only true remedy. This position, clearly derived from Sansone, also foreshadows the more general position of the PCI in relation to the divorce question: while it seemed unlikely to instigate the introduction of a divorce law, the party would support the initiatives of others, on the basis that reality had already thrown up situations in which a divorce law made sense.[58]

If this position in some ways continued the PCI's anxieties about the political inexpedience of the divorce question, it can also be read as part of a more open campaign to educate Italian women about the changing reality of Italian family life, and in particular, the position of women within it. This commitment becomes all the more visible in *Noi donne* in the early 1960s, when it published an increasing number of articles that broached previously taboo subjects such as divorce and contraception. *Noi donne*, read by hundreds of thousands, if not millions of women, played a key role in breaking such taboos and preparing the ground for a broader social debate in the later 1960s.

A key theme in *Noi donne*'s coverage of questions relating to the family and women was a determination to uncover disparities between the realties of contemporary family life and the outdated laws that governed it. For example, in March 1960 its pages proclaimed the "the pill" had arrived in Europe. The four-page article's headlines contrasted the illegality of promoting contraception in Italy (it had been a crime under fascism and remained so after the advent of the republic) with a reality that made it more and more necessary that parenthood should be carefully planned. For *Noi donne*, the pill represented the progress of science against the obscurantism epitomized by fascist prohibition of the discussion of contraception.[59]

The sense of social transformation conveyed by this early article on the pill continued throughout 1960. In May the magazine presented the results of on-the-spot interviews held with men and women on the streets all over Italy. Asked what they thought was "urgent for women," the answers selected for publication naturally all pointed toward women's liberation: access to work, economic independence, greater equality within marriage, and a divorce law. These responses obviously reflect *Noi donne*'s editorial position with more certainty than they do the feelings of the Italian population, but at least large numbers of readers were being given an impression of a rising chorus proclaiming the need for change in the realm of the private sphere in Italy.[60]

The following month a series of more sustained articles covered women's contemporary concerns. Again, the theme was the structural transformation of society and its implications for women. The third article in the series "Non è più lo stesso cuore" (It is no Longer the Same Heart), focused on family relationships. A boxed section in larger print highlighted that with the increase in women's employment, "a cyclone has passed over the habits, customs and affections of the Italians." The article proper begins with the claim the family used to be a pyramid with the father at the top, but today, the family is no longer so, because both mentalities and hearts have changed. The author seized on claims from all around that the family was in crisis, suggesting that the negative connotations of the word "crisis" reflected conservative nostalgia for male authority. In the writer's view, what nostalgic conservatives had dubbed a crisis was in fact simply a welcome and overdue erosion of that authority, leading to the need for an earnest search for a new framework for the modern family.[61]

Such expressions of the changing nature of the family, though not strictly about divorce, became more and more common from the early 1960s. Eventually they coalesced into a new world view for large numbers of people, in which divorce was a necessary and logical corollary of the new concept of the family. A month later the idea of a salutary crisis appeared again in an article about women's work. Claiming that the entry of women into the workforce had thrown "this old society into crisis," the article forecast growth toward an attractive future, which would show that this "crisis" had been decisive in the transformation of Italy.[62] Essentially this was a Marxist view of history, but emptied of cataclysm, one in which the decisive revolutions took place on a personal scale.

The high point of *Noi donne*'s 1960 crusade to heighten awareness of contemporary family problems appeared in the form of a three-part, in-depth inquiry in the summer of that year. The first article's dramatic illustration shows a modern kitchen with a woman head-down on her ironing board, while her husband stands with his back to her. The scene bespeaks a quiet desperation that the article claims must not be ignored simply because the majority of marriages may not be touched by such desperation. It recounts several contemporary cases in which marriage problems have resulted in suicide or murder, reporting on cases from Milan to Palermo. To these tragic incidents the author adds the specter of those whom the newspapers never mention and the statistics never register: those who suffer infernal marriages in silence, as if they were buried alive. This was the reality that had to be confronted in any discussion of divorce.[63]

The crisis of the family that had been such a feature of *Noi donne*'s view of 1960 was in fact nothing more than the disparity between the political establishment's inflexible approach to the civil code and a society that was in the process of transforming itself through economic development. What would become evident over the first half of the 1960s was a widening public sense that these transformations contrasted with the governments' apparent aversion to addressing them in terms of the law. At the end of 1960, *Noi donne* introduced a new regular rubric, "Tribuna per voi" (The Court for You), offering legal advice that drew attention to the need for the nation's legal arenas to be more receptive to the needs of ordinary people. Maria Bassino, a lawyer, presided over this column, which gave legal advice each fortnight. Unsurprisingly, the first edition of the new rubric dealt with the family, which the title described as a "burning issue."

The feature published six letters that show women caught between two different worlds: on the one hand, the possibilities offered by work opportunities, notions of equality and the like, and on the other, static customs and an unresponsive legal system. For example, one woman had been offered a teaching post in a distant town. Her husband had the possibility of transferring his job but would not countenance a move. He told his wife it was her duty to be where her husband chose to be. Another dispute concerned a husband imposing his choice of occupation on a couple's son, one with which the mother did not agree. These cases illustrate the tensions that could arise when the civil code granted the husband authority in such matters, which effectively overrode the notions of marital equality enshrined in the 1947 constitution.

Naturally, there was also a letter about the hardships created by the impossibility of divorce: "A.M." of Turin wrote that her husband had emigrated to the United States, where he had divorced her and married someone else. A.M., who described herself as still young and eager to marry again, was condemned to a sort of premature widowhood by Italian law, which insisted that she was a married woman. A.M. was one of those thousands of matrimonial outlaws—and all Maria Bassino could do was promise to dedicate a future edition of "Tribuna per voi" to "this pressing question."[64]

Luigi Sansone's notion of matrimonial outlaws had sunk into the popular imagination in Italy and provided a structure onto which to place the many clamorous examples mentioned in the press. It was inevitable that eventually this structure would one day be seen as a key to the interpretation of a widespread crisis afflicting the Italian family. By 1961, it was evident that discussing the family in crisis was no longer the rhetorical ploy only of a progressive, partisan women's magazine. In March, the *Osservatore romano* revealed that the Catholic hierarchy was deeply concerned about changes that were afoot, through a series of four articles on the family. The overall theme of the first of these was the weakening of family ties in modern society.[65]

A later article decried the deleterious consequences of the Reformation, whose "rationalism" and "materialism" had led to profound changes in the concept of marriage in many European nations. This was clearly a reference to the widespread introduction of divorce by the late nineteenth century. Though in Italy in 1961 marriage laws were still protected from the modern incursions of rationalism and materialism, the overall tenor of the articles is a battening down of the hatches against the most iniquitous law ever to threaten marriage: divorce. The articles amounted to an announcement that the Church would continue its "great battle" against this tendency, aiming to correct it with a "restoration" of the family based on indissoluble marriage.[66] It is evident that at the highest levels, the Catholic Church acknowledged the way modern life's changes seemed to threaten family ties, but at this stage its response was to present a reinforcement of the Catholic conception of marriage as the best antidote.

The Church clearly still saw Italy as one of the last bastions against modernity's incursions and expressed a determination to protect it. This was not, in effect, a gauntlet, but it was certainly a battle line. The intransigent defense of indissoluble marriage expressed in the *Osservatore romano* responded only to the vaguest sense of incipient change. No one had proposed a divorce law in parliament for several years, and even then, Sansone and Nenni's proposal had thudded comfortingly against the sandbank of parliamentary procedures. Only *Noi donne* regularly mentioned the word in its pages. In a way then, the *Osservatore romano* was shadow-boxing. But between 1961 and 1965 the shadow of divorce law would take on a more physical form.

The fact that public concern was widening is shown by a series of no fewer than 15 articles appearing in Rome's *Messaggero* newspaper in the summer of 1961. Gathered under the general title of "An inquiry into the Italian family," in fact the series as a whole places emphasis on the idea that Italy, with some singular features, was a slightly tardy participant in a crisis that is evident throughout the Western world. The main theme is an alarming increase in the number of failed marriages, which in Italy had moved from perhaps 3,000–4,000 per year in the 1930s, to perhaps

50,000 per year more recently. But as the author rightly pointed out, the real figures were unclear, because without a divorce law there was no real motive to officialise a separation. The overall question behind the articles was the extent to which the transformation of women and gender relationships underlay the increase in marital problems.[67]

A series of cartoons accompanied the articles, illustrating their main points. One in particular sums up the issue that had been the subject of *Noi donne*'s first legal advice column: the effective inequalities between men and women in marriage. Frame one shows a couple standing next to a yardstick, announcing that husband and wife are equal. Frame two shows the man looking menacingly at his nervous wife, holding up a book almost as large as he is, entitled *Law*. The caption announces that the husband is "more equal" than his wife. The final frame shows husband and wife taking off in different directions, little strokes of friction forcing them apart. The caption here seems to sum up the friction between real and legal Italy: "With the passing of time, this de-facto inequality creates a series of artificial tensions that aggravate the crisis rather than dissolve it."[68] Yet in their entirety these articles are not partisan or programmatic. They simply alerted a wide audience to a process of change in family life that seemed to be inevitable, irreversible, and international.

The Political Background

Although the reemergence of the divorce question had autonomous dynamics, related principally to the economic transformation of Italian society and the increasingly visible crisis of the family, the beginnings of broad discussions about divorce in both legal and real Italy also occurred in the context of a changing political atmosphere in the early 1960s. As Paul Ginsborg has shown succinctly, the atmosphere changed for Italy at an international as well as local level, with the most important local shift being an effective thawing of relations between the Christian Democrats and the left-wing parties.[69]

At an international level, the inauguration of the first Catholic president of the United States, John F. Kennedy, initiated a warmer era in the Cold War, and contributed to the potential for dialogue between the Catholic center and the Socialist Left of Italian politics. Another factor was the brief but influential papacy of John XXIII (1958–1963). John XXIII steered the Church away from the conservatism of his predecessor, Pius XII, and nurtured dialogues between Catholicism and diverse religious and ideological beliefs. The clearest indication of this was the second ecumenical Vatican Council, opened in October 1962. In his opening address,

John XXIII urged that the Catholic Church should meet the needs of the modern world, rather than "merely reiterating the vetoes of the past."[70]

These broader developments provided a background, rather than the motive force, for the beginnings of the Center-Left coalitions that governed Italy through the 1960s, but these also owed much to the electoral exigencies of the DC and the PSI themselves. The delicacy of the new political status quo was in fact far from propitious for major reforms in Italian society. For this reason it would be mistaken to assume that a new international constellation represented by the Kennedy administration and a new local constellation represented by a succession of Center-Left governments in Italy in the 1960s made the introduction of a divorce law any more likely. It can even be argued that the opposite was the case, as both major parties of the Left, the PSI and the PCI, became increasingly conditioned by their relationship with the Christian Democrats. If the progress of these relationships was like walking on eggshells, this partly explains the minimal reforms achieved in Italian society by the Center-Left governments. Anything that threatened extremely delicate coalition governments was avoided, and this is why deeply divisive political issues such as the divorce law did not form part of any party program.

In an historical sense this was no different from several other junctures in Italian politics: in 1903 Giolitti had dropped the divorce question as inexpedient; in 1923 Mussolini had abolished a long-standing divorce law in the newly acquired eastern provinces of Italy; in 1946 Togliatti had been at pains to underline how little interest the Communists had in introducing a divorce law. The emergence of the Center-Left in Italian politics from the early 1960s initially, at least, simply repeated this well-established pattern. The divorce question in Italy was ultimately resolved despite, not because of, the nature of Italian politics, and as at other times in the previous hundred years, initiatives on such issues would largely be taken by individuals.

The political inertia on the divorce question in the early 1960s was pithily summed up in an article presented in a monthly broadsheet entitled *Il Divorzio*. The broadsheet was subtitled *Monthly for the reform of personal and family law*, and had been founded in 1958, the year of the divorce proposal by Sansone and Nenni. As the Center-Left coalitions emerged in the early 1960s, the publication assessed the chances of the divorce question being pressed by a political party. The article was sparked by speculation in the Socialist newspaper *Avanti!* that the Liberals too were pro-divorce. *Il Divorzio* asked rhetorically "too?—but which other parties were also pro-divorce?" Apart from the Radicals, who were plagued by internal dissent, which other party dared declare itself pro-divorce these days? Certainly not the PSI preoccupied as it was with the success of its "five-year plans" for a coalition with the DC. Briefly mentioning the other parties, the conclusion claims that there was still no sign whatsoever of anyone in parliament with anything new to say about divorce. Moreover, the problem of reforming family law in Italy would only be soluble once the Christian Democrats realized that they did not speak for all Italians and ceased being a confessional party.[71]

In 1962, *Il Divorzio* had good reason to be pessimistic about the likelihood of the divorce question making headway in parliament. The same number gave even more coverage to the opening of the Second Vatican Council, suggesting that the pomp and circumstance of the opening sessions confirmed the Church's attachment to the notion of temporal power. It also noted that in relation to the family and marriage the Council seemed to be preparing to confront the "errors that threaten [marriage] directly, such as divorce, and indirectly such as Malthusianism and artificial fertility." In other words, in relation to marriage and reproduction, *Il Divorzio* only perceived continuing intransigence from the Church, not the familiar notion of Vatican II representing a new attitude.[72] Yet, within three years, the pessimism of *Il Divorzio* in 1962 would begin to look as if it belonged to another era, as the prospects for the introduction of a divorce law brightened considerably.

The Need for Reform: Gradualist or Radical?

The question was, who had any plans to confront the crisis of the family? *Il Divorzio* had acknowledged that the Radicals were the only party who dared declare themselves in favor of divorce, but it had dismissed them because of their internal disagreements. *Noi donne*, on the other hand, had spotted the Radicals early on as potential allies in the cause of women's liberation and revision of family law. The magazine gave extensive coverage to the Radical Party's second congress, held in Rome in May 1961. The party was founded to "defend the laic state and the social progress of the country." Thanks to the efforts of a relatively large number of women in the upper ranks of the group, one of the final motions at the congress concerned a commitment to equal rights regardless of sex, and reform of family institutions.

At a programmatic level, due to a motion presented by Maria Adele Michelini Crocioni and Anna Garofalo, this translated to the reform of family law, and the abolition of three articles of the criminal code: 553, which prohibited "propaganda" about contraception; 559, which made adultery a crime; and 587, which made "honor" an extenuating factor in certain crimes. More broadly, the motion aimed to introduce a divorce law, as well as opening all areas of public employment to women. In short, the Radicals had a program by which they wanted to make Italian society secular and modern. Of all their plans, it was the initiative for a divorce law that was to assure the party its place in history.

However, between the inauspicious early 1960s and the more propitious later years of that decade, something had to change. *Il Divorzio* had portrayed a political environment whose attitude to divorce ranged from timorous indifference to vociferous hostility, and this seems an accurate appraisal. How was it that this climate, characterized by London's *Times* as one in which there was "not the remotest chance that [. . .] the introduction of divorce will be seriously considered," [73] changed to one in which divorce was perhaps the most exhaustively debated issue of the day?

The hard political ground described by *Il Divorzio* and the *Times* softened because of a series of uncoordinated and almost imperceptible changes, like the slow advance of a new season. At an almost subterranean level lay the continued rapid development of the Italian economy and the structural changes that entailed: the internal migration of Italians from south to north, and from rural areas to the cities; increasing industrialization and urban concentration; and increasing participation of women in the workforce.

Evidence of broadening concern about the future of families in society had been growing for some time. The family became a frequent theme of lawyer's conferences, not only groups of women lawyers, but also, for example, a meeting of senior magistrates in 1963—noteworthy enough for it to be reported in the press as far away as London.[74] Whereas the theme of the family had been evident on an occasional basis in the very early 1960s in newspapers as diverse as the *Osservatore romano* and *Il Messaggero*, it received more specific coverage, and from the specific point of view of the protagonists of change—women themselves—in women's journals.

Popular and progressive women's journals such as *Noi donne* placed themselves at the forefront of a campaign to promote such reconsiderations, but there was concern at the Catholic end of the political spectrum as well. For example, the newly named organ of the Catholic women's organization, *Cronache e opinioni* (Chronicles and Opinions), was as convinced of the existence of a crisis in the family as its Marxist sibling. Catholic women were just as keen to encourage a reevaluation of the relationship between the family and society as left-wing women; and though the latter were keen to discuss divorce, while the Catholics were keen to reaffirm the value of indissolubility, both agreed that Italy's civil code must be "modified for the needs of today."[75] Though the women of the PCI would have been unlikely to agree with the Catholic Gioia di Cristofaro's assertion that the family was "a means of sanctification,"[76] both movements aimed to marshall women in the direction of greater dignity, freedom, and equality.[77]

Yet the two camps watched each other's representatives constantly and closely. When in 1963 the new pope, Paul VI, addressed the Sacra Rota Romana, the famous ecclesiastical court charged with adjudicating matrimonial causes, *Noi donne*'s editor breathed a sigh of relief because finally her belief that the family was in crisis had been recognized by at least one voice of authority. Up until now, wrote Benedetta Galassi Beria, it had been as if the crisis were some sort of mirage, perceptible only to a few cranks like the women of the PCI, and quite invisible to "serious, responsible people." Paul VI's acknowledgment of the rising number of marriage failures was a sign that at last influential people recognized the validity of *Noi donne*'s claims. Galassi Beria had no qualms in agreeing with Paul's insistence on the need to rediscover moral values in an increasingly materialistic society, though in her view the value of the pope's message was not his solution, but his recognition of the problem.[78]

From about 1963 onward the general trend would be toward wider discussion of the crisis of the family, though no one knew where it would go, because no one spearheaded the debate. It simply surfaced with greater frequency in ever increasing circles. The name of the problem was the crisis of the family, but its solution as yet had no name. One end of the political spectrum proffered moral values. Another offered the promise of law reform—but both felt uncertain. Between these extremes lay public opinion and seemingly incommensurable worldviews.

What is clear is that the Italian people were becoming more and more familiar with the terms of a debate on marriage and the family. If these ideas were most persistently discussed by partisan (albeit popular) women's journals, by 1964 it was obvious that sensitive subjects like divorce were no longer taboo, and were being taken up by magazines with a more general readership. For example, in 1964 the best-selling *Annabella* surveyed its readers about what they would have requested from the Vatican Council. Of the 38,000 replies, 80 percent would have liked a review of the Church's stance on birth control (which most women practiced already), and three-quarters expressed themselves in favor of a divorce law.[79]

The significance of these views from a large number of ordinary Italian women was grasped by *The Times* in London, which had confirmed in 1963 that a divorce law in Italy was unlikely in any foreseeable future.[80] A year later *The Times* reported that on questions of the family "opinions had been changing rapidly in the past few years," and its attention to the subject was evidence of the scale of debate in Italy by 1964.

If the press, and particularly women's magazines, evidence rapidly changing opinions on a broad scale in the early to mid-1960s, mention should also be made of the influence of television. Television at this stage was not necessarily a molder of opinions, but it certainly helped to make the outside world more familiar to Italians who may not have had the chance to travel. Television had been introduced in Italy in early 1954, and at the end of that year there were a mere 80,000 sets in the whole country. By 1960 there were over two million, and by early 1964, the figure was well over four million.[81]

The television took its place alongside other consumer durables such as refrigerators, cars, and washing machines, indicating that Italy was rapidly assuming some of the same social and economic contours as other Western nations. But the television had a cultural effect that the washing machine could not have: by 1964 it had introduced to large numbers of Italians the pleasures, dangers, and oddities of life elsewhere. An example of the significance of this was given in one of the tenth-anniversary programs, which showed how an elderly southern woman, who had never ventured more than a few miles from her town of birth, and had never seen the sea, for example, knew all about life in New York City because she had seen it on television.[82]

If *The Times*' claim that Italian women had been "emancipated by television" was exaggerated, the implication that television would be an agent for the propagation of new ideas for large numbers of Italians (as elsewhere) was entirely accurate. What remained to be seen was for how long Italian family law would resist the gradually rising pressure, and when change did come, whether it would be gradualist or radical.

8

Loris Fortuna and the *Divorzisti*, 1964–1970

By the end of 1964, the possibility of divorce in Italy began to be imaginable, but only in a shadowy, unformed way, as one senses land from a ship that is approaching the coast. Perhaps this change is only perceptible in retrospect—often in history certainty about a coming event is acquired only after it has happened. Yet, the year 1964 does seem to mark a change, the beginning of more concrete hopes. One publication from that year signals this change. This was a book by the president of the National Association of Magistrates, Mario Berutti, entitled simply *Il divorzio in Italia*. The title itself was arresting, since there was no divorce in Italy. The book put a divorce law back on the agenda, and it was not mealy-mouthed about the reasons for the absence of a divorce law in Italy. As Berutti put it, there was no such law "because the Catholic Church does not allow it."[1] Berutti's book, written for a wide readership, sounded a battle cry against the "anachronistic institution of indissoluble marriage,"[2] and against the institution that stood in the way.

Berutti provides an account of the bizarre side-effects of indissoluble marriage, mentioning the "ingenious frauds," the "grotesque compromises," and "hideous crimes" that constituted the reality behind the Italian people's apparently blithe acceptance of marital indissolubility.[3] He was not at all surprised by the recent success of Germi's *Divorzio all'italiana*, which he admired greatly.[4] Berutti left no stone unturned in an attempt to reveal the absurdities that could result from Italian marriage law. He decried the fact that many "outlaw families" created after separations, lay completely outside the law, even though they were tolerated by public opinion.[5] "Surrogate divorces" such as annulments attracted the usual criticism, the essence of which was that not all people were equal before an ecclesiastical court.

Even worse were the "unilateral" divorces, in which a foreigner obtains a divorce from an Italian in a foreign court, but the Italian spouse remains married as far as the law in Italy is concerned. No names were mentioned but the scenario was likely to bring to mind one of the most famous contemporary cases, in which Sophia Loren and Carlo Ponti had found themselves on trial for bigamy in 1962, and cleared their names only several years later. Overall, the book is charged with a new determination and a more direct sense of the root of Italy's problem. Berutti's book of 1964 made the sotto voce approach of *piccolo divorzio* seem timid and antiquated.

Although by 1964 most Italians could agree that reforms were needed, leftists found it much easier to embrace the idea than Catholics did. For Catholics the notion of historical determination sat uncomfortably with the idea of an institution they argued had reached perfection in the form of indissoluble monogamy under the tutelage of Christian teaching. This discomfort became evident whenever the question of reform arose. For example, in an article on new aspects of the family in the Catholic women's periodical, *Cronache e opinioni*, the fundamental argument was a defense of the immanent indissolubility of the family. This was always a platform, a bottom line, and any reforms had to proceed from this principle.[6]

In the context of the ongoing debate about the family, the voice of a young Socialist deputy calling for a divorce law in parliament at the end of 1964 might have had no more significance than any of the myriad ideas circulating at the time, and still less than the many ill-fated proposals for a divorce law that had come and gone during the past 86 years.[7] But there was a difference between even the 1950s, when Luigi Sansone had presented the most recent of those ill-fated proposals, and 1964. The terrain for a debate on divorce had been tilled by discussions about the crisis of the family, and a large number of Italians were ready to listen to, and participate in, a debate on divorce. This, combined with the singular determination of the young deputy and his motley allies, transformed the divorce issue from a vague mélange of ideas about the Italian family into a concrete program.

Loris Fortuna

Loris Fortuna was born in Brescia, Lombardy, in 1924. A child of the fascist era, by 1944 he was a fully fledged partisan operating in Friuli, the easternmost part of Italy, which was only acquired in 1919. Fortuna was captured and sent to a concentration camp in Bavaria. After his release he returned to

Italy, joined the PCI, and became one of the leaders of the Friuli workers' movement; he was one of many who left the PCI after the Soviet invasion of Hungary in 1956. He subsequently joined the PSI, and in 1963 he was elected as deputy for the seat of Udine.[8]

When Fortuna presented what would become his famous proposal to introduce a divorce law in early October 1965, the time was particularly ripe. The first example of this, low-key but persistent, was the climax of *Noi donne*'s long campaign for state intervention in the crisis of the family. Throughout the summer of 1965 *Noi donne* ran the longest series of articles yet presented on this subject. It began on 17 July with a questionnaire on the family, but subsequent articles focused exclusively on divorce.[9] On 25 September the last of the six extended articles appeared. Each one involved discussions with women in different parts of Italy, and the overall impression was that many Italian women, whether they had a personal interest in divorce or not, were more than ready to welcome a revision of the law regulating marriage.[10]

As if to underline that Italian women were not alone in their interest in the reform of family law, the summer of 1965 also witnessed a second popular magazine taking up a pro-divorce position. This was *ABC*, a weekly tabloid-style magazine aimed at men, published on Sundays, and as irreverent as *Noi donne* was earnest. Superficially (particularly on the cover) it was a titillating publication that seemed determined to take on the asphyxiating moral rectitude represented by the Italian establishment. It was iconoclastic, very male gendered, and a peculiar mixture of bawdiness and political commitment. As a self-appointed agent of modernity in what it decried as a backward nation, one of its hobby horses was divorce, revealed with the launch of a new rubric entitled "Lettere di separati" (Letters from the Separated) in September 1965.[11]

If the interest shown by *ABC* and *Noi donne* suggests a ferment of concern about family law "from below," a chance event "from above" also helped to draw public attention to the question of family problems in Italy. On 19 September, as the second Vatican Council entered its closing phase, Elias Zoghby, an Egyptian bishop, proposed that the circumstances giving rise to annulment of marriage be broadened, for example, to offer more protection to an innocent spouse who is the victim of abandonment or adultery.[12] Elements of the press seized upon Zoghby's suggestions as a sign that the monolithic anti-divorce position of the Catholic Church might finally be cracking.[13] After inadvertently becoming the darling of Italy's pro-divorce lobby, Zoghby explained that he had never meant to question marital indissolubility, but rather had wished to draw attention to the Orthodox Church's different interpretation of the sacred texts on marriage.[14]

Whatever Zoghby had meant, his words were taken as a sign by more Italians than ever that the divorce question had finally matured. It was in this context that Loris Fortuna presented his proposal to introduce a divorce law to parliament on 1 October 1965. The proposal was entitled "Cases for the dissolution of marriage." Fortuna dwelled for more than a third of his explanation of the proposal on its historical precedents, from Morelli to Sansone, but he also stressed the recent social development of the country, and the need to bring Italian legislation into line with the rest of Europe. Fortuna argued that the legal isolation of Italy had become particularly important given the increasing mobility of the new era and the increasing number of marriages between Italians and other nationalities.[15]

As with all previous proposals, Fortuna's allowed divorce in specific cases: when one spouse was committed to prison for five years or more, regardless of the crime, or any crime involving incest or prostitution; when mental illness was a mitigating factor in any of those crimes; when a spouse had abandoned the conjugal home for more than five years, or if there had been uninterrupted de facto separation for the same period; when one spouse had been in a mental institution for more than five years; and finally, when one spouse had obtained a divorce or annulment outside Italy. These were of course very restricted cases, with an emphasis on the innocent victim, even though divorce was possible by mutual consent after five years of separation. None of these circumstances was particularly novel; in fact, they are remarkably similar to those presented by Fortuna's predecessors, even as far back as Salvatore Morelli in 1878.

At first there was little indication that the fate of Fortuna's proposal would be any different from those that preceded it. The major newspapers reported the proposal dutifully, but without any particular sense of its potential success. Three of the four parties in the governing coalition (the Socialists, the Democratic Socialists, and the Republicans) were, "by cultural tradition," in favor of divorce, but this tradition was subordinate to the need to maintain a successful government with the Christian Democrats. In this system of precarious alliances the press obviously judged that there was no reason to foresee the sudden constitution of a pro-divorce front at the parliamentary level.[16] What distinguished Fortuna's proposal from its predecessors was not so much the way it was received inside parliament, but the response in civil society. For the first time in Italian history a coherent "secular front" began to coalesce around the divorce question. Hitherto, anti-divorce politicians had always been able to count on the Italian public's antipathy toward divorce. By the autumn of 1965, this antipathy was no longer monolithic.

Allies and Ambivalence

If the pages of *Noi donne* were correct to hail Fortuna's proposal as a signal that resistance to a divorce law could no longer act as a brake against progress,[17] it was in fact the men's magazine *ABC* that made a concerted effort to provide pro-divorce sentiment with the contours of a mass movement. *ABC* had already begun its special page for "Letters from the Separated" a few months earlier, and the magazine soon formed a friendly alliance with Loris Fortuna. This alliance took on more immediacy after Fortuna presented his proposal in parliament, announced boldly on *ABC*'s front cover (usually adorned with scantily clad women). Inside, *ABC* proclaimed that Loris Fortuna had "interpreted the popular will" with his proposal and now "it is up to us" to show the strength of that popular will.[18]

In order to do so, *ABC* provided its readers with a ready-printed postcard addressed to Fortuna at parliament in Rome. The card congratulated Fortuna for his proposal and expressed solidarity. Senders had to fill in their name, address, and profession, add a 30 lire stamp, and mail it.[19] The following week's issue announced a "plebiscite of consensus" over divorce on its cover, and a smaller heading indicated that the "referendum postcard" was also available in that issue. Inside, a report claimed that Fortuna had received 3,500 cards within 36 hours of the issue going on sale.[20] These antics, always accompanied by an irreverent tone, convey a sense of the effervescent optimism of the early days of what was to become a full-scale campaign to introduce divorce.

Fortuna's alliance with *ABC*, which was to last at least a decade, was one of two crucial partnerships, without which the proposal would never have become law. The second ally was the Radical Party—an almost "nonexistent" party of about 100 members, an extra-parliamentary force that had won no seats in the 1963 election.[21] Committed above all to civil liberties, social progress, and secularizing the Italian state, two of the party's key figures, Marco Panella and Mauro Mellini, saw Fortuna's divorce proposal as a worthy cause and an expedient political vehicle. From the autumn of 1965 the Radical Party became Fortuna's indefatigable, though not uncritical, supporter. Because of their political freedom, the Radicals became the main publicists behind the divorce campaign, much more so than Fortuna's own party, whose freedom of action was limited by its political alliance with the Christian Democrats.

The Radical Party launched its new alliance with the divorce cause by organizing a debate entitled "The Prospects for Divorce in Italy" at the Eliseo Theater in Rome, on 12 December 1965. The participants were Radical Party member and lawyer Mauro Mellini, PCI member Luciana

Castellina, Giovanni Battista Migliori of the Christian Democrats, and Loris Fortuna. By all accounts the discussion was extremely lively, with the lone opponent of divorce, Migliori, being howled down by the public.[22] The excitement reached a climax at the end with the public crying, "Organize! National meetings! Regional committees!" while Mellini announced that the divorce question must become the rallying cry for a new kind of political pressure group in Italy, unfettered by party agendas.[23]

The clamor of the meeting, the press attention, and Mellini's closing words about the need for extra-parliamentary pressure groups mark the Eliseo debate as a seminal event in the postwar history of Italian divorce proposals. But while the event presaged the new vitality and optimism of an extra-parliamentary "secular front," it also made clear the very real political complexities that optimism alone would not be able to overcome. The most obvious was Migliori's implacable "No" to divorce on behalf of the Christian Democrats; but also clear was the lack of unity among the lay parties. One poignant indication of this was Fortuna's comment that he hoped his party would not desert the divorce question in the name of other "solidarities"[24]—an indication of his fear that some colleagues would place questions of political opportunity before principles.

The PCI's position provides an example. Luciana Castellina had taken the opportunity of the debate to announce that her party was preparing a broader plan for reform of family law, which would contain a less restrictive proposal for divorce than Fortuna's. Representing the PCI's official line, she announced that her party intended to direct the institution of the family away from its bourgeois mold, and was not interested in supporting a divorce law that was an imitation of the ones in "Western capitalist countries."[25] Not only did this underline the gulf between the PCI and the PSI, it also showed that the Unione Donne Italiane and the magazine *Noi donne*, which had always supported the idea of *piccolo divorzio*, were out of step with the official PCI. One Rita S. summed up the frustration of many regarding the PCI's position in a letter to *Avanti!* after the Eliseo debate. She wrote that in her view the PCI used the need to "study," "research," "prepare," and "improve," as dilatory tactics. She found it absurd that the PCI chose to raise more issues and questions when they could simply support a divorce proposal that had a high probability of success.[26]

Although the equivocation of the PCI was problematic, it was by no means the most serious obstacle Fortuna's proposal faced. Between October 1965 and the Eliseo debate in December, the proposal slowly made its way through the parliamentary procedures that would decide whether it would go the way of its predecessors, or successfully arrive at a parliamentary discussion. On 1 April 1966, Fortuna appealed to the

Chamber to make sure that his proposal should not be allowed to sink behind the scenes among the parliamentary committees.[27]

ABC reported the full text of the speech, which mentioned 31,293 postcards and thousands of letters Fortuna had received from the Italian public. These were of course the result of the "postcard referendum" initiated by *ABC* itself, and they acted as an important signal that the divorce question now animated the public. Many of these had come from the south, with 1,306 from Naples, 875 from Palermo, and 410 from Cagliari. These were low numbers compared with 3,466 from Milan and 4,640 from Rome, but they were sufficient to demonstrate that the divorce question was not a dead letter in the *Mezzogiorno*, as had often been claimed.[28]

Outside parliament, divorce activity moved at a faster pace. A key moment was the Radical Party's founding of the "Lega italiana per il divorzio" (The Italian League for Divorce), which became known as the LID, on 4 April 1966.[29] This was the lobby group adumbrated by Mellini at the Eliseo the previous December. An early member of the Radical Party and founding member of the LID, Angiolo Bandinelli, recounted that by using this acronym on its stationery, members' privacy was protected from the prying eyes of postal deliverers, janitors, and neighbors. Bandinelli also stressed that many members, particularly women, came to the LID's meetings furtively, often with real fear in their eyes.[30] This is a salutary reminder that even if the taboo of divorce had been broken in public debate, many people still felt its weight in their personal lives.

Like *ABC*, the LID worked hard to make sure that the divorce question resisted the commonly leveled criticism that it was of no interest outside the major urban centers of the northern half of the peninsula. As well as establishing offices in the major cities (Rome, Milan, Turin, and Naples), the League set up branches in the smaller centers, such as Genoa, Bolzano, Vicenza, Taranto, Bari, Syracuse, and Cagliari. There was often LID representation in even smaller towns, though this may have consisted of only one person.[31] By April 1966, the combination of *ABC, Noi donne*, the Radical Party, and the LID successfully made divorce into a public talking point, just as Fortuna's proposal began to make its way through the parliamentary procedures.

On the anti-divorce side, between the initial presentation of Fortuna's proposal and April 1966 the Catholic press did not seem to take the threat particularly seriously, but the publicity gained in that month was sufficient to change that. For example, on the same day as a LID debate in Milan, that city's Catholic daily, *L'Italia*, wrote that it would soon publish a series of articles on the negative aspects of divorce. The writer, Monsignor Guzzetti, was bellicose, insisting that a reform of this importance required an electoral mandate, such as a referendum.[32] A few days later, the Italian Episcopal

Conference (CEI) issued a document that also noted the recent publicity about divorce. It called on Catholics to stand firm in their defense of the family and moral values.[33] Diana De Vigili summarized the sentiment of the Italian Catholic world at the time as a sense of outrage that parliament could even consider the introduction of a divorce law while the Christian Democrats were in government.[34] Clearly, the enduring presence of the divorce question in Italian politics was going to test the nature of the relationship between the Catholic world and the Christian Democrats.

The Parliamentary Quicksands

Inside parliament, Fortuna's proposal was in the hands of the fourth parliamentary committee, the Justice Committee, whose task it was to assess the legal implications of the proposed law. The composition of this and the other parliamentary committees reflected the distribution of seats in parliament, last determined by the 1963 election. The lay parties taken as a whole had a majority, but the largest single party remained the Christian Democrats. The committees appear to have been used as arenas for a degree of subtle internal filibustering, or at the very least for the raising of endless legal technicalities designed to ensnare a proposal and prevent it from returning for parliamentary debate before the end of the legislative session. This was the fate that had befallen nearly all previous proposals for divorce, and it was a fate Fortuna was determined his own proposal should avoid. The publicity conducted by *ABC* and the LID served to apply continual pressure, without which it is unlikely the proposal would have seen the light of day after passing through the committees.

Even so, its passage was hardly brisk. The proposal was received at the assigned committee on 11 March 1966, more than six months after it was announced in parliament. On 5 May, the chair of the committee, Alessandro Reggiani, a Social Democrat who was personally in favor of divorce,[35] issued a report summarizing the proposal and asking his fellow committee members to comment on whether divorce might have any implications for the constitution.[36] The challenge was now to fix a date for these deliberations, but despite a written request from Fortuna and several other deputies on 13 July,[37] discussions began only after the summer recess, on 15 September.

It was on this day that Christian Democrat deputy Stefano Riccio fired a weapon the Catholic world hoped would stop Fortuna's proposal at an early stage: the claim that a divorce law would be incompatible with the Italian constitution. Riccio claimed that because for most people marriage was regulated by the Lateran Pacts (as a result of which the Italian state granted full civil validity to church marriages), and because article 7 of the constitution incorporated the Lateran Pacts into the Italian constitution, a divorce law would be unconstitutional.[38] A further point was that a government provision for the dissolution of canonical marriages would amount to a unilateral alteration of the Lateran Pacts, which according to the treaty's wording, could only be changed by mutual agreement.

These lines of argument against the introduction of a divorce law had been raised earlier by the Vatican itself. In August 1966 the Vatican's secretary of state had sent a note to the Italian ambassador to the Holy See, complaining that the introduction of a divorce law that could dissolve Catholic marriages would be a violation of the concordat. The note also requested that the "grave apprehensions of the Holy See" be made known to the Italian government.[39] The use of formal diplomatic channels for this complaint, rather than the more common method of applying pressure to members of the Christian Democratic Party,[40] was perhaps a measure of the gravity of these apprehensions. Though the contents of the note seem never to have gone beyond the desk of the prime minister, Aldo Moro,[41] there was not a soul in Italy who needed the Vatican's apprehensions about divorce to be spelled out.

The problem of whether a divorce law would clash with either the constitution or the Lateran Pacts raised serious questions about the relationship between the Italian state and its official church. The Lateran Pacts had solved the Roman Question, but the incorporation of the pacts into the 1947 constitution had created a "Vatican Question" that was equally complex. Until the 1960s, even anticlerical Italians had accepted this as a cultural fact of Italian life, but the social and economic developments of the 1960s gave increasing cause to question the relationship.[42] One of the reasons for the divorce question's extraordinary resonance in Italy in the 1960s and 1970s was that it highlighted the blurred boundary between church and state. The divorce issue was not only about whether marriages could be dissolved; it was about the very nature and composition of the Italian state. Both sides knew this only too well, which is why it was fraught with difficulties.

The procedure became even more complex when one Christian Democrat deputy suggested that the proposal be sent to the Committee for Constitutional Affairs so that a determination could be made about the potential incompatibility with the constitution. Such a move epitomized the way in which a proposal could lose all momentum, mired in the deliberations of various parliamentary committees. It was the last thing Fortuna wanted and he argued that the law did not threaten the concordat because technically a divorce would only involve the civil effects of a canonical marriage. Like all those on the lay side of the political fence,

Fortuna strenuously defended the Italian government's right to legislate on the civil affairs of its citizens without having to defer to ecclesiastical law.[43] His pleas were in vain: the proposal went to the Committee for Constitutional Affairs in October 1966.

Although Fortuna was relatively powerless to influence the course his proposal took within parliament, it was at this point that the LID organized a mass rally in favor of divorce. Held on Sunday 13 November in Rome's Piazza del Popolo, this was the first of several festive rallies that would be held to publicize the divorce cause over the coming years, aiming to make sure that however mired the proposal might become in parliament, it was kept in public view. The LID sponsored busses to bring divorce supporters from all over Italy, and the rally ended in front of the nearby headquarters of Italy's state broadcasting system, RAI (Radio Audizioni Italiane), to protest the minimal amount of air-time given to the divorce question.[44] Overall the rally was a clear sign that for the first time in Italy, personal issues such as divorce were becoming broadly political matters in the eyes of the public.

It is difficult to assess the extent to which such publicity influenced the minds of politicians at this early stage, but it seems safe to say that without it, Fortuna's proposal would have been less likely to make its way over various parliamentary obstacles. Contingent factors were also relevant, and it so happened that the Committee for Constitutional Affairs was presided by Renato Ballardini, a Socialist who sympathized with the divorce cause and was keen to assert the legislative autonomy of the state. From the outset, he took the line that the divorce law proposed by Fortuna did not clash with the constitution in any way. Beyond the now familiar problem of article 7 of the constitution, Catholics had raised another objection: article 29 of the constitution stated that "the Republic recognizes the rights of the family as a natural society founded upon marriage." Some Catholics began to argue that this concept of the family as a "natural society" had been derived from religious doctrine. For this reason, they argued, even though the word "indissoluble" had not been specified in the constitution, allowing a law that specifically made it dissoluble would be an offense to the religious concept of the family as a natural society. Ballardini asserted that in fact the notion of the natural society was entirely secular and had been so from the outset.[45]

Despite Ballardini's attempt to circumscribe the scope of his committee's deliberations, ideological arguments about what the Constituent Assembly had intended by the family as a "natural society" quickly came to the fore. This was an essentially political debate over whether the legislator should be more concerned with the overall good of the community or protecting the civil rights of individuals. The Christian Democrat Attilio Ruffini exemplified the former argument, claiming that the Assembly had specifically rejected a private, contractual conception of marriage. He claimed that they had done this by emphasizing the communitarian idea of a "natural society" that was antecedent to the state, one whose essence and ends transcend the individual wills of the spouses.[46] Others, such as Raffaele Di Primio (PSI) claimed that the preparatory deliberations of the Assembly showed that its view was that the family was dependent upon the will of the spouses.[47]

Although such profound disagreements had little chance of being resolved through debate, ultimately the question was decided by a vote. Ballardini provided a convincing summary, arguing that in regard to marriage the state's sole obligation under the constitution was to confer civil effects upon a religious marriage, and that divorce was not incompatible with that obligation. On 19 January 1967, the committee agreed by a majority vote that divorce was not incompatible with the Italian constitution.[48] This was a landmark decision, demolishing one of the Christian Democrats' main arguments. As it turned out, it by no means dissolved their "profound conviction that the constitution sanctioned the principle of indissoluble marriage."[49]

Enemies and Stasis

What the decision did very well was prompt a new round of publicity, both national and international, as the divorce question in Italy took a significant step from the realm of constitutional theory back toward parliamentary debate. The pope began to make public utterances against divorce just as the Constitutional Affairs Committee moved toward its vote. On 8 January, at the traditional Sunday blessing in St Peter's Square, Paul VI asked the crowds to pray that "the laws which protect the family remain steadfast." In another message, to the Church Family Front Organization, the pope praised the indissolubility of marriage and hoped that married couples would "accept their trials."[50] After the committee's vote the pope made a much-reported speech to the ecclesiastical court that deals with marriage annulments, the Sacra Rota. He openly attacked "the avidity of those people who aspire to introduce divorce into the legislation and habits of nations which have the good fortune to be immune, almost as though it were a disgrace not to have such an institution." *The Times* of London reported that the pope "had unashamedly entered the Italian political scene in a more direct manner than has been known for years."[51]

The pope's entry into the political fray also drew much attention in Italy itself. Catholic newspapers such as the *Osservatore romano* and *Il Popolo* defended the right of the pope to speak as the spiritual leader of Christianity, while the lay papers, particularly *Avanti!*, deeply criticized this example of religious interference in Italian political life.[52] *ABC* claimed that the pope had described the legitimate vote of parliamentary deputies as a "pronunciamento." Outside parliament the tensions of a religious war were beginning to brew, with the leader of the Catholic world interpreting the actions of parliament as insurrectionary.[53] *ABC*'s answer was to call for a return of the spirit of the Risorgimento, with "all free Italians against confessional Italy."[54] *ABC* was given to slightly high-flown language at times, but it is no exaggeration to interpret the 1960s divorce debate as the final battle over questions that had been raised in the 1860s and left hanging ever since.

For the purposes of Fortuna's proposal the January 1967 vote by the Constitutional Affairs Committee quashed the constitutional argument and, with this obstacle removed, the proposal returned to the Justice Committee, where reports were to be completed and a vote taken on whether it could proceed to parliamentary discussion. These procedures were tedious, and the proposal dragged through the first half of 1967 with seemingly endless repetition of two irreconcilable views on marriage and on whether the government's first duty was to individuals or the state as a whole. As the committee's debates still did not seem anywhere near resolution by July 1967, Fortuna and several other deputies made a formal complaint about the procedure that allowed only one deputy to air views at each meeting.[55]

Reading between the lines, it was easy to see Fortuna's fears about the fact that the legislature had only 10 months to run; and it was important that the proposal be returned for discussion before the end of that period. Meanwhile, Catholic forces sought to translate Paul VI's exhortations of January 1967 into a more effective bulwark against an incursion into the laws protecting families. The first approach, that of asserting the constitutional incompatibility of a divorce law, had failed. The second approach, the idea of a popular referendum that had been mooted a year earlier, began to take on the contours of a major strategy during the Italian Bishops' Conference in April 1967.

If the anti-divorce side was marked by a new sense of resolution, their opponents suffered from disunity and failing momentum in the spring of 1967. After the great victory of the green light from the Constitutional Affairs Committee in January, they made no headway. On 9 March, a group of Communists, including Nilde Jotti, presented their own proposal for a divorce law. Contrary to the claims made by Luciana Castellina at the Eliseo debate in 1965, it was even more restrictive than Fortuna's already *piccolo* proposal, because it would allow a couple to divorce only after five years of official, not just de facto, separation.[56] This meant that couples who had lived apart for years unofficially would have to ask a court to recognize their separation before their five-year period began.

The lack of forward movement in the divorce campaign was also indicated by its spasmodic coverage in *ABC*, which, after an outraged article about the pope's use of the word "pronunciamento," published only a handful of articles on the divorce cause between March and June 1967. Two were about rising pro-divorce sentiment in the Catholic world,[57] and one was about yet another scandalous annulment of a movie star's marriage by the Sacra Rota. This was the marriage of Vittorio Gassman and Nora Ricci, on the grounds that Gassman "did not believe in the indissolubility of marriage" on the wedding day. As *ABC* was only too happy to point out, such annulments made a mockery of the Vatican's position against divorce.[58] As De Vigili has noted, just as the Catholic hierarchy was calling for unity, there were signs that in 1967 it could no longer count on the discipline of earlier decades.[59]

Fortuna had much the same problem, except that the lay forces had never been able to count upon internal unity. The Communist divorce proposal was just one indication of the lack of a united front on the issue, and it placed a spanner into the already grinding mechanisms of parliamentary procedure. As one Christian Democrat deputy in the Justice Committee eagerly pointed out, the PCI had previously undertaken not to make a proposal of its own while Fortuna's was being considered.[60] The situation had all the hallmarks of an initiative that had fallen into parliamentary quicksands, when the proposal unexpectedly reached a turning point. On 23 June, the president of the Justice Committee decided to combine the two proposals and discuss them together.[61]

A "Secular Front"?

Suddenly, divorce was back on the agenda. On 2 July *ABC* published an interview with Fortuna in which he said there was new hope. He lamented the lay parties' collective lassitude, but apportioned blame only to the Christian Democrats, who, with their 37–38 percent of seats, dominated the governing parties by threatening a government crisis, and intimidated their coalition partners with the possibility of exclusion from a future government. Above all Fortuna urged the lay parties to unite behind his cause, and announced that he and 23 other deputies had petitioned Goffredo Zappa, the head of the Justice Committee, to resume discussion and arrive at a vote.[62]

A good sign that the lay parties were beginning to fall into line came at a meeting of the National Council of the Liberal Party between 30 June and 2 July. The LID had arranged a silent demonstration outside the party's headquarters in Rome, and during the course of the meeting the Liberal Party renounced the prevarications of its leader, Giovanni Malagodi, and officially declared itself a pro-divorce party supporting Fortuna's proposal.[63]

This was encouraging, but it was only a start, and *ABC* announced an ambitious campaign to collect 500,000 pro-divorce signatures from the public. This was to be another "postcard referendum," and in the issue of 9 July *ABC* included a seven-page insert dedicated to the divorce campaign. The insert contested the Catholic claim that divorce was harmful to children, by presenting case studies in which *ABC* journalists had interviewed children living in the "cage" of "irregular" relationships after separation of their parents. The sentiments it documented amounted to exactly the same argument the Italian *divorzisti* had used from Morelli onward: children suffer when their parents' relationships fail, but they suffer much more when there is no legal way to overcome marital failures, leaving violence and subterfuge as the only alternatives. The entire insert was poignantly illustrated with photographs from the pro-divorce rally that had been held at the Piazza del Popolo in Rome on 13 November 1966. These show a true mass event, with thousands of people crowding the piazza, many holding witty placards. One in particular stands out for its sense of history: "1929 Mussolini says YES; 1967 Italy says NO, to the Concordat."[64]

Although in effect discussions in the Justice Committee did not get underway again until after parliament's summer recess, together Fortuna and *ABC* succeeded in applying sufficient pressure to relaunch the stranded proposal. Once again the main task faced by Fortuna and his allies was organizing the unwavering support of members of the lay parties, idealized by *ABC* as a *fronte laico*.[65] Despite the renewed determination of Fortuna's campaign from the summer of 1967, the fate of the proposal was to hang by a thread for an entire year. This is because once parliament's work resumed in the autumn of that year, the end of the legislature was already looming, to be followed by elections scheduled for May 1968. At this stage Fortuna resigned himself to the fact that divorce was unlikely to be discussed in parliament in the current legislature, and instead dedicated himself to the less ambitious task of gaining the Justice Committee's approval for the proposal.[66]

The period between October 1967 and the end of the session was fraught with intense but ultimately unproductive negotiations. Fortuna was intent on the construction of a resilient "lay front," but this was to come only at a price. Much of his effort went into convincing his own Socialist Party to adopt a clear policy decision in favor of divorce. *ABC* rightly claimed that Nenni, the Socialists' leader, was barely distinguishable from Moro, in that he approached the divorce question not as an issue affecting Italian society, but as an irritating problem that destabilized the coalition.[67]

Always attentive to the political implications of the question, socialist deputies had finally been directed to support divorce by the end of October. The difficulty Fortuna had in mustering the support of his own party was perhaps greater than that involved in obtaining the full support of the other main lay parties, the Liberals and the Communists. Here again the autumn of 1967 was an important period. For the price of several compromises that made the law even less radical (for example, the Liberals wanted a period of eight years between separation and divorce, not five) Fortuna gained clearer support from both those parties.[68]

Not long after this the Justice Committee began discussing the individual articles of Fortuna's proposal. The fragility of the *fronte laico* was revealed by the vote on the first two lines of the proposal, which said "Marriage can be dissolved at the request of one of the spouses in the following cases." The committee approved this principle by 21 votes to 20. This vote, however exiguous the pro-divorce margin, seemed to imbue the *divorzisti* with great optimism. For example, with characteristic hubris *ABC* announced that "finally there is a secular majority,"[69] and an important year ended on the high note provided by the first national congress of the LID, held in Rome on 9 and 10 December.

Political Instability and Violence

The one-vote victory at the end of 1967 was in fact far less of a triumph than Fortuna had aimed for a year earlier. But it did mean that the divorce campaign entered the election year of 1968 with high hopes, and the optimism was further fuelled by the Justice Committee's vote in favor of the proposal's second article on 10 January.[70] Fortuna had originally hoped that parliament would discuss the divorce law prior to the end of the legislature, in case the election returned an anti-divorce majority. In fact the elections, held in May 1968, resulted in only fractional adjustments to the balance of power among the political parties, and if anything slightly strengthened the pro-divorce majority.[71] One change worth noting is that the number of women elected to parliament (as both deputies and senators) fell from 30 to 27.[72]

Even though there had been no clear electoral shifts, the 1968 election heralded a period of volatile political instability that exceeded anything previously witnessed in postwar Italian politics. All across Europe the gathering clouds of labor and student unrest are probably the best remembered backdrop to this. In Italy these clouds burst with the "long hot autumn" of 1969, and the beginnings of political terrorism quickly followed. In terms of relationships among the parties, Fortuna's divorce proposal remained the most dangerous loose cannon on the coalition's decks,[73] yet it was also destined to be the clearest step toward reform and an embracing of the social ferment of those years. At the opening of the new legislature, the passage of Fortuna's bill, barely altered but nevertheless presented afresh as the first proposal to be discussed by the new parliament, was still by no means a foregone conclusion.[74]

A new hurdle was the contemporaneous presentation of yet a third proposal for a divorce law at the opening of the new legislature, authored by the Liberal Antonio Baslini, and signed by 18 other deputies. The appearance of an alternative proposal, slightly more restrictive than that of the socialists, further underlined the volatility of Fortuna's *fronte laico*, so carefully constructed during the second half of 1967. For a short time the emergence of a competing proposal threatened to divide the ranks of the *divorzisti*, and when it was announced in October 1968, Marco Panella resigned his position as secretary of the LID.

This might well have led to the unraveling of the entire "divorce front," had it not been for the timely intervention of *ABC*. *ABC* promptly organized a meeting between Fortuna, Panella, and Baslini, with the aim of reconstructing its much vaunted *fronte laico*. The magazine reported the entire debate to its readers, accompanying the text with a photograph that shows the three men sitting on comfortable sofas like old friends.[75] Soon after this the two parliamentarians reached an agreement and the two texts were fused into one proposal, which became known as the "Fortuna-Baslini."[76] Panella also resumed his leadership of the LID.

If magazines such as *ABC* did their utmost to smooth over the cracks in the pro-divorce alliance, the parliamentary archives, by contrast, reveal at least some of the extraordinary complexities of what Ginsborg referred to as the "long preparatory tunnel of the state bureaucracy" that preceded any significant reforms.[77] In the case of divorce, the parliamentary tunnel was particularly tortuous. As things stood after the elections, and after the summer recess, Fortuna's divorce proposal once again descended into the complex depths of the parliamentary committees. Despite having cleared these obstacles only a few months earlier, the process had to be repeated in the new legislature.

The president of the Justice Committee, now a Christian Democrat, took the opportunity to raise once again the assertion that divorce would be unconstitutional, and referred the proposal to the Constitutional Affairs Committee for a second time. Again that committee decided a divorce law would not be unconstitutional. It accepted the arguments made by Renato Ballardini to the effect that marital stability and unity did not in themselves amount to indissolubility, and that the state must recognize and provide for situations in which families fall short of those ideals.[78]

These arguments were not new: they had been at the center of a long struggle for the moral, if not legal jurisdiction over the Italian family since the introduction of civil marriage in 1866. The Church had won a major victory in 1929, but four decades later, the majority view in parliament, and as time would tell, amongst the Italian people, was starting to swing the other way. On 5 February the committee voted in favor of Ballardini's arguments, and the "Fortuna-Baslini" returned to the Justice Committee, freed of constitutional obstacles a second time.[79]

By late April 1969, that committee had decided the proposal was fit for debate in parliament. The extreme complexity of the route by which the proposal finally arrived on the threshold of parliament could easily obscure the fact that its mere arrival was of historic significance: when, on 29 May 1969, the Chamber of Deputies began to debate the divorce proposal, it was the first time in Italian history that it had done so. It was just over 90 years since Salvatore Morelli had made his first attempt.

Divorce in the Chamber

There was light at the end of the preparatory tunnel: the proposal faced debate in a parliament that had a theoretical majority of pro-divorce deputies, and to a lesser extent, senators. The broad alliance opposing the introduction of divorce engaged several strategies to defeat it. The most visible and perhaps the most discussed was one that had been outlined at the Bishops' Conference in 1967: a popular referendum to be used to abrogate the divorce law if it were introduced by parliament. Provision for abrogative referenda had been written into the constitution, but the specific law had never been drafted or approved. The Christian Democrats now began to expedite this process, so that they would have a weapon against the divorce law if it were introduced. This strategy reflected the Church hierarchy's and Christian Democrats' firm conviction that the great majority of Italians remained opposed to divorce.[80]

Loris Fortuna and the *divorzisti* were deeply skeptical about the referendum strategy. In a general sense Fortuna correctly underlined the anti-democratic potential of a vulgar plebiscitary clout each time parliament passed a law that concerned a minority of the population. In a more specific sense he was concerned that parliamentary debate of the referendum proposal should not take priority over the divorce law itself.[81] Despite the referendum's implications for Italian democracy, it was not Fortuna's principal concern as parliament took up the divorce issue for the first time. His main goals were that the debate should proceed unhindered by further delaying tactics and arrive at a vote, and that the lay deputies should vote in favor of divorce.

The potential obstacles were personified by Giulio Andreotti, now president of the Christian Democrats' parliamentary group, and coordinator of the party committee delegated to strategize a response to the divorce proposal. From 1969 to 1974, Andreotti was to be one of the leading figures in the battle against the divorce law. His determination to undermine it even on the territory of the very parties that supported it was indicated in May 1969, shortly before the parliamentary debate began. Addressing a delegation of the Centro Italiano Femminile (the principal association of Catholic women in Italy) in Rome, Andreotti assured them that every Christian Democrat deputy was already fully engaged in an action of "enlightenment" that aimed to convince the lay deputies to vote on divorce according to their conscience, rather than their party line.[82] Another aspect of Andreotti's strategy is revealed by the sheer number of Christian Democrat deputies who signed up to speak against divorce in the parliamentary debate. The extraordinarily high number of 108 deputies compares with fifteen Socialists, eight Communists, and seven Liberals.[83] No doubt the divorce proposals animated the passions of DC deputies more than most, but there is also more than a hint of filibustering tactics in their numbers.

Though the Christian Democrats represented an imposing political machine, they were slightly outnumbered in parliament, and they fought a rearguard action that played on the fear of change. This was also a characteristic of the anti-divorce campaigns coordinated by Catholic organizations in the parishes, which plastered walls with posters carrying slogans such as "La S ... Fortuna delle donne" (The Mis ... Fortune of woman), playing on Fortuna's own name, and "The destruction of the family." Fortuna noted the clerical targeting of women, describing it as a "psychological terrorism without precedent or limit."[84] Though it sounded histrionic, Fortuna's characterization of the wide clerical ferment as a new Vendée rebellion was not far off the mark: from parliament down to the smallest parish the anti-divorce campaign was of a character that made Fortuna's energetic offensive look all the more heroic.

For the pro-divorce lobby, parliament's summer recess was framed by two very different propaganda events, both of which once again owed their coordination to *ABC*. The first was marked by the plucky style that characterized the magazine: the edition of 20 June included a "divorce policy," a form that readers could fill out to initiate a divorce action. *ABC* guaranteed free legal advice to all applicants via a network of "matrimonial experts" all over the country, and, even more importantly, promised that the magazine would pay 50 percent of each applicant's legal costs for their eventual divorce. These costs were expected to be about 200,000 lire, compared to the "many millions" necessary for an annulment by the Sacra Rota.[85]

Subsequent issues of *ABC* announced the success of the initiative, which, despite a substantial increase in the print-run, had allegedly caused the magazine to sell out faster than any previous number. The editors invited those who had not been able to obtain one to apply directly to the editorial offices for their own copy of the "divorce policy."[86] This publicity stunt provides little or no quantitative evidence, but in qualitative terms it demonstrates the energy, imagination, and commitment of *ABC*'s editors. Of course, it was easier to offer assistance to make use of a law that did not yet exist, but that was the cheeky element of the whole ploy. It is not known whether *ABC* made good its promise once the law was passed.

At the end of that summer the LID and *ABC* jointly organized the second event, a mass pro-divorce rally in Rome just as parliament was about to reopen. The numerous placards summed up several themes that traversed the whole debate. They ranged from mild imprecations warning lay deputies that "Absentees are deserters" and statements such as "Women have no fear of divorce," to much harsher references to the "clerico-fascist" alliance, an epithet that had become part of the antiauthoritarian rhetoric of the long hot autumn. One placard showed a priest arm in arm with a fascist thug, announcing "The couple who will never divorce." Another showed a map of Italy placed horizontally, like a dog's bone, between the shark-like teeth of a priest whose jaws have the unmistakable outline of Mussolini.[87]

Throughout October and November, as students and workers assembled and rebelled all over Italy, the Chamber of Deputies debated the divorce law at great length. No deputy said anything starkly new, but these were nevertheless historic months in the annals of parliament. It was slow going as 167 deputies had enrolled to speak, and in a typical all-day session there was time only for a handful of speeches.[88] These were often tedious; the excitement lay in the fact that a vote on perhaps the most contentious issue ever debated in parliament was now a certainty. When the time to vote finally arrived on 28 November, at the end of two months of discussion, it delivered a clear triumph for divorce: of the 608 deputies present, 325 voted in favor of divorce, while 283 voted against. This provided a safe margin of 42. To the exultation of Fortuna and his colleagues, and no doubt many Italian "matrimonial outlaws," the proposal was transmitted to the Senate on 2 December 1969.

Divorce in the Senate
The transmission of the proposal to the Senate coincided with the beginning of one of the most volatile political seasons ever witnessed in postwar Italy.

On 12 December 1969, a terrorist bomb detonated in a bank in Milan killed 17 people and wounded 88. The police hastily announced that anarchists were to blame,[89] but the bombing soon came to be seen as the harbinger of a "strategy of tension," masterminded not by the Left, but by the "occult" Far Right, whose intention it was to bring to power an authoritarian government that would sweep out the chaos of the long hot autumn.[90] The bombing did indeed launch a period of tension, and the divorce proposal, although it had no direct relationship with the civil unrest of the period, became inextricably identified with the subsequent period of political instability.

The final year of the proposal's passage through parliament can be analyzed, like Braudel's Mediterranean, on several levels. Most obvious in the Italian press was the way divergent political positions over divorce complicated coalition politics at a time of knife-edge tension.[91] But it is at the levels beneath the choppy surface of day-to-day Italian politics that the true themes surrounding the divorce question most clearly played themselves out. The essence, as always, was the Church's struggle to maintain the best of both worlds the Lateran Pacts had offered in relation to marriage: for the state to provide Christian marriage with a range of safeguards and guarantees that in turn protected marriage from the state itself. In a penultimate attempt to defend marriage from that threat, the Vatican moved to prevent the proposal from passing through the Senate.

The Vatican made its moves in various ways, but the two most influential were a diplomatic note to the Italian ambassador to the Holy See, and a papal address at St Peter's on the forty-first anniversary of the Lateran Pacts, on 11 February 1970. The pope made clear his view that the introduction of a divorce law would "wound" church-state harmony,[92] and would amount to a unilateral alteration of the pacts by Italy.[93] This was also the essence of the diplomatic note which put forward the idea of two regimes of marriage: one Catholic, which would remain indissoluble, and the other purely civil, which could be dissolved.[94] News of this note was leaked to members of parliament, many of whom were offended by the interference it represented.

This of course only strenghtened the resolve of *divorzisti* such as Fortuna, who was absolutely determined that the Vatican proposal for two matrimonial regimes should not even be considered. His regular column in *ABC* fulminated against the "re-emergence of the temporal power of the popes."[95] Cartoons made the point even more clearly, with one showing two of the pope's Swiss guards on their way to arrest Fortuna.[96]

The pope's public pleas also attracted international attention. Because this undisguised Vatican pressure on the Italian parliament came just when Prime Minister Mariano Rumor and his cabinet resigned, and was likely to influence the construction of a new coalition, it was interpreted both inside and outside Italy as an attempt on the part of the papacy to change the course of Italian politics. Silvio Lanaro has written that efforts to form a new government were "paralyzed" by Vatican pressure, the sole aim of which was to block the approval of divorce.[97] For contemporary newspapers in Britain and the United States the undisguised Vatican pressure on the Italian parliament was remarkable.[98]

By the time Rumor's third cabinet took formal shape in late March, the Christian Democrats and the Socialists had reached an agreement over an older Catholic solution to the divorce question: the Christian Democrats would not block the passage of the proposal through the Senate in return for the smooth passage of the proposed law on the referendum.[99] The Christian Democrats, in a minority on this position, had to content themselves with the idea that ultimately the Italian people would settle the controversy. What this parliamentary bargain meant in reality was a resumption of the work of the Senate's Justice Committee, which had been at a standstill since the resignation of the cabinet in early February. The committee resumed its deliberations in April, and by mid-May referred the proposal to the assembled Senate with its approval. Compared with the obdurate opposition of previous debates, the Christian Democrats now only put up symbolic resistance.

Toward Victory

The result was that the final six months of 1970, in retrospect at least, had something of the quality of a funfair slide that led the proposal inexorably through the process, albeit with some heart-wrenching diversions. The relative smoothness with which the debate recommenced in the Senate in June could easily belie the continuing threats represented by various forms of Vatican pressure upon the government. These included a final diplomatic note, dated 13 June (a week before the Senate resumed its discussion), and yet more direct pressure that finally caused the third and final resignation of Mariano Rumor on behalf of his cabinet on 6 July.[100]

Some members of the Christian Democrats would no doubt have liked the president, Giuseppe Saragat, to dissolve the legislature and call early elections, but Emilio Colombo was able to assemble a new cabinet on 6 August, a coalition of the same parties that had constituted Rumor's government.[101] Meanwhile, with the government in disarray as a direct result of Vatican pressure, according to Fortuna,[102] he and the LID launched a final campaign that was more openly anticlerical than ever. It began with a successful mass rally in Rome on 10 July, dotted with placards such as "Italia sì, Vaticano no."[103]

In the same vein, the imminence of the Senate's vote gave 20 September 1970, the hundredth anniversary of the invasion of Rome by Italian soldiers at Porta Pia, a particularly intense quality that year. Fortuna argued that Italians should not see the day as a mere academic celebration, but as one that marked the renewal of a determined struggle against the "creeping clericalism of the day."[104] The LID organized a rally in Rome's Piazza Navona to mark the occasion, accompanied by a month-long outdoor exhibition of anticlerical posters and art. It was full of satirical taunts to the Church. One poster showed a military tank, with "Concordat" written in large letters along its side, rolling over the Italian people. Another advertised "Last rides on the Sacra Rota—reduced prices." A week after the festivities Fortuna announced portentously that the approaching vote in the Senate would either signal a relaunch of a secular republic, or the continuation of clerical dominance in Italy.[105]

The real message here was of course to the senators of the lay parties, reminding them to vote according to their party policy. The last few days of the Senate's discussion were tense for everyone. The proposal came incredibly close to the rocks of disaster on 1 October, when a Christian Democrat senator proposed an order of the day postponing transition from general debate to a discussion of the articles. The Senate voted instead to pass to the next stage, but only by a margin of two votes (155 to 153).[106]

This tiny majority, slimmer than the theoretical pro-divorce majority, provoked serious recriminations among political groupings. At the last minute, and apparently to avoid another impasse that seriously threatened the cohesion of the government, Senator Giovanni Leone proposed modifications to the entire proposal, making divorce a slightly more arduous process than it would have been under the proposal already approved by the Chamber of Deputies. In consultation with Fortuna, senators representing the lay parties accepted these in order to save the law. In particular, article 1 would now oblige the judge to attempt a reconciliation of the couple; article 3 extended the waiting time after separation from five to six and sometimes even seven years in particular cases; and article 4 provided for the judge to consult the couple's children about the divorce. In short, an already very cautious divorce law became even more so.[107] The Senate held its final vote on the proposal at the end of the day on 9 October. It approved the law by 164 votes to 150, a fairly comfortable margin, and, given the political convulsions the proposal had caused since January, this was a modest triumph for the divorce cause.

But the battle was not yet over. Because the law had been modified by the Senate, it had to return to the Chamber of Deputies for a second approval with the new wording. Given that the composition of the Chamber had not changed since the first vote, and that the proposal had been made even more cautious, in some ways this final step was no more than a symbolic final hurdle. Nevertheless, in the Italian parliament even a symbolic hurdle could take many days to jump. The discussion was drawn out over three weeks. The final session alone, begun on 24 November, continued across six further days, coming to a final vote at 5.40 in the morning on 1 December 1970. The length of the session was an absolute record. It attests to the perceived importance of the divorce question and to the passions surrounding it; and it underlines the virtual indissolubility of this particular political knot. But close to dawn on that morning in December, after several deputies had collapsed from exhaustion, a parliamentary vote of 319 for divorce, and 286 against, made Italian history: the nation now had a divorce law.[108]

Let the People Decide, 1970–1974

A few minutes after the parliamentary vote, a small group of tired people, mostly members and office bearers of the LID, erupted into jubilation on the piazza in front of Rome's Pantheon, not far from the parliament itself. The LID caravan had been parked there for several days, and the group had kept up a vigil throughout the Chamber's final sitting. A fuzzy photograph, appearing on the front page of a pro-divorce newspaper a few days later, captured the moment at 5.45AM. It shows a happy group of unremarkable people, mostly middle-aged or elderly, neither revelers nor revolutionaries.

They held lighted candles, fêting a long-term matrimonial "outlaw" and member of LID, an elderly woman named Argentina Marchei. She was chosen, for no particular reason except perhaps her seniority, to personify all those who stood to gain from the divorce law. Among many triumphant placards, the most prominent proclaimed "Argentina Marchei has won. Paul VI has lost." The diminutive Argentina herself, probably unused to the attention, stands demurely at the center of the adulation.[1] The photograph and the proclamation captured much of the spirit of the pro-divorce campaign over the previous five years: relatively ordinary citizens who claimed the right to decide when their marriages were beyond redemption, and who had been radicalized by the obdurate opposition to their claims.

Once the law had been gazzetted on 18 December, people like Argentina who had been separated for more than five years started to flow into the courts to initiate their divorce proceedings. The numbers were not great. Even after some years, in fact, there were no signs that the divorce law had undermined the foundations of the Italian family, as its opponents had feared, with divorce numbers always significantly lower in Italy than in other European countries.[2] Within a few years, it would be clear that the divorce law had not unraveled Italian society.

The fact that it was not going to do so seemed evident in the story surrounding the first two Italians to get divorced. An "obscure couple" from Modena, Giorgia Benassi and Alfredo Cappi were the very opposite of the film stars whose marriage failures had previously grabbed the attention of the press. Even a pro-divorce magazine like *Noi donne*, which sent a special correspondent to cover the historic occasion, struggled to find anything historic about the pair and their divorce. They were ordinary people who just wanted to get on with their separate lives.[3]

The history of divorce in Italy might have settled into similar obscurity, a regrettably necessary piece of legislation, utilized by a minority of citizens. But the legislation had been the result of a parliamentary bargain by which it would be subject to a popular referendum. The inexorable pursuit of this goal by a small group of hard-line anti-*divorzisti* ultimately added a symphonic coda to what had hitherto been merely a drawn-out, discordant piece for Chamber ensemble. Their efforts kept Italy's divorce question at the top of the political agenda and in the news for another four years, and ultimately the referendum probably came closer to testing the coherence of the Italian political fabric than any other issue since 1946.

The National Committee for a Referendum on Divorce

After the prolonged parliamentary debate, few politicians of any stripe were in a hurry to enact the referendum bargain. Nevertheless, on the day the law was passed, Professor Gabrio Lombardi founded the National Committee for a Referendum on Divorce (CNRD). Lombardi was Professor of Roman Law at the Catholic University of Milan. After receiving a form of blessing from the Italian bishops, and following a precedent that had been set in the 1880s in response to Tommaso Villa's first divorce proposal, Lombardi's committee made use of a dense network of Catholic social organizations, collecting 1,370,134 signatures (far more than the 500,000 officially required to initiate the process), which were handed to the Court of Cassation in June 1971.[4]

Technically this meant a referendum should have been held in the spring of 1972, but the law on popular referenda was a marvel of Italian complexity. Among its many provisions was one specifying that if the parliamentary legislature was dissolved before the end of its five-year term, any procedures for a referendum already in train could only be resumed a year after the general elections.[5] As it happened, the legislature was dissolved, in February 1972, at least in part with the specific intention of postponing the referendum.[6] This dissolution, the first in the history of the republic, was followed by elections in May, which meant that procedures for the referendum could not be resumed until May 1973. Because of further complications, ultimately the earliest the referendum could be held was in the spring of 1974.[7]

The general election of 1972 did not offer the hoped-for change in voting patterns. There was only one real shift, and one that was to be significant for the divorce referendum: the neofascist Movimento Sociale Italiano (MSI), with Giorgio Almirante as its new leader, almost doubled its share of the vote, from 4.4 percent in 1968 to 8.7 percent in 1972. Not only was the sudden electoral success of this carefully ostracized black sheep of Italian politics troubling for the other parties, it also meant that the elections failed to turn in a more stable coalition. The first cabinet, a Center-Right coalition led by Andreotti, failed within a year, and was succeeded by a Center-Left coalition led once again by Mariano Rumor.[8]

This political scenario was to provide the background for a referendum that remained a menacing prospect for all the major parties. In a general sense it threatened the clerical-lay alliance that had been the basis of all Italian governments since the 1950s. As the recent years of the divorce debates had shown, the question sorely tested the coherence of this alliance, but the electoral character of Italy offered no workable alternative. The divorce law's passage had created uncomfortable new alliances by default: the Christian Democrat Party shared its anti-divorce position only with the neo-fascist MSI. The Socialists, Republicans, Social Democrats, and Liberals found themselves bedfellows with the Communists.[9]

Conversely, Communist strategy since Togliatti had carefully avoided ideological confrontations with the DC, and this approach was just about to find its clearest expression with Enrico Berlinguer's conception of the "historic compromise" in October 1973.[10] The DC, on the other hand, whose midwifery had brought the concept of a referendum into the parliamentary light during 1970, also had compelling reasons to avoid fostering its own child. The most obvious was the political undesirability of doing anything that might throw them into the arms of the MSI, which would tarnish their image and alienate the party's left wing.

The DC feared the referendum for other reasons, too. Many of its supporters voted for the DC primarily for economic, not religious reasons, and the party could not be certain of those constituents' support on a question of religious conscience. Furthermore, the party itself had factions and the referendum may have brought these to the surface in a way that would be irreparable.[11] Even though it was clear that none of the major parties viewed the prospect of a referendum with any relish, once the CNRD had set the initiative in motion by June 1971, despite the interruptions and delays of the election, it developed its own momentum. As one politician lamented, it was "a car with no reverse gear."[12]

There was only one faint possibility of avoiding it, and that was by an alteration to the divorce law that would render it acceptable to at least some of the anti-*divorzisti*. Despite the unlikelihood of this, the Communist Senator Tullia Carrettoni submitted a proposal for a new divorce law, intended to replace the Fortuna-Baslini, on 2 December 1971. This was clearly designed to soften the clerical objection to the original law. It proposed the removal of nonconsummation as a motive for divorce; limitations on divorces granted to Italians whose spouse had obtained a divorce abroad; and a seven-year waiting period for those requesting divorce a second time.[13] The proposal, which many felt smacked of an arrangement between the PCI and the DC,[14] did not attract the necessary support to proceed.[15] After the elections of May 1972, the referendum seemed unavoidable.

What this scenario reveals above all is that nearly all Italy's politicians approached the referendum from the point of view of its political rather than moral implications. This was certainly not the case amongst those who were ultimately to settle the controversy—the Italian people. The fact that the referendum was delayed by three and a half years after the introduction of the law was undoubtedly very significant for its outcome. The delays gave the law time to prove itself and to take its place in the mental landscape of the Italians. As a result, the familiar correspondence between political and moral stances, one that would have seen the Italian people vote according to the directives of their preferred political parties, had time to be eroded.

The most important exemplars of this shift were Catholics who were either neutral or openly pro-divorce in the years between 1970 and 1974. During the early stages of the referendum dilemma, the DC's left wing made it clear to the party's leader, Amintore Fanfani, that to them liberty was just as important as the principle of indissoluble marriage. Before the vote, one of the main Catholic trade union organizations, CISL (Confederation of free Italian sindacalists), chose to take no clear stand either for or against divorce, and advised its members to vote according to their conscience.[16] Ambiguous neutrality was one thing, but there were also Catholics who openly sided with the pro-divorce campaign. In February 1974 the youth branch of the Association of Christian Italian Workers (ACLI) declared itself pro-divorce, and later that month nearly a hundred prominent liberal Catholics formed a pro-divorce committee. This committee acknowledged the need to safeguard the indissolubility of marriage, but not to a level of intransigence that excluded all possibility of dissolution in obvious cases of complete marital failure.[17]

The emergence of open Catholic dissent on the divorce question had great implications for the moral fabric of the nation, and newspapers hastened to bring it to the attention of the public.[18] The climax of this tendency concerned the Church's treatment of the abbot of one of Rome's Benedictine communities, three weeks before the referendum. Dom Giovanni Franzoni had declared himself in favor of divorce, and was promptly suspended "a divinis" (one step short of excommunication).[19] Unwittingly, the Church created a divorce martyr, and unsurprisingly, Dom Franzoni became the darling of *ABC* magazine.[20]

"No" Means "Yes"

Pro-divorce Catholics became known as "Catholics for the NO," which begs the question why, in the context of the referendum, "no" meant "yes, I am in favor of divorce." Because the referendum asked the Italian people whether they wanted to abolish an existing law, those who wanted to abolish the law had to vote "yes," while those wishing to retain it needed to vote "no." There was great potential for confusion, particularly as voters were asked to mark the ballot paper with a cross over the word they wished to choose. The campaign advertisements paid great attention to making sure people knew how to vote. The Catholics had the best mnemonic: one of their posters said simply "YES, as on your wedding day." In the weeks prior to the campaign "no" and "yes" could only mean being for or against divorce; widespread sensitivity to the new connotations of "yes" and "no" is best exemplified by the fact that in Italy the Eurovision Song Contest that year could not be televised until after the referendum, because the Italian entry was a song simply entitled "Sì!"[21]

Divorce and Feminist Consciousness

If the simple passing of time between the introduction of divorce and the referendum was one reason more people were likely to vote no, a further very important factor was the establishment of women's movements inspired by second-wave feminism in Italy during the early 1970s. These movements made defense of the divorce law into more of a women's issue than it had been in the 1960s, despite the pioneering efforts of *Noi donne*. The social revolution of the 1960s had initiated a broad debate on the institution of the Italian family and had helped to open it up for negotiation. Many publications for women, regardless of political hue, had agreed on the need for this debate since the 1960s or even earlier. It so happened that the introduction of a divorce law was the first major change to family law in Italy since 1865. It is important to recognize that the referendum was the most concrete question on which women were able to give an electoral opinion.

The importance of the divorce referendum as a turning point in a new feminist consciousness in Italy has been curiously underestimated in feminist historiography, possibly because it was overshadowed by the abortion debate that followed a few years later.[22] Yet the divorce referendum campaign brought women together as women, into the piazzas of Italy, to defend a law they knew would eventually prize open the oyster of the Italian family for further public debate.[23] The official literature of the two principal women's organizations, CIF and UDI, indicates that women had understood this from the advent of the republic, even if their views on the matter were diametrically opposed.

By the early 1970s divorce was a mainstream question for women, and the referendum was a turning point in women's collective consciousness.[24] The nascent feminist press of the era makes this clear. The first feminist magazine to be sold commercially in Italy, *Effe*, was to cry after the victory of the referendum, "Women's NO was not a battle cry to protect the unity of the family; it was a YES to their own liberation from the family-ghetto which the Christian Democrats saw as their rightful place."[25] In the lead-up to the referendum, *Effe* published at least one article of several pages on divorce in each issue, and the double issue of April–May 1974 had various articles amounting to 14 of its 55 pages dedicated to the divorce referendum. *Effe*'s attitude toward the referendum was captured by the cover of that issue, which showed a radiantly smiling rustic-looking woman at her market stall, holding a banner above her head in outstretched arms, proclaiming "Women say NO." She was not the sort of woman who was likely to write articles for *Effe*, but her picture suggested the solidarity of the women's front, across generations and classes, determined to protect the divorce law.[26]

If *Effe* represented the beginnings of an autonomous feminist press in Italy, *Noi donne* was one of the pioneers. Its approach to the divorce referendum represented the climax of a pro-divorce trajectory that had been evident from the late 1950s, when it had been the first magazine to air the question among ordinary readers. Prior to the referendum, and particularly in early 1974, *Noi donne* dedicated hundreds of pages to the defense of the divorce law, pages that give the impression of a sort of permanent pro-divorce fair all over Italy. Yet it was also a very serious matter, and true to *Noi donne*'s well-established tradition of letting Italian women speak for themselves, it sent reporters to all corners of the nation to find out what they thought about marriage and divorce, and how they planned to vote in the referendum.

The articles ranged from a 10-page "Speciale," interviewing four couples (two from Rome, one from Naples, and one from Turin) on the eve of their weddings,[27] to in-depth inquiries about the women of Sicily. On the cover of the Sicilian special number, a photograph of a group of head-scarfed women congregating on a humble doorstep evokes the indomitable social conservatism of the south. The main title, "What is the truth?" was posed between the Sicilian novelist Sciascia's claim "They are matriarchs," and the anti-*divorzisti*'s claim "They are weak." Inside, in a 15-page illustrated survey, we learn that they are in fact women of iron, but who generally see divorce as a means of resolving some of the difficult situations created by "the chances of life."[28] In other words, these women fit neither of the clichéd extremes ascribed to them by men. Instead, they demonstrated that they were perfectly capable of independent thought, and had a nuanced understanding of the modern world.

These are just two examples of a collection of surveys and inquiries that gave a human face to a political battle that was in full swing in the daily newspapers, among politicians, and on television. Of course, *Noi donne* was pro-divorce and so the human face they chose to present was only one side of the story. But even more mainstream women's magazines, glossy paeans to fashion and consumerism, such as *Grazia* and *Annabella*, weighed in on divorce shortly before the referendum. Normally such magazines steered clear of contentious issues because their readership covered a wide political spectrum, but in the spring of 1974 the divorce referendum dominated the whole nation, and it would have been very odd to stay completely silent.

Annabella, a popular middle-class glossy, had published two articles on divorce when it was introduced in 1970, but although it spoke to "modern" women, it was not greatly concerned, as *Noi donne* was, with actually modernizing them.[29] At the time of the referendum *Annabella* published just one article on the question, with the title "For heaven's sake don't take divorce away from us." It asked women not to allow themselves to be bamboozled by the political speculation, but to remember simply that the Fortuna-Baslini law was there to resolve marital situations that were beyond redemption. The article interviewed four women who had obtained, or were awaiting, "salvation" via divorce, to illustrate the law's utility.[30]

If the referendum was an important moment in the development of a new sense of self-confidence among Italian women, it was partly because their vote was crucial: they outnumbered men in the electorate by a margin of 1.7 million.[31] A century earlier Catholics had rightly been confident that the majority of Italian women would have been firmly against divorce, and the same had been true 50 or even 30 years earlier, when they had first obtained the right to vote. By 1974, however, no one was sure what women thought, and as a result, they were a major focus of the referendum campaign.[32] One poster printed by the LID showed a woman kneeling to tie her husband's shoelaces. The caption announced "NO, you are not a slave. If he knows you can leave he won't treat you like this."[33]

Those against divorce, on the other hand, sought earnestly to convince women of the age-old notion that marriage was a form of protection, while the option to dissolve it represented an advantage only for men. Showing how the intensity of the campaign sometimes resulted in a complete lack of restraint, one particularly scandalous article in *Il Segno*, the official organ of the Archbishopric of Milan, claimed that divorce was like Thalidomide, in that it may make women feel better, but it resulted in deformed children.[34]

Less outrageously lacking in taste but similarly scaremongering were some of the rhetorical tactics of the anti-divorce campaign's most prominent figure, Amintore Fanfani. Secretary of the Christian Democrats, by April 1974 Fanfani had also become the central figure of the referendum.[35] He chose to complete his indefatigable campaign tour of the length and breadth of Italy in the south, heartland of support for the Christian Democrats and supposed bastion of family values, where he touched both the economic and moral nerves of the Mezzogiorno. For example, in Taranto, he asked a theater packed with "madri di famiglia" (family mothers) to think about their men folk: "Today, after a little affair, they come back. Tomorrow, with divorce, who knows?"[36] Who knows whether these women were impressed by this exhortation to continue to accept the notion that their husbands' adulterous behavior was the lesser of two evils?

Fanfani ended his tour, and his campaign, in Sicily, where arguably the final chapter in the Italian divorce debates had begun, with *Divorzio all'italiana*. There, in the mountain town of Caltanisetta, he told an audience of farmers and peasants that if the divorce law were to be affirmed, the next thing would be "marriages between homosexuals, and perhaps . . . your own wives will leave you to escape with some young girl."[37] On the first point Fanfani was not far off the mark, but for the wrong reason. He tried to imply that marriages were like atoms, and once split, the calamitous results would only be limited by the imagination. It would in fact be a long time before homosexuals anywhere began to lobby for official recognition of their partnerships, but it is true that those claims lie on the same continuum as divorce: the divorce question in 1970s Italy was about whether to give individuals more choice over what constitutes a family. The same issue lies at the heart of contemporary campaigns by homosexuals for recognition of their relationships by the state.

The Referendum

Over the weekend of 12 and 13 May 1974, the Italian people voted overwhelmingly in favor of retaining the discretion that had been given to them by the Fortuna-Baslini law. The vote in favor of the law was 59.1 percent, while 40.9 percent voted to abolish it. The results varied significantly by region,[38] but taken in four main geographical groupings the variations were not as large as expected: in the north, 64.8 percent favored divorce; in central Italy, 65.2 percent were in favor; in Sardinia and Sicily, 51.7 percent were in favor; and only the mainland south registered a minority in favor of divorce, of 47.9 percent.[39]

The closeness of the vote in the south was a surprise to most observers, and the pro-*divorzisti* considered it a great victory over traditional southern loyalty to the Christian Democrats. Fortuna took the opportunity in his "victory speech" to suggest that the notion of the south as the ball and chain around Italy's foot should be thrown out once and for all. He exulted that with an overall balance of more than five million votes in favor of divorce, Italians had shown that they were inferior to no other nation. He stressed that it was the victory of a people, not a faction. For Fortuna, as for many others, this result represented a new page for Italy. He concluded: "You see, when a battle is honest, it is not always the case that the electorate must vote Christian Democrat."[40]

The victory of divorce was unarguably a significant defeat for the Christian Democrats, and less directly, the Roman Catholic Church.[41] At a stroke it called into question the political and cultural hegemony these twin pillars of Italian society had enjoyed since the foundation of the republic. The results of the referendum acted as a sort of census of the extent to which the Italian people had become secular. The fact that the DC had seriously miscalculated that extent cast a shadow over its ability to continue in its historic role of political synthesis that had long been the basis of its success.[42]

The question was what, if anything, would replace that synthesis. For the lay parties the referendum result was the most portentous political moment since 1946. It blocked the advance of the nascent right and remarginalized the MSI, which had used the referendum as an anti-Communist crusade. The victory certainly opened new prospects for the construction of a lay-progressive electoral front. It gave the PCI the confidence that it could be the leader of such a front, and opened a path to the electoral victory of 1976 and the "historic compromise." The passing of time, however, has shown that in political terms the new alternative did not materialize as many had hoped and expected.[43]

Apart from the actual preservation of the Fortuna-Baslini law, what the referendum undoubtedly achieved was twofold. In a prospective sense, even if it did not make a clean sweep of a set of sclerotic political arrangements, the result paved the way for substantial changes in Italian law in several areas. The first and most direct was the new family legislation of 1975.

This was first radical overhaul of Italian civil law in more than a century, and, with the divorce law, brought Italian legislation into line with developments in the rest of Europe and the Western world.[44] The second was the 1978 law decriminalizing abortion. Ultimately, too, the divorce law paved the way for a renegotiation, in 1984, of the 1929 concordat.

In a retrospective sense, the 1974 referendum allowed the Italian people to complete the unfinished business of 1947. In that year the Constituent Assembly had timorously kept the possibility of introducing divorce in Italy open, by voting against the constitutionalization of indissoluble marriage. With an Orwellian twist, the referendum of 1974 finally swept away the fears of 1947, with representatives of both sides of the argument keenly aware that divorce was an unsettled question of that important year.[45]

As Simona Colarizi has written, by 1974 the battle over divorce seemed simply "a challenge between old and new, between reaction and progress, and the majority of Italians voted for modernity."[46] If the ideal of modernity is responsible liberty for all, across a continuum linking political, civil, religious, and private spheres, the 1974 referendum showed not that Italians had finally been made modern, but that they had made themselves modern—to the surprise of a large proportion of the Italian political class. In the heart of the troubled 1970s, it was above all reason for Italians to be optimistic about the future of Italy, as they had been in 1947.

Conclusion

Divorcing Tradition

In Rome in early 2006, the headquarters of the *Messaggero* newspaper displayed a selection of half a dozen historic front pages in the large windows facing the busy Via del Tritone. These included the 1946 announcement that Italy had become a republic, a photograph of Neil Armstrong's footprint on the moon in 1969, and images of the terrorist attacks on New York City in September 2001. Amongst those epoch-making events also stood the front page announcing the result of the divorce referendum of May 1974, with the letters "NO" so large they occupied almost half the page. It might seem odd that a referendum on an aspect of Italian marriage law should be chosen to keep company with events such as the birth of a new political system, or the shattering horror of 9/11, but it is a reminder of the stature of May 1974 in the history of the Italian nation and for the identity of its people.

Part of the stature of the referendum derives from the sheer length of the debate over divorce, whose roots went back to the French Revolution. To continue the botanical metaphor, in Italy itself the debate bore a first indigenous shoot with Melchiorre Gioia's prize-winning study of 1803, became a branch of argument in the early decades of the nation, was lopped during fascism, grew back with the republic, reached maturity by 1970, and received a popular preservation order in 1974. But it was not only the duration of the divorce question that warranted its inclusion in a journalistic hall of fame (indeed, Italians today are often surprised to learn their nation debated divorce at all in the nineteenth century). It owes its particular place in Italian history to the fact that the divorce question acted as a litmus test for two historic struggles that seemed finally to have been resolved by the referendum of 1974.

In the first place, debating divorce created an arena that underlined the need for a clearer definition of the relationship between the Italian state and the Roman Catholic Church. The Roman question had been opened in 1870 and settled by the Lateran Pacts of 1929, but it gradually opened again in the 1950s and 1960s, at least in part because of unresolved questions such as divorce. Secondly, the divorce issue had always brought forth ideological tensions over the definition of the relationship between individual needs and collective interests. In the Italian case, the very duration of the divorce debates resulted partly from the difficulties of establishing the identity of that collectivity. Officially that identity became national in 1860, but the majority of Italians did not identify their interests, collective or individual, with the nation in those early years. If they were to do so, and it was the dream of Risorgimento visionaries such as Mazzini that they should, they would need to be wooed, cajoled, and made into Italians.

The institutions of marriage and the family, and the debates around them, played a fundamental role in that process. During the struggle to unify Italy, those who sought to win Italian hearts and minds for the cause of national unity made vital use of the metaphors of *parentela*, or kinship, as part of a strategy to convince Italians of the natural logic of creating a "national" family.[1] Mazzini's rallying cry, "Patria, famiglia, libertà!" is perhaps the most succinct example of the way in which the supposed continuum between family and fatherland was put to political use. Once that formula had been realized politically, the nation's legislators aimed to sculpt the body politic, to use Nancy Cott's memorable phrase,[2] by unifying marriage laws across the new *patria*.

The civil code of 1866, by conferring recognition only upon civil marriages, reveals Italian legislators attempting to stake a claim to territory over which the Catholic Church had held jurisdiction for many centuries. Two things contributed to the failure of this attempt: first, no law enforced the precedence of civil over religious marriage, with the result that many Italians simply ignored the former; second, the similarity between the civil law model and ecclesiastical law meant that marriage under the new code was a departure in name only—effectively, the new state administered a religious concept of marriage. The introduction of civil marriage did very little to establish a convergence between custom and law, or to make Italians in a new way. Nevertheless, in terms of the relationship between the state and the Church, it muddied, rather than clarified, the waters.

In 1878, Salvatore Morelli promoted divorce legislation in an attempt to clarify that relationship and rectify the limits of civil marriage. His proposal aimed to erase from marriage all vestiges of its canon-law past and make it an entirely secular institution. The secular ideals personified by Morelli were carried forward, albeit in less radical guises, by his successors in the Liberal era, Villa, Berenini, Zanardelli, and Commandini. From the outset, the Church demonstrated determined opposition, manifested through a series of well-coordinated campaigns against dissoluble marriage that showed the lay organizations of Catholicism well understood how to make use of the mechanisms of liberal democracy. Catholic opposition to divorce was augmented by the parliamentary resistance of an ill-defined mélange of secular conservatives, personified by Antonio Salandra. Representing a long line of secular conservative thought, Salandra insisted that the misery of a small number of individuals in failed marriages did not outweigh the collective benefits of preserving the indissolubility of marriage. The combined opposition of conservative and religious interests successfully undermined all efforts to introduce a divorce law in Italy before World War I.

This is a clear sign that in the early twentieth century Italy took a divergent path from the European countries that had provided its main political models, particularly France, Great Britain, and Germany. The clearest aspect of this divergence was the increasing involvement of the Catholic Church in Italian politics, an involvement that had existed subtly since the unification, but became more direct from the early 1900s. The orthodox historical interpretation of this change is that the pope permitted Catholics to enter parliament as an antidote to the spread of socialism, just at the point when Italy's dominant political grouping, the constitutional liberals, began to feel that the Church would make an easier political ally than the increasingly unwieldy and divided Socialist Party. In this view, the failure of divorce reform at about the same time was simply one small consequence of the political exigencies of the era. What this interpretation overlooks is the motive force of the divorce issue itself in pressing the Church to countenance a cohabitation with the state. That cohabitation set the tone of Italian politics for much of the twentieth century.

With the rise to power of Mussolini, what had originally been a cohabitation of convenience became a fully fledged *connubio*; but even before the Lateran Pacts triumphantly solved the problem of the relationship between the state and the Church, Mussolini's fascist ideology began to refashion the relationship between individual and collective interests. Fascism reversed the supposed liberal ideal of a minimal state serving to protect the freedoms of the individual, and in its place subordinated individual interests to those of a glorified state. Families too, were to serve the interests of the state. An individualistic law like divorce had no place in a scheme that sought to create each family as a microcosm of Mussolini's ideal state: hierarchical, fecund, and indissoluble. The Lateran Pacts of 1929 handed back to the Church its much-prized jurisdiction over the institution of marriage, and symbolically closed the divorce debates over which Catholic and conservative pressure, aided by the ambiguous official liberal position, had effectively triumphed earlier in the century.

The collapse of fascism at the end of World War II made way for Italy's democratic renewal. The first representatives of the Italian people under the republic envisaged the renewal as being one that would sweep away the vestiges of fascism and bring a more democratic basis to what they saw as the primary human association—the family. Yet, however thorough the democratic renewal might have been, it also established fundamental continuities with the past. Chief among those was the prestige and influence of the Catholic Church, whose continued power was now guaranteed by the incorporation of the Lateran Pacts into the Italian constitution. Even though the Constituent Assembly vigorously debated the democratization of the family, ultimately, as Anna Rossi-Doria argued, the model emerging from these debates bore the hallmarks of Catholic hegemony over the concept of the family unit.[3] In legal terms at least, this left the family more hierarchical and indissoluble than might otherwise have been the case.

The last-minute cancellation of the word "indissoluble" from the constitution's description of marriage and the family in 1947 may have been an important victory for the secular parties, but it was a pyrrhic victory that pales in significance beside the essential continuity of the legal regulation of family life, not just from the fascist era, but from the 1860s. The Constituent Assembly made no changes to the civil code, and as a result many of the equalities promised by the constitution, particularly between husbands and wives, remained merely symbolic. Thus women suffered a more stringent definition of adultery than men, and had to make their homes where their husbands chose; the father held ultimate authority over the couple's children—who belonged to their mother's husband, even if he was not their biological father. Similarly, illegitimate children, neither of whose parents were married, bore a formal stigma that made them perpetual second-class citizens. Finally, the constitution may not have prescribed marriage as indissoluble but, according to the civil code, death remained the only event that could dissolve wedlock.

This rigid imprint marked the Italian family throughout the 1950s, and the political dominance of the Christian Democrats made attempts to revise it unlikely to succeed. The efforts of socialists such as Luigi Sansone and Giuliana Nenni to raise interest in the introduction of a divorce law in the 1950s fell upon deaf ears in the Italian parliament. Nevertheless Sansone's work, particularly in disseminating the concept of "matrimonial outlaws"—those who had fallen foul of Italy's stringent marriage laws, often through no fault of their own—provided a kernel that gave new life to ideas that gradually broke the taboo against discussion of divorce. Others, such as Domenico Peretti Griva, writers for the women's magazine *Noi donne*, and authors for the journal *I problemi di Ulisse*, added their voices to Sansone's from the mid-1950s. By the early 1960s, Italy began to debate divorce openly again.

This debate took place in the context of increasing awareness that economic development and the mass movement of people across regional and even national boundaries was putting great strain upon families that were still regulated by an inflexible concept of what the institution of the family should be. Women's associations in particular, whether secular or Catholic in inspiration, showed great sensitivity to the fact that women bore the brunt of most of these stresses and strains, as they attempted to reconcile family responsibilities, economic pressures, and work opportunities in an increasingly complex world. In 1961, Pietro Germi's film, *Divorzio all' italiana*, provided an elegant sign of the times, addressing the transformation of traditional gender roles, regional disparities, and discrepancies between the law and reality.

By the mid-1960s more and more Italians could see that family law needed to adapt to the social and economic changes brought about by Italy's miraculous postwar development. The fact that divorce became a warhorse for those who sought to introduce such family-law changes owed much of its motive force to the vision, determination, and political acumen of Loris Fortuna. The very nature of the divorce question was equally important: by raising the church-state question, it also appealed to the growing cohort of those who wished to revisit an issue that even the Vatican, through the second ecumenical council, seemed to suggest was ripe for debate. Secondly, in the context of a nation that had begun to take on sociological contours similar to those of its northern European neighbors, the whole question of the relationships between individuals, families, and the state, also appealed to those whose agenda included renegotiating those arrangements.

The Radical Party, deeply committed to such issues, saw in divorce the perfect vehicle for its causes. Fortuna's proposal for a divorce law in October 1965 soon resulted in the birth of an unlikely extra-parliamentary team to support the parliamentary campaign. The team, led by Radical Party activists Marco Panella and Mauro Mellini, alongside Fortuna, consisted of the newly founded Lega Italiana per il Divorzio and the indefatigable weekly magazine *ABC*. This "divorce front" represented an important novelty in Italian lobbying: a politically transverse pressure group committed to a single cause—a cause that had the potential to destabilize the postwar political order.

The divorce question owed its destabilizing potential at least partly to the nature of Italy's political system, particularly after Center-Left coalitions became the norm from 1963. Christian Democrats and Socialists were the most common coalition partners, but the numerical dominance of the Christian Democrats, and the close relationship between that party and the Vatican, meant that Italy, despite the outward trappings of modernity, was not modern in spirit. The political wrangling that surrounded the entire divorce question from the mid-1960s until the 1974 referendum illustrates the realization of its destabilizing potential. On several occasions cabinets had to resign, and in 1972, with the government in deadlock over the prospect of a referendum on divorce, for the first time in the history of the republic the president had no alternative but to dissolve the legislature and call early elections. These events illustrated the seismic force of the divorce question in Italian politics, and the extent to which it was mired in considerations of political opportunity rather than principle.

Ironically, the disruptive effects of the divorce question seemed more evident inside parliament than in Italian society. After the introduction of the law in December 1970, Italians made sensible, responsible use of divorce and it became clear that it was not going to be the moral undoing of the nation. This partly explains the referendum decision of the Italian people, particularly that of many Catholics, not to abolish divorce law. The other major factor was the collective opinion of Italian women. During the economic miracle large numbers of women began to claim liberation from a legal position that had remained largely unchanged since the nineteenth century. These women, equipped for the first time with some measure of economic independence, eventually made divorce into the first broadly shared feminist issue.

In this sense, Anna Kuliscioff's claim in 1892 that the only true basis for liberation of Italian women would be a degree of economic wherewithal had been correct. She had only been wrong to place her faith in the idea that a socialist revolution would obviate women's need for "bourgeois" reforms like divorce. In fact the reform represented by the introduction of divorce in the 1970s and the popular mandate of 1974 amounted to a revolution in its own right. Subsequently, the introduction of divorce made way for a thoroughgoing revision of family law in 1975, the first major revision of the civil code in 110 years. Their action to save the divorce law gave women the collective confidence to address the abortion issue, which became another milestone in Italian feminist politics. Such changes shifted the framework for the debating of Italian family legislation from the nineteenth century to the twenty-first.

Recently, Paul Ginsborg summed up two competing models of the family in the present century. The first is a family that is "isolated, impermeable, and self-referential." The second is a family that is "porous, open, curious, desirous of interaction with other realities." Under the second model, the very nature of what constitutes a family would always be open for debate. As Ginsborg points out, while the realities of a global economy press families toward that more fluid model, representations of the ideal family in the West remain more and more desperately anchored in the first.[4] Although this position may underestimate the very changes that have taken place in families, and even their representation, over the past three decades or so, Ginsborg's scheme for the twenty-first century echoes the tensions that lay at the heart of Italy's debates on marriage and the family from 1860 to 1974. Toward the end of the nineteenth century, advocates of divorce law such as Morelli, Villa, and Zanardelli argued strenuously for a family model that responded to and interacted with changes in the outside world, while those who were against divorce argued that indissoluble families represented the best defense against the iniquities such changes might bring.

From the 1920s to the 1950s there was a long interlude while that position held sway, but between the 1960s and 1974, the majority of Italians gradually came to accept the idea that the opening of a dialogue between the family and changing society would be beneficial, not detrimental, to individual lives. Their popular vote in 1974 was certainly a landmark in a long debate, the end of the unfinished business of 1947 and even the 1860s. It closed an epoch in the history of the making of modern Italians, which is why *Il Messaggero*'s front page on the referendum more than deserved its place in the window over four decades later. But it was by no means the conclusion of anything more than a very long chapter. In May 1974, Italians voted themselves out of an isolation that the nation's conservatives had found splendid, and Italy entered a more European, global, and ongoing debate about the relationship between the intimate decisions of private life and the collective good. The only anathema in that debate is dogma.

Notes

Introduction

1. Archivio del Museo Centrale del Risorgimento, Rome, Archivio Garibaldi, busta 684, folder 1. Giacomo Emilio Curàtulo, *Garibaldi e le donne* (Rome: Imprimerie Polyglotte, 1913), pp. 293–313; Silvia Alberti de Mazzeri, *Le donne di Garibaldi* (Milan: Editoriale Nuova, 1981), pp. 162–163. The episode is also mentioned briefly in Denis Mack Smith, *Garibaldi. Una grande vita in breve* (translation of 1956 edition, Milan: Mondadori, 1995), p. 74, and Christopher Hibbert, *Garibaldi and his Enemies: The Clash of Arms and Personalities in the Making of Italy* (reprint of 1965 edition, Harmondsworth: Penguin Books, 1987), pp. 165–173.

2. Curàtulo, *Garibaldi e le donne*, p. 301.

3. According to an article by Alessandro Luzio in the *Corriere della Sera* (Milan) of 12 January 1914, p. 3, Garibaldi is alleged to have claimed in April 1860 before setting off for Sicily that he needed action, "to overcome the two-edged pain in [his] soul—wounded by the cession of Nice and by a shattered dream of love."

4. Garibaldi married Anita Ribeiro in Uruguay in the 1840s, and she had died while they were escaping from Rome after the revolution of 1848. She therefore entered the pantheon of Risorgimento martyrs.

5. Giuseppe Mazzini, *The Duties of Man and Other Essays* (London: Everyman, 1955), pp. 61–62.

6. Nancy Cott, *Public Vows: A History of Marriage and the Nation* (Cambridge, MA: Harvard University Press, 2000), esp. pp. 1–6.

7. On this dilemma, see, for example, Raffaele Romanelli, "Individualismo, famiglia e collettività nel codice civile della borghesia italiana," in Raffaella Gherardi and Gustavo Gozzi, *Saperi della borghesia e storia dei concetti fra Otto e Novecento* (Bologna: Il Mulino, 1995), p. 351; and Raffaele Romanelli, "Famiglia e diritto: Dall'ideologia del codice civile ai grandi numeri della statistica giudiziaria," *Quaderni storici* 91, no. 1 (1996): 41–67.

8. Alberto Mario Banti convincingly analyzes the evolution of this relationship in *La nazione del Risorgimento. Parentela, santità e onore alle origini dell'Italia unita* (Turin: Einaudi, 2000), p. 119.

9. Among the classic works are Arturo Carlo Jemolo, *Chiesa e stato negli ultimi cento anni* (Turin: Einaudi, 1948); Giovanni Spadolini, *L'opposizione cattolica da Porta Pia al '98* (reprint of 1954 edition, Florence: Edizioni della Cassa di Risparmio di

Firenze, 1991); Giorgio Candeloro, *Il Movimento cattolico in Italia* (Rome: Edizioni Rinascita, 1953).

10. In a representative case, the fate of divorce in the early twentieth century is relegated to a footnote by Filippo Mazzonis in "Dai democratici cristiani al patto Gentiloni," *Storia della società italiana*, Part 5, Vol. XX: *L'Italia di Giolitti* (Milan: Teti Editore, 1981), p. 355n.

11. Paul Ginsborg, *A History of Contemporary Italy: Society and Politics 1943–1988* (London: Penguin, 1990), p. 101.

12. Giorgio Fenoaltea, *Il divorzio. Tema con variazioni* (Rome: Campitelli, 1946), p. 40.

13. Giuseppe Passalaqua, *Il divorzio e la chiesa* (Naples: n.p., 1947).

14. Luigi Scremin, *Matrimonio divorzio e biologia umana* (Milan: Istituto di Propaganda Libraria, 1948), pp. 9 and 129. Incidentally, among the same author's other works was a pamphlet entitled *Il vizio solitario*, offering parents advice on how to teach their sons to avoid "the solitary vice."

15. Domenico Riccardo Peretti-Griva, *La famiglia e il divorzio* (Bari: Laterza, 1956).

16. Mario Berutti, *Il divorzio in Italia* (Milan: Edizioni di comunità, 1964), pp. 8–10.

17. Ibid.

18. Mauro Mellini, *Così annulla la Sacra Rota. Divorzio di classe nell'Italia clericale* (Rome: Samonà e Savelli, 1969); Leopoldo Piccardi, ed., *Il divorzio in Italia* (Florence: La Nuova Italia, 1969); Annamaria Galoppini, "Il problema del divorzio nella storia della legislazione italiana," *Rivista trimestrale del diritto e procedura civile*, XXIV, no. 2 (June 1970), pp. 532–567; Antonio Fappani, *La polemica divorzista in Italia* (Brescia: Queriniani, 1970); Mauro Mellini, *Le sante nullità. La vera alternativa: Divorzio o Sacra Rota?* (Rome: Edizioni Savelli, 1974); Francesco Perego, *Divorziare in nome di dio* (Venice-Padua: Marsilio Editori, 1974).

19. Alessandro Coletti, *Il divorzio in Italia. Storia di una battaglia civile e democratica*, 2nd ed. (Rome: Edizioni Savelli, 1974).

20. Pietro D'Avack, ed., *Studi sul divorzio* (Padua: CEDAM, 1972); Maria Grazia Lulli, "Il problema del divorzio in Italia dal sec. XVIII al codice del 1865," *Il diritto di famiglia e delle persone* Anno III, no. 4 (October–November 1974), pp. 1230–1247; Francesco Perego, *Divorziare in nome di dio* (Venice-Padua: Marsilio Editori, 1974); Tito Lucrezio Rizzo, "I progetti di divorzio dall'avvento al potere della sinistra alla fine del Secolo XIX," *Il diritto di famiglia e di persone* (1975), pp. 948–961; Simonetta Nelli, *Lo scioglimento del matrimonio nella storia del diritto italiano* (Milan: Giuffrè Editori, 1976); Annamaria Galoppini, "Profilo storico del divorzio in Italia," *Il diritto di famiglia e delle persone*, Anno IX, 1980, pp. 594–666; Lesley Caldwell, *Italian Family Matters: Women, Politics and Legal Reform* (Basingstoke: Macmillan, 1991), esp. Chapters 3 and 4.

21. Diana De Vigili, *La battaglia sul divorzio. Dalla Costituente al Referendum* (Milan: Franco Angeli, 2000).

22. Roderick Philips, *Family Breakdown in Late Eighteenth-Century France: Divorces in Rouen, 1792–1803* (Oxford: Oxford University Press, 1980); *Putting Asunder: A History of Divorce in Western Society* (Cambridge: Cambridge University Press, 1988).

23. Antony Copley, *Sexual Moralities in France, 1780–1980: New Ideas on the Family, Divorce and Homosexuality* (London: Routledge, 1989).

24. Francis Ronsin, *Les divorciares. Affrontements politiques et conceptions du mariage dans la France du XIXe siècle* (Paris: Aubier, 1992).

25. Mary Poovey, *Uneven Developments: The Ideological Work of Gender in Mid-Victorian England* (Chicago: University of Chicago Press, 1988), pp. 51–52.

26. Lawrence Stone, *The Road to Divorce: England, 1530–1987* (Oxford: Oxford University Press, 1990).

27. A. James Hammerton, *Cruelty and Companionship: Conflict in Nineteenth-Century Married Life* (London and New York: Routledge, 1992).

28. See for example, Mary Gibson, *Prostitution and the State in Italy, 1860–1915* (New Brunswick, NJ: Rutgers University Press, 1986); Lucetta Scaraffia and Gabriella Zarri, eds., *Donna e fede. Santità e vita religiosa in Italia* (Rome-Bari: Laterza, 1992); Margherita Pelaja, *Matrimonio e sessualità a Roma nell'Ottocento* (Rome-Bari: Laterza, 1994); Michela De Giorgio and Christiane Klapisch-Zuber, eds., *Storia del matrimonio* (Rome-Bari: Laterza, 1996).

29. Lucetta Scaraffia, "«Il Cristianesimo l'ha fatta libera, collocandola nella famiglia accanto all'uomo» (dal 1850 alla «Mulieris Dignitatem»)," in Lucetta Scaraffia and Gabriella Zarri, eds., *Donne e fede*, pp. 441–493.

30. Conversely, for a consideration of the notion that divorce may have threatened masculine privileges within marriage, see Mark Seymour, "Keystone of the Patriarchal Family? Indissoluble Marriage, Masculinity and Divorce in Liberal Italy," *Journal of Modern Italian Studies* 10, no. 3 (2005): 297–313.

Chapter 1   Making Italians

1. *Atti del Parlamento Italiano. Discussioni della Camera dei Deputati*, 2 April–28 December 1860 (Turin: Botta, 1861), p. 488.

2. Roderick Philips, *Putting Asunder: A History of Divorce in Western Society* (Cambridge: Cambridge University Press, 1988), pp. 34–36.

3. Dominique Lepetit, *L'histoire de France du divorce de 1789 à nos jours* (Cherbourg: Isoète, 1996), pp. 28–30.

4. John A. Davis, *Conflict and Control: Law and Order in Nineteenth-Century Italy* (Atlantic Highlands, NJ: Humanities Press International, 1988), p. 122.

5. While providing an indication of the extent to which the divorce law was used in one part of Italy between 1809 and 1815, an article on the subject by Benedetto Croce shows the way that brief period when divorce was permitted in Italy became symbolically important during the campaigns to introduce divorce after unification. Benedetto Croce, "Il divorzio nelle province napoletane: 1809–1815," *La scuola positiva*, Anno 1, nn. 11–12 (15–30 October 1891), pp. 481–497.

6. Eugenio Barsanti, "Matrimonio," *Enciclopedia giuridica italiana* 10 (Milan: Società Editrice Libreria, 1921), pp. 1–85.

7. Alberto Aquarone, *L'Unificazione legislativa e i codici del 1865* (Milan: Giuffrè Editore, 1960), p. 40.

8. Anna Maria Istasia, "La questione femminile nelle discussioni parlamentari postunitarie: Il codice civile del 1865," *Dimensioni e problemi della ricerca storica*, n. 2 (1991): 168.

9. Judith Jeffrey Howard provides a detailed analysis of the position of Italian women under the new civil code in "The Woman Question in Italy, 1861–1880," (Ph.D. diss., University of Connecticut, 1977), ch. 4.

10. Paolina Schiff, *La donna e la legge civile* (Milan: Tipografia Bellini, 1880), p. 5.

11. Christiane Klapisch-Zuber, "Introduzione," in Michela De Giorgio and Christiane Klapisch-Zuber, eds. *Storia del matrimonio* (Rome-Bari: Laterza, 1996), p. xvi.

12. Carlo Francesco Gabba, *Studi di legislazione civile comparata in servizio della nuova codificazione italiana* (Milan: Tipi di Alessandro Lombardi, 1862), p. 214. It is worth noting that in this work Gabba declared himself in favor of divorce, writing that it was the next logical step after the introduction of civil marriage (p. 233). He later became one of the most prestigious scholars to lend his voice to the anti-divorce cause.

13. See for example, the opinions of Broferio, in *Atti del Parlamento Subalpino. Discussioni della Camera dei Deputati*, Session of 1852, Vol. V: 4 March 1852–21 November 1853 (Florence: Botta, 1868), pp. 1309ff.

14. For example, Peringotti, ibid., p. 1298; De Viry, ibid., p. 1315.

15. 94 in favor, 35 against, 3 abstentions, ibid., p. 1444.

16. *Atti del Parlamento Subalpino. Discussioni del Senato del Regno*, Session of 1852, March 1852–21 November 1853 (Florence: Botta, 1868), p. 262.

17. Ibid., p. 265.

18. Ibid., p. 280.

19. Ibid., pp. 299–300.

20. Ibid., p. 348.

21. Ibid., p. 349.

22. Giuseppe Piola, "Matrimonio (diritto civile)," *Il Digesto italiano. Enciclopedia metodica e alfabetica di legislazione, dottrina e giurisprudenza*, Vol. XV, Part 1 (Turin: Unione Tipografico Editrice Torinese, 1903–1907), p. 1092; Gabba, *Studi di legislazione civile*, p. 215.

23. Harry Hearder, *Italy in the Age of the Risorgimento, 1790–1870* (London and New York: Longman, 1983), p. 215.

24. *Atti del Parlamento Italiano. Discussioni della Camera dei Deputati*, Session of 1860, 2 April–28 December 1860, p. 488.

25. *Atti del Parlamento Italiano. Discussioni del Senato del Regno*, Session of 1861–62, Vol. III (Florence: Botta, 1870), p. 2713.

26. Ibid., p. 2711.

27. *Atti del Parlamento Italiano. Discussioni del Senato del Regno*, Session of 1863, July 1863, p. 245.

28. Ibid., p. 246.
29. Ibid., pp. 248–249.
30. *Atti del Parlamento Italiano. Senato del Regno. Progetti di legge, relazioni e documenti diversi*, Session of 1863–64, 25 May 1863–16 May 1865 (n.p., n.d.), p. 1264.
31. Ibid., p. 1265.
32. *Atti del Parlamento Italiano. Discussioni del Senato del Regno*, Session of 1863, p. 249.
33. *Atti del Parlamento Italiano. Discussioni della Camera dei Deputati*, Session of 1863–64–65, Vol. X: 5 January–22 February 1865, 2nd ed. (Rome: Camera dei Deputati, 1890), p. 8198.
34. *Indice generale degli Atti Parlamentari, 1848–1897* (Rome: Tipografia della Camera dei Deputati, 1898), Part 1, p. 427.
35. See, for example, D. Agostino Romani, *Beni recati alla società dal Cristianesimo e mali prodotti dall'eresia. Con cenno sul divorzio amesso dai moderni politici* (Rome: Tip. Di Filippo Cairo, 1863).
36. Gabba, *Studi di legislazione civile*, p. 232.
37. Melchiorre Gioia, *Teoria civile e penale del divorzio. Ossia necessità, cause, nuova maniera d'organizzarlo seguita dall'analisi della legge francese 30 venosto Anno XI relativo allo stesso argomento* (Milan: Piriotta e Maspero, 1803).
38. Gabba, *Studi di legislazione civile*, p. 233.
39. Ibid., p. 238.
40. Carlo Coscioni, *I prolegomeni al nuovo codice civile italiano* (Naples: Tipografia dell'Arno, 1863), p. v.
41. Ibid., p. ix.
42. Ibid., p. xiv.
43. Giuseppe Consolo, *Del divorzio nei rapporti colle leggi civili e colla libertà dei culti riconosciuti nello stato* (Padua: Tipografia A. Bianchi, 1864), p. 10.
44. Ibid., p. 15.
45. Elviro Naclerio, *Il divorzio e le leggi: Considerazioni* (Naples: Tipografia Carlo Zomack, 1867), p. 32.
46. Ibid., p. 12.
47. Ibid., p. 21.
48. Ibid., pp. 24–26 and 29.
49. Ibid., p. 47.
50. Ibid., pp. 48–49.
51. Attilio Pagliaini, *Catalogo generale della libreria italiana dall'anno 1847 a 1899* (Milan: Associazione Tipografico-Libraria Italiana, 1901), pp. 649–650.
52. Franca Pieroni Bortolotti, "Introduzione" to Anna Maria Mozzoni, in Franca Pieroni Bortolotti ed., *La liberazione della donna* (Milan: Gabriele Mazzotta Editore, 1975), p. 9.
53. Anna Maria Mozzoni, *La donna in faccia al progetto del nuovo codice civile italiano* (Milan: Tipografia Sociale, 1865), p. 7.
54. Ibid., pp. 24–25.
55. Bortolotti, "Introduzione," p. 13; Annarita Buttafuoco, *Cronache femminili. Temi e momenti della stampa emancipazionista in Italia dall'Unità al fascismo*

(Siena: Dipartimento di Studi Storico-Sociali e Filosofi, Università degli Studi di Siena, 1988), p. 10.

56. Bortolotti, "Introduzione," p. 13.

57. Maria Alimonda Serafini, *Matrimonio e divorzio. Pensieri* (Salerno: Stabilimento Tipografia Nazionale, 1873).

58. *Enciclopedia biografica e bibliografica "italiana,"* Series VI: *Poetesse e scrittrici,* Vol. II (Rome: Istituto Editoriale Italiano, 1942), pp. 247–248.

59. Oscar Greco, *Bibliografia femminile italiana del XIX secolo* (Venice: Tipografia Issoglio, 1875), pp. 448–456.

60. Serafini, *Matrimonio e divorzio,* p. 11.

61. Ibid., p. 19.

62. Ibid., p. 12.

63. Ibid., p. 13.

64. Ibid., p. 14.

65. Ibid., p. 18.

66. Ibid., p. 21.

67. Domenico Di Bernardo, *Il divorzio considerato nella teoria e nella pratica* (Palermo: Tipografia A. Natale, 1875), p. 1.

68. Ibid., p. 230.

69. Ibid., p. 232.

70. Ibid., p. 234.

71. Ibid., p. 239.

72. Ibid., p. 244.

73. Ibid., pp. 247–248.

74. Ibid., p. 249.

75. Ibid., p. 285.

76. Ibid., p. 684.

77. Francesco Meleri, *Il divorzio. Romanzo sociale* (Crema: Tipografia Sociale, 1876), pp. 17–21.

78. Ibid., p. 259.

79. Giuseppe Ricciardi, *Il divorzio* (Naples: Tipografia S. Pietro, 1876), p. 66.

80. Ibid., pp. 9–11.

81. Ibid., pp. 16–17.

82. Ibid., pp. 32–33.

83. Ibid., p. 36.

84. Ibid., p. 61.

85. Ibid., p. 64.

86. Ibid., p. 67.

Chapter 2   Unmaking Marriage?

1. Anna Maria Isastia, "L'attività parlamentare di Salvatore Morelli," in Ginevra Conti Odorisio, ed., *Salvatore Morelli (1824–1880). Emancipazionismo e democrazia nell'Ottocento europeo* (Naples: Edizioni Scientifiche Italiane, 1992), p. 114.

2. Francis Ronsin, *Les Divorciaires: Affrontements politiques et conceptions du mariage dans la France du XIXe siècle* (Paris: Aubier, 1992), p. 178.

3. Alfred Naquet, *Le divorce* (Paris: E. Dentu, 1877).

4. Ronsin, *Les Divorciares*, pp. 188–190.

5. Ginevra Conti Odorisio, "Pensiero politico e questione femminile ne *La donna e la scienza* di Salvatore Morelli," in Odorisio, ed., p. 42.

6. *Atti del Parlamento Italiano. Discussioni della Camera dei Deputati*, Session of 1878, Vol. II: 13 May–17 June (Roma: Tip. Eredi Botta, 1878), p. 1099.

7. Maria Teresa Guerra Medici, "Un salentino nel Risorgimento italiano. Gli anni di formazione," in Odorisio, ed., pp. 136–141.

8. Ibid., pp. 139–140.

9. Salvatore Morelli, *La donna e la scienza, o la soluzione del problema sociale*, 3rd ed. (Naples: Società Tipografico-Editrice, 1869), p. 10.

10. Ibid., pp. 16–17.

11. Ibid., p. 24.

12. Ibid., p. 25.

13. Odorisio, "Pensiero politico," p. 48. Morelli had come into contact with these ideas while he was in prison.

14. Morelli, *La donna*, p. 11.

15. Paul Ginsborg, "Family, Civil Society and the State in Contemporary European History: Some Methodological Considerations," *Contemporary European History* 4, no. 3 (1995): 259.

16. See Morelli, *La donna*, p. 129.

17. *Atti del Parlamento Italiano. Discussioni della Camera dei Deputati*, Session of 1878, Vol. II: 13 May–17 June, p. 1100.

18. Ibid., p. 1102.

19. Morelli, *La donna*, p. 129.

20. *Atti del Parlamento Italiano. Discussioni della Camera dei Deputati*, Session of 1878, Vol. II: 13 May–17 June, p. 1100.

21. Anne Taylor Allen, "Feminism, Social Science and the Meanings of Modernity: The Debate on the Origin of the Family in Europe and the United States, 1860–1914," *American Historical Review* 104, no. 4 (1999): 1087.

22. *Atti del Parlamento Italiano. Discussioni della Camera dei Deputati*, Session of 1878, Vol. II: 13 May–17 June, p. 1100.

23. Ibid., pp. 1100–1101.

24. Ibid., p. 1103.

25. Ibid.

26. Ibid., p. 1105.

27. Ibid.

28. Ibid., p. 1106. The approval was given by the deputies standing: no figures were recorded.

29. See for example, *La Nazione* (Florence), 26 May 1878. Note also, that Milan's Socialist newspaper, *La Plebe*, made no mention of divorce at this time. When it did finally bring up the issue, it was on 10 August 1878, in response to the campaign in France. It published a long editorial on the hypocrisy of bourgeois marriage.

30. *Osservatore romano* (Rome), 18 May 1878.

31. *Osservatore romano*, 26 May 1878.

32. Guido Verucci, *L'Italia laica prima e dopo l'Unità 1848–1876. Anticlericalismo, libero pensiero e ateismo nella società italiana* (Rome-Bari: Laterza, 1981), p. 302.

33. *La Capitale* (Rome), "Il divorzio," 24 May 1878.

34. *La Capitale*, "Il divorzio," 28 May 1878.

35. Archivio Storico della Camera dei Deputati, Disegni e Progetti di Legge, Incarti delle Commissioni (henceforth, ASCD, DPLIC), busta 265. N.B. the papers within the *buste* are unnumbered.

36. Ibid.

37. Ibid.

38. See, for example, Coreale's comments, Ufficio II, or the votes of Ufficio V, ASCD, DPLIC, 265.

39. Comment by Napodario, Ufficio VII, and conclusions of Ufficio VII's deliberations, ASCD, DPLIC, 265.

40. There is no record of ninth *ufficio*'s meeting, but Morelli, introducing his second proposal for a divorce law, claimed that the commission was in majority against: *Atti del Parlamento Italiano. Discussioni della Camera dei Deputati*, Session of 1880, 8 March 1880 (Rome: Camera dei Deputati), p. 569.

41. Archivio del Museo Centrale del Risorgimento Italiano, Archivio Garibaldi, busta 684, folder 15, folio 7.

42. Ibid., 684/7(2).

43. Ibid., 684/6(1).

44. Ibid., 684/1(15).

45. Ibid., 684/6(1).

46. Ibid.

47. Ibid., 684/7(10).

48. Ibid., 684/12(4), p. 10.

49. Ibid., 684/12(4), p. 11.

50. Ibid.

51. Ibid.

52. Ibid., 684/12(4), p. 21.

53. Ibid., 684/12(4), p. 25.

54. Ibid., 684/12(4), p. 32.

55. Ibid., 684/12(4), p. 40.

56. Ibid.

57. Ibid., 684/12(4), p. 56.

58. Ibid., 684/12(4), p. 57.

59. Ibid., 684/12(4), pp. 41–42.

60. Archivio di Stato di Roma, Corte di Apello, Sentenze Civili, busta 86, sentenza 492/79, pp. 17–35.

61. Ibid., p. 21.

62. Ibid., p. 24.

63. Ibid., p. 25.

64. Ibid., pp. 30–32.

65. Ibid., p. 33.

66. See, for example, *Corriere della sera* (Milan), 27–28 January and 29–30 January 1880, and *La Nazione*, 1 February 1880.

67. *La Capitale*, 6 January 1880.
68. Ronsin, *Les divorciares*, p. 196.
69. Ibid., pp. 199 and 215.
70. Alexandre Dumas (figlio), *La questione del divorzio* (Milan: Ferdinando Garbini Editore, 1880).
71. The encyclical was published in Italian in *La Voce della verità* (Milan) on 20 February 1880.
72. Ronsin, *Les divorciares*, pp. 209–211.
73. *Atti del Parlamento Italiano. Camera dei Deputati. Raccolta degli atti stampati per ordine della Camera*, Session of 1880, 17 February–2 May 1880, Vol. II: nn. 34–100 (Rome: Camera dei Deputati, 1880), no. 65.
74. *Atti del Parlamento Italiano. Discussioni della Camera dei Deputati*, Session of 1880, 17 February–2 May 1880 (Rome: Camera dei Deputati, 1880), p. 570.
75. Ibid., pp. 578–579.
76. See, for example, *Corriere della sera*, 10–11 March 1880.
77. Ibid., 9–10 March 1880.
78. *La Voce della verità*, 10–11 March 1880.
79. *Osservatore romano*, 10 March 1880.
80. Isastia, "L'attività parlamentare," p. 117.
81. Fiorenza Taricone, "Salvatore Morelli e Anna Maria Mozzoni," in Odorisio, ed., p. 183.
82. Ibid., p. 182.

Chapter 3   Divorce Italian Style?

1. Marina Beer, "Miti e realtà coniugali nel romanzo italiano fra Ottocento e Novecento," in Michela De Giorgio and Christiane Klapisch-Zuber, eds., *Storia del matrimonio* (Rome-Bari: Laterza, 1996), pp. 439–463. Beer claims that while Italian literature did portray unhappy marriages and scandals such as adultery, novels that featured marriage breakdown were extremely rare. She mentions Giovanni Verga's novel *Eros* (1875) and Carolina Invernizzo's *La maestra del pianoforte* (1892) as the only ones, and claims that no novel would actually portray divorce in a positive light until the early twentieth century. This is not strictly correct, since Francesco Meleri's 1875 novel (analyzed in chapter 1, pp. 30–31) specifically promoted divorce, and the popular novelist Cordelia (the pen-name of Virginia Treves) published *Catene* (*Chains*), the story of a woman whose marital problems would have been solved by a divorce law, in 1882.

    To this list must be added Federico De Roberto's *I viceré*, first published in 1894 but set at the time of Italian unification, and one of the Risorgimento's great novels. The story of an ancient Sicilian dynasty's determination to survive the unification, one of its most remarkable episodes is a scandalous double annulment by an ecclesiastical court, enabling two lovers to marry. The annulments take place after unification but before the civil code of 1865 standardized Italy's law. Above all, the episode underlines the minutely complex interrelationship between centers of local power (in this case the Uzeda family) and the Church. Connections of blood, land, politics, and money ensure that strictly black-letter scruples are overlooked when the petitioners for an annulment are members of an elite caste. Federico De Roberto, *I viceré* (Turin: Einaudi, 1990), pp. 371–382.

2. See Domenico Rizzo, "Marriage on Trial: Adultery in Nineteenth-Century Rome," in Perry Willson, ed., *Gender, Family and Sexuality: the Private Sphere in Italy, 1860–1945* (Basingstoke: Palgrave Macmillan, 2004), pp. 20–36.

3. *Atti del Parlamento Italiano. Discussioni della Camera dei Deputati*, Session of 1880, 8 March 1880 (Rome: Camera dei Deputati), p. 570.

4. Ibid.

5. Little attention has so far been given to this very interesting subject. One noteworthy exception is an essay that examines the way the Church exercised its power to make exceptions in the marriage law among the poor of Rome before Italian unification: Margherita Pelaja, "Marriage by Exception: Marriage Dispensations and Ecclesiastical Policies in Nineteenth-Century Rome," *Journal of Modern Italian Studies* 1, no. 2 (1996): 223–244.

6. *Acta Sanctae Sedis. Ephemeridis (1865–1908). Index generalis* (Rome: Typis Editricis Romanae, 1909), pp. 387–397.

7. Roderick Philips claims that those who have studied the question see little reason to believe that in the past annulments were used as a substitute for divorce. Philips, *Putting Asunder*, p. 9.

8. For example, cases treated "economically" (i.e., at no charge) appear frequently in *Analecta Juris Pontificiae. Dissertations sur différents sujets de droit canonique, liturgie theologie et histoire* (Rome: Librairie de la Propagande), for example Vol. 12, p. 897 (1871); Vol. 14 (1875), p. 444; Vol. 15 (1876), p. 825; Vol. 21 (1882), p. 699.

9. Paolo Ungari, *Il diritto di famiglia in Italia. Dalle Costituzioni "giacobine" al Codice civile del 1942* (Bologna: Il Mulino, 1970), p. 145.

10. *Atti del Parlamento Italiano. Camera dei Deputati. Raccolta degli atti stampati per ordine della Camera*, Session of 1873–74, Vol. II: nn. 29–71 (Rome: Camera dei Deputati, 1874), no. 48.

11. "Istructio S. Poenitentiariae Apostolica circa Contractum Quem Matrimonium Civile Appellant," *Acta Sanctae Sedis* I, Appendix XVIII (Rome: Ex Tipografia Polyglotta, 1898), p. 511.

12. *Analecta juris pontificiae* 21 (1882), p. 699.

13. By contrast, during the 1960s the number of annulments in Italy rose to about 300 a year, thus resparking the old debates about annulments being divorces for those favored by the Church. See Mauro Mellini, *Così annulla la Sacra Rota. Divorzio di classe nell'Italia clericale* (Rome: Savonà e Savelli, 1969), p. 118.

14. Philips, *Putting Asunder*, pp. 13–14.

15. Italy, *Codice civile* (Turin: Unione Tipografico-Editrice, 1888), pp. 57–59. Personal separation was regulated by articles 148–158 of Book I.

16. Federico Ciccaglione, "Separazione personale," in *Il Digesto italiano. Enciclopedia metodica e alfabetica di legislazione, dottrina e giurisprudenza*, Vol. 21, Part 2 (Turin: Unione Tipografico-Editrice, 1896), p. 855.

17. These and the following statistics are all from *Atti del Parlamento Italiano. Camera dei Deputati. Raccolta degli atti stampati per ordine della Camera*, Session of 1880–81, Vol. VII: nn. 126–181 (Rome: Camera dei Deputati, 1882), no. 159-A (henceforth referred to as Law no. 159-A), pp. 16–46.

18. Ciccaglione, "Separazione personale," p. 867.

19. Ibid., p. 825.

20. Law no. 159-A, p. 16.

21. Because Rome became part of the Italian nation only during 1870, and the statistics on personal separation for Rome run only from 1871, it cannot be included in this analysis of regional variations.

22. Law no. 159-A, p. 38.

23. Ibid., p. 41.

24. Ibid.

25. Procedure gleaned from the Rome records of personal separation, Archivio di Stato di Roma, Archivio del Tribunale Civile e Penale di Roma, "Separazione di coniugi" (henceforth ASR, TCP, SC).

26. See for example, Elviro Naclerio, *Il divorzio e le leggi: Considerazioni* (Naples: Tipografia Carlo Zomack, 1867), pp. 46–47.

27. Direzione Generale della Statistica, *Annali di statistica. Appendice agli atti della commissione per la statistica giudiziaria e notarile (sessione del luglio 1898). Divorzi e separazioni personali dei coniugi. Relazione*, by Augusto Bosco (Rome: Tipografia nazionale di G. Bertero, 1908), p. 7.

28. Law no. 159-A, p. 38.

29. This was a common sum among the workers applying for personal separation in the 1870s–1890s.

30. ASR, TCP, SC, 1882, busta 16, fasc. 2.

31. Ibid., 1882, busta 16, fasc. 9.

32. Rizzo, in "Marriage on Trial," pp. 29–30, presents an interesting analysis of the way the threat of criminal prosecution for adultery could be used to exert pressure in separation cases.

33. ASR, TCP, SC, 1882, busta 16, fasc. 36.

34. Ibid., 1884, busta 18, fasc. 23.

35. Ibid., 1882, busta 16, fasc. 35.

36. Ibid., 1887, busta 21, fasc. 55.

37. Ibid., 1892, busta 26, fasc. 6.

38. For example, ibid., 1887, busta 21, fasc. 16 and 18.

39. Ibid., 1892, busta 26, fasc. 14.

40. Ibid., fasc. 1.

41. Pietro Germi, dir., *Divorzio all'italiana* (Rome, 1961).

42. *Atti del Parlamento Italiano. Discussioni della Camera dei Deputati*, Session of 1880, 8 March 1880 (Rome: Camera dei Deputati), p. 571.

43. *Atti del Parlamento Italiano. Camera dei Deputati. Raccolta degli atti stampati per ordine della Camera*, Session of 1880–81, Vol. VII: nn. 126–181 (Rome: Camera dei Deputati, 1882), Law no. 159 (henceforth Law 159), p. 29.

44. Murder figures from p. 29 of the appendix to Villa's proposal; population figures from Table XIX of Villa's 1880 proposal, all Law no. 159. N.B. Population

figures refer to the area covered by a particular court, not only the city where the court was located.

45. *Atti del Parlamento Italiano. Discussioni della Camera dei Deputati*, Session of 1880, 8 March 1880 (Rome: Camera dei Deputati), p. 571.
46. *Corriere della sera* (Milan), 30 September–1 October 1879.
47. See the *Corriere della sera* of 2–3 October 1879.
48. Ibid., 1–2 October 1879.
49. Ibid.
50. Ibid., 30 September 1879.
51. Ibid.
52. Ibid., 30 September–1 October 1879.
53. Ibid., 4–5 October 1879.
54. Ibid., 2–3 October 1879.
55. Ibid., 30 September–1 October 1879.
56. Ibid., 4–5 October 1879.
57. Ibid., 2–3 October 1879.
58. Ibid., 1–2 October 1879.
59. Ibid., 3–4 October 1879.
60. Ibid., 4–5 October 1879.
61. Ibid., 5–6 October 1879.
62. Ibid., 16–17 October 1879.
63. Ibid., 17–18 October 1879.
64. Ibid., 18–19 October 1879.
65. Ibid., 19–20 October 1879.
66. Ibid.
67. Ibid., 22–23 October 1879.
68. Ibid.
69. Ibid., 31 October–1 November 1879.
70. *La Capitale* (Rome), 2 November 1879.
71. *Corriere della sera*, 1–2 November 1879.
72. *La Capitale*, 3 February 1880.
73. *Corriere della sera*, 27–28 October 1879.

Chapter 4   Real Italy versus Legal Italy

1. Silvano Montaldo has superbly reconstructed the interplay between divorce, Villa's biography, and his view of nation-building in "Il divorzio: famiglia e *nation building* nell'italia liberale," *Il Risorgimento* no. 1 (2000): 5–57.
2. Alfredo Canavero, *I cattolici nella società italiana. Dalla metà dell'800 al Concilio Vaticano II* (Brescia: Editrice La Scuola, 1991), p. 89.
3. *Atti del Parlamento Italiano. Discussioni della Camera dei Deputati*, Session of 1880, Vol. III: 17 February–2 May 1880 (Rome: Camera dei Deputati), p. 578.
4. If a proposed law was presented to parliament by the government it was referred to as a *disegno*, or draft; if a law was proposed by an individual deputy,

it was referred to as a *proposta*, or proposal. In the latter case the parliament had to vote on whether to take the law into consideration or not. Naturally, a government draft did not require such approval.

5. *Osservatore romano* (Rome), 23 January 1881.
6. *Osservatore romano*, 29 January 1881.
7. *Il Messaggero* (Rome), 29 January 1881.
8. Biblioteca del Seminario Patriarcale Venezia, Archivio dell'Opera dei Congressi (henceforth BSPV, AOC), busta 30, letter from Salviati to Aquaderni, 13 January 1881.
9. BSPV, AOC, busta 30, letter from Salviati to unidentifiable correspondent, 15 January 1881.
10. Ibid., letter from Salviati, 17 January 1881.
11. Ibid., Scipione Salviati, untitled circular, 17 January 1881.
12. Ibid., undated petition [January 1881].
13. Giovanni Spadolini, *L'opposizione cattolica da Porta Pia al '98* (reprint of 1954 edition, Florence: Edizioni della Cassa di Risparmio di Firenze, 1991), p. 3.
14. Ibid., p. 31.
15. Angelo Gambasin, *Il movimento sociale nell'Opera dei Congressi (1874–1904). Contributo per la storia del cattolicesimo sociale in Italia* (Rome: Editrice Università Gregoriana, 1958), p. 20–21.
16. Canavero, *I cattolici nella società italiana*, pp. 52–53.
17. Gambasin, *Il movimento sociale*, pp. 33–34.
18. Ibid., p. 33.
19. Ibid., p. 54.
20. Canavero, *I cattolici nella società italiana*, pp. 70–71.
21. In 1897 the Catholic social movement boasted 188 diocesan committees, 3,982 parish committees, 708 youth sections, 17 university clubs, 588 rural banks, 24 daily newspapers, 115 periodicals, 688 working women's societies, and 116 youth clubs. Gabriele De Rosa, *Il movimento cattolico in Italia. Dalla Restaurazione all'età giolittiana* (Rome-Bari: Laterza, 1988), p. 127.
22. Arturo Carlo Jemolo, *Chiesa e stato negli ultimi cento anni* (Turin: Einaudi, 1948), p. 402.
23. Ibid., p. 403.
24. Gambasin, *Il movimento sociale*, p. 18.
25. Ibid., p. 19.
26. *Atti del Parlamento Italiano. Camera dei Deputati. Raccolta degli atti stampati per ordine della Camera*, Session of 1880–81, Vol. VII: nn. 126–181 (Rome: Camera dei Deputati, 1882), Law no. 159, pp. 29–100 (henceforth Law 159).
27. Ibid., p. 37.
28. Ibid., Art. 4, p. 25.
29. Ibid., Art. 5, p. 5.
30. Ibid., Art. 7, p. 6.
31. Ibid., Art. 8, p. 6.
32. Ibid., p. 1.
33. Ibid., p. 7.

34. *Atti del Parlamento Italiano. Camera dei Deputati. Raccolta degli atti stampati per ordine della Camera*, Session of 1880–81, Vol. VII: nn. 126–181 (Rome: Camera dei Deputati, 1882), Law no. 159, pp. 29–100 (henceforth Law 159), p. 7.

35. Ibid., p. 8.

36. Ibid.

37. Ibid., p. 10.

38. Ibid., p. 12.

39. Ibid.

40. Because a man was considered an adulterer by the Italian law only if he kept a concubine in the marital home or "notoriously" elsewhere, it was very difficult for a separated husband to be found guilty of adultery.

41. Law no. 159, p. 23.

42. The right for the public (anyone, including women, over majority age) to petition the government went back to the 1848 Statuto, and was put to use most spectacularly by the Opera dei Congressi's campaigns against divorce.

43. ASCD, DPLIC, busta 321, f. 366.

44. Ibid., f. 366.

45. Ibid., f. 369.

46. Ibid., f. 407.

47. Ibid., ff. 376–389. It is not absolutely clear by what majority, as the vote of one *ufficio* was not recorded, but it appears that not less than six of the nine *uffici* voted in favor of the law.

48. *Atti del Parlamento Italiano. Camera dei Deputati. Raccolta degli atti stampati per ordine della Camera*, Session of 1880–81, Vol. VII: nn. 126–181 (Rome: Camera dei Deputati, 1882), Document 159-A (henceforth, Document no. 159-A).

49. Antonio Salandra, *Il divorzio in Italia* (Rome: Forzani e Co., 1882), p. iv.

50. Ibid., p. iv.

51. Ibid., pp. 55–56.

52. Tunis was home to more than 9,000 Italians at the time, and a mere 200 French. It was also the part of the African landmass closest to Italy, and the French occupation was considered an affront to Italy's national prestige. Martin Clark, *Modern Italy, 1871–1982* (London and New York: Longman, 1984), p. 46.

53. Salandra, *Il divorzio in Italia*, p. 41 et seq.

54. Ibid., p. 83.

55. Ibid., p. 102.

56. Ibid., p. 113.

57. Ibid., e.g. p. 81.

58. Ibid., p. 180.

59. *Atti del Parlamento Italiano. Discussioni della Camera dei Deputati*, Session of 1882–86, Vol. III: 9 March –27 April 1883 (Rome: Camera dei Deputati, 1886), p. 2189.

60. *Atti del Parlamento Italiano. Camera dei Deputati. Raccolta degli atti stampati per ordine della Camera*, Session of 1882–86, 22 November 1882–27 April 1886, Vol. VI: nn. 56–90, Law no. 87 (Rome: Camera dei Deputati, 1886).

61. Ibid., p. 2.

62. ASCD, DPLIC, busta 370.
63. Domenico Giuriati, *Le leggi dell'amore* (Turin: Roux e Favale, 1881). The author expresses a favorable view of divorce at, for example, p. 22 et seq.
64. *Atti del Parlamento Italiano. Camera dei Deputati. Raccolta degli atti stampati per ordine della Camera*, Session of 1882–86, 22 November 1882–27 April 1886, Vol. VI: nn. 56–90, Document no. 87-A (Rome: Camera dei Deputati, 1886), p. 16 (henceforth Document 87-A).
65. Ibid., p. 5.
66. Ibid., p. 10.
67. Ibid., p. 16.
68. Ibid.
69. The best account of these events is in Francis Ronsin, *Les divorciares. Affrontements politiques et conceptions du mariage dans la France du XIXe siècle* (Paris: Aubier, 1992), pp. 236–265; see also Evelyn M. Acomb, *The French Laic Laws, 1879–1889* (New York: Octagon Books, 1967), pp. 193–196.
70. Document 87-A, p. 6.
71. Ibid., p. 33.
72. Melchiorre Gioia, *Teoria civile e penale del divorzio. Ossia necessità, cause, nuova maniera d'organizzarlo seguita dall'analisi della legge francese 30 venosto Anno XI relativo allo stesso argomento* (Milan: Piriotta e Maspero, 1803).
73. *L'Opinione* (Rome), 24 June 1884.
74. *La Nazione* (Florence), 24 June 1884.
75. Alessandro Coletti, *Il divorzio in Italia. Storia di una battaglia civile e democratica*, 2nd ed. (Rome: Edizioni Savelli, 1974), p. 42.
76. Ferdinando Cordova, *Massoneria e politica in Italia 1892–1908* (Rome-Bari: Laterza, 1985), pp. 1–3. For a broad overview of the relationship between anti-clericalism and the Masons, see also Adrian Lyttelton, "An Old Church and a New State: Italian Anticlericalism 1876–1915," *European Studies Review* 13 (1985): 225–248.
77. *Il Divorzio. Organo del comitato centrale per la propugnazione del divorzio* (Rome, 1890–91); there is unfortunately no trace of this first series, which appeared from November 1890 until the new series began in May 1891. The unlikelihood of finding copies is confirmed by Olga Majolo Molinari, *La Stampa periodica romana dell'Ottocento* (Rome: Istituto di Studi Romani Editore, 1963), p. 310.
78. *Il Divorzio. Rivista critica della famiglia italiana*, no. 1, Rome, May 1891.
79. Ibid., p. 1.
80. Ibid., p. 2.
81. Ibid., pp. 2–4.
82. *Il Divorzio*, no. 2, June 1891, p. 15.
83. Ibid., pp.13–14.
84. *Il Divorzio*, Anno II, nn. 2–4, p. 23.
85. *Corriere della sera*, 10–11 September 1891.
86. *Il Divorzio*, July–October 1891, p. 3.
87. *Corriere della sera*, 8–9 September, 1891.
88. *La Nazione*, 1 September 1891.
89. *Corriere della sera*, 9–10 September 1891.

90. *Corriere della sera*, 9–10 September 1891.

91. Carlo Francesco Gabba, *Studi di legislazione civile comparata in servizio della nuova codificazione italiana* (Milan: Tipi di Alessandro Lombardi, 1862), p. 233.

92. Carlo Francesco Gabba, *Il divorzio nella legislazione italiana*, 3rd ed. (Turin: Unione Tipografico-Editrice, 1891), pp. 5–6: Gabba criticizes the liberal doctrine of abstract liberty, which he sees as the font of the divorce creed.

93. *La Nazione*, 13 September 1891.

94. Ibid.

95. *Corriere della sera*, 12–13 September 1891.

96. *Il Messaggero*, 13 September 1891.

97. Ibid.

98. *Osservatore romano*, Rome, 10 September and 13 September 1891.

99. *Osservatore romano*, 15 September 1891.

100. *Atti del Parlamento Italiano. Discussioni della Camera dei Deputati*, Session of 1890–92, Vol VI: 19 March–15 June 1892 (Rome: Camera dei Deputati, 1892), p. 7722.

101. Ibid., p. 7723.

102. Ibid., p. 7726.

103. Ibid., p. 7729.

104. Ibid., p. 7730. The *Osservatore romano* claimed that the law was favored only by a weak majority (*Osservatore romano*, 5 April 1892), while the *Messaggero* claimed that only six or seven deputies voted against the law (*Il Messaggero*, 5 April 1892).

105. *Il Messaggero*, Rome, 6 April 1892.

106. *Il Divorzio*, Anno II, nn. 2–4, p. 24.

107. Ibid., p. 25.

108. ASCD, DPLIC, busta 558.

109. BSPV, AOC, busta 30, Circular, 29 March 1892.

110. ASCD, DPLIC, busta 558, f. 12.

111. Ibid., f. 34.

112. Ibid., f. 17.

113. *La Tribuna*, 19 December 1892.

114. *Osservatore romano*, 6 January 1893.

115. *Atti del Parlamento Italiano. Discussioni della Camera dei Deputati*, Session of 1892–93, 25 January–21 March 1893 (Rome: Camera dei Deputati, 1893), p. 839.

116. Ibid., p. 849.

117. Ibid., p. 852.

118. Ibid.

119. Ibid., p. 855.

120. Ibid., p. 856.

121. Ibid., p. 857.

122. Ibid., p. 860.

Chapter 5   Divorce between Liberalism and
Socialism, 1900–1902

1. Enrico Decleva, "Anticlericalismo e lotta politica nell'Italia Giolittiana. I: L' «esempio della Francia» e i partiti popolari (1901–1904)," *Nuova rivista storica*, Anno LII (May–August 1968), pp. 291–354.
2. Malcolm O. Partin, *Waldeck-Rousseau, Combes and the Church: The Politics of Anti-Clericalism, 1899–1905* (Durham, NC: Duke University Press, 1969), pp. 22–23; Maurice Larkin, *Church and State after the Dreyfus Affair: The Separation Issue in France* (New York: Barnes and Noble, 1973), p. 71.
3. Partin, *Waldeck-Rousseau*, p. 67.
4. Ferdinando Cordova, *Massoneria e politica in Italia, 1892–1908* (Rome-Bari: Laterza, 1985), p. 116.
5. John McManners, *Church and State in France, 1870–1914* (New York: Harper and Row, 1972), pp. 60–61.
6. Adrian Lyttelton, "An Old Church and a New State: Italian Anticlericalism 1876–1915," *European Studies Review* 13, no. 2 (April 1983): 229–230.
7. *Il Secolo* (Milan), 13–14 August, 1901.
8. Ernesto Nathan, "Circolare n. 61," *Rivista della Massoneria italiana*, Anno XXX, nn. 3–5 (February–March 1899), p. 35.
9. *Atti del Parlamento Italiano. Camera dei Deputati. Raccolta degli atti stampati per ordine della Camera dei Deputati*, Sessione 1900–02, Vol. 9: nn. 332–386 (Rome: Camera dei Deputati, 1902), Law no. 369, p. 2 (henceforth Law no. 369).
10. Francesco Filomusi Guelfi, "Della naturalizzazione, della separazione, e del divorzio di una donna francese o italiana" (Turin: Unione Tipgrafico-Editrice,1876), (extract from *Giurisprudenza italiana*, Vol. XXVIII, 1876).
11. Ibid., p. 3.
12. *Corriere della sera* (Milan), 22–23 September 1879; *La Nazione* (Florence), 26 September 1879.
13. Maurizio Roccarino, *Il divorzio e la legislazione italiana. Stato odierno della questione* (Turin: Bocca Editori, 1901), p. 118.
14. Ibid.
15. Francesco Filomusi Guelfi, *Il divorzio tra stranieri in Italia. Nota* (Fano: Tipografia Sorciniana, 1884), p. 41 (reprint from *Il Foro italiano*, Anno IX).
16. For example, Manfredi Siotto Pintor, "Il divorzio degli italiani naturalizzati stranieri," p. 4 (offprint from *Annali dell'Università di Perugia*, new series, Vol. 1, fasc. 1, 1903).
17. *Il Foro italiano*, 1901, Vol. XXVI, pp. 85–88.
18. Ibid., pp. 1179–1186.
19. A search through the major newspapers of the era revealed no commentary, even in the special columns dedicated to judicial matters.
20. [Corte di Cassazione, Turin], *Il regime matrimoniale italiano e il divorzio* (Turin: Unione Tipografico-Editrice, 1900).
21. Cordova claims that there were "tempestuous polemics" in the liberal press (Cordova, *Massoneria*, p. 115), which seems to be something of an exaggeration.

It is true that in the specialist legal journals many authors expressed very divided opinions, but it hardly appears to have been the subject of particular attention by the newspapers.

22. *Atti del Parlamento Italiano. Discussioni della Camera dei Deputati*, Session of 1900, Vol. 1: 16 June–8 December 1900 (Rome: Camera dei Deputati, 1900), p. 1542. The fact that Berenini was motivated by the question of foreign divorces is indicated in Agostino Berenini, "Il divorzio innanzi alla Camera," *La Rassegna nazionale*, 15 December 1901, pp. 405–417.

23. *Atti del Parlamento Italiano. Discussioni della Camera dei Deputati*, Session of 1900, Vol. II: 10 December 1900–7 February 1901, p. 1542.

24. Marina Addis Saba, *Anna Kuliscioff. Vita privata e passione politica* (Milan: Mondadori Editori, 1993), p. 135 et seq. Kuliscioff did not countenance marriage even when, as a result of her role in the worker uprisings of 1898, she risked deportation to her native Russia.

25. Anna Kuliscioff, "Il sentimentalismo nella questione femminile," *Critica sociale* Anno 1 (1892): 142.

26. Socialists from Saint-Simon onward were used to being criticized for spreading the gospel of "free love." In an article in the same issue of *Critica sociale*, "Avvocato F.T." (presumably Turati) specified that the socialists promoted "free unions," not free love. *Critica sociale* Anno 1 (1892): 154–155.

27. Kuliscioff, "Sentimentalismo," p. 142.

28. *Atti del Parlamento Italiano. Discussioni della Camera dei Deputati*, Session of 1900–01, Vol. IV: 7–30 March 1901 (Rome: Camera dei Deputati), pp. 2376–2379.

29. Ibid., pp. 2587–2592.

30. Ibid., pp. 2389–2392.

31. *Osservatore romano* (Rome), 13 March 1901.

32. *Il Messaggero* (Rome), 12 March 1901 and 18 March 1901, respectively.

33. *Osservatore romano*, 16 October 1901.

34. *Il Secolo*, 14–15 October 1901

35. *Il Secolo*, 26–27 October 1901.

36. *Corriere della sera* (Milan), 4–5 November 1901.

37. Ibid., 6–7 November 1901.

38. Ibid., 4–5 November 1901; the same idea was also repeated by the *Corriere* on 18–19 November.

39. *Il Secolo*, 17–18 November 1901.

40. *Atti del Parlamento Italiano. Discussioni della Camera dei Deputati*, Session of 1900–01, Vol. VII: 27 November–22 December 1901 (Rome: Camera dei Deputati, 1902), p. 6476.

41. Ibid.

42. Ibid.

43. Ibid., p. 6478.

44. Ibid., p. 6477.

45. Law no. 369.

46. *Atti del Parlamento Italiano. Discussioni della Camera dei Deputati*, Session of 1900–01, Vol. VII: 27 November–22 December 1901, p. 6478.

47. Ibid.
48. Ibid., p. 6480.
49. Ibid., p. 6481.
50. Ibid., p. 6483.
51. Ibid.
52. Ibid., p. 6484.
53. *Avanti!* (Rome), 6 December 1901, p. 1.
54. Ibid., p. 2.
55. Archivio Storico Della Camera dei Deputati, Disegni e Proposte di Legge, Incarti delle Commissioni (henceforth ASCD, DPLIC), busta 746, 10 December 1901.
56. The unprecedented nature of this appeal was noted by *La Stampa* (Turin), on 17 December 1901. The text of the *Allocution*, in Italian translation, was published in *Il Divorzio* (Rome: Opera dei Congressi Cattolici, January 1902), a one-off broadsheet, not to be confused with the serial of the same name published by a pro-divorce committee in 1891–1892.
57. Alfredo Canavero, *I cattolici nella società italiana. Dalla metà dell'800 al Concilio Vaticano II* (Brescia: Editrice La Scuola, 1991), p. 116.
58. Biblioteca del Seminario Patriarcale Venezia, Archivio Opera dei Congressi (henceforth BSPV, AOC), busta 30, Petition, 17 December 1901.
59. BSPV, AOC, busta 30, telegram from Milan, 29 December 1901.
60. Ibid., letter from a priest, Gozzegno, 26 January 1902.
61. Ibid., letter from Castelnuovo del Zappa, 13 January 1902.
62. Ibid., undated letter among others from early 1902, S.Croce del Pino.
63. Ibid., postcard from Coronari to Paganuzzi, 17 December 1901.
64. *Il Divorzio*, Rome, January 1902, "Il divorzio e i cattolici," p. 1.
65. Ibid., p. 2.
66. Ibid., p. 4.
67. *Avanti!*, 7 January 1902.
68. Ibid., 17 January 1902.
69. Ibid., 9 January 1902.
70. Ibid., 10 January 1902.
71. Ibid., 11 January 1902.
72. ASCD, DPLIC, busta 746.
73. Ibid.
74. In one of the few monographs on the history of divorce in Italy, Alessandro Coletti found this disparity very strange, and indeed, it does seem inexplicable if there was any truth in *Avanti!*'s reports about the huge meetings in favor of divorce. Alessandro Coletti, *Il divorzio in Italia. Storia di una battaglia civile e democratica*, 2nd ed. (Rome: Edizioni Savelli, 1974), p. 71.
75. *Atti del Parlamento Italiano. Camera dei Deputati. Raccolta degli atti stampati per ordine della Camera dei Deputati*, Sessione 1900–1902, Vol. 9: nn. 332–386 (Rome: Camera dei Deputati, 1902), Document no. 369-A, p. 16.
76. Ibid.
77. Ibid., pp. 3–4.
78. Ibid., p. 6.

79. *Atti del Parlamento Italiano. Camera dei Deputati. Raccolta degli atti stampati per ordine della Camera dei Deputati*, Sessione 1900–1902, Vol. 9: nn. 332–386 (Rome: Camera dei Deputati, 1902), Document no. 369-A, p. 7.
80. Ibid., p. 8.
81. *La Stampa*, 29 January 1902.

Chapter 6   From the Failure of Reform
to the Lateran Pacts, 1902–1929

1. Annarita Buttafuoco, *Cronache femminili. Temi e momenti della stampa eman-cipazionista in Italia dall'Unità al fascismo* (Siena: Dipartimento di Studi Storici, Sociali e Filosofici, Università degli Studi di Siena, 1988), p. 22.
2. *Corriere della sera* (Milan), 28–29 January 1902.
3. *La Stampa* (Turin), 19 February 1902; *Osservatore romano* (Rome), 19 February 1902.
4. *La Stampa*, 17 February 1902.
5. *Il Secolo* (Milan), 21 February 1902.
6. Ibid., 22 February 1902.
7. *Osservatore romano*, 22 February 1902.
8. *Corriere della sera*, 21–22 February 1902.
9. Reported in *Corriere della sera*, 21–22 February 1902.
10. *Avanti!* (Rome), 21 February 1902.
11. *Il Secolo*, 22–23 February 1902.
12. *La Stampa*, 21 February 1902.
13. *Avanti!*, 22 February 1902.
14. Ibid.
15. *Il Messaggero* (Rome), 22 February 1902.
16. Pasquale Murmura, *Conferenza sul divorzio tenuta nel Teatro di Catanzaro addì 11 maggio 1902* (Monteleone: Tipografia Passafaro, 1902), p. 9.
17. Ibid., p. 10.
18. Ibid., p. 29.
19. See chapter 1.
20. Benedetto Croce, "Il divorzio nelle province napoletane: 1809–1815," *La Scuola positiva*, Anno 1, nn. 11–12 (15–30 October 1891), pp. 481–497.
21. Hartmut Ullrich, "La campagna per il divorzio nella Napoli inizio secolo e l'at-tegiamento di Benedetto Croce," *Rivista di studi crociani* (1970), pp. 320–344.
22. Ibid., p. 331.
23. Enrico Corradini, "L'agitazione ecclesiastica contro il divorzio," *La Rassegna nazionale* VIII, no. 3 (1 February 1902): 204.
24. Ibid., p. 203.
25. Ibid., p. 209.
26. Gaetano Mosca, "Pro e contro il divorzio," repr. in *Partiti e sindacati nella crisi del regime parlamentare* (Rome-Bari: Laterza, 1949), p. 297; (orig. in *Corriere della sera*, 12 February 1902).
27. Ibid.
28. Ibid., p. 299.

29. Ibid.
30. Giovanni Marchesini, *Il principio del matrimonio e il divorzio* (Padua-Verona: Fratelli Drucker, 1902).
31. L. M. Bossi, *La legge sul divorzio considerata dal lato ginecologico. Conferenza tenuta all'Associazione Medica Lombarda* (Naples: Tipografia Jovene, 1902), pp. 9–11.
32. Emilio Federici, *Divorzio e socialismo* (Venice: Tipografia Emiliana, 1902), p. xii.
33. Salvatore Brandi, *La follia del divorzio. Fatti e note* (Rome: Civiltà Cattolica, 1902), p. 10.
34. Ibid., p. 3.
35. Fiorenza Taricone, *L'associazionismo femminile italiano dall'Unità al fascismo* (Edizioni Unicopli, Milan, 1996), p. 10.
36. Ibid.
37. Ibid., p. 8.
38. Sibilla Aleramo noted "that no one dared" to include it among the issues for discussion at the Congress: "Appunti sulla psicologia femminile italiana," unpublished essay of 1910 appearing in Sibilla Aleramo, *La donna e il femminismo. Scritti 1897–1910*, ed. Bruna Conti (Rome: Edizioni Riuniti, 1978), p. 157.
39. *Avanti!*, 5 February 1902.
40. Franca Pieroni Bortolotti, Introduction to Anna Maria Mozzoni, *La liberazione della donna* (Milan: Mazzotta Editore, 975), p. 13.
41. Teresa Labriola, *Del divorzio. Discussione etica* (Rome: E. Loescher, 1901).
42. Ibid., p. 25–26.
43. Ibid., p. 35–37.
44. Ibid., p. 42.
45. Ibid., p. 54.
46. Ibid., p. 60.
47. Ibid., p. 63.
48. Sibilla Aleramo, *Una donna* (Milan: Feltrinelli, 1996). The novel was not published until 1906.
49. Grazia Deledda, *Dopo il divorzio. Romanzo* (Turin-Rome: Roux e Viarengo, 1902), pp. 7–9.
50. Ibid., p. 21.
51. Ibid., p. 136.
52. Ibid., p. 159.
53. Ibid., p. 161.
54. Fiorenza Taricone, *Teresa Labriola. Biografia politica di un'intellettuale tra Ottocento e Novecento* (Milan: Franco Angeli, 1994), p. 88.
55. Anna Franchi, *Avanti il divorzio. Romanzo* (Milan: Remo Sandron, 1902).
56. Anna Franchi, *Il divorzio e la donna* (Florence: G. Nerbini Editore, 1902).
57. Ibid., p. 20
58. Ibid., pp. 12–13.
59. Ibid., p. 21.
60. Laura Lilli, "La stampa femminile," in Vittorio Castronovo and Nicola Tranfaglia, eds., *Storia della stampa italiana*, Vol. 5: *La stampa italiana del neo-capitalismo* (Rome-Bari: Laterza, 1976), p. 261.
61. Lucetta Scaraffia, "«Il Cristianesimo l'ha fatta libera, collocandola nella famiglia accanto all'uomo» (dal 1850 alla «Mulieris dignitatem»)," in Lucetta

Scaraffia and Gabriella Zarri, eds., *Donne e fede. Santità e vita religiosa in Italia* (Rome-Bari: Laterza, 1994), p. 469.

62. Luisa Anzoletti, *Il divorzio e la donna italiana*, 2nd ed. (Milan: L. F. Cogliati, 1902).
63. Ibid., p. 6.
64. Rosanna De Longis, *La stampa periodica delle donne in Italia. Catalogo 1861–1985* (Rome: Commissione nazionale per la realizazzione della parità tra uomo e donna, 1987), p. 12.
65. Ibid., p. 75–77.
66. Ibid., p. 81.
67. *Atti del Parlamento Italiano. Camera dei Deputati. Raccolta degli atti stampati per ordine della Camera*, Session of 1902–04, Vol. IV: nn. 151–212 (Rome: Camera dei Deputati), Law no. 207.
68. Noted in *Avanti!*, 30 November 1902.
69. For example, *La Stampa*, 26 November 1902; *Avanti!*, 27 November 1902.
70. *Osservatore romano*, 2 December 1902.
71. *Avanti!*, 30 November 1902.
72. *Raccolta degli Atti Stampati*, 1902–1904, Law no. 207, p. 33.
73. Archivio Storico della Camera dei Deputati, Disegni e proposte di legge incarti delle commissioni (henceforth ASCD, DPLIC) busta 772, Verbali degli uffici (ufficio II).
74. Ibid., ufficio III, 2 December 1902.
75. Ibid., ufficio I, 2 December 1902.
76. Ibid., Di San Giuliano, ufficio VI, 2 December 1902; Maurigi, ufficio VIII, 2 December 1902.
77. See, for example, the citation of *Le Figaro* in *Il Divorzio* (Rome: Opera dei Congressi Cattolici, January 1902).
78. ASCD, DPLIC 772, Scalini, ufficio IX, 2 December 1902.
79. Ibid., for example Sorani (III), Bianchi (V), De Amicis (VI), Salandra (VIII), all 2 December 1902.
80. Ibid., Socci (II), 2 December 1902.
81. Ibid., Borciani (I), 2 December 1902.
82. For example, ibid., Pozzo (I), 2 December 1902; see also Giovanni Giolitti, *Memorie della mia vita*, Vol. I (Milan: Treves, 1922), p. 173.
83. ASCD, DPLIC 772, meeting of 10 December 1902.
84. Ibid., meeting 16 December 1902. There was a total of only eight votes because L. Bianchi was absent. He was in favor of divorce but even if he had been present the overall vote would still have been against divorce.
85. See, for example, *La Stampa*, 17 December 1902.
86. *Osservatore romano*, 25 and 31 December 1902.
87. *Avanti!*, 18 December 1902.
88. The article is unsigned, but was attributed to Leonida Bissolati by A.C. Jemolo in *Chiesa e stato negli ultimi cento anni*, p. 510, and also by Alessandro Coletti, *Il divorzio in Italia*, p. 70.
89. *Atti del Parlamento Italiano. Camera dei Deputati. Raccolta degli atti stampati per ordine della Camera*, Session of 1902–04, Vol IV: nn. 151–212 (Rome: Camera dei Deputati, 1904), Document no. 207-A, *Relazione* by Antonio Salandra, p. 5.

90. Ibid., p. 9.
91. Ibid., p. 23.
92. Giovanni Spadolini, *Giolitti e i cattolici (1901–1914)* (Florence: Le Monnier, 1971), p. ix.
93. Emilio Gentile, *Storia dell'Italia contemporanea*, Vol. II: *L'età giolittiana 1899–1914* (Naples: Edizioni Scientifiche Italiane, 1977), p. 92.
94. Ibid., p. 91.
95. Francesco Gaeta, *Storia d'Italia*, Vol. 21: *La crisi di fine secolo e l'età giolittiana* (Turin: UTET, 1982), p. 286.
96. Gentile, *Storia dell'Italia contemporanea*, p. 100.
97. Giorgio Candeloro, *Il Movimento cattolico in Italia* (Rome: Edizioni Rinascita, 1953), p. 310.
98. Giovanni Giolitti, *Memorie della mia vita*, Vol. I (Milan: Treves, 1922), p. 173.
99. Spadolini, *Giolitti e i Cattolici*, p. 27.
100. Gaeta, *Storia d'Italia*, p. 191.
101. See, for example, Gaeta, *Storia d'Italia*, p. 91; Giorgio Candeloro, *Storia dell'Italia moderna*, Vol. 7: *La crisi di fine secolo e l'età giolittiana* (Milan: Feltrinelli, 1974), p. 196; Gentile, *Storia dell'Italia contemporanea*, p. 102.
102. Candeloro, *Il Movimento*, pp. 312–313.
103. Geremia Bonomelli, *Sul divorzio* (Cremona: Tipografia S. Giuseppe, 1881).
104. Candeloro, *Il Movimento*, pp. 312–313.
105. Ibid., p. 314.
106. Gaeta, *Storia d'Italia*, p. 192.
107. Alessandro Coletti, *Il divorzio in Italia. Storia di una battaglia civile e democratica*, 2nd ed. (Rome: Edizioni Savelli, 1974), p. 74.
108. Ibid., p. 76.
109. Ibid., p. 78.
110. Camera dei Deputati, *La XXIV Legislatura (27 novembre 1913–29 settembre 1919), Indice* (Rome, 1919), p. 236.
111. Agreeing to resist the introduction of the divorce law was one of three undertakings asked of Liberal deputies in return for votes from Catholics. See Filippo Meda, "I cattolici italiani e le ultime elezioni politiche," *Nuova Antologia* 169 (1914), p. 297.
112. Gentile, *Storia dell'Italia contemporanea*, p. 101.
113. *Atti del Parlamento Italiano. Discussioni della Camera dei Deputati*, XXVI Legislatura, 9 June 1923 (Rome: Camera dei Deputati, 1923), p. 9928.
114. The law extending the Italian civil code to the newly acquired territories was published in the *Gazzetta ufficiale* on 21 March 1924. It seems fitting that one of Mussolini's later publication glories was a lavish edition of the writings of the great nineteenth-century Italian thinker Alfredo Oriani. Oriani's anti-divorce epistle of about 400 pages, originally written in 1886 as a response to the pro-divorce position of Alexandre Dumas, was republished under Mussolini's auspices in 1942. See Alfredo Oriani, *Opera Omnia. Vol. VIII: Matrimonio*, ed. Benito Mussolini (Bologna: Licinio Capelli Editori, 1942).

Chapter 7   Remaking Italians? From Fascism
to the Republic, 1929–1964

1. Arturo Carlo Jemolo's balanced interpretation of this marriage of convenience pays particular attention to the Catholic attitude to fascism, which was more complex than the fascist attitude to Catholicism. See A. C. Jemolo, *Church and State in Italy, 1850–1950*, trans. David Moore (Oxford: Blackwell, 1960), p.188.

2. Feminist scholarship from the 1990s has emphasized the convenient overlap between fascist and Catholic ideals of the family, but also their contrasts, and in particular, the ways in which ultimately fascism failed to coopt the family. See, for example, Victoria De Grazia, *How Fascism Ruled Women: Italy 1922–1945* (Berkeley: University of California Press, 1992), esp. chap. 4; and Cecilia Dau Novelli, *Famiglia e modernizzazione in Italia fra le due guerre* (Rome: Edizioni Studium, 1994).

3. Simona Colarizi, *Storia del novecento italiano. Cent'anni di entusiamso, di paure, di speranza* (Milan: BUR, 2000), p. 312.

4. *Noi donne*, 15 May 1945, cover.

5. Sandro Bellassai portrays the tensions and ambiguities of the PCI's position on divorce well in *La morale comunista. Pubblico e privato nella rappresentazione del PCI (1947–1956)* (Rome: Carocci Editore, 2000), pp. 158–168.

6. Palmiro Togliatti, "La famiglia centro di solidarietà umana elementare," in *I comunisti e la famiglia, 1945–1974* (Rome: Partito comunista italiano, 1974), pp. 11–14.

7. Nilde Jotti, Assemblea Costituente, *Commissione per la Costituzione, Discussioni, Prima sottocommissione* (Rome: Camera dei Deputati, n.d.) (henceforth AC CC), 30 October 1946, p. 332.

8. See Paolo Ungari, *Storia del diritto di famiglia (1796–1975)*, (Bologna: Il Mulino, 2002), p. 239.

9. Corsanego, AC CC, 30 October 1946, p. 331.

10. La Pira, AC CC, 7 November 1946, p. 355.

11. AC CC, 7 November 1946, p. 358.

12. AC CC, p. 355.

13. There was a poignant personal story behind these debates, since it was in 1946 that Togliatti, married to Rita Montagnana since 1924, formed what was to be a lifelong relationship with Nilde Jotti. See Aldo Agosti, *Palmiro Togliatti* (Turin: UTET, 1996), pp. 319–320.

14. AC CC, p. 360.

15. La Pira, AC CC, p. 369.

16. AC CC, p. 376.

17. Camera dei Deputati, *La Costituzione della Repubblica nei lavori preparatori della Assemblea Costituente. Vol II, Sedute dal 17 aprile 1947 al 19 maggio 1947* (Rome: Tipolitografia Edigraf, 1976 reprint based on 1970 edition), Nitti, 21 April 1947, p. 1040 (henceforth *Costituzione della Repubblica*).

18. *Costituzione della Repubblica*, 21 April 1947, p. 1040.

19. *Costituzione della Repubblica*, 17 April 1947, pp. 945–947.

20. *Costituzione della Repubblica*, 21 April 1947, pp. 1101–1104.
21. *Costituzione della Repubblica*, 23 April 1947, p. 1174. Grilli has occasionally been claimed as a member of the PCI, but he was a member of the PSI, and later the PSLI, the Partito Socialista dei Lavoratori Italiani.
22. *Costituzione della Repubblica*, 24 April 1947, pp. 1201–1204.
23. Historians of a previous generation, such as Federico Chabod, remind us that the most distinctive new feature of politics in postwar Italy was the "azione dei cattolici." See *L'Italia contemporanea (1918–1948)* (Turin: Einaudi, 1961), p. 186.
24. Togliatti's (and thus the PCI's) stance toward the Lateran Pacts came from the same convictions as his view on divorce: a great fear of alienating large numbers of Catholic masses from the progressive aims of the PCI. See Agosti, *Palmiro Togliatti*, pp. 335–336.
25. Anna Rossi-Doria, "Le donne sulla scena politica," in *Storia dell'Italia repubblicana. Vol. I: La costruzione della democrazia. Dalla caduta del fascismo agli anni cinquanta* (Turin: Einaudi, 1994), p. 845.
26. Cited by Rossi-Doria, "Le donne sulla scena politica," p. 846.
27. A. C. Jemolo, *Church and State in Italy, 1850–1950*, trans. David Moore (Oxford: Basil Blackwell, 1960), p. 322. This translation was of the abridged 1955 edition of the original work published in Italy in 1948.
28. Luigi Sansone, "Ecco il mio progetto del 'piccolo divorzio,'" *L'Europeo*, 24 October 1954, p. 15.
29. Ibid.
30. Penny Morris, "From Private to Public: Alba de Céspedes' Agony Column in 1950s Italy," *Modern Italy* 9, no. 1 (2004): 11–20, 14.
31. Luigi Sansone, *I fuorilegge del matrimonio* (Milan-Rome, Edizioni Avanti!, 1956), p. 5.
32. Camera dei Deputati, *Disegni e proposte di legge-relazioni*, Legislature II, 1953–58, Vol. X, Law no. 1189 (Rome: Tipografia della Camera dei Deputati, n.d.), p. 3 (henceforth Law no. 1189).
33. Law no. 1189, p. 5.
34. Law no. 1189, pp. 8–9.
35. Sansone explained that his first proposal fell foul of parliamentary vicissitudes in his 1958 proposal for a divorce law, made to the Senate: Senato della Repubblica, III Legislatura, *Atti interni, Disegni di legge*, Vol. 1, n. 2 (Rome: Tipografia del Senato, 1963).
36. Sansone, *I fuorilegge del matrimonio*, pp. 14–16.
37. Ibid., p. 27.
38. Ibid., p. 25.
39. Domenico Peretti Griva, *La famiglia e il divorzio* (Bari: Laterza, 1956).
40. Maria Casalini, *Le donne della sinistra (1944–1948)* (Rome: Carocci, 2005).
41. *Noi donne*, 10 January 1954, p. 10.
42. *Noi donne*, 31 January 1954, pp. 6–7.
43. Concetto Marchesi, "Variazioni sul divorzio," *Noi donne*, 7 July 1955, pp. 8–9.
44. "I fuorilegge del matrimonio," *Noi donne*, 13 January 1957, pp. 6–7.

45. "Che ne pensate del piccolo divorzio?" *Noi donne*, 27 January 1957, pp. 16–17 and 37. Article 3, "Matrimoni perduti," 3 February 1957, pp. 30–31; Article 4, "Il dito sulla piaga," 10 February 1957, p. 23; Article 5, "Un centro di studi per le delusioni matrimoniali," 24 February 1957, pp. 30–31; Article 6, "La salvezza del matrimonio è anche nel 'piccolo divorzio,' " 3 March 1957, p. 13.

46. Giovanni Cesareo, "Il matrimonio è la tomba dell'amore?" *Noi donne*, 19 July 1959, pp. 28–31.

47. Lidia Failla, "La famiglia russa ha cessato di esistere con la creazione delle scuole internato," *Cronache*, December 1958, p. 5.

48. Elisa Bianchi, "La donna nella famiglia e nel lavoro," *Cronache*, July–August 1960, p. 1.

49. Maria Luisa Zavattaro Ardizzi, "La posizione giuridica della donna nella famiglia," *Cronache*, July–August 1960, p. 6.

50. Bianchi, see note 48.

51. Pietro Germi, dir., *Divorzio all'italiana* (Irvington, NY: Criterion Collection, 2005), videorecording of 1961 motion picture, titled *Divorce Italian Style* in English.

52. The film prompted discussion of this relic of medieval law and much has been written about its continuation in the Italian criminal code until 1981. See, for example, Marzio Barbagli, *Provando e riprovando. Matrimonio, famiglia e divorzio in Italia e in altri paesi occidentali* (Bologna: Il Mulino, 1990), p. 49.

53. Stewart Klawans, "The Facts (and Fancies) of Murder," sleeve note, *Divorce, Italian Style*, videorecording, Criterion Collection, 2005.

54. Giorgio Moscon, *Divorzio all'italiana di Pietro Germi* (Rome: Edizioni FM, 1961), p. 43.

55. Maria Maffei, "Il 'divorzio' di Daniela," *Noi donne*, 23 July 1961, pp. 38–41.

56. Giovanni Cesareo, "L'intoccabile divorzio," *Noi donne*, 12 June 1960, p. 15.

57. The four articles were: Ercole Graziadei, "Il divorzio nel mondo bianco," pp. 52–60; Pietro Grismondi, "I progetti sul divorzio," pp. 61–71; Arturo Carlo Jemolo, "Il divorzio, il Concordato, la Costituzione," pp. 88–92, and Pietro D'Avack, "Il problema del divorzio nel diritto matrimoniale italiano," pp. 93–105, all in *I problemi di Ulisse*, Vol. 37, no. 7 (1960).

58. PCI, Direzione, Sezione femminile, "La nostra posizione su alcuni problemi inerenti la famiglia," Rome 18 January 1960, typescript, Archivio UDI, FaDi 60.1/1.

59. Giovanni Cesareo, "È arrivata in Europa la pillola del controllo," *Noi donne*, 20 March 1960, pp. 18–21.

60. Giulietta Ascoli, "Urgente per la donna," Part I, *Noi donne*, 15 May 1960, pp. 12–15, and part II, 22 May 1960, pp. 30–33.

61. Luisa Melograni, "Non è più lo stesso cuore," *Noi donne*, 12 June 1960, pp. 28–31.

62. Giovanni Cesareo, "Dal lavoro nasce il futuro," *Noi donne*, 3 July 1960, pp. 14–17.

63. Giovanni Cesareo, "Il divorzio: Discutiamone I," *Noi donne*, 17 July 1960, pp. 18–21.

64. Maria Bassino, "Tribuna per voi: La famiglia, qualcosa che scotta," *Noi donne*, 4 December 1960, pp. 16–19.

65. Vincenzo Fagiolo, "Origine ed istituzione del matrimonio," *Osservatore romano*, 18 March 1961, p. 3.

66. Vincenzo Fagiolo, "Indissolubilità del matrimonio," *Osservatore romano*, 6 April 1961, p. 3.

67. Paolo Glorioso, "La grave crisi matrimoniale anche in Italia scaturisce dalla trasformazione della donna?" Article 1 in a series of 15 from *Il Messaggero*, July 1961 (clippings without page numbers or dates held in Archvio UDI, Fa-Di 61.1/2).

68. Paolo Glorioso, "I diritto della famiglia e del matrimonio secondo la Costituzione italiana," article 6 in a series of 15, *Il Messaggero*, 1961 (Clipping in Archivio UDI, Fa-Di 61.1/2).

69. Paul Ginsborg, *A History of Contemporary Italy: Society and Politics, 1943–1988* (London: Penguin Books, 1990), p. 258.

70. Ginsborg, *Contemporary Italy*, p. 261.

71. "I liberali per il piccolo divorzio?," *Il Divorzio*, October 1962, p. 1. The organization behind the publication of this broadsheet was the Movimento Italiano per il Divorzio (the Italian Movement for Divorce), known as the MID. Founded as an official political party in 1958, it competed in the election of that year (" 'Divorce Party' for Italian Election," *The Times*, 31 March 1958, p. 7), though with negligible results. Apart from its broadsheet, copies of which are extremely rare, the movement appears to have left virtually no trace on the historical record, and it is not mentioned by Alessandro Coletti or Diana De Vigili, the principal scholars of divorce in Italy. It was a movement whose time was not yet ripe, and it was presumably superceded by the pro-divorce movement founded in the 1960s.

72. "Condannti a peccare," *Il Divorzio*, October 1962, p. 1.

73. "Reforming Mussolini's Penal Code," *The Times*, 11 September 1959, p. 11.

74. "Marriage Law Under Scrutiny," *The Times*, 25 October 1963, p. 10.

75. Giuliana Ricca, "La famiglia nella realtà d'oggi," *Cronache e opinioni*, March 1963, p. 9. The publication changed its name from *Cronache* to *Cronache e opinioni* in 1962.

76. Gioia di Cristofaro, "Famiglie d'oggi," *Cronache e opinioni*, July–August 1963, p. 14.

77. For a reevaluation of these women's movements, particularly their relationship with more outspoken liberation movements after 1968, see Wendy Pojmann, "Emancipation or Liberation? Women's Associations and the Italian Movement," *The Historian* 67, no. 1 (March 2005): 73–96.

78. Benedetta Galassi Beria, "Il Papa e il matrimonio" (editorial), *Noi donne*, 28 December 1963, p. 5.

79. "Calls for Marriage Reform in Italy," *The Times*, 4 December 1964, p. 11.

80. "Marriage Law Under Scrutiny," *The Times*, 25 October 1963, p. 10.

81. "Women Emancipated by Television," *The Times*, 10 January 1964, p. 9.

82. Ibid.

Chapter 8   Loris Fortuna and the *Divorzisti*, 1964–1970

1. Mario Berutti, *Il divorzio in Italia* (Milan: Edizioni di Comunità, 1964), p. 142.
2. Ibid., p. 7.
3. Ibid., p. 57.
4. Ibid., p. 60.
5. Ibid., p. 73.
6. Giorgio Battistacci, "Nuovi aspetti della società familiare," *Cronache e opinioni*, June 1964, p. 2.
7. "Calls for Marriage Reform in Italy," *The Times*, 4 December 1964, p. 11.
8. Angiolo Bandinelli, "Loris Fortuna," in *Il Parlamento Italiano, 1861–1988. Vol XX, 1969–1972: Fra stato sociale e contestazione. Da Rumor ad Andreotti.* (Milan: Nuova CEI, 1992), pp. 65–66.
9. "La famiglia moderna e i suoi problemi", *Noi donne*, 17 July 1965, pp. 14–15. The second article in the series appeared under the title "Il divorzio e le donne" (*Noi donne*, 24 July 1965, pp. 18–21), and this became a generic heading for the subsequent four articles.
10. Luisa Melograni, "Il divorzio e le donne: l'indissolubilità nasce dal cuore," *Noi donne*, 25 September 1965, pp. 38–40.
11. Diana De Vigili, *La battaglia sul divorzio. Dalla Costituente al Referendum* (Milan: Franco Angeli, 2000), p. 40.
12. Alessandro Coletti, *Il divorzio in Italia. Storia di una battaglia civile e democratico*, 2nd ed. (Rome: Giulio Savelli, 1974), p. 139.
13. For example, Milla Pastorino wrote "This is the first time a chink has been opened on the indissolubility of marriage by an official of the Catholic Church," in "Divorzio in Parlamento," *Noi donne*, 16 October 1965, p. 10.
14. De Vigili, *La battaglia sul divorzio*, p. 40.
15. Camera dei Deputati, *Disegni e proposte di legge—relazioni*, Vol XL, n. 2630 (Rome: Stabilimenti Tipografici Carlo Colombo, 1969), pp. 1–10.
16. De Vigili, *La battaglia sul divorzio*, pp. 19 and 21.
17. Milla Pastorino, "Divorzio in Parlamento," *Noi donne*, 16 October 1965, pp. 10–11.
18. "Un passo avanti," *ABC*, 10 October 1965, pp. 10–11.
19. Ibid.
20. "La legge: Plebiscito dei consensi," *ABC*, 17 October 1965.
21. De Vigili, *La battaglia sul divorzio*, p. 43.
22. Paolo Meucci, "Tavola rotonda sul progetto Fortuna per il divorzio," *Il Giorno*, 13 December 1965, p. 3.
23. "Dibattito al Ridotto del Eliseo. I divorzisti decisi a scendere in campo (fuori o dentro i schieramenti politici)," *Paese Sera*, 13 December 1965 (clipping without page no. in Archivio UDI, Fa-Di 65.3/2).
24. Ibid.
25. "I communisti contrari al «piccolo divorzio»," *Corriere della Sera*, 13 December 1965 (clipping without page number from Archivio UDI, Fa-Di 65.3/2).

26. Rita S., letter to *Avanti!*, 2 January 1966 (clipping without page number from Archivio UDI, Fa-Di 66.3/4).

27. De Vigili, *La battaglia sul divorzio*, p. 46.

28. "Divorzio: testo integrale dell'on. Fortuna alla Camera," *ABC*, 10 April 1966, pp. 10–12.

29. "Fondata la Lega italiana per il divorzio," *ABC*, 10 April 1966, p. 13.

30. Interview with Angiolo Bandinelli, Rome, 12 November 2003.

31. Coletti, *Il divorzio in Italia*, p. 136.

32. Cited in De Vigili, *La battaglia sul divorzio*, p. 49.

33. Ibid., p. 48.

34. Ibid.

35. Ibid., p. 51.

36. Archivio Storico della Camera dei Deputati, Disegni e Progetti di Legge, Incarti delle Commissioni (henceforth, ASCD, DPLIC), Vol. 811, Proposta di legge Camera, n. 2630, *Bollettino delle giunte e delle commissioni parlamentari*, 5 May 1966, p. 6. The files documenting the passage of a controversial proposal through the parliamentary committees, which could take years, are often voluminous, and the items in a file are not numbered. Often, key events are marked by a page extracted from the *Bollettino delle giunte e delle commissioni parlamentari*, as on this occasion. When this is the case, *Bollettino* and the date will be indicated.

37. ASCD, DPLIC, Vol. 811, Proposta di legge Camera, n. 2630, *Bollettino delle giunte e delle commissioni parlamentari*, 13 July 1966, p. 3.

38. ASCD, DPLIC, *Bollettino*, 15 September 1966, pp. 4–5.

39. De Vigili, *La battaglia sul divorzio*, p. 53.

40. Ibid., p. 53.

41. Ibid. De Vigili underlines that neither parliament nor subsequent heads of government were informed about this or the two further notes from the Vatican. It is likely that Moro and others were concerned to protect the Vatican from accusations of interfering with Italian politics. The need to avoid such accusations also explains the more usual methods of interference via pressure on individual DC deputies.

42. An example is Fortuna's mention of the "Vaticanization of the state," in "Un'intervista con l'onorevole Loris Fortuna," *ABC*, 15 January 1967, p. 14.

43. ASCD, DPLIC, 811, *Bollettino* of 15 September 1966, p. 6.

44. "Si è svolta a Roma una grandiose manifestazione indetta dalla Lega Italiana per il DIVORZIO," *Noi donne*, 26 November 1966, p. 19.

45. ASCD, DPLIC, 811, *Bollettino* of 19 October 1966, p. 1.

46. ASCD, DPLIC, 811, *Bollettino* of 9 November 1966, p. 1.

47. ASCD, DPLIC, 811, *Bollettino* of 14 December 1966, p. 3.

48. ASCD, DPLIC, 811, *Bollettino* of 19 January 1967, p. 3.

49. For example, Tozzi Condivi, ASCD, DPLIC, *Bollettino* of 19 January 1967, p. 4.

50. "The Pope Opposes Divorce Moves," *The Times*, 9 January 1967, p. 7.

51. "Clash with Italian Parliament," *The Times*, 24 January 1967, p. 7.

52. De Vigili, *La battaglia sul divorzio*, pp. 56–57.

53. "Italia: Colonia del Vaticano," *ABC*, 5 February 1967, p. 7.

54. "Nasce il secondo Risorgimento," *ABC*, 12 February 1967, p. 7.

55. ASCD, DPLIC, 811, *Bollettino* of 13 July 1967, p. 6.

56. Camera dei Deputati, IV Legislatura, *Documenti—Disegni di Legge e relazione*, n. 3877 (Rome: Stabilimenti Tipografici Carlo Colombo, 1969).

57. "Divorzio e civiltà del benessere," *ABC*, 19 March 1967, p. 7, and "Gli studenti cattolici favorevoli al divorzio," *ABC*, 4 June 1967, p. 12.

58. Mario Gatti, "Il divorzio benedetto è solo per i ricchi," *ABC*, 21 May 1967, pp. 46–47.

59. De Vigili, *La battaglia sul divorzio*, p. 62.

60. DPLIC, *Bollettino* of 28 June 1967, p. 7.

61. De Vigili, *La battaglia sul divorzio*, p. 65.

62. "Fortuna dice: Siamo più forti," *ABC*, 2 July 1967, p. 12.

63. "Divorzio alla riscossa," *ABC*, 2 July 1967, pp. 12–13. See also De Vigili, who interprets the *L'Astrolabio* announcement of Republican support as the beginnings of a "fronte laico," or secular front, p. 66.

64. "Drammatico: i figli in 'gabbia,' " Insert in *ABC*, 9 July 1967, pp. I–VII.

65. For example, "Divorzio: Fronte laico contro i clericali," *ABC*, 8 October 1967, p. 6.

66. De Vigili, *La battaglia sul divorzio*, p. 66.

67. "Ambiguo «sì» socialista alla legge sul divorzio," *ABC*, 22 October 1967, p. 9.

68. In De Vigili's analysis, by October 1967 these parties were concerned to ensure that they could also claim fractional parternity over the law, or in her words, so that the future law owed something to them too, pp. 70–71.

69. "Finalmente c'è una maggioranza laica," *ABC*, 3 December 1967, p. 5.

70. De Vigili, *La battaglia sul divorzio*, p. 71.

71. The Christian Democrats won 39.1% of the total vote, an increase of 0.8%. The PCI won 26.9%, which was an increase of 1.6%. The Socialists, now split between the United Socialist Party (PSU) and the left-wing PSIUP, gained 19% between them, about 1% less than their combined vote at the previous elections. See Ginsborg, *Contemporary Italy*, p. 326.

72. Bruna Bellonzi, "Le donne in Parlamento," *Noi donne*, 8 June 1968, pp. 8–10. Seventeen women had seats in the Chamber of Deputies. Eight were members of the DC, eight were members of the PCI, and one was a Socialist.

73. Piero Craveri, *La Repubblica dal 1958 al 1992*, Vol XXIV of *Storia d'Italia* (Turin: UTET, 1995), p. 429.

74. In Giuseppe Tamburrano words, divorce entered Italian legislation as a result of an "extremely complex process," consisting of "Vatican pressures, secret dealings between the DC, high prelates, and exponents of the lay parties including the communists, and parliamentary wrangling." Giuseppe Tamburrano, *Storia e cronaca del centro-sinistra* (Milan: Feltrinelli, 1990), p. 382, quoted by Silvio Lanaro, *Storia dell'Italia repubblicana* (Venice: Marsilio, 1992), p. 354.

75. "Il fronte laico non si spezza," *ABC*, 1 November 1968, pp. 14–18.

76. Angiolo Bandinelli, "Antonio Baslini," in *Il Parlamento italiano, 1861–1988. Vol. XX, 1968–1972: Fra stato sociale e conestazione. Da Rumor ad Andreotti* (Milan, Nuova CEI, 1992), pp. 67–68.

77. Ginsborg, *Contemporary Italy*, p. 327.
78. ASCD, DPLIC, Vol. 979, *Bollettino* of 5 February 1969, p. 4.
79. Ibid.
80. De Vigili, *La battaglia sul divorzio*, p. 86.
81. For example, "Qui Loris Fortuna," *ABC*, 25 April 1969, p. 45. There were several other expressions of concern.
82. De Vigili, *La battaglia sul divorzio*, p. 86.
83. ASCD, DPLIC, 979, a hand-written note entitled "La situazione al 30 maggio, ore 20" (The situation on 30 May, 8 PM).
84. Loris Fortuna, "Prepararsi in tempo per i referendum sul divorzio e sul Concordato," *ABC*, 11 July 1969, p. 28.
85. "Ecco la polizza per divorziare con centomila lire," *ABC*, 20 June 1969, pp. 40–41.
86. "Enorme successo della polizza ABC divorzio," *ABC*, 27 June 1969, p. 34.
87. "Divorzio: Chi diserta tradisce," *ABC*, 3 October 1969, pp. 4–5.
88. See, for example, ASCD, DPLIC, Vol. 979. On 30 October 1969, four deputies spoke; on 31 October, eleven spoke.
89. Ginsborg, *Contemporary Italy*, p. 333.
90. Simona Colarizi, *Storia del novecento italiano*, p. 411.
91. De Vigili provides an excellent account of the behind-the-scenes lobbying as Mariano Rumor struggled to piece together a coalition capable of resolving a range of contentious questions, divorce chief among them, pp. 93–107.
92. "Pontiff Warns against Bill to Legalize Divorce," *New York Times*, 12 February 1970, p. 8.
93. Peter Nichols, "Vatican-State Rift on Divorce Widens," *The Times*, 16 February 1970, p. 4.
94. De Vigili, *La battaglia sul divorzio*, p. 95. See also Ministero degli Affari Esteri, *Documenti diplomatici sulla interpretazione dell'art. 34 del Concordato tra l'Italia e la Santa Sede* (Rome: Ministero degli Affari Esteri, 1970), which reprints the diplomatic notes between Italy and the Holy See on this question.
95. Loris Fortuna, "Qui Loris Fortuna," *ABC*, 20 March 1970, p. 29.
96. "Papa Montini è tornato al pugno duro di Pacelli," *ABC*, 27 March 1970, p. 4.
97. Lanaro, *Storia dell'Italia repubblicana*, p. 353.
98. For example, Peter Nichols, "Saragat May Call Elections to End Italian Crisis," *The Times*, 2 March 1970, p. 5. For a detailed analysis of the British and U.S. press response to the Italian divorce campaign, see Mark Seymour, "Condiscendenza con affetto. Le 'due culture' e la questione del divorzio in Italia vista dagli anglofoni (1900–1974)," *Genesis* 4, no. 1 (December 2005): 45–72.
99. Lanaro, *Storia dell'Italia repubblicana*, p. 354. There is general consensus on the nature of this arrangement as a political bargain, or "gentleman's agreement." See, for example, Nicola Tranfaglia, "La modernità squilibrata. Dalla crisi del centrismo al «compromesso storico»," in *Storia dell'Italia repubblicana*, Vol. II, *La trasformazione dell'italia: Sviluppo e squilibri, 2. Istituzioni, movimenti culture* (Turin: Einaudi, 1995), p. 92. See also Costantino Mortati, *Istituzioni di diritto pubblico*, Vol. II (Padua: CEDAM, 1976), p. 841.

100. De Vigili, *La battaglia sul divorzio*, p. 105.
101. Ibid., p. 108.
102. See, for example, Loris Fortuna, "Divorzio. Italiani, attenti: Ci vogliono imbrogliare!" *ABC*, 21 August 1970, pp. 4–5.
103. *ABC*, 17 July 1970, pp. 4–5.
104. Loris Fortuna, "Venti settembre: Senza peli sulla lingua," *ABC*, 4 September 1970, p. 28.
105. Loris Fortuna, "Qui Loris Fortuna," *ABC*, 25 September 1970, pp. 4–5.
106. Archivio Storico del Senato della Repubblica, Assemblea, V Legislatura (1968–1972), ddl n. 973, 1 October 1970.
107. An article-by-article comparison of the law before and after the Senate modifications is provided in Camera dei Deputati, *Atti parlamentari. Disegni di Legge*, N. 1-B (Rome: Camera dei Deputati, n.d.).
108. Camera dei Deputati, *La V Legislatura della Repubblica. La Legislazione italiana dal 20 maggio 1968 and 7 maggio 1972. Vol. I* (Rome: Camera dei Deputati, n.d.), p. 757.

Chapter 9   Let the People Decide, 1970–1974

1. "Divorzio!" *Notizie radicali*, 10 December 1970, p. 1.
2. See Guido Maggioni, *Il divorzio in Italia. Storia dell'applicazione di una legge nuova* (Milan: Franco Angeli, 1990). Divorces in Italy between 1970 and 1986 averaged 15,000 per year, compared with 73,000 in France, and 134,000 in United Kingdom, p. 8.
3. Adriano Panniccia, "I primatisti del divorzio," *Noi donne*, 16 January 1971, pp. 10–11.
4. Martin Clark, David Hine, and R. E. M. Irving, "Divorce—Italian Style," *Parliamentary Affairs* 27, no. 4 (1974): 333–358.
5. Ibid., 342.
6. Orazio M. Petracca, "Il primo scioglimento anticipato delle Camere," in *Il Parlamento italiano, 1861–1988. Vol. XX, 1968–1972: Fra stato sociale e contestazione. Da Rumor ad Andreotti* (Milan: Nuova CEI, 1992), pp. 221. See also Pietro Scoppola, "Una crisi politica e istituzionale," in *Storia e problemi contemporanei*, special number, *Rileggendo gli anni settanta*, May–August 2002, p. 26; and Ginsborg, *Contemporary Italy*, p. 335.
7. Clark et al., "Divorce—Italian Style," p. 343.
8. Ginsborg, *Contemporary Italy*, pp. 336–337.
9. Clark et al., "Divorce—Italian Style," p. 343.
10. Ginsborg, *Contemporary Italy*, p. 355.
11. Clark et al., "Divorce—Italian Style," p. 344.
12. De Vigili, *La battaglia sul divorzio*, p. 153.
13. Camera dei Deputati, *La V legislatura della Repubblica. La legislazione dal 20 maggio 1968 al 7 maggio 1972*, Vol. I (Rome: Camera dei Deputati, n.d.), pp. 799–800.
14. A prominent 1970s feminist, Adele Cambria, wrote a damning denunciation of the extent to which the PCI's attitude to divorce was conditioned by

motives of political opportunity: "Sacra famiglia DC-PCI: divorzio e paura," *Compagna* 1, no. 1 (January 1972): 8–9.

15. De Vigili, *La battaglia sul divorzio*, pp. 144–145.

16. Clark et al., "Divorce—Italian Style," p. 350.

17. Sandro Magister, *La politica vaticana e l'Italia, 1943–1978* (Rome: Editori Riuniti, 1979), p. 424.

18. For example, "Il «nì» dell'Azione Cattolica sul divorzio," *Corriere della Sera*, 20 April 1974, p. 2; and "Un quarto dei parroci romani non suona la campana del «sì»," *Corriere della Sera*, 24 April 1974, p. 3.

19. Clark et al., "Divorce—Italian Style," p. 351.

20. "Dom Franzoni licenziato," *ABC*, 16 May 1974, p. 14.

21. "Stand on Your Head to Vote," *The Economist*, 4 May 1974, pp. 51–52.

22. For example, Elda Guerra traces the "new subjectivity" of feminists as it developed from the late 1960s to the 1980s without a mention of the divorce law, the referendum, or women's responses to it: "Una nuova soggettività: Femminismo e femminismi nel passaggio degli anni Settanta," in Teresa Bertilotti and Anna Scattigno, eds., *Il femminismo degli anni Settanta* (Rome: Viella, 2005), pp. 25–67.

23. Several studies published by British and U.S. scholars not long after the referendum underlined the importance of the event as the catalyst for widespread discussion of feminist issues in Italy. See, for example, Lesley Caldwell, "Church, State and Family: The Women's Movement in Italy," in Annette Kuhn and AnnMarie Wolpe, eds., *Feminism and Materialism: Women and Modes of Production* (London: Routledge and Kegan Paul, 1978), pp. 69 and 71; Dinah Dodds, "Extraparliamentary Feminism and Social Change in Italy, 1971–1980," *International Journal of Women's Studies* 5, no. 2 (1982): 150; Joanne Barkan, "The Genesis of Contemporary Italian Feminism," *Radical America* 18, no. 5 (1984): 31–37. In a summary of UDI's congresses from 1945 to 1982, Pina Nuzzo, director of UDI Nazionale in Rome, wrote "Women knew how to find the most effective arguments (the personal is the political) to make the campaign for the NO into a mass campaign. Women came out of this experience with a greater capacity to stand on the political stage and with the impetus necessary to confront the abortion question." ("Info-Memo 1945–1982, Rome," unpublished typescript, Rome, 2002, Archivio UDI). Although anecdotal evidence suggests that there is nothing far-fetched about Nuzzo's claim, the divorce question and its relationship to the women's movement has received virtually no attention from Italian feminist historians.

24. For example, Miriam Mafai claimed that the referendum was the first victory of the new feminist movement: "That day, with that vote, the Church's secular domination of women's sentiments and women's bodies, ended," Miriam Mafai, "Divorzio: Quando l'Italia si scoprì laica," *La Repubblica*, 8 May 2004, p. 35. Although the focus of her essay is the abortion debate, Paola Gaiotti di Biase also refers to the importance of the divorce law as a preparatory step for women: "Cattoliche e cattolici di fronte all'aborto e il mutamento degli equilibri della Repubblica," *Genesis* 3, no. 1 (2004): 59–66.

25. "Hanno vinto le donne," *Effe*, June 1974, p. 39. Thirty-five thousand copies of this issue were printed.

26. *Effe*, April–May 1974, cover.

27. "Vogliamo una famiglia vera," *Noi donne*, 24 February 1974, pp. 17–27.

28. Gabriella Lapasini, "Speciale: La donna siciliana," *Noi donne*, 7 April 1974, pp. 29–43.

29. Marta Schiavi, "Per un anno si divorzierà solo a Milano?" *Annabella*, 4 November 1970, pp. 29–32; and Magister, "Si può divorziare anche in chiesa!" *Annabella*, 15 December 1970, pp. 29–32.

30. "Per carità non toglieteci il divorzio," *Annabella*, 4 May 1974, pp. 55–59.

31. The electorate consisted of 19,605,000 women and 17,890,000 men. Clark et al., "Divorce—Italian Style," p. 352.

32. For example, a newspaper article in January 1974 reported that only 30 % of women wished to abolish the divorce law, but this was so different from similar polls taken a few years earlier that there was considerable doubt about the most recent poll. Miriam Mafai, "Solanto 30% delle donne per l'abolizione del divorzio," *Paese sera*, 20 January 1974 (clipping without page number, Archivio UDI, Fa-Di 74.3/13).

33. "Cronache del «sì» e del «no»," *Corriere della sera*, 20 April 1974, p. 5.

34. Reported in Alfonso Amadeo, "La posizione della donna di fronte al referendum," *Corriere della sera*, 9 May 1974 (clipping without page number, Archivio UDI, Fa-Di 74.3/14).

35. Fanfani's position in relation to the referendum remains ambiguous. As the figure who ultimately decided that the referendum would go ahead, he was widely attributed with having done so for reasons of personal ambition, seeing it as an opportunity to strengthen his leadership of the DC. Diana De Vigili tempers this judgment, regarding the decision as unavoidable (see De Vigili, *La battaglia sul divorzio*, pp. 162–163). On the other hand, Fanfani's commitment to the anti-divorce cause once the decision had been made is unquestionable.

36. Antonio Padellaro, "Fanfani cerca un'argine al Sud contro i «no» del Settentrione," *Corriere della sera*, 25 April 1974, p. 11. According to *ABC*, Fanfani also made thinly veiled threats that a vote in favor of divorce in the south would result in an end to the flow of economic subsidies: Carlo Vettori, "Il ricatto di Fanfani: COLERA," *ABC*, 18 April 1974, pp. 20–21.

37. Antonio Padellaro, "Fanfani parla del referendum ma ascolta gli intrighi siciliani," *Corriere della Sera*, 28 April 1974, p. 11.

38. "Come hanno votato gli italiani," *Avanti!*, 14 May 1974, p. 3, lays out the results city by city for the entire nation.

39. De Vigili, *La battaglia sul divorzio*, p. 178.

40. Loris Fortuna, "Il 'Guittone d'Arezzo' ha fatto il suo tempo," *ABC*, 23 May 1974, p. 24. For more on the position in the south, see also "Il sud ha votato no a Fanfani e Almirante," *ABC*, 23 May 1974, p. 26.

41. One of the most poignant expressions of the defeat was a minute from the Italian Ambassador to the Holy See, Gian Franco Pompei, to Aldo Moro, on 14 May 1974: "The Church and her inexpert advisors expected this confrontation to heal a wound, but instead it remains confirmed and consolidated

indefinitely." Gian Franco Pompei, *Un ambasciatore in Vaticano. Diario 1969–1977*, ed. Pietro Scoppola (Bologna: Il Mulino, 1994), p. 379.

42. Pietro Scoppola, "Una crisi politica e istituzionale," p. 26; Enzo Santarelli, *Storia critica della repubblica. L'Italia dal 1945 al 1994* (Milan: Feltrinelli, 1996), p. 233; Lanaro, *Storia dell'Italia repubblicana*, p. 359.

43. Tranfaglia, "La modernità squilibrata," pp. 108–109.

44. Paolo Ungari, *Storia del diritto di famiglia, 1796–1975* (Bologna: Il Mulino, 2002), p. 247.

45. On the weekend of the referendum the *Osservatore romano* reprinted one of the key debates on the divorce question from the proceedings of the Constituent Assembly in 1947: "Una polemica alla Costituente," *Osservatore romano*, 13–14 May 1974, p. 7. In November 1975, *Noi donne* drew a direct line between women's NO to fascism during the Resistance and the NO of the divorce referendum: Rosa Brunelli, "Mille volte NO," *Noi donne*, 9 November 1975, pp. 14–15.

46. Colarizi, *Storia del novecento italiano*, p. 429.

Conclusion

1. Alberto Mario Banti, *La nazione del Risorgimento. Parentela, santità e onore alle origini dell'Italia unita* (Turin: Einaudi, 2000), p. 119.

2. Nancy Cott, *Public Vows: A History of Marriage and the Nation* (Cambridge, MA: Harvard University Press, 2000), p. 5.

3. Anna Rossi-Doria, "Le donne sulla scena politica," in *Storia dell'Italia repubblicana. Vol. I: La costruzione della democrazia. Dalla caduta del fascismo agli anni cinquanta* (Turin: Einaudi, 1994), p. 845.

4. Paul Ginsborg, *Il tempo di cambiare. Politica e potere della vita quotidiana* (Turin: Einaudi, 2004), pp. 109–110.

Bibliography

Sources

Archives

Archivio Storico della Camera dei Deputati, Rome.
    Collection: Disegni e Progetti di Legge: Incarti delle Commissioni.
Archivio Storico del Senato della Repubblica, Rome.
    Collection: Assemblea, Disegni di legge, V Legislatura (1968–1972).
Archivio di Stato di Roma, Rome.
    Collection: Archivio del Tribunale Civile e Penale di Roma.
    Collection: Corte di Apello, Sentenze civili.
Archivio Centrale dell'Unione donne in Italia (UDI), Rome.
    Collection: Famiglia-Divorzio.
Biblioteca del Seminario Patriarcale, Venice.
    Collection: Archivio dell'Opera dei Congressi.
Archivio del Museo Centrale del Risorgimento, Rome.
    Collection: Archivio Garibaldi.

Italian Parliamentary Records
(in chronological order)

Atti del Parlamento Italiano. Discussioni della Camera dei Deputati. Session of 1860 (VII Legislature), 2 April–28 December 1860. Turin: Botta, 1861.
———. Senato del Regno. Discussioni. Session of 1861–62 (VII Legislature), Vol. III. Florence: Botta, 1870.
———. Discussioni della Camera dei Deputati. Session of 1861–1862 (VII Legislature), 2 April–21 May 1863 (n.p., n.d.).
———. Camera dei Deputati. Progetti di legge, relazioni e documenti diversi. Session of 1863–64 (VIII Legislature), (n.p., n.d.).
———. Discussioni della Camera dei Deputati. Session of 1863–64–65 (VIII Legislature), Vol. X: 5 January 1865–22 February 1865. 2nd ed. Rome: Camera dei Deputati, 1890.
———. Camera dei Deputati. Raccolta degli atti stampati per ordine della Camera. Session of 1873–74 (XI Legislature), Vol. II: nn. 29–71. Rome: Camera dei Deputati, 1874.

Atti del Parlamento Italiano. Discussioni della Camera dei Deputati. Session of 1878 (XIII Legislature), Vol. II: 13 May–17 June 1878. Rome: Tip. Eredi Botta, 1878.

———. *Camera dei Deputati. Raccolta degli atti stampati per ordine della Camera.* Sessione of 1880 (XIII Legislature), Vol. II: nn. 34–100. Rome: Camera dei Deputati, 1880.

———. *Discussioni della Camera dei Deputati.* Session of 1880 (XIII Legislature), 17 February–2 May 1880. Rome: Camera dei Deputati, 1880.

———. *Camera dei Deputati. Raccolta degli atti stampati per ordine della Camera.* Session of 1880–81 (XIV Legislature), Vol. VII: nn. 126–181. Rome: Camera dei Deputati, 1882.

———. *Discussioni della Camera dei Deputati.* Session of 1882–86 (XV Legislature), Vol. III: 9 March–27 April 1883. Rome: Camera dei Deputati, 1886.

———. *Camera dei Deputati. Raccolta degli atti stampati per ordine della Camera.* Session of 1882–86 (XV Legislature), Vol. VI: nn. 56–90. Rome: Camera dei Deputati, 1886.

———. *Discussioni della Camera dei Deputati.* Session of 1890–92 (XVII Legislature), Vol VI: 19 March–15 June 1892. Rome: Camera dei Deputati, 1892.

Indice generale degli Atti Parlamentari, 1848–1897. Rome: Camera dei Deputati, 1898.

Atti del Parlamento Italiano. Discussioni della Camera dei Deputati. Session of 1900–01 (XXI Legislature), Vol. 1: 16 June–8 December 1900. Rome: Camera dei Deputati, 1901.

———. *Discussioni della Camera dei Deputati.* Session of 1900–01 (XXI Legislature), Vol. II: 10 December 1900–7 February 1901. Rome: Camera dei Deputati, 1901.

———. *Discussioni della Camera dei Deputati.* Session of 1900–01 (XXI Legislature), Vol. IV: 7 March–30 March 1901. Rome: Camera dei Deputati, 1901.

———. *Discussioni della Camera dei Deputati.* Session of 1900–01 (XXI Legislature), Vol. VII: 27 November–22 December 1901. Rome: Camera dei Deputati, 1902.

———. *Camera dei Deputati. Raccolta degli atti stampati per ordine della Camera.* Session of 1900–02 (XXI Legislature), Vol. IX: nn. 332–386. Rome: Camera dei Deputati, 1902.

———. *Camera dei Deputati. Raccolta degli atti stampati per ordine della Camera.* 2nd Session of 1902–04 (XXI Legislature), Vol IV: nn. 151–212. Rome: Camera dei Deputati, 1904.

La XXIV Legislatura (27 novembre 1913–29 settembre 1919). Indice. Rome: Camera dei Deputati, 1919.

Atti del Parlamento Italiano. Discussioni della Camera dei Deputati. Session of 1921–1923 (XXVI Legislature). Rome: Camera dei Deputati, 1923.

Assemblea Costituente. *Commissione per la Costituzione. Discussioni. Prima Sottocommissione dal 26 luglio al 19 dicembre 1946.* Rome: Tipografia della Camera dei Deputati, n.d.

Camera dei Deputati. *La Costituzione della Repubblica nei lavori preparatori della Assemblea Costituente. Vol II, Sedute dal 17 aprile 1947 al 19 maggio 1947.* Rome: Tipolitografia Edigraf, 1976 (reprint based on 1970 edition).

Camera dei Deputati, *Disegni e proposte di legge-relazioni.* Legislature II, 1953–58. Rome: Tipografia della Camera dei Deputati, n.d.

Senato della Repubblica. *Atti interni. Disegni di legge.* Legislature III, 1958–1963. Rome: Tipografia del Senato, 1963.

Camera dei Deputati. *Disegni e proposte di legge-relazioni.* Legislature IV, 1963–68. Rome: Stabilimenti Tipografici Carlo Colombo, n.d.

Camera dei Deputati. *Disegni e proposte di legge-relazioni.* Legislature V, 1968–72. Rome: Stabilimenti Tipografici Carlo Colombo, n.d.

Camera dei Deputati. *Discussioni.* Legislature V, 1968–72. Rome: Camera dei Deputati, n.d.

Camera dei Deputati. *La V Legislatura della Repubblica. La Legislazione italiana dal 20 maggio 1968 and 7 maggio 1972.* Vol. I. Rome: Camera dei Deputati, n.d.

Senato della Repubblica. *Atti interni. Disegni di legge.* Vol XXXIX, Legislature V. Rome: Tipografia del Senato, 1972.

Other Government Publications

Camera dei Deputati. *Ricerca sul diritto della famiglia.* Rome: Camera dei Deputati, 1966.

Direzione Generale della Statistica. *Annali di Statistica. Appendice agli Atti della Commissione per la Statistica Giudiziaria e Notarile (Sessione del luglio 1898). Divorzi e separazioni personali di coniugi.* Rome: Tipografia di G. Bertero, 1908.

Italy. *Codice civile.* Turin: Unione Tipografico-Editrice, 1888.

Ministero degli Affari Esteri. *Documenti diplomatici sulla interpretazione dell'art. 34 del Concordato tra l'Italia e la Santa Sede.* Rome: Ministero degli Affari Esteri, 1970.

Sardinia. *Atti del Parlamento Subalpino. Discussioni della Camera dei Deputati.* Session of 1852, Legislature IV, Vol. V: 4 March 1852–21 November 1853. Florence: Botta, 1868.

Sardinia. *Atti del Parlamento Subalpino. Discussioni del Senato del Regno.* Session of 1852, Legislature IV: 4 March 1852–21 November 1853. Florence: Botta, 1868.

Sardinia. *Codice civile per gli stati di S. M. il Re di Sardegna.* Turin: Stamperia Reale, 1837.

Serials

ABC (Milan).

Annabella (Milan).

Avanti! (Rome).

Battaglia divorzista (Rome).

Compagna (Rome).

Cronache e opinioni (Rome).

Corriere della sera (Milan).

Critica sociale (Milan).

Effe (Rome).

Grazia (Milan).

Il Divorzio. Rivista critica della famiglia italiana (Rome).

Il Foro italiano (Rome).

Il Messaggero (Rome).

Il Secolo (Milan).

L'Europeo (Milan)

L'Opinione (Rome).

L'Osservatore romano (Rome).

La Capitale (Rome).

La Nazione (Florence).

La Repubblica (Milan).

La Stampa (Turin).

La Tribuna (Rome).

La Voce della verità (Milan).

Liberazione (Rome).

New York Times (New York City).

Noi donne (Rome).

Rivista della Massoneria italiana (Rome).

The Economist (London).

The Times (London).

Published Sources

Acomb, Evelyn Martha. *The French Laic Laws (1879–1889)*. New York: Octagon Books, 1967.

Acta Sanctae Sedis. Ephemeridis (1865–1908). Index generalis. Rome: Typis Editricis Romanae, 1909.

Addis Saba, Marina. *Anna Kuliscioff. Vita privata e passione politica*. Milan: Arnoldo Mondadori Editore, 1993.

Agosti, Aldo. *Palmiro Togliatti*. Turin: UTET, 1996.

Aguilar, Luigi. *Il divorzio condannato dalla religione e dal diritto naturale privato e pubblico*. Turin: Tipografia Salesiana, 1879.

Ajcardi, Enrico. *Divorzio? Brevi considerazioni giuridiche e sociali intorno a questa istituzione*. Rome: Tipografia Befani, 1881.

Alberti de Mazzeri, Silvia. *Le donne di Garibaldi*. Milan: Editoriale Nuova, 1981.

Aleramo, Sibilla. *Una Donna*. Reprint of 1906 edition. Milan: Feltrinelli, 1996.

―――. *La donna e il femminismo. Scritti 1897–1910*. Ed. Bruna Conti. Rome: Edizioni Riuniti, 1978.

Analecta Juris Pontificiae. Dissertations sur différents sujets de droit canonique, liturgie theologie et histoire. Rome: Librairie de la Propagande, 1871–1882.

Anzoletti, Luisa. *Il divorzio e la donna italiana: discorso*. 2nd ed. Milan: Tipografia Editrice L. F. Cogliati, 1902.

Aquarone, Alberto. *L'Unificazione legislativa e i codici del 1865*. Milan: Giuffrè Editore, 1960.

Ardigò, Achille. "La disintegrazione della famiglia nella sociologia dell'800 (Spencer, Marx, Engels, Tönnies, Durkheim). Note di sintesi." *Studi di sociologia* (January–March 1965): 215–231.

Avignone, G. B. *Del matrimonio civile. Memoria.* Milan: Tipografia di Alessandro Lombardi, 1861.

Ballerini, Giuseppe. *Matrimonio e divorzio (a proposito dell'attuale progetto di legge).* Siena: Tipografia S. Bernadino, 1902.

Banti, Alberto M. *La nazione del Risorgimento. Parentela, santità e onore alle origini dell'Italia unita.* Turin: Einaudi, 2000.

Barbagli, Marzio. *Provando e riprovando. Matrimonio, famiglia e divorzio in Italia e in altri paesi occidentali.* Bologna: Il Mulino, 1990.

Barbagli, Marzio, and Chiara Saraceno. *Separarsi in Italia.* Bologna: Il Mulino, 1998.

Bardari, Renato Luciano. *Divorzio e separazione. Memoria, per la laurea in Giurisprudenza.* Naples: Tipografia Giannini, 1880.

Barkan, Joanne. "The Genesis of Contemporary Italian Feminism." *Radical America* 18, no. 5 (1984): 31–37.

Bellassai, Sandro. *La morale comunista. Pubblico e privato nella rappresentazione del PCI (1947–1956).* Rome: Carocci Editore, 2000.

Berenini, Agostino. "Il divorzio innanzi alla Camera." *La Rassegna nazionale* VII, no. 5 (1901): 405–417.

Bertillon, Jacques. *Etude démographique du divorce et de la séparation de corps dans les differents pays de l'Europe.* Paris: G. Masson, 1883.

Berutti, Mario. *Il divorzio in Italia.* Milan: Edizioni di comunità, 1964.

Bianchi, Emilio. *Il divorzio. Considerazioni sul progetto di legge presentato al Parlamento Italiano.* Pisa: Tipografia T. Nistri, 1879.

Billia, L. Michelangelo. *Nessun caso di divorzio.* Florence: Uffizio della *Rassegna Nazionale,* 1893.

Binchy, Daniel A. *Church and State in Fascist Italy.* Oxford: Oxford University Press, 1970 (repr. 1941 ed.).

Binion, Rudolph. "Fiction as Social Fantasy: Europe's Domestic Crisis of 1879–1914." *Journal of Social History* 27, no. 4 (1994): 679–699.

Bonavita, Francesco. *La legge sul divorzio spiegata al popolo. Conversazione tra Luigi fabbro e Maddalena sua moglie.* Florence: G. Nerbi Editore, 1902.

Bonomelli, Geremia. *Sul divorzio.* Cremona: Tipografia S. Giuseppe, 1881.

Bosworth, R. J. B. *Mussolini's Italy: Life under the Fascist Dictatorship, 1915–1945.* New York: The Penguin Press, 2006.

Bossi, Luigi M. *La legge sul divorzio considerata dal lato ginecologico. Conferenza tenuta all'Associazione Medica Lombarda.* Naples: Stabilimento Tipografico Jovene, 1902.

Brandi, Salvatore. *La follia del divorzio. Fatti e note.* Rome: Civiltà Cattolica, 1902.

Brunelli, Giovanni. *Divorzio e nullità di matrimonio negli stati d'Europa.* Milan: Giuffrè Editore, 1937.

Brunelli, Ignazio. *Indissolubilità o divorzio?* Bologna: Tipografia Zamovani e Albertazzi, 1891.

Buttafuoco, Annarita. *Cronache femminili. Temi e momenti della stampa emancipazionista in Italia dall'Unità al fascismo.* Siena: Dipartimento di Studi Storico-Sociali e Filosofici, Università degli Studi di Siena, 1988.

Caldwell, Lesley. "Church, State and Family: the Women's Movement in Italy." In *Feminism and Materialism: Women and Modes of Production*. Ed. Annette Kuhn and AnnMarie Wolpe. London: Routledge and Kegan Paul, 1978, pp. 68–95.

———. *Italian Family Matters: Women, Politics and Legal Reform*. Basingstoke: Macmillan, 1991.

Canavero, Alfredo. *I cattolici nella società italiana. Dalla metà dell'800 al Concilio Vaticano II*. Brescia: Editrice La Scuola, 1991.

Candeloro, Giorgio. *Il movimento cattolico in Italia*. Rome: Edizioni Rinascita, 1953.

———. *Storia dell'Italia moderna*. Vol. 7: *La crisi di fine secolo e l'età giolittiana*. Milan: Feltrinelli, 1974.

Capecchi, Vittorio, and Marino Livolsi. *La stampa quotidiana in Italia*. Milan: Bompiani, 1971.

Casalini, Maria. *Le donne della sinistra (1944–1948)*. Rome: Carocci, 2005.

Cassuto, Dario. *Le sentenze estere di divorzio e il giudizio di delibazione*. Turin: Unione Tipografico-Editrice, 1901.

Castronovo, Valerio. *La stampa italiana dall'Unità al fascismo*. Rome-Bari: Laterza, 1973.

Castronovo, Valerio, and Nicola Tranfaglia. *Storia della stampa italiana*. Vol. 5: *La stampa italiana del neocapitalismo*. Rome-Bari: Laterza, 1976.

Cenni, Enrico. *Il divorzio considerato come contro natura e antigiuridico*. Florence: Tipografia Cellini, 1881.

Cesarini, Grazia, and Ghita Marchi. *La stampa femminile dal '700 ad oggi*. Rome: Edizioni «Noi Donne», 1952.

Chadwick, Owen. *A History of the Popes, 1830–1914*. Oxford: Clarendon Press, 1998.

Chester, Robert. *Divorce in Europe*. Leiden: Martinus Nijhoff, 1977.

Cimbali, Enrico. *Due riforme urgenti. Il divorzio e la ricerca della paternità naturale*. Turin: Unione Tipografico Editrice, 1902.

Clark, Martin. *Modern Italy, 1871–1982*. London and New York: Longman, 1984.

Clark, Martin, David Hine, and R. E. M. Irving. "Divorce—Italian Style." *Parliamentary Affairs* 27, no. 4 (1974): 333–358.

Colarizi, Simona. *Storia del novecento italiano. Cent'anni di entusiasmo, di paure, di speranza*. Milan: BUR, 2000.

Coletti, Alessandro. *Il divorzio in Italia. Storia di una battaglia civile e democratica*. 2nd ed. Rome: Edizioni Savelli, 1974.

Consolo, Giuseppe. *Del divorzio nei suoi rapporti colle leggi civili e colla libertà dei culti riconosciuti nello stato*. Padua: Tipografia A. Bianchi, 1864.

Conti, Augusto. *Osservazioni sopra un libro del Prof. Gabba contro il divorzio e sopra i danni della legge proposta alle Camere*. Florence: Tipografia del Vocabolario, 1885.

Conti Odorisio, Ginevra, ed. *Salvatore Morelli (1824–1880). Emancipazionismo e democrazia nell'Ottocento europeo*. Naples: Edizioni Scientifiche Italiane, 1992.

Contro il divorzio. Bolletino II del Comitato centrale per la difesa del matrimonio. Florence: Loescher e Seeber, 1894.

Contro il divorzio. Pubblicazione del Comitato studentesco antidivorzista torinese. Torino: n.p., 1903.

Cordelia [Virginia Treves]. *Catene*. Reprint of 1882 edition. Milan: Fratelli Treves, 1903.

Cordova, Ferdinando. *Massoneria e politica in Italia. 1892–1908*. Rome-Bari: Laterza, 1985.

Corradini, Enrico. "L'agitazione ecclesiastica contro il divorzio." *Rassegna nazionale* VIII, no. 3 (1902): 195–209.

Corte di Cassazione. *Il regime matrimoniale italiano e il divorzio*. Turin: Unione Tipografico-Editrice, 1900.

Coscioni, Carlo. *I prolegomeni al nuovo codice civile italiano*. Naples: Tipografia dell'Arno, 1863.

Cott, Nancy. *Public Vows: A History of Marriage and the Nation*. Cambridge, MA: Harvard University Press, 2000.

Craveri, Piero. *La Repubblica dal 1958 al 1992*. Vol XXIV of *Storia d'Italia*. Turin: UTET, 1995.

Croce, Benedetto. "Il divorzio nelle province napoletane: 1809–1815." *La Scuola positiva* Anno 1, nn. 11–12 (October 15–30, 1891): 481–497.

Curàtulo, Giacomo Emilio. *Garibaldi e le donne*. Rome: Imprimerie Polyglotte, 1913.

D'Avack, Pietro Agostino. *Studi sul divorzio*. Padua: CEDAM, 1972.

Dau Novelli, Cecilia. *Famiglia e modernizzazione in Italia fra le due guerre*. Rome: Edizioni Studium, 1994.

Davis, John A. *Conflict and Control: Law and Order in Nineteenth-Century Italy*. Atlantic Highlands, NJ: Humanities Press International, 1988.

De Felice, Renzo, ed. *Storia dell'Italia contemporanea*. Vol. 2: *L'età giolittiana 1899–1914* by Emilio Gentile. Naples: Edizioni Scientifiche Italiane, 1977.

De Giorgio, Michela. *Le italiane dall'unità a oggi. Modelli culturali e comportamenti sociali*. 2nd ed. Rome-Bari: Laterza, 1993.

De Giorgio, Michela, and Christiane Klapisch-Zuber, eds. *Storia del matrimonio*. Rome-Bari: Laterza, 1996.

De Grazia, Victoria. *How Fascism Ruled Women: Italy 1922–1945*. Berkeley: University of California Press, 1993.

De Longis, Rosanna. *La stampa periodica delle donne in Italia. Catalogo 1861–1985*. Rome: Commissione nazionale per la realizzazione della parità tra uomo e donna, 1987.

De Matteis, Luigi. *Matrimonio e divorzio secondo natura e religione, tradizione e storia, diritto e civiltà*. Naples: Stamperia già del Fibreno, 1885.

De Rita, Giuseppe. *Amore, matrimonio, divorzio*. Campobasso: Tipografia Colitti, 1901.

De Roberto, Federico. *I vicerè*. Reprint of 1894 edition. Turin: Einaudi, 1990.

De Rosa, Gabriele. *Il movimento cattolico in Italia. Dalla Restaurazione all'età giolittiana*. Bari: Laterza, 1988.

De Siena, Pasquale. *Sulla indissolubilità del matrimonio*. Naples: Stamperia del Fibreno, 1871.

De Vigili, Diana. *La battaglia sul divorzio. Dalla Costituente al Referendum*. Milan: Franco Angeli, 2000.

Decleva, Enrico. "Anticlericalismo e lotta politica nell'Italia giolittiana. I: L'«esempio della Francia» e i partiti popolari (1901–1904)." *Nuova Rivista Storica* LII, nn. 3–4 (1968): 291–354.

Deledda, Grazia. *Dopo il divorzio. Romanzo.* Turin: Roux e Viarengo, 1902.

Di Bernardo, Domenico. *Il divorzio considerato nella teoria e nella pratica.* Palermo: Tipografia A. Natale, 1875.

Dodds, Dinah. "Extraparliamentary Feminism and Social Change in Italy, 1971–1980." *International Journal of Women's Studies* 5, no. 2 (1982): 148–160.

Dumas, Alessandro (figlio). *La questione del divorzio.* Milan: Ferdinando Garbini Editore, 1880.

———. *Perchè i preti combattono il divorzio?* Naples: Società Editrice Partenopea, 1902.

Enciclopedia biografica e bibliografica "italiana." Series VI: *Poetesse e scrittrici.* Rome: Istituto Editoriale Italiano, 1942.

Enciclopedia biografica e bibliografica "italiana." Series XLII: *Il Risorgimento Italiano,* Vol. IV: *Gli uomini politici.* Rome: Istituto Editoriale Italiano, 1942.

Enciclopedia biografica e bibliografica "italiana." Series XLIII: *Ministri, Deputati, Senatori dal 1848 al 1922.* Milan-Rome: Istituto Editoriale Italiano, 1940–1941.

Enciclopedia giuridica italiana. Milan: Società Editrice Libraria, 1900–1921.

Fappani, Antonio. *La polemica divorzista in Italia.* Brescia: Queriniana, 1970.

Federici, Emilio. *Divorzio e socialismo.* Venice: Tipografia Emiliana, 1902.

Fenoaltea, Giorgio. *Il divorzio. Tema con variazioni.* Rome: Campitelli, 1946.

Filomusi Guelfi, Francesco. *Contro il divorzio. Lettera al presidente del Comitato laico di Napoli Senatore S. Fusco.* 2nd ed. Rome: Tipografia Pallotta, 1903.

———. *Il divorzio tra stranieri in Italia. Nota.* Fano: Tipografia Souciniana, 1884. Extracted from *Il Foro Italiano,* Anno IX.

Fiore, Pasquale. *Sulla controvesia del divorzio in Italia. Considerazioni.* Turin: Unione Tipografico Editrice, 1891.

Franchi, Anna. *Avanti il divorzio.* Milan: Remo Sandron, 1902.

———. *Il divorzio e la donna.* Florence: G. Nerbini Editore, 1902.

Fumasi, Eleonora. *Mezzo secolo di ricerca storiografica sul movimento cattolico in Italia dal 1861 al 1945: contributo a una bibliografia.* Brescia: Editrice La Scuola, 1995.

Gabba, Carlo Francesco. *Il divorzio nella legislazione italiana.* Turin: Unione Tipografico-Editrice, 1891.

———. *I due matrimoni civile e religioso nell'odierno diritto italiano.* Pisa: Tipografia Nistri, 1876.

———. *Studi di legislazione civile comparata in servizio della nuova codifiazione italiana.* Milan: Tipi di Alessandro Lombardi, 1862.

Gaiotti di Biase, Paola. "Cattoliche e cattolici di fronte all'aborto e il mutamento degli equilibri della Repubblica." *Genesis* 3, no. 1 (2004): 55–86.

Galante, Vincenzo. *Il divorzio e le riforme alla legge sul matrimonio.* Naples: Tipografia Priore, 1903.

Galasso, Giuseppe, ed. *Storia d'Italia.* Vol. 21: *La crisi di fine secolo e l'età giolittiana,* by Francesco Gaeta. Turin: UTET, 1982.

Galoppini, Annamaria. "Il problema del divorzio nella storia della legislazione italiana." *Rivista trimestrale del diritto e procedura civile* XXIV, no. 2 (June 1970): 532–567.

———. "Profilo storico del divorzio in Italia." *Il diritto di famiglia e di persone* Anno IX (1980): 594–666.

Gambasin, Angelo. *Il movimento sociale nell'Opera dei Congressi (1874–1904). Contributo per la storia del cattolicesimo sociale in Italia.* Rome: Editrice Università Gregoriana, 1958.

Garroni, Adolfo. *Il divorzio nei suoi tre grandi rapporti: civili, religiosi e sociali.* Rome: L. Garroni, 1876.

Gentile, Emilio. *Storia dell'Italia contemporanea.* Vol. 2: *L'età giolittiana 1899–1914.* Naples: Edizioni Scientifiche Italiane, 1977.

Gibson, Mary. *Prostitution and the State in Italy, 1860–1915.* New Brunswick, NJ: Rutgers University Press, 1986.

Ginsborg, Paul. *A History of Contemporary Italy: Society and Politics, 1943–1988.* London: Penguin Books, 1988.

———. "Family, Civil Society and the State in Contemporary European History: Some Methodological Considerations." *Contemporary European History* 4, no. 3 (1995): 249–273.

———. *Il tempo di cambiare. Politica e potere della vita quotidiana.* Turin: Einaudi, 2004.

Gioia, Melchiorre. *Teoria civile e penale del divorzio. Ossia necessità, cause, nuova maniera d'organizzarlo seguita dall'analisi della legge francese 30 venosto Anno XI relativo allo stesso argomento.* Milan: Pirotta e Maspero, 1803.

Giolitti, Giovanni. *Memorie della mia vita.* Vol. I. Milan: Treves, 1922.

Giuriati, Domenico. *Le leggi dell'amore.* Turin: Roux e Favale, 1881.

Gortchakoff-Ouvaroff, Nathalie. *La femme e le divorce.* Pistoia: Tipografia Nicolai, 1891.

Greco, Oscar. *Bibliografia femminile italiana del XIX secolo.* Venice: Tipografia G. Issoglio, 1875.

Groppi, Angela. *I conservatori della virtù. Donne recluse nella Roma dei Papi.* Rome-Bari: Laterza, 1994.

Hammerton, A. James. *Cruelty and Companionship: Conflict in Nineteenth-Century Married Life.* London and New York: Routledge, 1992.

Hearder, Harry. *Italy in the Age of the Risorgimento, 1790–1870.* London and New York: Longman, 1983.

Hibbert, Christopher. *Garibaldi and his Enemies: The Clash of Arms and Personalities in the Making of Italy.* Reprint of 1965 edition. Harmondsworth: Penguin Books, 1987.

Howard, Judith Jeffrey. "The Woman Question in Italy, 1861–1880." Ph.D. diss., University of Connecticut, 1977.

Il Digesto italiano. Enciclopedia metodica e alfabetica di legislazione, dottrina e giurisprudenza. Turin: Unione Tipografico-Editrice, 1895–1912.

Il Divorzio. Rome: Opera dei Congressi Cattolici, 1902.

Il Matrimonio cristiano e le calunnie dei divorzisti. (Tra un socialista e un democratico cristiano). Rome: Società Italiana Cattolica di Cultura, 1903.

Il Parlamento Italiano, 1861–1988. Vol XX, 1968–1972: Fra stato sociale e contestazione. Da Rumor ad Andreotti. Milan: Nuova CEI, 1992.

Istasia, Anna Maria. "La questione femminile nelle discussioni parlamentari postunitarie: il codice civile del 1865." *Dimensioni e problemi della ricerca storica* no. 2 (1991): 167–183.

"Istructio S. Poenitentiariae Apostolica circa Contractum Quem Matrimonium Civile Appellant." *Acta Sanctae Sedis*, Vol. I, Appendix XVIII. Rome: Ex Tipografia Polyglotta, 1898.

Jemolo, Carlo Arturo. *Chiesa e stato in Italia negli ultimi cento anni.* Turin: Einaudi Editore, 1948.

———. *Church and State in Italy, 1850–1950.* Trans. David Moore. Oxford: Basil Blackwell, 1960.

———. *Il matrimonio nel diritto canonico. Dal Concilio di Trento al Codice del 1917.* Reprint of 1941 edition. Bologna: Il Mulino, 1993.

Klawans, Stewart. "The Facts (and Fancies) of Murder." Sleeve note, "Divorzio all'italiana," videorecording, Criterion Collection, 2005.

Labriola, Teresa. *Del divorzio. Discussione etica.* Rome: E. Loescher, 1901.

Lanaro, Silvio. *Storia dell'Italia repubblicana. L'economia, la politica, la cultura, la società dal dopoguerra agli anni '90.* Venice: Marsilio, 1992.

Larkin, Maurice. *Church and State after the Dreyfus Affair: The Separation Issue in France.* New York: Barnes and Noble, 1973.

Lepetit, Dominique. *L'histoire de France du divorce de 1789 à nos jours.* Cherbourg: Isoète, 1996.

Linati, Pier Maria. *Matrimonio e divorzio.* Parma: Tipografia Ferrari e Pellegrini, 1892.

Lombroso, Paola, and Mario Carrara. *Nella penombra della civiltà. (Da un'inchiesta sul pensiero del popolo).* Turin: Fratelli Bocca Editori, 1906.

Lulli, Maria Grazia. "Il problema del divorzio in Italia dal sec. XVIII al Codice del 1865." *Il diritto di famiglia e delle persone* Anno III, no. 4 (October–November 1974): 1230–1247.

Lyttelton, Adrian. "An Old Church and a New State: Italian Anticlericalism 1876–1915." *European Studies Review* 13 (1983): 225–248.

Mack Smith, Denis. *Garibaldi. Una grande vita in breve.* Translation of *Garibaldi: A Great Life in Brief*, 1956. Milan: Mondadori, 1993.

Maggioni, Guido. *Il divorzio in Italia. Storia dell'applicazione di una legge nuova.* Milan: Franco Angeli, 1990.

Magister, Sandro. *Chiesa extraparlamentare. Il trionfo del pulpito nell'età postdemocristiano.* Naples: L'Ancora del Mediterraneo, 2001.

———. *La politica vaticana e l'Italia, 1943–1978.* Rome: Editori Riuniti, 1979.

Majolo Molinari, Olga. *La stampa periodica romana dell'Ottocento.* Rome: Istituto di Studi Romani Editore, 1963.

Mammarella, Giuseppe. *L'Italia contemporanea (1943–1998).* Bologna: Il Mulino, 1998.

Manoukian, Agopik, ed. *I vincoli familiari in Italia. Dal secolo XI al secolo XX.* Bologna: Il Mulino, 1983.

Marchesini, Giovanni. *Il principio della indissolubilià del matrimonio e il divorzio.* Padua-Verona: Fratelli Drucker, 1902.

Marescalchi, Alfonso. *Il divorzio e la istituzione sua in Italia.* Rome: Tipografia della Mantellate, 1889.

Masini, Pier Carlo. "Un anarchico a Montecitorio." *Tempo Presente,* July 1968, pp. 7–15.

Mazzini, Giuseppe. *The Duties of Man and Other Essays.* London: J. M. Dent, 1955.

Mazzoleni, Angelo. *La famiglia nei rapporti coll'individuo e colla società.* Milan: Tipografia Salvi, 1870.

Mazzonis, Filippo. "Dai democratici cristiani al patto Gentiloni." *Storia della società italiana,* Part 5, Vol. XX: *L'Italia di Giolitti.* Milan: Teti Editore, 1981.

McManners, John. *Church and State in France, 1870–1914.* New York: Harper and Row, 1972.

Meda, Filippo. "I cattolici e le ultime elezioni politiche." *Nuova Antologia* 169 (1914): 295–309.

Meleri, Francesco. *Il divorzio. Romanzo sociale.* Crema: Tipografia Sociale, 1876.

Mellini, Mauro. *Così annulla la Sacra Rota. Divorzio di classe nell'Italia clericale.* Rome: Samonà e Savelli, 1969.

———. *Le sante nullità. La vera alternativa: divorzio o Sacra Rota?* Rome: Edizioni Savelli, 1974.

Monaldi, Monaldo. *L'istituto del divorzio in Italia. Studio giuridico sociale. Preceduto da un completo cenno storico sopra il matrimonio e il divorzio nelle antiche legislazioni.* Florence: Tipografia L. Nicolai, 1891.

Monastra, Giovanni. *La necessità sociale del divorzio in Italia.* Piazza Armerina: Tipografia G. Bologna La Bella, 1900.

Montaldo, Silvano. "Il divorzio: famiglia e *nation building* nell'italia liberale." *Il Risorgimento* no. 1 (2000): 5–57.

Morelli, Salvatore. *La donna e la scienza, o la soluzione del problema sociale.* 3rd ed. Naples: Società Tipografico-Editrice, 1869.

Morris, Penny. "From Private to Public: Albe de Céspedes' Agony Column in 1950s Italy." *Modern Italy* 9, no. 1 (2004): 11–20.

Mortati, Costantino. *Istituzioni di diritto pubblico.* Vol. II. Padua: CEDAM, 1976.

Mosca, Gaetano. "Pro e contro il divorzio." Reprinted from 1902 article in *Corriere della sera* (Milan), in Gaetano Mosca, *Partiti e sindacati nella crisi del regime parlamentare.* Rome-Bari: Laterza, 1949.

Moscon, Giorgio, ed. *Divorzio all'italiana di Pietro Germi.* Rome: Edizioni FM, 1961.

Mosse, George L. *Nationalism and Sexuality: Middle Class Morality and Sexual Norms in Modern Europe.* Madison, WI: University of Wisconsin Press, 1985.

Mozzoni, Anna Maria. *La donna in faccia al progetto del nuovo codice civile italiano.* Milan: Tipografia Sociale, 1865.

———. *La liberazione della donna.* Ed. Franca Pieroni Bortolotti. Reprint of 1864 edition. Milan: Gabriele Mazzotta Editore, 1975.

Murmura, P. *Conferenza sul divorzio tenuta nel Teatro di Catanzaro addì 11 maggio 1902.* Monteleone: Tipografia Passafaro, 1902.

Naclerio, Elvirio. *Il divorzio e le leggi: considerazioni*. Naples: Tipografia Carlo Zomack, 1867.

Naquet, Alfred. *Le divorce*. Paris: E. Dentu, 1877.

Nelli, Simonetta. *Lo scioglimento del matrimonio nella storia del diritto italiano*. Milan: Giuffrè Editore, 1976.

Noonan, John T. *Power to Dissolve: Lawyers and Marriages in the Courts of the Roman Curia*. Cambridge, MA: Belknap Press of Harvard University Press, 1972.

Oriani, Alfredo. *Opera Omnia. Vol. VIII: Matrimonio*. Ed. Benito Mussolini, 4th ed. Bologna: Licinio Capelli Editore, 1942 [1886].

Partin, Malcolm O. *Waldeck-Rousseau, Combes and the Church: The Politics of Anticlericalism, 1899–1905*. Durham, NC: Duke University Press, 1969.

Partito comunista italiano. *I comunisti e la famiglia, 1945–1974*. Rome: Partito comunista italiano, 1974.

Pasi, Antonia, and Paolo Scorcinelli. *Amori e trasgressioni. Rapporti di coppia fra '800 e '900*. Bari: Edizioni Dedalo, 1995.

Passalaqua, Giuseppe. *Il divorzio e la Chiesa*. Naples: n.p., 1947.

Pelaja, Margherita. "Marriage by Exception: Marriage Dispensations and Ecclesiastical Policies in Nineteenth-Century Rome." *Journal of Modern Italian Studies* 1, no. 2 (1996): 223–244.

———. *Matrimonio e sessualità a Roma nell'Ottocento*. Rome-Bari: Laterza, 1994.

Perego, Francesco. *Divorziare in nome di dio*. Venice-Padua: Marsilio Editori, 1974.

Peretti Griva, Domenico. *La famiglia e il divorzio*. Bari: Laterza, 1956.

Philips, Roderick. *Putting Asunder: A History of Divorce in Western Society*. Cambridge: Cambridge University Press, 1988.

Piccardi, Leopoldo. *Il divorzio in Italia*. Florence: La Nuova Italia, 1969.

Pieracini, Arturo. *Il divorzio. Risposta ad un opuscolo omologo dell'avv. E. Bianchi*. Pisa: Tipografia Mariotti, 1879.

Pieroni Bortolotti, Franca. *Alle origini del movimento femminile in Italia 1848–1892*. Turin: Einaudi Editore, 1963.

———. *Socialismo e questione femminile in Italia, 1892–1922*. Milan: Mazzotta Editore, 1974.

Pojmann, Wendy. "Emancipation or Liberation? Women's Associations and the Italian Movement." *The Historian* 67, no. 1 (March 2005): 73–96.

Polacco, Vittorio. *Contro il divorzio. Lezione tenuta il 2 maggio 1892 nella R. Università di Padova*. 2nd ed. Padua: Fratelli Drucker, 1902.

———. *La questione del divorzio e gli Israeliti in Italia*. Padua: Fratelli Drucker, 1894.

Pompei, Gian Franco. *Un ambasciatore in Vaticano. Diario 1969–1977*. Ed. Pietro Scoppola. Bologna: Il Mulino, 1994.

Poovey, Mary. *Uneven Developments: The Ideological Work of Gender in Mid-Victorian England*. Chicago: Chicago University Press, 1988.

Ricciardi, Giuseppe. *Il divorzio*. Naples: Tipografia S. Pietro, 1876.

Rifelli, Giorgio, and Corrado Ziglio. *Per una storia dell'educazione sessuale 1870–1920*. Florence: La Nuova Italia, 1991.

Rizzo, Domenico. *Gli spazi della morale. Buon costume e ordine delle famiglie in Italia in età Liberale*. Rome: Biblink Editori, 2004.

————. "Marriage on Trial: Adultery in Nineteenth-Century Rome." In *Gender, Family and Sexuality: the Private Sphere in Italy, 1860–1945*. Ed. Perry Willson. Basingstoke: Palgrave Macmillan, 2004, pp. 20–36.

Rizzo, Tito Lucrezio. "I progetti di divorzio dall'avvento al potere della sinistra alla fine del Secolo XIX." *Il diritto di famiglia e di persone* (1975): 948–961.

Robinson, Geoffrey. *Matrimonio, divorzio e nullità. Guida al processo di nullità matrimoniale nella chiesa cattolica*. Translation of *Marriage, Divorce and Nullity: A Guide to the Annulment Process in the Catholic Church*. Melbourne: Collins Dove, 1984; Padua: Edizioni Messaggero, 1994.

Roccarino, Maurizio. *Il divorzio e la legislazione italiana. Stato odierno della questione*. Turin: Bocca Editori, 1901.

Romani, Agostino. *Beni recati alla società dal Cristianesimo e mali prodotti dall'eresia. Col cenno sul divorzio amesso dai moderni politici*. Rome: Tipografia di Filippo Cairo, 1863.

Ronsin, Francis. *Les divorciares. Affrontments politiques et conceptions du mariage dans la France du XIXe siècle*. Paris: Aubier, 1992.

Rossi-Doria, Anna. "Le donne sulla scena politica." In *Storia dell'Italia repubblicana. Vol. I: La costruzione della democrazia. Dalla caduta del fascismo agli anni cinquanta*. Turin: Einaudi, 1994, pp. 777–846.

Sabbatucci, Giovanni, and Vittorio Vidotto, eds. *Storia d'Italia. Vol. 3: Liberalismo e democrazia, 1887–1914*. Rome-Bari: Laterza, 1995.

Salandra, Antonio. *Il divorzio in Italia*. Rome: Forzani e Co., 1882.

Sandonnini, Claudio. *Del matrimonio civile. Memoria seconda*. Modena: R. Tipografia Governatoria, 1861.

Sansone, Renato, ed. *I fuorilegge del matrimonio*. Milan-Rome: Edizioni Avanti!, 1956.

Santarelli, Enzo. *Storia critica della Repubblica. L'Italia dal 1945 al 1994*. Milan: Feltrinelli, 1996.

Saredo, Giuseppe. *Trattato di diritto civile italiano*. Florence: Tipografia Editrice dell'Associazione, 1869.

Scaraffia, Lucetta, and Gabriella Zarri, eds. *Donne e fede. Santità e vita religiosa in Italia*. Rome-Bari: Laterza, 1994.

Schiff, Paolina. *La donna e la legge civile*. Milan: Tipografia P. B. Bellini, 1880.

Scremin, Luigi. *Matrimonio divorzio e biologia umana*. Milan: Istituto di Propaganda Libraria, 1948.

Serafini, Maria Alimonda. *Matrimonio e divorzio. Pensieri*. Salerno: Stabilimento Tipografico Nazionale, 1873.

Seymour, Mark. "Condiscendenza con affetto. Le due culture e la questione del divorzio in Italia vista dagli anglofoni (1900–1974)." *Genesis* 4, no. 1 (December 2005): 45–72.

————. "Keystone of the Patriarchal Family? Indissoluble Marriage, Masculinity and Divorce in Liberal Italy." *Journal of Modern Italian Studies* 10, no. 3 (2005): 297–313.

Siotto Pintor, Manfredi. *Il divorzio al cospetto della scienza giuridica e sociale.* Perugia: Stabilimento Tipografico Bartelli, 1903.

———. *Il divorzio degli italiani naturalizzati stranieri.* Offprint from *Annali dell'Università di Perugia*, new series, Vol. I, no. 1, 1903.

Spadolini, Giovanni. *Giolitti e i cattolici (1901–1914).* Florence: Le Monnier, 1970.

———. *Giolitti: un'epoca.* Milan: Longanesi, 1985.

———. *L'Opposizione cattolica da Porta Pia al '98.* Reprint of 1954 edition. Florence: Edizioni della Cassa di Risparmio, 1991.

Stone, Lawrence. *Broken Lives: Separation and Divorce in England, 1660–1857.* Oxford: Oxford University Press, 1993.

———. *The Road to Divorce: England 1530–1987.* Oxford: Oxford University Press, 1990.

Suman, Giovanni. *Divorzio o indissolubilità?* Naples: Francesco Paolo Rizzi Editore, 1886.

Taricone, Fiorenza. *L'Associazionismo femminile italiano dall'Unità al fascismo.* Milan: Edizioni Unicopli, 1996.

———. *Il Centro italiano femminile. Dagli origini agli anni Settanta.* Milan: Franco Angeli, 2001.

———. *Teresa Labriola. Biografia politica di un'intellettuale tra Ottocento e Novecento.* Milan: Franco Angeli, 1994.

Taylor Allen, Ann. "Feminism, Social Science, and the Meanings of Modernity: The Debate on the Origin of the Family in Europe and the United States, 1860–1914." *American Historical Review* 104, no. 4 (1999): 1085–1113.

Tempia, Giovanni. *La riforma del matrimonio. Critica del divorzio.* Rome: Tipografia M. Lovescio, 1890.

Tonelli, Anna. *Politica e amore. Storia dell'educazione ai sentimenti nell'Italia contemporanea.* Bologna: Il Mulino, 2003.

Tranfaglia, Nicola. "La modernità squilibrata. Dalla crisis del centrismo al «compromesso storico»." In *Storia dell'Italia repubblicana*, Vol. II, *La trasformazione dell'italia: sviluppo e squilibri*, 2. *Istituzioni, movimenti, culture.* Turin: Einaudi, 1995, pp. 1–111.

Ullrich, Hartmut. "La campagna per il divorzio nella Napoli inizio secolo e l'atteggiamento di Bendetto Croce." *Rivista di studi crociani* (1970): 320–344.

Umbro, Teofilo. *Firmiamo, ovvero del divorzio.* Foligno: Tipografia degli Artigianelli, 1893.

Ungari, Paolo. *Il diritto di famiglia in Italia. Dalle costituzioni "giacobine" al Codice civile del 1942.* Bologna: Il Mulino, 1970.

———. *Il diritto di famiglia in Italia (1796–1975).* Bologna: Il Mulino, 2002.

Vaturi, Vittorio. *Per il divorzio: Discorso tenuto al Teatro Alfieri di Livorno il 20 agosto 1893.* Leghorn: Tipografia Italo Artufari, 1893.

Verucci, Guido. *L'Italia laica prima e dopo l'Unità, 1848–1876. Anticlericalismo, liberalismo e ateismo nella società italiana.* Rome-Bari: Laterza, 1981.

Villani, Carlo. *La questione del divorzio.* Naples: Fratelli Orfeo, 1891.

Wanrooij, Bruno. *Storia del pudore. La questione sessuale in Italia 1860–1940.* Venice: Marsilio Editori, 1990.

Wertman, Douglas A. "The Catholic Church and Italian Politics: The Impact of Secularisation." *West European Politics* 5, no. 2 (1982): 87–107.

Zamperini, Luigi. *Divorzio. Risposta alle circolari 7 e 21 marzo 1880 del Ministero di Grazia e Giustizia del Regno d'Italia relative a notizie statstiche sulle separazioni personali fra coniugi.* Verona-Padua: Drucker e Tedeschi, 1880.

Motion Picture

Germi, Pietro, dir. *Divorzio all'italiana (Divorce Italian Style)* [1961]. Irvington, NY: Criterion Collection, 2005. Videorecording.

Index